Property Investment Appraisal

Third edition

Andrew Baum

Professor of Land Management
Department of Real Estate and Planning
University of Reading Business School

and

Neil Crosby

Professor of Real Estate
Department of Real Estate and Planning
University of Reading Business School

Blackwell
Publishing

© 2008 by Andrew Baum and Neil Crosby

Blackwell Publishing editorial offices:
Blackwell Publishing Ltd, 9600 Garsington Road, Oxford OX4 2DQ, UK
  Tel: +44 (0)1865 776868
Blackwell Publishing Inc., 350 Main Street, Malden, MA 02148-5020, USA
  Tel: +1 781 388 8250
Blackwell Publishing Asia Pty Ltd, 550 Swanston Street, Carlton, Victoria 3053, Australia
  Tel: +61 (0)3 8359 1011

First published 2008 by Blackwell Publishing Ltd

2   2008

ISBN 978-1-4051-3555-9

Library of Congress Cataloging-in-Publication Data
Baum, Andrew E.
Property investment appraisal / Andrew Baum and Neil Crosby. – 3rd ed.
    p. cm.
  Includes bibliographical references and index.
  ISBN-13: 978-1-4051-3555-9 (pbk. : alk. paper)
  ISBN-10: 1-4051-3555-7 (pbk. : alk. paper) 1. Real property–Valuation–Great Britain.
2. Real estate investmen–Great Britain. I. Crosby, Neil. II. Title.

HD596.B385 2007
333.33'20941--dc22
                                                                2007009094

A catalogue record for this title is available from the British Library

Set in 10/12 pt Sabon
by Newgen Imaging Systems (P) Ltd, Chennai, India
Printed and bound in Singapore
by Utopia Press Pte Ltd

The publisher's policy is to use permanent paper from mills that operate a sustainable forestry policy, and which has been manufactured from pulp processed using acid-free and elementary chlorine-free practices. Furthermore, the publisher ensures that the text paper and cover board used have met acceptable environmental accreditation standards.

For further information on Blackwell Publishing, visit our website:
www.blackwellpublishing.com

Contents

Preface

This is the third edition of this text. It is over 10 years since we produced the second edition and 20 years since the first edition was published in 1988. We seem to be able to coincide editions with peaks and troughs in the UK property market – with, if readers will forgive our presumption, some benefit to the content.

The first edition was published when the market was booming. It had the stated aim of changing UK professional practice, a necessary objective in our view given that strong rental growth and high inflation rates had fundamentally undermined the applicability of the conventional valuation model to reversions and leaseholds. There was added justification, as valuation was becoming more important, property having established its place as a major asset class for financial institutions. Valuations had become subject to greater scrutiny from investors and analysts from other asset classes, and property valuation methods appeared archaic and static. Most UK texts of the time were little more than a set of cookbook routines predicated on the passing on of perceived wisdom, and no text had focused wholly on a critical examination of the basis and validity of that approach. We attempted to put market valuation processes into their historical perspective and argued that as markets changed so should methods.

By the time of the second edition, the UK market was just beginning to recover from the most significant property market crash in recent recorded history. The emphasis had changed from reversions to 'over-rented' property and how valuation models coped with falling or fallen markets. Models suggested as alternatives to conventional approaches in our first edition began being assimilated into UK professional practice due to the now-obvious failure of traditional methods to cope with over-renting caused by long leases and upwards-only rent reviews. It was beginning to dawn on investors and valuers that a cash flow might be secured against a tenant rather than the property, and understanding the security of that cash-flow tenant should be just as important as understanding property fundamentals in producing rational valuations.

In the third edition of this text – written amidst a booming and dangerously strong investment market, but one with complex reversions, over-rented property and leaseholds in ready supply – we develop those issues more fully. Our job is not yet done, as the conventional method is challenged but still reasonably dominant. We have therefore resisted a strong temptation to move the emphasis of the book away from valuation and into investment analysis, and we feel that there are many excellent texts from various parts of the world which do that job very well.

We have therefore retained the basic structure and thrust of the first two editions. We set out some basic investment and appraisal theory in Part One of the book and have added a chapter on building and modelling cash flows as a precursor to the investment material in Part Three. The heart of the book remains the critical examination of market valuation models, and it remains the case that no other book addresses this issue in detail.

Valuations are important. They are used as a surrogate for transactions in the construction of investment performance. While that situation exists, investors and other market operators need to rely on them. The German open-ended fund crisis at the end of 2005 is an illustration of the risks we take as professionals if valuations – and valuers – lose the trust of their market.

Andrew Baum and Neil Crosby
Reading, UK
March 2007

Part One
Introduction

Chapter 1
Property Investment Appraisal in its Context

1.1 What is appraisal?

The subject of this book is the appraisal of property investments. In choosing the term 'appraisal' we have two distinct applications in mind. By 'appraise' we mean

a. To fix a price for (an asset);
b. To estimate the amount, or worth or value, of (an asset)

The first of these meanings implies what is known, in the UK, as the valuation process or, in the US, as the appraisal process: the estimation of market value or the prediction of the most likely selling price. There is now widespread acceptance of the international definition of market value set out in the valuation standard of the International Valuation Standards Committee, commonly known as 'the White Book' (IVSC, 2005), which is now in its seventh edition. This definition is

> the estimated amount for which a property should exchange on the date of valuation between a willing buyer and a willing seller in an arm's length transaction after proper marketing wherein the parties had acted knowledgeably, prudently and without compulsion

Many nations also feel the need to have their own valuation standards, not least the UK, whose standards [maintained by the Royal Institution of Chartered Surveyors (RICS)] have been through a number of editions of what is commonly referred to as 'the Red Book'. The latest edition (RICS, 2003) is the fifth and has adopted the aforementioned basic international definition. There are even attempts to create regional standards (such as the European *'Blue Book'*, published by TEGOVA, The European Group of Valuers of Fixed Assets), and this has created some tension and rivalry between international, regional and national bodies, particularly in Europe. However, there is now very little disagreement, if any, on the general wording of the market value definition, even if there are some differences in interpretation. These differences will continue to diminish as the property investment market becomes more and more international.

The second of the two meanings, the estimation of worth or value, is not necessarily market-based. Since the second edition of this book in 1995 this concept has been developed and institutionalised, having entered UK valuation standards in the 1990s as the 'calculation of worth', and now defined in the White Book under the term 'investment value'. The term 'calculation of worth' has now – happily – been dropped by the RICS in favour of the international definition. The definition is as follows:

> the value of the property to a particular owner, investor or class of investor, for identified investment objectives. This subjective concept relates specific property to a specified investor, group of investors, or entity with identifiable investment objectives and/or criteria.

This definition does appear to fudge a major issue, specifically whether worth or value is to an individual investor or to a group of investors. This has significant implications about how it might be assessed in practice, as the value to an individual and the value to a group may not be the same.

Individual investors are influenced by a set of criteria by which the value of an asset might be assessed. For example, their tax situation, the rate at which they can borrow, how much equity capital they have to spare, what adjoining assets they own and the strengths and weaknesses of their existing investment portfolio are all factors that may lead them to perceive value in a particular property.

Hence, while all investors may agree upon such important variables as the size of the asset being appraised, the cash-flow implications of the lease and the likelihood of achieving planning permission for a change of use, individual investors will always be subject to different motivations. As will be shown later in this book, the distinction between value and worth can be important.

Further, it is possible that a group of investors will use the same criteria and share the same characteristics, and would as a result attach a similar value to a property asset. Identifying the possible buyer group is very relevant to appraisal, which is therefore the process of identifying a mixture of objectively measured market variables and the prospective owner's (or group of owners') subjective estimates of other relevant factors.

We use the term 'appraisal' to cover the process of estimating either market value (the prediction of the most likely selling price) or investment value (the estimation of worth to an individual or to a group of individuals). We would therefore encourage the use of the term 'market valuation' or 'valuation for pricing' for the former, and we would prefer to use 'investment value' for the latter. We hope this will not cause too much confusion, but the possibility of confusion unfortunately exists, grounded in the fact that the development of property terminology has been influenced by the isolation of the property world from the securities markets. There is no doubt regarding the meaning of valuation in the securities markets: it means the estimation of worth. Pricing is a function that is carried out by buyers, sellers and market makers. The price of a particular company in the stock market is publicly quoted, and large numbers of identical shares in that company can be bought and sold.

In property, however, there are no market makers. The price at which a transaction will take place has to be influenced by an expert opinion – a 'valuation' – because there is both insufficient market evidence and insufficient homogeneity of product for traders to be able to fix prices. It is therefore to be expected that at any one time different views of worth will be held by different individuals and these differences will fuel market turnover.

In addition to the main concepts of market value and investment value, each of which has been defined in the first section of this chapter, 'sustainable value' (mortgage lending value), a relatively new phenomenon used in the bank-lending process, has been developed in mainland Europe. It has found some favour, particularly within German banking systems, and the mortgage lending value basis has been adopted, along with market value, within the international banking regulatory process known as Basel 2. The concept sustainable value has been subject to intense criticism, as of it does not conform to any recognised economic concept of value and the definition is virtually incomprehensible. The implications for investors can be damaging and may have had some impact on the German open-ended fund crisis of 2005/2006, discussed later in this chapter. We see no merit in it and we think it should be abandoned.

1.2   What makes a good appraisal?

The stock (property) selection policies of both major and minor property investors often include an examination of the mismatch between estimates of market value and investment value in order to spot pricing anomalies, and any investor or advisor will benefit from a clear understanding of the difference between the market value of an asset and its worth to an investor or group of investors. If there is a difference, is this evidence of poor-quality appraisal?

It is widely believed that market valuations should primarily be *accurate*; that is, they should closely predict selling price. Accuracy may therefore be a relevant and useful test of the quality of a market valuation. Investment valuations, on the other hand, should primarily be *rational*; they should be professional and expert reflections of a combination of objectively measured market variables and the prospective owner's subjective estimates. We will argue in this book that *all* appraisals, including market valuations, should be rational. If they are, although accuracy can never be guaranteed, greater confidence in what will be perceived as professional and expert results will be generated.

The two earlier editions of this book had the stated aim of encouraging better, more rational practice in the appraisal of property investments. We have no evidence that valuation practices have improved so much that we can relax this aim for this edition. Nonetheless, despite difficulties in proving the point, we have little doubt that valuation practice has improved significantly in many ways. Appraisal methods have continued to be debated and, in the last 10–15 years, more research has been undertaken on the process of valuation.

This, coupled with the continuing development of standards, has resulted in many examples of better, more rational, valuations. For example, in the UK, academic and practitioner research has led, in addition to a continuing debate on techniques, to some major attempts to make the valuation process more transparent and objective (Baum *et al.*, 2000; Carsberg, 2002) and valuation reports more useful to clients (Crosby *et al.*, 1997; Waters, 1999). While this book focuses on appraisal methods, and not on behavioural aspects of the valuation process, we refer the reader to the ever-increasing literature on valuer–client relationships, client influence and conflicts of interest between stakeholders in different kinds of valuations such as borrowers, lenders, brokers, fund managers, trustees and shareholders; issues concerning bases of valuation and valuation reporting; and problems and pitfalls in the selection and instruction of valuers.

Nonetheless, we have already discussed the issue of different concepts and bases of valuation and introduced the debate concerning the accuracy of the results, and we will discuss this further in the context of recent studies into the valuation process. The issues we will refer to include the accuracy of valuations and the possibility of smoothing and lagging effects. As a relevant case study, we show how a combination of valuation smoothing, conceptual weaknesses and client influence may have added to the German open-ended fund crisis of 2005/2006.

1.3   Conventional and discounted-cash-flow approaches to appraisal

Recessions and property crashes in many regions of the world in the early 1990s led directly to an increased interest in valuation techniques from clients and valuers, and also from those whose role is to comment on valuation practice. This process had started at the time of writing the second edition of this text in 1994/1995, but, despite the criticism of conventional valuation techniques contained in that edition and others that have followed over the last 10 years, conventional approaches still dominate UK market valuation practice. This is in increasing contrast to other developed markets in which discounted-cash-flow (DCF) valuations dominate.

Why is the UK more wedded to comparative conventional techniques? Despite some high-rise development and the increasing importance of multi-let large-scale shopping centres, the UK still has much prime property investment stock let on long leases to single occupiers. The average value of a property (measured by the Investment Property Databank) is small at £13m in the UK, compared with over AUD100m (£40m) in Australia at the end of 2005. Within the universe measured by the National Council of Real Estate Investment Fiduciaries (NCREIF), the average value of property in the US is $45m (£23m), and, as in Australia, many of the properties are multi-let, multi-storey tower blocks and shopping centres. The turnover of the UK commercial property stock is high, estimated to be over 10% per annum (Key, 2004) and property interests are not complex.

Finally, the typical institutional UK lease has traditionally been the longest in the world, and has had the added benefit of upward-only rent reviews and 'triple net' rents. This has produced a simple, low-risk investment with limited variability of cash flow. In these circumstances the initial rent explains a large proportion of the value of the asset, and the development of a comparative valuation method based on capitalising the initial rent can be understood. Given these physical and leasing characteristics, it is no real surprise that UK valuations persist in adopting simple comparison-based valuation methods rather than DCF-based approaches to appraisal. But things are changing.

We set out in this edition to show that the cash-flow approach, described in detail in Chapter 3, with simple derivatives of it set out in Chapter 5, have significant advantages and no disadvantages compared with the simple conventional models. Time has not dimmed our enthusiasm for this argument. We believe that investment value can be identified by a rational analysis of market transactions, and we do not believe that having a relatively transparent, high-turnover market, as in the UK, gives valuers an excuse to develop simplistic rules of thumb to make up for the heterogeneous nature of the asset.

We will show later in this chapter that appraisal is by its nature not precise, and suggest that both the outcome of appraisal accuracy studies and appraisals themselves should be treated with caution. But even if it were possible to observe appraisal accuracy, and to establish that valuations are accurate indicators of market price, irrational techniques that happen to produce 'accurate' outcomes should not be defended. It should be the aim of an appraisal to achieve accuracy by means of rational techniques. If buyers or sellers were to become aware of an inefficient sub-sector of the property market, the pricing anomaly will be recognised, prices will change and market valuations based on irrational techniques will immediately become capable of dangerous inaccuracy. The 1980s' short leasehold market (see Baum and Butler, 1986) is an old example of the breakdown of conventional techniques. A lack of confidence in market valuations for pricing led to the use of sales by tender and the gradual, continuing adoption of an explicitly rational cash-flow model for short-leasehold appraisals.

In this edition, we add a further example by presenting a case study that illustrates how conventional market valuations can damage the interests of an owner when investment worth to a buyer or group of buyers is influenced by factors absent from comparable transactions (see Chapter 9). This case, based on an over-rented property sold in the early 1990s, is an equally pertinent example of how techniques can break down if they are not rational and grounded in finance. The valuation debate in the UK that followed the early 1990s was thought to be the catalyst for a major re-appraisal of valuation methods in the UK, but the long bull market that followed has reduced this threat and some valuers appear to have returned to their conventional roots.

A more long-lasting and potentially more permanent change may be driven by the changing nature of the UK commercial lease. For the first time, UK valuers have had to face up to shorter leases, and the more general issue of pricing different lease terms, because the standard institutional lease of the 1980s (25-year terms, 5-yearly upwards-only reviews, full repairing and insuring terms, and no break clauses) has been rejected by tenants. Pressure on landlords has also mounted from Government, keen to see more flexibility and choice. Valuers not facing up to the valuation issues of shorter, more flexible leases has been cited as one reason why landlords were reluctant to grant tenants more flexibility (DETR, 2000), and lease pricing has emerged as a significant issue for the UK valuation community (Crosby et al., 2005). We address this issue in detail in an appendix to Chapter 8.

Rational valuation does not necessarily imply a questioning of market price, but requires that changes in observed prices are reflected rationally in changes in meaningful variables, permitting the rational revaluation of other assets. We hope to show that conventional appraisal models do not permit this to happen. Lack of rationality is increasingly inappropriate in today's deregulated and international capital markets. A change towards rational valuation will facilitate increased market efficiency and the rapid assimilation of any observable changes in markets into prices and into appraisals.

1.4   Property investment appraisal and the capital markets

The first two editions of this text made a strong case for property investment appraisals being made in the context of the capital markets (equities and bonds) rather than appraisals and valuations being based solely on comparisons with other property investments. We are pleased to be able to say that we do not consider it necessary to make the case for a third time, as it is now accepted in both academic circles and practice that property is just another focus for investment funds and must compete directly with those alternatives (see Chapter 2). Significant amounts of the prime property stock of the UK is in the hands of the major financial institutions that make choices between and allocations to a variety of investment types, and analysis and pricing must be undertaken in the context of the price of those alternatives. The rise of institutional and property company investment in property has been documented elsewhere (see, for example, Investment Property DataBank (IPD) data) and is shown in Table 1.1. The proportion of funds that UK insurance companies and pension funds have invested in property declined from a peak of nearly 20% in 1981 until it hit the floor in 1999, since when it has recovered (by 2007) to an allocation of around 7% of invested assets.

Table 1.1 Asset allocation by UK financial institutions, 1977–2003.

Year	Life funds	Pension funds	Life and pension funds
1977	17.2	14.1	15.9
1978	19.7	13.9	17.2
1979	21.6	14.7	18.5
1980	23.2	14.7	18.8
1981	23.9	14.8	19.1
1982	20.1	12.2	15.9
1983	18.1	10.1	13.8
1984	16.3	9.1	12.3
1985	15.3	8.2	11.3
1986	13.7	7.2	10.0
1987	15.4	7.9	11.1
1988	17.1	8.9	12.4
1989	15.8	8.1	11.3
1990	15.1	8.9	11.6
1991	11.8	7.1	9.2
1992	9.3	5.2	7.1
1993	7.9	4.6	6.1
1994	8.9	5.5	7.1
1995	7.2	4.2	5.7
1996	6.6	4.0	5.3
1997	6.3	3.7	5.0
1998	5.9	3.5	4.8
1999	5.4	3.8	4.7
2000	5.3	4.3	4.9
2001	5.9	4.3	5.2
2002	6.3	5.2	5.8
2003	5.5	4.5	5.1

These values describe allocations of equity capital. However, the debt finance outstanding to property, having risen significantly in the 1980s and reduced after the property crash of 1990, has again risen significantly in the late 1990s and the first half of the first decade of this millennium. There has also been a boom in private property investment by high-net-worth individuals, and also in private equity property investment through unlisted property funds. These are new sources of capital provided by equally sophisticated investors driven by estimates of relative value. This broadening of the investor base increases the need for rational appraisal capable of cross-reference against other assets.

The performance of property against other mainstream asset classes has also been the subject of long-term scrutiny in the UK, and Table 1.2 sets out the relative returns estimated by IPD.

This table shows that (using geometric mean returns) equities (14% p.a.) have performed best over the long term, property has performed second best (12.4% p.a.) and bonds have performed third best (10.7% p.a.). But the volatility of property is much lower than the other two, as measured by the standard deviation of those returns. Equities delivered a standard deviation of 30.8%; bonds, 14.3%; and property, only 10.3%. In addition, property has performed well at different times compared with the other two asset classes, as indicated by the level of correlation between the three assets set out in Table 1.3.

The coefficient of correlation is 0.62 between equities and bonds, but is only 0.19 between property and equities and 0.05 between property and bonds. This suggests that the performance of equities and bonds is closely related, with bond and equity returns more likely to rise and fall together. A perfect positive relationship, where returns rise and fall in symmetry with each other, would produce a correlation coefficient of 1, while property and other markets move more randomly against each other. A completely random relationship equates to a correlation coefficient of 0, while a perfect but negative relationship that would produce the best diversification would be −1. The case that is often made for property is that it is therefore both of lower risk and a good diversifier of the portfolio.

However, there are problems with this argument based on valuation methods. The analysis clearly assumes that the performance figures are accurate and that there is a major difference between the performance of property and the other two asset classes. But the capital values of property used in the performance calculations are produced by valuations and are not transaction based; however, the capital values of equities and bonds are observed from transactions. It is argued that the way in which valuations are produced means they tend to lag the actual market movements, so producing a lagging effect in the performance figures, which also produces the lack of correlation. They also tend to smooth the peaks and troughs of the movement in prices, producing the low standard deviations. In other words, the evidence of diversification and low risk characteristics for property is

Table 1.2 Returns on mainstream asset classes, 1971–2006.

	Total return			Income return			Capital growth		
	Property	Equities	Gilts	Property	Equities	Gilts	Property	Equities	Gilts
1971	16.1	46.5	27.3	5.3	4.6	9.7	10.8	41.9	17.6
1972	29.4	16.4	-3.8	5.7	3.6	8.5	23.7	12.8	-12.3
1973	28.5	-28.1	-8.9	5.2	3.3	9.7	23.3	-31.4	-18.6
1974	-15.9	-50.1	-15.2	3.9	5.2	12.3	-19.8	-55.3	-27.5
1975	11.4	149.3	36.8	6.2	13.0	17.6	5.2	136.3	19.2
1976	9.4	2.3	13.7	6.3	6.2	14.8	3.2	-3.9	-1.1
1977	26.5	48.6	44.8	7.5	7.4	14.2	19.0	41.2	30.6
1978	25.7	8.6	-1.8	6.7	5.9	11.5	19.0	2.7	-13.3
1979	23.2	11.5	4.1	6.5	7.2	13.3	16.7	4.3	-9.2
1980	17.5	34.8	20.9	6.3	7.7	14.7	11.3	27.1	6.2
1981	15.0	13.6	1.8	5.9	6.4	13.9	9.1	7.2	-12.1
1982	7.5	28.5	51.3	5.6	6.4	15.1	1.9	22.1	36.2
1983	7.6	28.8	15.9	6.0	5.7	11.0	1.6	23.1	4.9
1984	8.9	31.6	6.8	6.3	5.6	10.2	2.5	26	-3.4
1985	8.3	20.2	11.0	6.5	5.0	10.6	1.9	15.2	0.4
1986	11.3	27.3	11.0	6.7	5.0	10.6	4.6	22.3	0.4
1987	26.0	8.0	16.3	7.3	3.9	10.1	18.7	4.2	6.2
1988	29.6	11.5	9.4	6.8	5.1	9.4	22.8	6.5	0.0
1989	15.4	36.1	5.9	5.8	6.1	9.6	9.6	30.0	-3.7
1990	-8.5	-9.7	5.6	5.4	4.6	10.1	-13.8	-14.3	-4.5
1991	-3.1	20.7	18.9	7.0	5.7	10.9	-10.2	15.1	8.0
1992	-1.7	20.5	18.4	7.9	5.6	9.7	-9.6	14.8	8.7
1993	20.3	28.4	28.8	9.9	5.1	9.5	10.4	23.3	19.3
1994	11.9	-5.9	-11.3	8.0	3.7	6.8	3.9	-9.6	-18.1
1995	3.6	23.8	19.0	7.5	5.3	8.7	-3.9	18.5	10.3

Continued

Part One

Table 1.2 (Continued)

	Total return			Income return			Capital growth		
	Property	Equities	Gilts	Property	Equities	Gilts	Property	Equities	Gilts
1996	10.1	16.7	7.7	8.1	5.0	7.1	2.0	11.7	0.6
1997	16.9	23.5	15.0	8.2	3.8	8.8	8.7	19.7	6.2
1998	11.7	13.8	19.4	7.4	2.9	7.9	4.4	10.9	11.5
1999	14.7	24.2	-3.2	7.3	3.0	6.1	7.4	21.2	-9.3
2000	10.5	-5.9	9.8	6.9	2.1	6.9	3.6	-8.0	2.9
2001	6.8	-13.3	3.9	6.7	2.1	6.3	0.1	-15.4	-2.4
2002	9.6	-22.7	10.3	7.0	2.3	6.0	2.6	-25.0	4.3
2003	10.9	20.9	1.8	7.0	4.3	5.6	3.9	16.6	-3.8
2004	18.3	12.8	6.6	6.9	3.6	5.9	11.4	9.2	0.7
2005	19.1	22.0	7.4	6.3	3.9	5.5	12.8	18.1	1.9
2006	18.1	16.8	-0.1	5.5	3.6	5.3	12.6	13.1	-5.5
Mean									
SD	10.2	30.3	14.3	1.1	2.0	3.1	10.1	28.9	13.0

Table 1.3 Correlations of returns on mainstream asset classes, 1971–2005.

	Equities	Property	Bonds
Equities	1.000		
Property	0.189	1.000	
Bonds	0.623	0.046	1.000

a mirage produced by the inability of valuations to correctly identify all price movements precisely. This issue is developed further in the next section of this chapter.

In assessing the attractions of property in the context of the alternative asset types, valuation, along with considerations of liquidity and the depreciation of property, have been cited as issues that have been used to disadvantage property in the asset allocation process. Research into these peculiar characteristics of property therefore focuses first on understanding the implications of these factors and then pricing any resulting performance differences between property and other investments. When these differences are dealt with in this way, they cease to be a reason not to include property in the portfolios of investors and become part of the issue of proper comparative pricing of the asset – and even an opportunity to make money through the identification of pricing anomalies, which hedge funds (for example) will increasingly try to do. In the UK, the recent introduction of a UK Real Estate Investment Trust, a well-established vehicle in the US and Australia for many years, and the development of derivative products are both illustrations of the driving together of property and the capital markets and the impossibility of property appraisal methods standing apart from these markets.

1.5   The appraisal process

Valuations play an important role in the property market. They are used in financial statements, for performance measurement purposes, in the banklending process and in the acquisition, sale and management process.

In financial statements, and in performance measurement and buy/sell decisions, it is important to be able to identify the most likely selling price (market value), and banks have also felt that it is important to know the likely current market value when deciding how much to lend against property that might have to be sold to pay off the loan. These two sources of instruction have been dominant, and valuers have therefore majored on assessing market value. Valuation methods have grown up with the implicit assuming that the process of valuation is a process of identifying the market value. For some valuers, this is the only valuation basis they use and understand.

However, market valuation requires that the valuer identifies a particular exchange price at a particular time. The valuation has no shelf life (although some court decisions have suggested a 3- or 6-month lifespan) and it cannot identify mis-pricing. As a result, it is not a useful tool in the analysis of markets. There is an established doctrine underpinning the identification of market value, specifically the best evidence of trading prices of other similar assets. This doctrine is underpinned by the courts and by the perceived best practice of other competent practitioners. 'Other similar assets' is invariably interpreted as other similar *property* assets, and the use of transactions in similar properties raises issues of physical structure, relative location quality and similarity of lease arrangements. Much of this text relates to how valuers can make better use of comparable material in market valuations.

However, more sophisticated investors and investment policies have led to major changes in the level of advice required from valuers and valuations. Over the last 30 years, the need for more detailed advice within both valuation calculations and reports has required valuers to extend their skills, and the need to consider investment value reflects this change. The price paid in the market place may not represent the value of a property to any individual investor, and this value needs to be identified at least partly by reference to the individual's subjective perception of what they will receive in return from ownership of the interest in property. This return could manifest itself in a number of ways over the holding period (which in itself could be different for different purchasers). The investment appraisal therefore requires an assessment of the likely income into the future set against the cost of acquiring, maintaining and enhancing the asset. The most widely used approach to this is a discounted cash flow, and Chapter 3 discusses the information needs of, and other technical issues concerning, cash-flow valuation. The value of the cash flow could be above, below or the same as the market value, and a mismatch of price and investment value could trigger a sale or purchase by certain investors. Most investment decisions are now underpinned by a combination of identifying the most likely exchange price and an analysis of that price to better understand investment value.

International and national valuation standards have become more and more demanding in regulating communication between clients and valuers. This communication involves the selection and appointment of the valuer as well as the reporting of the valuation itself. There has been an increasing concern over the valuer's relationship with clients, and a research literature is developing indicating reasons why valuations may not be totally objective.

1.5.1 Accuracy and bias

Do market valuations fulfil their primary objective of providing an accurate identification of the exchange price? Figure 1.1 illustrates the differences

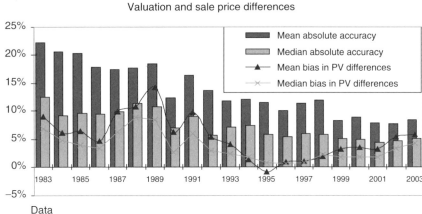

Data

Year	Mean absolute accuracy (%)	Median absolute accuracy (%)	Mean bias in PV differences (%)	Median bias in PV differences (%)
1983	22	13	9	7
1984	21	9	6	5
1985	20	10	6	4
1986	18	10	5	3
1987	17	10	10	6
1988	18	11	11	9
1989	19	11	14	8
1990	12	7	6	3
1991	17	9	10	6
1992	14	6	5	3
1993	12	7	4	2
1994	12	8	1	2
1995	12	6	−1	1
1996	10	5	1	1
1997	11	6	1	1
1998	12	6	2	2
1999	8	5	3	2
2000	9	5	4	2
2001	8	4	3	2
2002	8	5	5	3
2003	8	5	6	4

Figure 1.1   Valuation and sale price differences in UK, 1983–2003. PV differences = price–value differences. *Source*: RICS/IPD (2005).

between valuations and subsequent sale prices (adjusted for time differences) within the UK IPD between 1983 and 2003.

Ignoring whether the average valuation is higher or lower than the subsequent sale price, in the last 10 years the median difference between the valuation and the sale price is under 7%. Taking into account the direction of the difference the sale price has been around 3% higher than the valuation after adjusting for time differences.

This tends to suggest some lagging of valuations to actual sale prices. This is reinforced by the fact that in the boom years of the late 1980s valuations lagged further and further behind prices, indicating that they followed prices upwards at a lower gradient than the rate at which prices were rising. However, they also appeared to follow prices down at a lower rate than they were actually falling. After 5 years of falling and then static prices, valuations finally caught up, only to be left behind again as markets started to rise again post 1995. If valuations and prices are independent of one another, then these results have serious implications for correlation analysis and the making of the case for property.

However, Baum *et al.* (2000) found that valuations were not independent of prices and played an important part in deciding which properties are bought and sold. On this basis, it would be expected that prices would exceed valuations generally, as funds are less likely to sell or buy at prices that do not meet the last valuation or the next prospective valuation for the portfolio performance measurement system (from which the dataset is drawn). Some funds had difficulty getting trustee approval for selling at less than prior valuation, and some buying funds formally checked that their portfolio valuer would at least confirm the purchase price at the next prospective portfolio valuation before buying. Prospective sale prices at less than valuation would not be completed, and so the expected sample of sales would be biased towards prices that exceeded the prior or prospective market valuation. A positive bias in any accuracy study should therefore be expected.

At the micro-level, there is a consensus in the UK property market that individual valuations are prone to a degree of uncertainty. But it would appear that, at the macro-level, few analysts accept that appraisal-based indices reflect the true underlying performance of the property market. It is commonly held, for example, that such indices fail to capture the extent of market volatility and tend to lag underlying performance. As a consequence, issues such as the level and nature of valuation uncertainty and the causes and extent of index smoothing have generated a substantial research literature that reinforces the perception that valuations both lag the market and smooth the peaks and troughs of 'real' prices within indices.

The suggested reasons for this are as follows: anchoring, temporal aggregation, and comparable lagging.

Anchoring. In many jurisdictions, the fiduciary responsibility of the valuer towards the client is an important influence on valuer behaviour. Claims based on accusations of professional negligence are rare but not unknown. Judicial precedent is a powerful influence on the valuation process. It is not therefore surprising if a valuer, retained to produce a portfolio valuation on a 3-year contract, pays attention to his or her year-end 2006 valuation when undertaking the 2007 equivalent and ensures continuity by limiting the number and size of shocks a client might suffer. This can reduce changes in value from one period to the next.

Temporal averaging. Stock markets rise and fall on a daily basis, sometimes significantly. Price changes between the 31 December 2006 market and the 31 December 2007 market are fully reflected by the end-of-trading price on each day, and it is perfectly possible for the year-end 2006 market to be at a temporary low and the year-end 2007 market to be at a temporary high. In property, however, year-end valuations have to be undertaken over a period of up to 3 months, and even where the valuation date is set at 31 December an averaging effect is inevitable. This is likely to result in lower price volatility from year to year.

The lagging effect of comparable evidence. Real estate valuation is founded primarily on the use of comparable sales evidence. Similarity in property characteristics is paramount. The currency of the transaction may not be easy to control. Hence, the evidence used to value a property as on 31 December 2007 may be collected over the period from July to December. In a rising or falling market, this will again result in a lower variance of prices. Clayton *et al.* (2001) provide some Canadian evidence that valuers anchor on past valuations and comparables.

Existing research generates the following hypotheses:

- Valuations will be based upon the previous valuation plus or minus a perception of change.
- The perceived changes, unless the subject of very reliable transaction evidence, will be conservative.
- Valuations will be affected by procedures and precedents of a statutory and regulatory nature.
- The results of legal judgements will be a powerful influence on valuations.

However, many of these issues remain controversial and unresolved, partly because some of this research and commentary has ignored the real-world context in which valuations are produced and used. In particular, a presumption underlying much of the academic work undertaken to date is the independence of valuations from the market price-setting process. As indicated earlier, this may not be the case.

The fact that valuations may influence the properties that are bought and sold, and that the process itself may induce behavioural biases, may not be the only reason for a lack of independence of valuations from prices. Another issue is overt client pressure.

1.5.2   Client influence

Research has shown that valuers and valuations can be consciously or subconsciously moved by a variety of factors ranging from previous valuations and selective information to overt influence from clients or other stakeholders in the valuation outcome. In the bibliography we set out a number of further references to this work by authors such as Diaz, Gallimore, Wolverton, Levy, Hansz, Havard, McAllister, the authors of this book and others.

In bank-lending valuations, borrowers may need a valuation of a minimum amount to support an essential loan, brokers may need a valuation to justify a deal and individual lenders may need the business to earn commissions. In performance measurement valuations, individual fund managers may need a particular performance outcome to earn a bonus or carried interest, or to support a track record to win or retain fee-earning business. There is therefore a number of possible circumstances in which clients and other stakeholders in the outcome may want to put pressure on the valuer to report a specific outcome. For example, in early 2006, some German open-ended funds with unit prices set by valuations were subject to very high withdrawals from investors and one suggestion (Crosby, 2006b) is that this was happening because investors did not trust the manager-influenced valuation-based price levels.

There were a number of factors leading to this perception. First, although the German concept of sustainable value was not used for these particular valuations, the valuations were undertaken by valuers comfortable with this smoothing concept of value. Second, the stated objectives of the funds and a major marketing point were that these open-ended funds were designed to be much less volatile than other property funds (BVI, undated). Third, individual valuers were allowed to earn a large amount of the firm's income from one client, and each fund was counted as an individual fund for this purpose even if the individual funds were issued by the same financial house.

It has already been seen that valuations tend to lag price increases and falls, so that in a bear market it could be hypothesised that valuations would not follow price reductions down as quickly as they occurred. If this bear market continued for a long term, which was the case in Germany, valuations could become higher than prices.

It is not surprising, therefore, that investors would be nervous of this cocktail of moral hazards, with plenty of incentives for the funds to influence valuers, many of whom were comfortable with the positive smoothing concept. As the valuation process tends to smooth prices, some investors lost confidence in the valuation levels being reported. There was no secondary market, and units were traded at prices based solely on the valuation.

It is therefore important to regulate the valuation process in order to protect the valuer from undue pressure, create transparency in the process and the outcome and to maintain both actual and perceived valuer independence. Because of this pressure, regulation of the valuation process is increasing and will continue to do so to make valuations more objective and transparent. This brief discussion highlights the fact that valuation techniques are not applied in a vacuum, and that it is important to understand the role and purpose of the valuation, and the possible influences upon it.

Despite all of the interest and debate concerning valuation, starting with methods but more recently involving the process, there is evidence that valuation methods have, in the UK, resisted the trend evident in some other regimes towards more explicit approaches. Argument and discussion continue in the UK, and there is still a need to challenge the rationality of conventional approaches to market valuation based on direct comparisons within the property market. In a market with a large turnover of lettings and capital transactions, long leases and simple single-let properties, the argument for a simple comparison technique does have some logic. However, this fails to identify ongoing changes in lease structures, prevents more complex situations from being addressed and drives a wedge between market valuation and the appraisal of investment value. Traditional valuations in the UK failed to respond to both the short-leasehold valuation issue in the 1980s and the over-rented situation of the 1990s, causing mis-valuation of assets through technical incompetence. A similar danger has arisen within German open-ended funds, and affects all open-ended and traded funds priced at net asset value.

As a result we will continue to argue for a rational valuation model, and the rest of this book is our attempt to further develop this argument.

Part One

Chapter 2
Principles of Investment Analysis

2.1 Investment

In this book we are concerned with the appraisal of real-property investments. More specifically, we are concerned with the prediction of the most likely selling price of a real-property investment in the market or with the estimation of the worth, or investmetn value, of such an investment to a prospective purchaser.

What is it that distinguishes a real-property investment from other types of real property? The most useful distinction we can employ is between property acquired for occupation and that acquired for investment. The desire for shelter or a place to do business or to enjoy recreation may be contrasted with the desire for 'a vehicle into which funds can be placed with the expectation that they will be preserved or increase in value and/or generate positive returns' (Gitman, 2006).

Investment is 'the sacrifice of something now for the prospect of later benefits' (Greer and Farrell, 1996). How does an investment 'generate positive returns' or 'later benefits'? It can do this in two obvious ways:

a. By generating a flow of income
b. By generating a return of capital, whether it be less than, equal to or in excess of the initial sacrifice

There are less obvious benefits to investment ownership. In previous editions we referred to what has been called 'psychic income', defined as a positive feeling induced by investment ownership. Property, like fine art and racehorses, is said to produce this benefit. We prefer in this edition to add the acquisition of real and financial options as an often-hidden third benefit of property ownership, and will return to this later.

Subject to this qualification, investment (total) return is a function of income and capital return. Consideration of these factors is the essence of investment pricing and valuation. Before we approach this issue, with which investments can and should we compare property ownership?

2.2 Investment types

Property investments cannot be appraised in isolation, despite the fact that the education and development of the valuation profession in many countries may suggest that this is so. By its nature, appraisal is a comparative or relative process, and property investments must at some stage be appraised in comparison with alternative investment vehicles. It is necessary in property investment appraisal to understand something of the nature of alternative outlets and their relative strengths and weaknesses.

Four broad investment types will be briefly considered and analysed in comparison with property investment vehicles. These are

a. Bank deposits
b. Fixed-interest securities
c. Index-linked gilts
d. Equities or ordinary shares

The following analysis is rudimentary: further detail is provided by Rutterford and Davison (2007).

2.2.1 Bank deposits

Cash is regarded as a safe alternative outlet for investment funds and bank deposits and a useful starting point for a basic comparative investment analysis.

The common distinction between savings and investment does not help. As Sharpe and Alexander (1990) put it:

> A distinction is often made between investment and savings. The latter is defined as foregone consumption, with the former restricted to 'real' investment of the sort that increases national output in the future. While this distinction may prove useful in other contexts, it is not especially helpful for analysing the specifics of particular investments or even large classes of investment media. A deposit in a 'savings' account at a bank is investment in the eyes of a depositor.

In the UK, and for our purposes, bank deposits are identical in principle to the old building society accounts of the more common type. Each is characterised by the setting aside of cash in return for regular interest. This may be annual, 6-monthly (as is typical with many building society accounts) or more regular. While the capital invested may appear to grow in such an account, it is important to note that what is really happening is the addition of compound interest to a fixed (in monetary terms) capital sum.

Rates of interest are not typically guaranteed for any substantial period and may vary with no specified limits. Consequently, a summary of the means of generation of return in a bank deposit investment can be stated as follows:

a. Capital: The investment provides a return of capital of an amount exactly equal in money terms to the original investment.
b. Income: The investment provides a return in the form of interest that may vary upwards or downwards over time.

2.2.2   Fixed-interest securities

Conventional gilts and other fixed-interest securities that are not index-linked are typically a major component of the portfolios of major investors [for our purposes this means insurance companies or pension funds (institutions)]. Conventional fixed-interest securities may be divided into gilt-edged securities (gilts), which are UK government fixed-interest securities, and others, typically corporate fixed-interest securities (debentures, loan stocks and preference shares, the latter strictly being fixed-income securities providing dividends rather than interest). Our discussion and generalisations focus upon the particular characteristics of the much more common gilt, although the majority of comments made relate to all fixed-interest securities. A suitable generic term for this type of investment is 'bonds'.

Bonds are a means of borrowing cash. The UK government has in the past issued gilts for specific nationalisation programmes and named the gilt accordingly. Currently, gilts are issued for general financing of government responsibilities. The modern names are treasury, exchequer and funding.

Gilts are usually issued in amounts of £100 or £1000 nominal value and will normally sell upon issue at a price close to this figure. By this means, the issuer assumes immediate use of the capital that changes hands in return for a commitment to pay interest in two equal 6-monthly instalments on two pre-specified dates, and to repay the nominal value at a specific date in the future (except in the case of undated gilts, which carry no commitment to repay the capital invested).

The amount of interest is fixed and determined by the coupon, decided before the time of issue of the gilt. The coupon is a rate of interest; the amount of interest per annum is the product of the coupon and the nominal value of, usually, £100. The amount of interest per 6 months is therefore given by

$$\text{Interest per 6 months} = \frac{\text{coupon} \times \text{nominal value}}{2}$$

For example, Exchequer 12.25% 1994 pays interest of $\dfrac{12.25 \times 100}{2}$

$$= £6.13, \text{ per 6 months}$$

The payment of interest continues until redemption of the gilt. Short-dated gilts are identified by a redemption date within 5 years, mediums by redemption within 5–15 years, longs by redemption over 15 years away and undateds by unspecified redemption. For other than the latter types, the redemption date is specified at the date of issue; Exchequer 12¼% 2011, for example, is redeemed at a specified date in 2011. As time goes by, longs become mediums, mediums become shorts, and shorts disappear as they are redeemed. Undateds continue unchanged and are likely to remain so. While the government has the option to redeem after a given date, the six undated gilts that remain unredeemed all have coupons of between 2.5% and 4%, and no government will choose to replace these loans unless interest rates fall below current levels (they are around 4.5% at the beginning of 2007).

Thus, for redeemable fixed-interest gilts held until the redemption date, the cash flow to be produced by the investment can be predicted with certainty. Market prices will not, however, remain constant. Immediately after issue, the stock market price-fixing mechanism will begin to operate, and market prices will fluctuate. Simplistically, if interest rates rise immediately after issue, the coupon is likely to become low in relation to new issues, the amount of interest will be comparatively less and the price of the bond will fall. The opposite would occur if interest rates fell as they did in 1982 and throughout the 1990s, providing large capital gains for many bondholders.

The market value of a gilt (as quoted in the financial press on a daily basis) represents a mid-point price around which gilts can be bought and sold. Given this readily available information and the certain income flow, the internal rate of return (IRR) on fixed-interest securities held to redemption can be accurately computed.

Take again Exchequer 12¼% 2011. This has a redemption date of 22 March. Let us assume that on 1 October 2007 the £100 nominal value of this stock can be bought for £114.59. The timing and amount of expected cash flows are shown in Table 2.1. (Note that tax deductions are ignored; in addition, this example ignores accrued interest, which must be considered when the date of purchase does not coincide with an interest payment date.)

This cash flow produces a half-yearly rate of return of 3.06%; annualised, this represents a before-tax IRR or gross redemption yield of 6.21%. Note, however, that this would normally be quoted in nominal terms, that is, $2 \times 3.06\%$; see Table 2.1.

Cash-flow certainty is removed by the possibility of sale before redemption. As values move up and down, the prospect of selling the gilt to make a capital gain or loss arises. Given that future prices cannot be predicted,

Table 2.1   A gilt cash flow.

Date	£
1 October 2007	(114.59)
22 March 2008	6.25
20 September 2008	6.25
22 March 2009	6.25
20 September 2009	6.25
22 March 2010	6.25
20 September 2010	6.25
22 March 2011	6.25 + 100 = 106.25

Table 2.2   Typical gilt price information.

1995					Price £	+ or −	Interest yield	Redemption yield
High	Low	Stock						
118½	111¼	Exchange	12¼%	1999	114.59	+¾	10.69	6.12
Highest	Lowest	Stock	Coupon	Redemption	Price	Price	Interest	Nominal
trading	trading			year		move	only	gross
price in	price in					since last	yield	redemption
1995	1995					quote		yield

no certain calculation of internal rates of return can be made without an assumption that the gilt is held to redemption. It is, however, possible to be a little more positive by concluding that, while future prices (and therefore gains and losses) cannot be predicted, there is a tendency for the value of the gilt to approach £100 plus the last interest payment as the redemption date approaches. Over time, interest payments become less important and the redemption value becomes more important. The value of a gilt with 6 months to run should thus be close to £100 plus the final interest payment.

The financial pages of national newspapers quote gross redemption yields on the nominal basis noted here. They also quote *interest yields* expressing the relationship between the current price and the annual interest payments. For irredeemable gilts only the latter is, of course, presented. Table 2.2 shows a typical (mythical) extract.

The generation of return from government bonds can therefore be summarised as follows:

a. Capital: The investment provides a return of capital in an amount which may be more or less than the original investment. If held to redemption, the return will be the nominal value of £100; in any case, as the redemption date approaches the return of capital will tend towards this price.

b. Income: The investment produces an income in the form of interest, paid half yearly in arrears. Being determined by the coupon and the nominal value, this never varies: a bond is a fixed-interest investment.

2.2.3   Index-linked gilts

Index-linked government bonds were introduced in UK in the early 1980s. They are natural investments for pension funds with real liabilities, but their availability has been limited and high prices have on occasion been explained by a mismatch of demand and supply. Broadly speaking, they offer an income that is fixed in real, rather than monetary, terms and a redemption payment which is again fixed in real terms.

Parity with real values is attempted by tying interest payments and the redemption to the retail price index, albeit lagged by 8 months. (This is to cope with the problem of accrued interest, which is included in the price of all gilts. Without lagging the interest payment, given that it could never be predicted, the price could not be calculated.) The coupon is the nominal interest, typically around 2%.

The return on index-linked gilts is therefore the product of a nominal interest rate, an inflation-linked interest payment and an inflation-linked return of capital, normally a gain. While the calculation of the gross redemption yield is complex (Rutterford and Davison, 2007), it can be broadly estimated as $(1 + i) (1 + l) - 1$, where i = inflation rate and l = the liquidity preference or real return rate. Thus, a 2% index-linked stock, unless resold within a short period, has an unknown redemption yield in nominal terms, as this will depend upon the inflation rate between the time 8 months prior to purchase and 8 months prior to sale or redemption; but, if inflation is expected to average 3%, if the stock is held to redemption and if it is purchased at close to its nominal value of £100, then the expected redemption yield will be around $(1 + 0.03) (1 + 0.02) - 1 = 0.05060$, or 5.06%. These index-linked gilts would be attractive to any pension fund concerned with inflation risk if fixed-interest gilts produced a nominally fixed return of 5% or below when held to redemption (see the following).

The return generated by index-linked gilts is summarised as follows:

a. Capital: The investment provides a return of capital in an amount that may be more or less than the original investment. However, given positive inflation, a monetary capital gain would be expected. The return of capital depends on the rate of inflation intervening between dates 8 months prior to purchase and 8 months prior to redemption.

Assuming that the gilt is purchased at par on issue, the capital gain matches inflation, and so the price is maintained in real terms.

b.   Income: The investment provides a varying income equal to the nominal interest rate plus (minus) the lagged inflation (deflation) rate.

2.2.4   Ordinary shares (equities)

Ordinary shares, or equities, represent a share of ownership in a company. While they may or may not carry voting rights, all imply a fractional share in the equity value (total assets less debt) of a company. They are commonly issued with a nominal or par value of 25p.

Income is normally paid twice-yearly and is in the form of dividends (interim and final), which are determined by the company's profits and management policy, each of which may change from year to year. The income from shares, therefore, while it may have some relationship to the last declared dividend, is unpredictable.

An equity is 'irredeemable' in normal circumstances, other than by sale. The resale price is market determined and may be higher or lower than the purchase price. Again, therefore, capital return is unpredictable. Experience shows that the volatility of profits and dividend policy (among other factors) is reflected in the volatility of share prices. It should be borne in mind that there is no safety net as there is in the case of gilts with a guaranteed redemption; on the other hand, capital gain prospects are similarly unlimited.

Yield measures for ordinary shares are, as a consequence, largely unhelpful (although they are used a great deal by analysts). An IRR, always the most complete return measure, can only be estimated given a prediction of resale date, resale price and all intervening interim and final dividends, or by projecting dividends to infinity (see below). This is so hazardous that it is rarely attempted. The only yield measure in common use is the relationship of last year's interim and final dividend to the current quoted price. Even next year's dividend yield can only be an estimate.

Dividend yield is no measure of total return. Low dividend yields may imply expected increases in dividends, expected capital gains or both. Dividend yields are relatively volatile and do not form the basis of sound investment decision-making without the addition of a considerable volume of extra information. The price–earnings (P/E) ratio, a comparison of price per share with earnings per share, is a standard additional measure of the quality of the share, where a high P/E ratio may imply anticipated growth in earnings and therefore in share values. It can be used in the estimate of resale price in attempts to forecast holding-period return, or IRR. Resale price is a product of earnings per share and the P/E ratio at the resale point, which may show cyclical fluctuation and be capable of some qualified estimation. More usually, however, the predicted IRR of an ordinary shareholding reflects the rationality that the value, and therefore sale price, of a share must ultimately reflect all future anticipated dividends. Assuming annual dividends,

$$P_o = \frac{D_1}{1+r} + \frac{D_2}{(1+r)^2} + \frac{D_3}{(1+r)^3}$$

where P_o is the price in year O; D_1, D_2 and D_3 are expected dividends in years 1, 2 and 3; and r is the overall required return (target rate).

If dividends are expected to increase in a common ratio (g), the series becomes

$$P_o = \frac{D_1}{1+r} + \frac{D_1(1+g)}{(1+r)^2} + \frac{D_1(1+g)^2}{(1+r)^3}$$

Summating this geometric progression gives

$$P_o = \frac{D_1}{r-g}$$

[Those familiar with common presentations of property valuation mathematics (see, for example, Baum et al., 2006) may recognise ($r - g$) as a capitalisation rate and the preceding formula as the income approach or investment method: of that, considerably more will follow.]

Such a model may be employed for valuation (estimation of a likely selling price for a share that has never traded on the stock market, for example) or analysis (estimation of anticipated return, r). In either case it is instructive to note the effect of anticipated dividend or income growth.

For example, if shares are available for sale at £1.25, last year's total dividend was 8p and dividends are expected to increase at a rate of 7% p.a., this would produce an estimated IRR of 13.4%.

$$1.25 = \frac{0.08}{r-0.07}$$

$$r - 0.07 = \frac{0.08}{1.25}$$

$$r = 13.4\%$$

Such a model is naive, to say the least. It does, however, reveal a vital factor in property investment appraisal: anticipated growth in income and capital, g, and its effect upon initial yield. The initial or dividend yield in the example is low in comparison to the overall yield: this is fundamental and provides a central point of reference in this book. In the following, we develop this model further.

The return from ordinary shares is generated as follows:

a.   Capital: The investment may produce a return of capital which may exceed or be less than the original investment. All capital may be lost; however, at the same time, there is no limit on the possible amount received on sale.

b.   Income: The investment provides a varying income dependent upon earnings and management policy.

2.2.5   Property

Property (in the UK and many commonwealth countries) or real estate (in North America, Australia and increasingly elsewhere) may be acquired for many purposes other than investment. Broadly speaking, a distinction may be made between property owned for occupation (although there may be a simultaneous investment service performed by that property) and property owned for investment *per se*.

Property owned as an investment may be either freehold, connoting effective superior ownership, or leasehold, providing an inferior form of ownership subject to (a) superior landlord(s), either leaseholders or leaseholders and freeholder. (For fuller details of UK land tenure, see Gray and Symes, 1981, and Baum and Sams, 2007.)

The distinction between freehold and leasehold property considerably complicates a generalised view of property investment returns. While ownership of a freehold interest indicates perpetual ownership of indestructible land together with the more transient structure built upon it, ownership of a leasehold indicates a wasting asset. Yet this is too simplistic: some leases retain their value after the lease-end because of the phenomenon of key money (Fraser, 1984; Baum and Yu, 1985) and the automatic renewal ensured by the operation of the 1954 Landlord and Tenant Act, and some freeholds exhibit a declining quality. Nonetheless, it is fair to generalise the permanent nature of a freehold and the temporary nature of a leasehold. It is in these two forms that property investments are almost universally held in the UK, especially by larger scale investors. Figures 2.1 and 2.2 show the general relationship of the capital values over time of freehold and leasehold investments in a period of inflation.

It can be seen from Figure 2.1 that in a period of inflation a freehold property investment may be expected to show a profit upon resale. Deterioration and obsolescence may contribute to a declining (although difficult to measure) building component value, so that refurbishment or redevelopment may

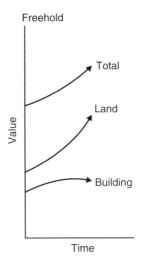

Figure 2.1   Term structure of property investment values – freehold.

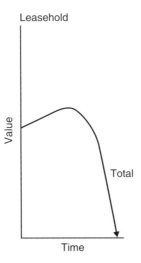

Figure 2.2   Term structure of property investment values – leasehold.

be necessary to maintain performance, but the general trend of value is upward.

A 25-year lease in the same property, on the other hand, would by now almost certainly have peaked in value and would be entering a period of rapid decline to zero. The same is broadly true of any investment in lease-hold commercial property.

Nonetheless, the problem of building depreciation or obsolescence of free-hold buildings should not, as has usually been the case in the property world, be understated. Poorly designed buildings located in low-land-value areas will produce a more rapid fall off in performance than carefully restored and refurbished buildings in the West End of London. Not to distinguish between these vastly different investment types would be most dangerous, and in this text we suggest approaches to the problems.

The income produced by a property investment is in the form of rent reduced by operating expenses of various types. While operating expenses will be incurred both regularly (management, service provision) and infrequently (repairs), rent will normally be received at regular intervals, quarterly in advance being typical in the UK. Analogous to the stock market and its differentiation between cum-dividend and ex-dividend investments is the apportionment procedure applied to rents received in advance in respect of a full rent period during which the property is sold. Apportionment of the rent that relates to the period between completion and the next rent date is in the favour of the purchaser and is in effect deducted from the purchase price (Bornand, 1985).

The payment of rent is governed by the provisions of the lease. There is no standard arrangement in the English-speaking world: US leases are of varying types but rarely for longer than 10 years and often for 3-year periods; Australian leases of grade A and premium offices appear similar to the US. Leases in the Far East are often shorter still. The UK has now lost its formerly standard 25-year lease with a modern tendency towards 5, 10 or 15 year leases, but it is now not uncommon for industrial and office leases to include breaks, normally timed at the 5-year review date. Given that in continental Europe 5- and 10-year leases are very common, the UK lease is decreasingly at odds with standard practice elsewhere.

The regularity with which rents may be increased also differs throughout the world. While in the US, Hong Kong and Singapore the 3-year lease is usually at a fixed rent and the Australian office and retail leases include annual fixed or consumer-price-index-based reviews, the UK lease usually fixes rents for 5-year intervals with upward-only reviews, and continental European leases often have rents indexed annually. Longer North American leases may have rents tied to the rate of inflation or, more often, to tenant's turnover; this is rare in the UK. The pattern of rental in the typical prime UK investment property is therefore stepped upwards (in a period of inflation or growth) at 5-yearly intervals. Rents at each review point are renegotiated in line with the open market rental or estimated rental value (ERV).

[Change to the UK commercial leasing regime has been one of the most important property market issues of the last 15 years since the property crash of 1990, and readers wanting a more detailed insight into this issue are referred to two reports for Government produced by the University of Reading (DETR, 2000; Crosby *et al.*, 2005)].

In summary, therefore, the return from property is generated as follows:

a. Capital: The investment may produce a return of capital by resale, which may exceed or be less than the original investment. In freehold investments, there is an effective limit (land value) to any loss; in leaseholds, a decline to nil value must eventually be suffered.

b. Income: The investment provides a varying income depending upon rental values, themselves a product of the demand for use of the property and the supply of alternatives. Variance of the income is reduced by leases and long review periods; upward-only reviews will produce, at worst, a level income.

2.2.6 Summary

To summarise this broad overview of five investment types, it is useful to identify similarities.

Ordinary shares and property are fundamentally different from bank deposits and fixed-interest securities in two major respects. First, ordinary shares and property are both what Sharpe and Alexander (1990) calls real or equity investments, representing ownership of tangible assets. Bank deposits and fixed-interest securities are not real investments, but are investments in money itself. This difference gives rise to a second difference: broadly speaking, equity or real investments perform well in periods of inflation (they are inflation-proof to some degree), while money investments perform badly (inflation-prone). The period of significant inflation witnessed in the UK from the 1950s until the early 1990s was a major cause of a rise in property and share prices in relation to alternative non-equity investments. To illustrate the opposite effect, falling inflation expectations through the 1990s fuelled excellent returns for bonds; see Table 1.2.

Sitting uncomfortably between these pairings is the index-linked gilt, which is not a real investment, but which will perform well in inflationary periods. Table 2.3 illustrates this.

There are, of course, many other examples of investments that demonstrate or question those classifications. Leaseholds producing a fixed-profit rent are inflation-prone real investments, as are fixed freehold ground rents,

Table 2.3 A classification of investments.

	Real investments	**Monetary investments**
Inflation proof	Equities	
	Properties	Index-linked gilts
Inflation prone		Bank deposits
		Fixed-interest securities

for example. During the first part of the 1990s these inflation-prone property investments were joined by the large number of over-rented properties, let on long leases with upward-only rent reviews. So this limited list of five investment types is neither finite nor comprehensive. It does, however, serve to set property investment in a context of alternative investment opportunities.

2.3   Qualities of investments

What is a good investment? A simple answer to this seemingly simple question is 'one which produces a high return'. Previously we have identified returns as deriving from two sources: income and capital return. A good investment is one that produces high levels of these in comparison with the price paid.

But most investments are traded in an atmosphere of uncertainty. It is not possible to predict with accuracy what the level of return will be. Even fixed-interest gilts held to redemption produce a return that is uncertain in real terms and dependent upon future inflation levels for purchasing power value.

Investors will attempt to reduce uncertainty to its minimum by market research and other means. Information that is freely available is impounded into prices, and so investments promising a high return will (all other factors being equal) sell for more. Jacob and Pettit (1984) described this 'efficient market hypothesis' as follows.

Market participants, acting in their own self-interest, use available information to attempt to secure more desirable (higher returns, ceteris paribus) portfolio positions. In doing so they collectively ensure that price movements in response to new information are instantaneous and unbiased and will 'fully reflect' all relevant information. Competition among participants to secure useful information will drive security prices from one equilibrium level to another so that the change in price in response to new information will be independent of prior changes in price, so that price changes follow a 'random walk' in response to the information.

Investors in the five categories summarised in Chapter 1 will typically hold some information which is not uncertain. This will be:

a. The price of the investment.
b. The current income produced. For bank deposits, this is the current interest rate; for fixed-interest gilts, the coupon; for index-linked gilts, the next interest payment (based on the retail price index already published); for ordinary shares, the last dividend payment; and for property, the current contract rent.

Absolute certainty over the current income level leads to the use of the *initial yield* as a common market measure by which investments can be related. This is given by

$$\frac{\text{net current income}}{\text{price}}$$

The level of this initial yield will be determined by several factors that determine the quality of an investment. A high-quality investment is expected to produce a low initial yield because the market would bid a high price in relation to the level of current income, which depends upon a series of considerations or features that are unrelated to the current income level, and which are considered in the following sections.

2.3.1   Income and capital growth

The current income level may not be a good indicator of future income levels. Consequently, the initial yield may not indicate the continuing income yield that will be produced by an investment over its holding period. Where that yield is expected to increase, the initial yield may be low, the result of a higher price being paid.

Fixed-interest gilts produce a fixed income. The price should reflect that fact. There is no prospect of income growth or, conversely, of monetary income loss. The initial yield is a perfect indication of the continuing income yield ('running yield').

Index-linked gilts, on the other hand, produce an index-linked income. As long as inflation is expected to be positive, income growth may be anticipated and the initial yield should therefore be lower, ceteris paribus, than for fixed-interest gilts.

Ordinary shares produce dividends that depend upon (a) profits and (b) management dividend and reinvestment strategy. The latter is often used to smooth away variations in the former, so that a broad relationship between inflation and dividends may be theorised via profit levels, and in an inflationary era the profits of an average company might be expected to increase.

For property, a similar relationship might be theorised between inflation and rents. Investment Property Databank (IPD) data shows that, while the all-property rental value long-term index has grown from 100 in 1975 to 367 in 2003, the retail prices index has grown to 496 in the same time period. However, this hides the performance of different segments of the market. Retail has shown real growth in rents with an index of 593, equating to 0.65% p.a. real growth over inflation. However, offices and industrial property have not performed as well, showing real shortfalls of 2.26% and 1.24% p.a. respectively.

Theorising over-simplistically, a supply artificially restricted by planning controls may be set against increasing demand as behaviour patterns change and population increases to cause real rental growth. A similar effect may be translated into real dividend increases for ordinary shares; it is not present for fixed-interest (conventional) gilts. However, this ignores the effects of depreciation in property assets, and real losses could be caused by a lack of understanding of how obsolescence in buildings affects rental values and the need for periodic capital expenditure.

There may also be monopoly profits that accrue to property owners. Property interests are unique: although the impact of heterogeneity will vary according to circumstances, extra gains may be made by exploiting the resulting monopoly position. An extreme example of this is marriage value. The owner of a mid-length leasehold interest will almost certainly be unable to sell to an investor at a price that matches the gain which the freehold reversioner could make by its surrender. Monopoly profits may accrue as a result to both freeholder and leaseholder. Other 'special purchasers' may appear: immediate neighbours, or even funds that are especially keen to buy a south-east prime shop, for example, for portfolio balance.

Less clear-cut is the gain made upon re-zoning or betterment. This may be diluted by competition, but the siting of a new motorway or the real-location of land planned for commercial development may well produce capital gains in excess of inflation and a reasonable real growth. These can also be termed monopoly profits: they may be the product of the exploitation of monopolistic information or of monopolistic land ownership. This can also be called the exploitation of 'real options' (see 2.3.4 below).

Finally, gearing or leverage, the use of borrowed funds to exaggerate capital and income growth, is particularly suited to property investment. Simple house purchase illustrates this strategy. Suppose a house purchaser has a choice of an all-cash buy for £500 000 or a £300 000 interest-only 10% loan and £200 000 equity input. Suppose prices increase by 50% over 3 years. The following comparison (shown in Table 2.4) emerges.

Table 2.4 Geared and ungeared returns.

	All cash	60% Mortgage
House value in 3 years	£750,000	£750,000
Equity in 3 years	£750,000	£450,000
Less initial equity	£500,000	£200,000
Less interest payments (compounded)	£0	£93,000
Equity gain	£250,000	£150,700
Equity gain (as % of initial equity)	50%	75.35%

A 75% capital increase resulting from gearing may be compared with an ungeared 50% gain. This particular investor would be best advised to buy additional similar property elsewhere – if it can be found – and make 75% on the whole £500,000 currently available for investment by repeating the gearing level.

Such gains can be maximised by increasing the gearing level in times of high price increases, where interest rates are low and where taxation rules are favourable. The risk of financial failure resulting from interest rate increases or falling prices is at the same time increased by such a policy (a risk cruelly exposed over the first 3 years of the 1990s for those borrowing high percentages of outlay at the peak of the market pricing cycle); but the general inflationary trend since the Second World War and the particular experience of 1960–1972, when many massive gains resulted from such policies (Marriott, 1967; Rose, 1985), provides an example of a sustained period that demonstrated the benefits of gearing. The period of low interest rates in the context of a recovering property market in the period of 1997–2007 is another illustration of how fortunes can be (and were) made through leverage. While equities may be geared (e.g. by the use of options), property is the perfect asset in this respect.

These four constituents of growth have produced many valuable property companies and underpin the popular nature of property investment. Income growth is directly translated into capital growth, and it might be surmised that (ceteris paribus) the geared purchase of property in an improving area close to a new development or traffic improvements in a period of inflation is an excellent investment, examples of which have been common over the last 50 years.

2.3.2   Operating expenses

Once the purchase of an investment has been completed, the investor must face the prospect of continued expense necessitated by ownership. For bank deposits, such operating expenses are nil, apart from the investor's own time spent in checking accounts. For securities, the management of a given investment (rather than a portfolio) is again reduced to keeping an eye on the financial pages. For property, on the other hand, operating expenses derive from several sources – repair and maintenance costs, insurance premiums, rent review fees, management (rent collection, periodic inspection, services management) fees, shortfalls in service charges, rates (in some circumstances), re-letting fees, refurbishment costs, dilapidations claims and various legal expenses arising out of disputes with the public, tenants or adjoining owners- and contribute to a potentially high annual expenditure for the property investment owner, and may increase required initial yields.

2.3.3   Liquidity, marketability and transfer costs

Liquidity (for our purposes) is the ease and certainty with which an asset can be converted to cash at, or close to, its market value. Bank deposits are almost perfectly liquid; gilts are usually convertible to cash within one day; equities may be transformed to cash within a week to a month. Property, on the other hand, is illiquid. A quick sale will not usually be possible unless a low price is accepted. Even then, the period between a decision to sell and receipt of cash can be as long as 3 months. Lizieri *et al.* (2004) analysed nearly 200 transactions from three funds in three separate years, representing three different market states, and found that the median period for the time from putting a property on the market until completion of the sale was nearly 6 months.

Contributing to property's illiquidity is a trio of factors. Marketability describes the reserve of potential buyers for an investment and the speed and ease with which they may be contacted. For large property investments – buildings worth more than £50m, say – the number of potential buyers may be small. For unusual investments (e.g., Land's End) the potential market may be difficult to target and advertising may be highly inefficient. On the other hand, the stock exchange ensures the marketability of most gilts and equities.

The indivisibility of property as an investment contributes to its lack of marketability and therefore to its illiquidity. The possibility of sale of part of an investment reduces the impact of this problem and enables flexible financial management. Property can be physically divided, divided into freehold and leaseholds, or split into time shares, but it remains in general a fundamentally indivisible investment, with a high minimum outlay. This explains the rapid growth of the unlisted property fund market in the late 1990s and early part of the new millennium (see www.propertyfundsresearch.com). However, until syndication and other forms of fractional ownership become much more widespread and popular in the UK, the purchase and sale of small units of a property investment will not normally be possible. This is not true of the alternatives.

The transfer costs necessitated when a decision to sell is finally translated into cash are higher than those associated with the alternatives. Stamp duty, conveyancing fees and agents' fees on purchase are higher than conveyancing fees and agents' fees on sale: these may total 5% and 2.5%, respectively. A more likely transfer cost for equities is around 0.1% for a reasonable volume and is likely to be less for gilts.

Illiquidity and its associated costs may therefore be said to be highest for property in comparison to the chosen alternatives. It has been argued (Fraser, 1985b) that the infrequency of property trading as compared with trading frequency in the stock market (see Chapter 4, Table 4.3) reduces the importance of this factor, but infrequency of trading probably results from illiquidity. The fact remains that cash tied up in property is, pound for pound, less liquid than cash tied up elsewhere. This has two implications: first, it increases the chances of an investor becoming financially embarrassed and put out of business by lenders; second, it decreases the chances of attractive alternatives being acquired. For property companies, the illiquidity of property may be said to be much more of a problem than it is for the larger institutions. In any case, it should increase required initial yields.

2.3.4   Real options

For many smaller investors, property has an appeal unmatched by the alternatives. For some, this may be a prestige value: for others, it may be the opportunity for exercising positive management and, while perhaps increasing return, offering self-employment. Driving past farmland may hold more appeal for some (even fund managers) than reading the financial pages; building naming rights may be a more tangible example of the psychic income that may be derived from property ownership. Whatever its effect – noticeable in some cases, non-existent in others – psychic income is a positive input into the quality of property as an investment, which may reduce the required initial yield.

A more rational explanation of this phenomenon is the possibility that property ownership brings with it the possibility of making money from a variety of activities. Freehold ownership confers a series of rights upon property owners, ranging from the right to remove a tenant for the purposes of one's own occupation to the right to apply for permission to redevelop the property for the same or an alternative use. Farmland on the edge of a city without permission for residential use may appear to have no value beyond agricultural value, but there is always the possibility that at some point in the future permission will be granted. This is a real option.

Another example of a real option value attaching to property is land with permission for development where the development is not viable. Its current use value may appear to define the best price that should be paid. But the viability of development can always change – and where property values are volatile, this can happen in significant quantity. In fact, volatility in property values will add more value to the real option, because the upside value will become greater and can be exploited when it does, while the downside need not be suffered.

Generally, property provides real options where cash, fixed-interest securities, index-linked gilts and equities do not. Property can also provide more traditional financial options through asymmetrical (upward-over) rent review clauses, an example of which is illustrated in Chapter 9. Options will generally reduce, or can be used to explain, low initial yields.

2.3.5   Tax efficiency

The tax efficiency of an investment refers to the degree to which a gross return is reduced to a net return for the individual investor. The different and complex tax positions of individuals, institutions and companies alike make it difficult to generalise regarding the relative tax efficiency of different real estate investments. However, property in general can be very income tax efficient because the use of debt or leverage can reduce taxable rental income. This will reduce initial yields. An example of this is provided in Chapter 3.

2.3.6   Risk

2.3.6.1   Introduction

Of very great importance is the degree of risk attached to an investment. Some finance texts view risk as the major determinant of return; modern portfolio theory (MPT) contributes to this importance by regarding the investment decision as a trade-off between expected returns and risk (Brigham and Ehrhardt, 2005). Branch (1985) is more circumspect, suggesting that 'investors will generally trade off some expected return for a reduction in risk'. A simple conclusion may be drawn: risk increases the required initial yield.

But what is risk? Reilly and Brown (2002) suggest that it is 'uncertainty regarding the expected rate of return from an investment'. Is there anything intrinsically unattractive about uncertainty when the expected rate of return may be much higher, or much lower, than expected? The answer to this question is supported by empirical rather than theoretical evidence. The typical investor is demonstrably risk-averse.

Experiments carried out in university classes usually bear this out. Despite the unreality engendered by the lack of real money in such an environment the following game is a useful test of risk-aversion. The tutor offers for sale 10 tickets, each of which gives the right to a cheque. Five cheques for £50 and five cheques for £100 are to be distributed on a random basis with a 50/50 chance of each being handed over in return for a ticket in any one case. The class holds 15–20 students. Tickets are sold by means of sealed tender, so that only the 10 highest bids are successful. Unsuccessful bidders lose no money.

The prices obtained for tickets always indicate risk-aversion. £75 would not be an unrealistic offer, balancing a chance of £25 profit with an equal chance of £25 loss. But students rarely bid up to £75. One such series of bids from 15 students is as shown:

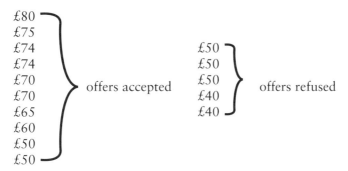

£80
£75
£74
£74
£70
£70   } offers accepted
£65
£60
£50
£50

£50
£50
£50   } offers refused
£40
£40

In a more competitive market place, the successful £50 bidders would be less fortunate. The £80 bidder showed some property market optimism and a confidence in his luck. The £75 bid was, as suggested above, a neutral offer but the other bids illustrate risk-aversion. They equated the 50% chance of a considerable gain with the 50% chance of a much smaller loss. The median bid of £60 equated a £40 gain with a £10 loss. (The two £40 bids show an excessive degree of suspicion over the sincerity of the tutor.)

Thus, uncertainty regarding the expected rate of return from an investment is seen as unattractive and results in devaluation. Ten certain £75 returns would have produced £750; the tickets offered netted only £668 for the same eventual cost to the offeror. Risky investments are less valuable.

2.3.6.2   Systematic and specific risk

Finance theory has firmly promoted the idea that there are two main types of risk. Systematic risks are endemic to an asset class. Specific risk is not; and by diversifying a portfolio within one type of asset class, specific risk can ultimately be removed, because a very large portfolio, one which approximates to the entire universe of the asset type, will tend to produce no surprises that the asset class as a whole does not suffer.

The sources of property risk are manifold, and many are unique to this investment form. Some are generic to property as an asset, and can be called systematic risks; some are unique to single assets, and can be called specific risk; and some can be either, depending on the appropriate definition of the asset class. We call these semi-systematic risks. Some can be either systematic or specific: systematic at the national level, or specific at the local level. (We return to this issue later in the chapter.)

2.3.6.3   Systematic risks

a. *Legislation risk* is the chance of changes in case law and statute law that directly affect investment returns. Certain property investors have suffered in this respect in past decades by the introduction and extension of the Rent Acts, the Leasehold Reform Act, value added tax (VAT), the Town and Country Planning Act and others (Baum and Sams, 2007) and the current debate on UK commercial lease reform is perceived by some of the protagonists as producing a shift in value from one group to another by the threat of legislation.

Property is therefore especially prone to legislation risk. Equities are not exempt from this: health and safety regulations can have a massive impact upon drug companies, for example. Nonetheless, the experience of some residential landlords upon extension of the Rent Acts and the introduction of the Leasehold Reform Act 1967, while probably of limited impact, sharply focused property investment as a high legislation risk sector.

b. *Liquidity risk* is uncertainty affecting the speed at which an asset can be converted to cash at, or close to, its market value. Bank deposits are almost perfectly liquid; gilts are usually convertible to cash within 1 day; equities may be transformed to cash within a week to a month. Property, on the other hand, is illiquid. A quick sale will not usually be possible unless a low price is accepted. This contributes directly to property risk (Baum, 1988b; Lizieri *et al.*, 2004).

2.3.6.4   Systematic/specific risks

a. *Structural risk* is the chance of high repair costs, high maintenance costs, or refurbishment becoming necessary, and eventually rebuilding becoming necessary, either through structural failure or economic or functional obsolescence. Such risks are not paralleled in other markets other than indirectly and even then in a highly diversified manner. For example, there may be a structural risk attached to the performance of ordinary shares in a heavy industry company with one old manufacturing plant, but this risk type would be much reduced in the case of a chain of retail shops, where many more units (if owned freehold) would diversify such risk and reduce its impact upon performance.

Despite considerable output (reviewed in Baum *et al.*, 2005), much work remains to be completed in the general area of property depreciation and obsolescence. It is not currently easy to generalise about the life of building types. It is, however, possible to say that freehold interests in prime shop units are much less prone to structural risk (often the buildings are old yet solidly constructed, having transcended the usual cycle of redevelopment; they are simple, ground floor cubes; and the responsibility for shop fronts, fittings and so on is transferred to the tenant) than are modern offices or industrial units (where the nature of occupation, the nature of construction and technological impact upon industry reduce economic life). It is also clear that land is less likely to depreciate in normal circumstances so that property investments with a proportionately larger land value are less prone to obsolescence and hence to structural risk. Office buildings in the City of London (for example) are less prone to structural risk than similar buildings in Houston, where land values are less protected by physical boundaries and planning restrictions, and are in any event lower due to the relative eminence of the City of London as a financial centre.

Other structural risks may be passed on to tenants in the form of full repairing and insuring leases, but the ultimate responsibility for obsolescence and fundamental defects rests with the property owner who consequently shoulders a risk unique to this form of investment. Hence, there is both a systematic risk of depreciation and obsolescence and a specific risk of structural failure

b. *Taxation risk* describes the chance of imposition of new taxes upon the investment type or of alterations in current taxes. Property can be uniquely prone to taxation risk. The increases in stamp duty imposed in the early budgets of Gordon Brown are a clear example of this.

Prior to massive institutional investment, it was possible to generalise that the person in the street was much less likely (aside from home ownership) to be a property investor than a stock market investor; that is still true in terms of direct investment. Property is easily identified as a taxation target and attacking it is not electorally disastrous, as long as home ownership for the less well-off is avoided. This fact in itself explains the tax incentives given to single house ownership (now limited to the still-important capital gains tax exemption) in a context of relative disincentive for private property investment. Taxes upon UK property investments apparently affect only the corporate sector and the wealthy. (Many institutional funds are tax exempt.)

More importantly, taxes such as a tax on development land value can have an enormous impact upon return. The introduction of a capital gains tax in the UK in 1965 was of great redistributive effect; the indexation of capital gains tax in 1982 has reduced this impact. The effect of the introduction of VAT on rents was forecast to be significant although its actual impact was much less than predicted.

Various income tax reliefs for particular categories of property investment – woodlands, for example, or industrial buildings – are constantly in danger of adjustment or abolition. Taxation risk for property is a major factor that is less likely to attack the alternative markets.

In the specific risk category, local authority rates are constantly under the public eye and are unlikely to vary greatly; however, while they tax occupation rather than ownership, it is clear that occupier tax increases should cause rent (and return) reductions. The introduction of rate-free (for 10 years) Enterprise Zones, for example, increased property values within the zones (albeit at the expense of immediately surrounding areas: see, for example, MacGregor *et al.*, 1985); and the introduction of the Uniform Business Rate and the Rating Revaluation in 1990 had an impact on relative values, although Mehdi (2003) suggests that this impact was not immediate.

The impact of Stamp Duty rises on monthly valuations was not immediate (McAllister *et al.*, 2003).

c. *Planning risk* is the risk that central (systematic risk) or local (specific risk) government planning policies (in the broadest sense, including transport policy, regional policy, power policy and so on) impinge negatively or positively upon property investment values. At the regional level, policies of redistribution (such as the siting of government departments in depressed areas) will have broad effects; at the local level, proposals for such traffic improvements as the M25 and the Channel Tunnel have an immediate impact upon values. At the individual level, particular planning decisions have an enormous impact upon value. The downside corollary is a speculative purchase of land with development potential which eventually settles upon someone else's land, and it is of course downside risk that equates with most investors' perception of risk as an investment quality.

The effect of planning is so enormous that further elucidation is probably unnecessary. Let it suffice to say that the effects upon other sectors of the investment market are less pronounced.

2.3.6.5   Semi-systematic risks

a. *Sector risk* is the chance that sectoral price movements affect the subject investment. Such a risk is certainly present in the ordinary share market, where the choice of sector may be vital. Electricals may underperform industrials and chemicals; within that sector, micro-electronics may underperform household goods.

A property's sector risk is more sharply focused than this. Given the 'lumpiness' of property investment, where large sums of money may be tied up in one investment, property is particularly prone to sector risk.

Performance differences occur between sectors caused by changes in rents and capitalisation rates. For example, although shop average yields fell between 1977 and 1985, industrial yields rose by nearly 200 basis points [the ICHP (Investors Chronicle Hillier Parker, now CBRE) average industrial yield was 8.5% in 1977 and 10.2% in May 1985].

This combination of rental growth or decline and capitalisation rate change can cause significant short-term variations in total returns. For example, the ICHP index of returns to City offices fell from 1058 to 530 between November 1989 and May 1993. During the same period the industrial index rose from 1284 to 1395.

b. *Locational risk* is a similar factor to sector risk, but its relative importance is a complex empirical issue. The average IPD total return over the period 1980 to 2003 shows significant variation across the regions. Average total returns ranged from 8.9% pa for all offices to 10.1% p.a. for all industrials. However, retail total returns ranged from 10.5% in Scotland to 17.7% in

Northern Ireland, office total returns ranged from 7% in Wales to 11.7% p.a. in the East Midlands and industrial total returns ranged from 11.5% in the East to 14.5% in Wales.

Overlaid upon this is international risk. UK funds have been seen to spread their property investments in recent decades through the UK, Europe and North America. Both the relative performance of property rental values and yields in these areas and exchange rate fluctuations contribute to a pronounced sector risk in individual property investment that cannot so easily be diversified away by exploiting the lower unit of investment that typifies other markets. (On the other side of the coin, depending upon the nature of the liabilities of the investor, international diversification can be an efficient reducer of risk in the portfolio context: see page 260 and Wurtzebach and Baum, 1993.)

2.3.6.6 Specific risks

a. *Legal risk* is the chance that the title to an investment is unsatisfactory or that it is discovered that a right exists over the subject land which affects its value. It is the risk that a rent review notice is missed; or, conversely, that a request for an excessive rent is not challenged in time by a tenant. These possibilities are generally unique to property. Each will be someone's loss balanced by someone's gain; to all, they represent risks.

b. *Tenant risk* is the chance that the tenant will affect returns by his actions. The most serious concern of the investor will be the chance of voids, meaning the possibility of the tenant vacating the premises and paying no rent. Even where long leases are signed by tenants, the possibility of bankruptcy must be considered. Legal actions are expensive and ponderous where actions to recover rent are undertaken.

Tenants may fail to perform repairing and insuring obligations. They may cause physical damage to or stigmatise a property. They may alienate adjoining owners or other tenants.

These prospects lend a risk to property that is near-unique. Perhaps the closest parallel is the risk of investing in ordinary shares that derives from bad management policies; it is much reduced, if it can be paralleled at all, in government securities and bank deposits.

Tenant risk acts upon the gross income. Sector risk has a similar effect but also acts directly on yields and thus capital values. Structural risk has an impact on the cost of operating the investment and may also reduce resale value and hence capital return. Legislation risk may affect both rents and yields independently (e.g. Rent Acts). Taxation risk may act upon income or expenses allowed against income (income or corporation tax) and capital return (capital gains tax). Planning risk may change income flow, capital return and even psychic income through restricting the owner's use of the property asset. Legal risk may result in inadequate rent or an alteration in yield through defective title.

2.3.6.7   Business and financial risk

In contrast to the aforementioned risk classifications, designed for application to property and within which there are direct and indirect applications to alternative markets, finance theory applies three broad categories of risk to investment. Reilly and Brown (2002) summarise these as follows:

a.   Business risk: The uncertainty of income flows caused by the nature of the firm's business.
b.   Financial risk: The uncertainty introduced by the method of financing an investment.
c.   Liquidity risk: The uncertainty introduced by the secondary market for an investment. How long will it take to convert the investment into cash, and what price will be received?

Applying these classifications to property is approached by imagining each property investment as an individual business. Business risk is then a derived risk reduced enormously by fixed rents in leases or between rent reviews and by upward-only rent reviews. Liquidity risk has already been covered. Financial risk affects property acquired by using some borrowed funds, and is the corollary of a geared purchase. While all investments are sensitive to some extent to interest rate fluctuations, it can be seen that property that is highly geared (as it often is) carries with it a high financial risk.

In summary, property is subject to many risks, several of which are unique to this sector. General risk classifications that are applied to the alternatives show property to be prone to all general categories but relatively protected from business risk by leasing practice. These general classifications are of very limited value in explaining property risks, and the fuller examination that preceded this classification may be of considerably more value. This depends, however, on the appropriate definition of risk.

2.3.6.8   Nominal or real risk?

Risk may be analysed in terms of nominal income (what is the possibility of variations in the actual income and capital returns from the expected?) or in terms of real income (what is the possibility of variations in the real value or purchasing power of actual and capital returns from the expected?). The choice is a significant one and depends greatly upon the liabilities of the investor.

A comparison of property with (for example) fixed-interest gilts is simpler on the former basis, while a comparison with index-linked gilts is simpler when predicated on the latter basis.

Example 2.1

Assume a suitable target rate for a purchase of index-linked gilts is 13%. Three years ago, a 5-year index-linked gilt, coupon 3%, was issued with interest paid annually in arrears at a price of £100. Inflation over the last 3 years until now, when the gilt was resold, has run at 5% p.a. Inflation between the current resale date and the redemption date is expected to run at 10% p.a.

The income is given as (£100 × c) where c = coupon, increasing at a rate of $(1 + i)$, where i = compound inflation rate from issue to year of income.

In the last 3 years, the annual income is as follows:

Three years ago: £100 × (0.03) × (1.05) = £3.15
Two years ago: £100 × (0.03) × (1.05)^2 = £3.31
Last year: £100 × (0.03) × (1.05)^3 = £3.47

In the next 2 years it is expected to be as follows:

Year 1: £100 × (0.03) × (1.05)^3 × (1.10) = £3.82
Year 2: £100 × (0.03) × (1.05)^3 × (1.10)^2 = £4.20

The expected resale price in 2 years' time is given by £100 $(1 + d_1)$ $(1 + d_2)$ $(1 + d_3)$ $(1 + d_4)$ $(1 + d_5)$.

This is £100 $(1 + 0.05)$ $(1 + 0.05)$ $(1 + 0.05)$ $(1 + 0.10)$ $(1 + 0.10)$ = £140.07.

Currently, an investor with a target rate of 13% would pay a price given by

$$\frac{£3.82}{1.13} + \frac{£4.20}{(1.13)^2} + \frac{£140.07}{(1.13)^2}$$

$$= \quad £3.38 + \quad £3.29 \quad + £109.70 = £116.37$$

For the original purchaser, his return is the IRR (r) of the following income flow:

$$- £100 + \frac{£3.15}{1 + r} + \frac{£3.31}{(1 + r)^2} + \frac{£3.47}{(1 + r)^3} + \frac{£116.37}{(1 + r)^3}$$

The IRR (r) = 8.33% p.a.; this is a real return not of 3% p.a. but of 3.17% p.a.

Alternatively, were inflation expected at 2% p.a. from now on, the price paid by the new investor would be different, thereby affecting the price and IRR received by the original investor. If the new investor still required a 13% return, the price would fall. The income would fall to £3.54 in the first year and £3.61 in the second year, and the redemption value would fall to £120.44. The new investor would only pay £100.29. The achieved IRR for the first investor would become 3.40% p.a.; this is a real return not of 3% p.a. but of −1.5% p.a. However, the new investor would not require a return of 13% as this high level is generated by high inflation expectations; an 8% reduction in inflation expectations would probably result in a similar fall in target rate to 5%. This is the

Example 2.1 (Continued)

Table 2.5 A real and nominal risk hierarchy.

Risk	Real	Nominal
Low	Index-linked gilts	Fixed-interest gilts
	Equities	Bank deposits
	Property	Property
	Bank deposits	Index-linked gilts
High	Fixed-interest gilts	Equities

2006 situation with nominal and index-linked redemption yields; nominal rates are below 5% and real rates are considered low at around 2% with inflation expectations running in the region of 2–3%.

The price paid for the last 2 years would be £115.89, which would be similar to the previous price and give the original investor an IRR of 8.2%, delivering the original real return coupon of 3%.

The real risk of index-linked gilts therefore depends upon the timing of a sale prior to redemption and upon future expectations of inflation. However, this risk is largely eliminated by the close relationship between target rates and inflation.

Bank deposits display almost negligible money risk but have considerable real risk produced largely by the propensity of the fixed capital return to be reduced in real value by inflation, and the imperfect and only very indirect linkage between interest rates and inflation.

The nominal risk of a UK property investment, which is reduced by the fixed nature of rents between reviews, is probably on a par with its real risk, which is reduced by a broad correlation between inflation and rental values and between rental values and capital values, so that property represents a medium-risk investment type in either context.

Real risk might be a preferable basis for investment comparison. But we are sure that, at present, property investment appraisals should be carried out in a manner that lends itself to investment comparison, and that comparison is most practicable by using nominal values in cash-flow predictions. Consequently, we err on the side of a nominal risk hierarchy (Table 2.5) for the rest of this book. In these terms, fixed-interest bonds held to redemption are least risky; bank deposits are next; property, with the levelling of return produced by leasing practice, is exceeded by index-linked gilts and equities in terms of nominal risk.

The nominal risk of fixed-interest gilts if held to redemption is almost nil, determined by the prospect of government default. There is some money risk if a sale before redemption is possible. Real risk is, on the other hand, quite high due to the fixed nominal income produced and the possibility of variations in the real value of money.

The nominal risk of equities is higher, as dividends and share prices vary. Real risk should intuitively be less than for fixed-interest gilts due to a broad correlation between inflation and dividends and between dividends and share prices, although empirical evidence may be found to dispute this.

The nominal risk of index-linked gilts is considerable, even if held to redemption, because of uncertainties regarding future inflation levels, while the real risk is very low, created only by lagging of the inflation linking. If a sale before redemption is a possibility, additional real risk is experienced as a result of future inflation expectations, themselves subject to change, being reflected in price and altering the inflation-linked nature of the return (see Example 2.1).

2.3.6.9   Systematic or specific risk?

Fraser (1985b) produced evidence based on the JLW (Jones Lang Wootton, now Jones Lang LaSalle) Property Index for his proposition that, whether measured in money or real terms, and whether measured in terms of downside risk or overall risk, property has been the least risky investment category of the three major institutional investment vehicles (fixed-interest gilts, equities and property). At the individual property level, it is impossible to reconcile this empirical evidence with *a priori* reasoning. One would expect to be correct in a presumption that, in money terms at least, property is riskier than fixed-interest gilts held to redemption. Fraser's analysis relates to portfolios of property and gilts rather than the individual constituent assets. The JLW Property Index was constructed by forming a hypothetical portfolio of actual office, shop and industrial properties. Many of the risks that attach to individual property investment have been diversified away. For example, falling values in one location would compensate rising values in another, thus smoothing out variations. An investor cannot access this level of diversification in practice, as Table 2.6 (from Baum and Struempell, 2005) shows.

Huge amounts of capital are required to replicate the performance of a property sector. For example, over £1 billion would have been needed to invest in a sufficient number of London offices to perform sufficiently similar to the IPD London office index over the period 1991–2004 so that the standard deviation of excess return (for tracking error, see Baum and Struempell, 2005) was limited to 2%.

Similarly, the extremely stable real-value profile of rent indices masks considerable variations in the three broad sectors of offices, shops and industrials. Even within those categories there are many more inter-regional, inter-city and inter-property variations hidden away. Consequently, the use of indices containing a large number of properties, which may be outside the scope of a typical investor, will present a misleading risk-less view of property as an asset. The reliance of such indices upon smoothed valuations – see Chapter 8 – compounds this problem.

Table 2.6 Capital required to track property segments.

Capital required (£m) for segment	5% Tracking error	4% Tracking error	3% Tracking error	2% Tracking error
Standard shops	28	42	74	157
Retail warehouses	86	129	259	1,013
Shopping centres	118	158	237	434
Other retail	40	60	100	169
London offices	152	243	455	1,229
South East offices	36	50	86	172
Provincial offices	36	58	87	166
Office parks	40	60	110	210
Industrials	32	51	90	212

Source: Baum and Struempell (2005).

Markowitz (1959) developed a basic portfolio model that showed how risk may be reduced within a portfolio by combining assets whose returns demonstrated less-than-perfect positive correlation.

What follows is a simplistic and non-technical introduction to MPT and the capital asset pricing model (CAPM), predicated in terms of a single-period expectations model. A simple numerical example at page 53 illustrates the principle. Readers who require a full discussion of MPT should refer to a standard text on finance.

Given that the typical investor is risk-averse, the combination of two or more investments whose returns fluctuate over time and in different conditions, but in opposite directions, can reduce risk without at the same time reducing return. Thus, if it can be shown that, as industrial properties decline in value, shops increase in value, and vice versa, then a two-asset property portfolio is superior to that of either individual asset. The investor de-values a risky asset; two risky assets in combination would be worth more than the sum of the two individual values.

Measuring risk by use of standard deviations (see Chapter 8) and return by IRR or NPV, it is possible to plot on a graph the risk–return combination of two equally priced and perfectly negatively correlated investments. Let us imagine that these are the shop and industrial investments referred to above.

Imagine that the shop (X) has an expected IRR of 14% and a standard deviation of IRRs of 24%; and that the industrial property (Y) has an expected IRR of 18% and a standard deviation of IRRs of 52%. Whether an investor would choose X or Y would depend upon his risk–return indifference: a risk-averse investor (A) would choose X; a risk-seeking investor (B) would choose Y (see Figure 2.3).

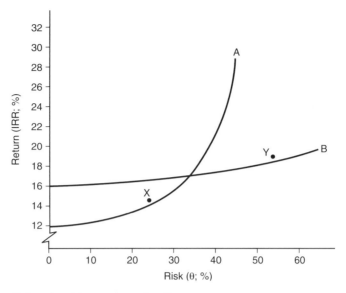

Figure 2.3   The risk–return trade-off.

Let us further imagine that investments X and Y are infinitely divisible, and that the purchaser's available funds can be expended in any combination of X and Y from 100% X to 100% Y (this may be possible through the unitisation or syndication of property investments). Given their perfect negative correlation, a 50:50 combination will have nil risk; the return will be the average of the two IRRs, that is, 16%.

Figure 2.4 shows all possible combinations, joined in a continuous line. Note that investor A would choose 100% X or any combination of X and Y up to a maximum amount of the risky asset Y given by the point O. Investor B would choose 100% Y or any combination of Y and X up to a maximum amount of the low-return asset X given by point P. Note that both A and B can narrow down their choice further. For either, less than 50% of investment Y produces a two-investment portfolio that has a higher return, and for a lower risk! This choice should be a portfolio combination between points V and O. There is an efficient set of combinations shown by that part of the curve connecting points V and Y, known as the efficient frontier (see Figure 2.5). All other combinations can be disregarded.

We must now relax the simple assumption of a two-property portfolio. Given a much larger choice of property, equity and other risky investments, any two or more of which may be combined, a whole set of efficient frontiers may be constructed (see Figure 2.6).

It can be noted that all risk–return combinations of IJ are bettered by alternatives. In addition, certain parts of all other curves are bettered at

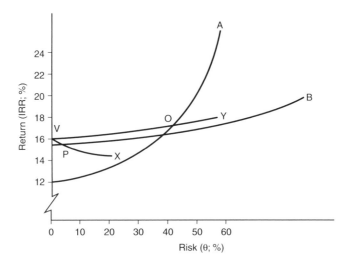

Figure 2.4   Risk and return in a two-asset portfolio.

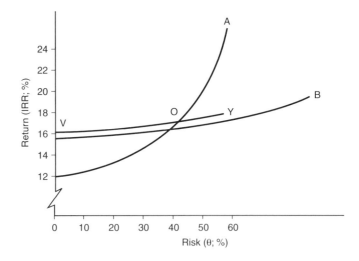

Figure 2.5   The efficient frontier.

some point. A new efficient frontier of portfolios may be constructed roughly along a line reconnecting points A and H.

It can also be seen that 100% of the least risky asset A and 100% of the highest return asset H are alternative positions on the efficient frontier. In between there may be any number of combinations of two or more property (and equity) assets. The investor's choice will depend upon his risk return indifference.

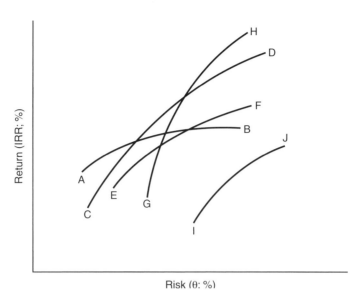

Figure 2.6   Multi-asset portfolio efficient frontiers.

Any point along line AH is a risk–return trade-off. But some risk-free investments may be found. For some investors, it may be preferable to invest wholly in risk-free investments. What happens to the efficient frontier if risk-free assets are combined with an efficient portfolio of risky investments? It can be shown that the standard deviation of a portfolio that combines a risk-free asset and a portfolio of risky assets is the linear proportion of the standard deviation of the risky asset portfolio. In other words, given a standard deviation of 0 for a risk-free investment, a 50:50 combination of that risk-free investment with the risky portfolio will produce a risk of 50% of the risky portfolio. A new linear efficient frontier may be constructed (see Figure 2.7). Assume the risk-free return is 12.5%.

It is clear from Figure 2.7 that one set of combinations (RV) dominates all other possibilities (including, for example, RS). Depending on the investor's risk return indifference, a point along this line should be selected. This (slightly modified) is known as the capital market line.

By definition, all portfolios on the capital market line are efficiently diversified. It is not possible to reduce risk for an increased or equal return even by adding further negatively correlated investments. The risk of this portfolio is the risk of the whole market (systematic): there is no residual or non-market risk, and it is now the volatility of the market which produces risk for the portfolio.

Adding further investments will not affect the unsystematic risk of the portfolio, which has been diversified away. It may, however, have an effect upon its systematic risk. How volatile is a new investment in relation to the

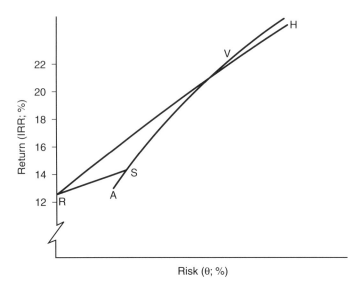

Figure 2.7   The efficient frontier with a risk-free asset.

market portfolio? If it exaggerates the upturns and downturns in the portfolio, it is a risky asset and should only be purchased if the rate of return it
promises is sufficiently high: that is, one that suggests that positive abnormal
returns will be made.

β is the measure of volatility of an investment in relation to the market
portfolio, that is, a portfolio comprising every known asset weighted in
terms of market value. A (β) of 1.0 implies that as the market increases
in value by 10%, the expected value of the new investment increases by
10%. A (β) of 2.0 implies that as the market increases in value by 10% the
expected value of the new investment increases by 20%. A (β) of 0.5 implies
that as the market increases in value by 10% the expected value of the new
investment increases by 5%.

We have already discussed the possibility of investing in a (monetary) risk-
free asset, say, fixed-interest government bonds held to maturity. The rate of
return on such an investment can be called the risk free rate (RFR).

The market portfolio is not risk free. It is free of unsystematic risk; therefore, all it contains is systematic risk. The return on the whole market will
vary in value over time in relation to the return on the risk-free investment.
The expected return on the market portfolio [$E(R_m)$] should therefore be
higher than the RFR. It comprises the RFR plus an expected risk premium
[$E(R_p)$].

$$E(R_m) = RFR + E(R_p)$$

or

$$E(R_m) = RFR + (\beta) [E(R_m) - RFR]$$

The return on a risky investment can be similarly derived. It should comprise the RFR plus a risk premium that reflects the systematic risk of the investment relative to the market. Where an investment is twice as risky as the market, the expectation is that it should earn twice the risk premium. The measure of this relative riskiness is (β). Thus, the return on a risky investment of (E_a) is given by:

$$E_a = RFR + (\beta)\ (R)$$

Empirical studies in the UK (e.g. DTZ's annual Money Into Property report) have shown that R has in recent years been close to 2.5%. Given a RFR (the return on short-term Treasury Bills or the redemption yield on short dated government bonds, in either case with maturity matching the single period which forms the basis of the model) of around 4.5% at the time of writing, the expected return (r) on the market (m) can be estimated:

$$r_m = 0.045 + 0.025$$

$$= 7.0\%$$

The required return on risky investments can also be calculated. Let us assume (without necessarily recommending the use of CAPM in the property market: see Chapter 9) that an historic examination of the performance of property investments in relation to the whole market has produced estimates of β for offices, shops and industrials. Brown and Matysiak (2000b) attempted exactly this type of analysis. Let us assume that the results are as follows:

Shops: (β) = 0.3
Offices: (β) = 0.4
Industrials: (β) = 0.5

(Note that all three categories are less risky than the market, a result that would support Fraser's examination based on the JLW Property Index described on page 47).

The expected or required returns are as follows:

Shops: r_s = RFR + (β) (R)
                     = 0.045 + 0.3 (0.025)
                     = 5.25%
Offices: r_o = RFR + (β) (R)
                     = 0.045 + 0.4 (0.025)
                     = 5.5%
Industrials: r_i = RFR + (β) (R)
                     = 0.045 + 0.5 (0.025)
                     = 5.75%

These are surprisingly low required returns – see the following – and the implications of such an analysis for property investment appraisal are enormous. However, the theoretical basis of the CAPM is not accepted without question; its application to property is not necessarily settled; and tests for β in the UK property market are rare and uncorroborated. Despite these reservations, much can be learnt about the behaviour of the property market from this theory.

Several sources of individual property investment risk were identified earlier in this chapter, and at a portfolio level it is clear that many are in the nature of unsystematic risks that can be diversified away by balanced portfolio construction.

*Tenant risk*s are largely the risks of voids leading to nil rents and can be normalised by the purchase of a large number of properties. As the number of investments held increases, the chance of a total void (say 10%) approaches the certainty of a partial 10% void across the portfolio. As long as the expected cash flow reflects this prospect, risk is now negligible.

Sector risk and *locational risk* can be diversified away, to some extent, by their very nature. While it may not be possible to construct a property portfolio that mirrors the performance of national indices (Brown and Matysiak, 2000b; Hoesli and MacGregor, 2000), balancing by type, by region and by city will result in considerable risk reduction.

Planning risk can be diversified away. We have already referred to shifting value: one planning refusal may be balanced by a permission elsewhere; and planning risk can be neutralised by holding property in many locations.

Legal risk is similar and can be largely removed by diversification. As one bad title is suffered it may be that another legal right that is valuable but was not paid for is discovered. Not wholly unsystematic, however, are the following.

Taxation risk can affect all property in the same (negative or positive) manner. The introduction of a new tax on property ownership is an example of how all property may be prone to a taxation risk that is itself systematic.

Legislation risk is similar. Imagine the effect on values of a new Law of Property Act, which abolishes freehold ownership or nationalises land. The 1993 Department of the Environment Consultation Paper, which threatened to outlaw upward only rent reviews, was forecast to immediately reduce commercial and industrial property investment values by over 4%, with a long-term reduction of over 10% (Crosby *et al.*, 1993). The risk is again systematic.

Equally, *liquidity risk*, the uncertainty affecting the speed at which an asset can be converted to cash at, or close to, its market value, is systematic.

Structural risk is, in some respects, diversifiable. A spread of building types, construction materials and so on will convert the possibility of excessive loss into the certainty of a normal burden of repair and rebuilding. However, the impact of fashion upon building design may not be altogether unsystematic. While a balanced portfolio might reduce the risks of technological change and its impact upon industrial design, more basic changes in architectural practice may affect all properties in the same manner. For example, natural light may be found to be less efficient for all properties than a new type of artificial lighting. All buildings would then become obsolete to a greater or lesser extent. New lift designs might have a similar, though less dramatic, effect. And micro-technology might eventually change the pattern of property employment so drastically that all sectors of the market are prone to the same risk.

In conclusion, property as an investment is (like all investments) prone to both unsystematic and systematic risks. While the former may be diversified away, the latter cannot. The effect of balanced portfolio construction is thus to reduce but not abolish property investment risk. Is it possible to generalise about this? Is the high individual risk of property irrelevant; or is the lower portfolio risk the correct measure?

Much depends upon the behaviour of the typical investor in the particular sub-market under consideration. Does the investor practise a policy of diversification within the property market? Does he have sufficient funds to do this properly?

The answers to these questions can only be provided by reference to the particular. If the prime institutional investment market is the sub-market under consideration, then the answer to the first question is probably positive, but to what extent, and in how rational a manner, may be difficult to judge. The answer to the second question is that it is extremely unlikely. Given the current minimum level of investment necessary to purchase prime investment property, few, if any, funds can diversify internationally, regionally, by city and by property type in order to diversify away tenant risk, sector risk, planning risk, legal risk and some structural risk. Even the largest insurance companies may not be in this position. The analyst's strategy must therefore be to identify the most likely purchaser, the relevant conception of risk and its effect upon the likely selling price or return to that purchaser. The vast majority of transactions in the UK property market involve purchasers and vendors who are not able to avoid unsystematic risk. For this reason we do not propose to proceed with portfolio analysis as the basis for undertaking appraisals in the major part of this text. We will, however, use the theory again (in Chapter 9) in an illustrative example.

2.4   Initial-yield analysis and construction

Early in this chapter we explained the use of the initial yield as the popular measure of the quality of an investment. Because the initial income level of an investment is usually known or can be predicted with some certainty it can be compared with price to produce a readily understood yield measure.

$$\text{Initial yield} = \frac{\text{current income}}{\text{price}}$$

It should now be recognised that a series of features that affect the quality of the investment affect the initial yield level through the operation of market demand and the price determination process. As market conceptions of any or all of income and capital growth, liquidity, operating expenses and risk change for the better, the effect upon price will be positive. Given no change in current income, which is determined largely irrespective of these considerations, the effect must be upon initial yield.

The initial yield is therefore a highly complex measure of the quality of an investment. In theorising what the level of initial yield should be for an investment, a process of yield construction may be undertaken.

Irving Fisher's classic work on interest (Fisher, 1930) and work by Meiron Gordon in the 1950s (Gordon, 1958) established the basis for yield construction. Following Fisher, required total returns can be broken down into rewards for three factors: time preference or impatience (l); expected inflation (i) and risk (rp). A rate can be constructed from these inputs so that the required return $I = [(1 + l)\,(1 + i)\,(1 + rp) - 1]$.

Simplifying this, a RFR can be constructed from l and i, and the rate on risk-free investments such as short-term treasury bills combines rewards for these two factors, so that:

$$\text{RFR} = (1 + l)\,(1 + i) - 1$$

and the required return (r) is given by:

$$r = (1 + \text{RFR})\,(1 + rp) - 1$$

(Note that an approximation is given by $r = \text{RFR} + rp$. This is the format adopted in the illustration of the following yield construction.)

Following Gordon, the initial return (k) available on an investment can be related to the required total return (r) simply in terms of the net income growth (g) that is anticipated (see also page 27), so that

$$k = r - g$$

Combining Fisher and Gordon, the following equation can be constructed:

$$k = \text{RFR} + r - g$$

This is the basis for a process of yield construction, but some further development is necessary, especially for property as an unusual asset class. It is unusual because it depreciates over time, both as the result of physical deterioration and as the result of obsolescence (Baum *et al.*, 2005). Given that in the preceding equation income growth is a market expectation referring to movement in an index, an extra reward is required to compensate for depreciation (*d*). Hence, following Baum (1988a):

$$k = \text{RFR} + r - g + d$$

Hence, the first step in a process of yield construction for a property investment is to find a risk-free (or neutral) rate obtainable elsewhere in the investment market. What return is available from investments that are free of income and capital growth in nominal terms, absolutely liquid, free of operating expenses and risk free?

Of the alternatives presented in Chapter 1, the closest proxy for the RFR is the redemption yield on fixed-interest gilts. The cash flow is certain, removing growth and risk; the investment is liquid; and it is cheap to manage. In Chapter 1, we showed how the effective IRR (redemption yield) of a hypothetical Exchequer 12¼% 2011 gilt could be calculated as 6.21%. In 2007 we are familiar with redemption yields of close to 4.5%. This will serve as our RFR. (Arguably, the index-linked gilt yield is a closer approximation to a RFR for investors who are concerned with real returns.)

The initial yield on our property investment (let us assume a prime shop) can be constructed by a normative process as follows. The RFR is adjusted in a series of stages to account for the factors that affect shop properties. (All figures used have no logical or empirical foundation; they are for illustration only.)

A risk adjustment (a risk premium, *rp*) may first be applied. Given that the gilt is risk free, and (whether viewed in an individual or portfolio sense) that the shop investment is risky and illiquid, assume *rp* = 3%. Adding 0.5% for operating expenses, the required return is 8%.

Rental growth prospects for the market have a reducing effect on initial yield. Assume that the consensus long-term forecast is for nominal rental growth of 3% p.a.

The expected depreciation rate for a prime shop is probably very low because of high site values and the tenant's tendency to regularly refit the premises. Assuming a rate of 0.5%, the result is a required initial yield of 5.5%.

Neutral/ risk-free yield	Risk and illiquidity	Operating expenses	Growth	Depreciation	Initial yield
4.5%	3.0%	0.5%	−3.0%	0.5%	5.5%

A positive process of yield analysis, using market information to observe what actually happens in practice, would show that, in 2007, 4.5% would be a more typical initial yield accepted for a prime shop. What could explain this?

a. If the adjustments used reflect the preferences of an individual investor, he or she should not purchase the investment at the market price.

b. The market price and initial yield suggest that successful bidders for the property are less pessimistic about risk, and illiquidity, or are more optimistic about net growth, or a combination of both factors is in operation. For example, if a portfolio risk measure is used and a smaller (2%) risk premium is viewed as necessary, illiquidity is not a problem due to intended infrequency of trading, and the growth prospects are considered to be 1% p.a. better, then the construction (normative) process can be equated with the analytical (positive) process as follows:

Neutral/ risk-free yield	Risk and illiquidity	Operating expenses	Growth	Depreciation	Initial yield
4.5%	2.0%	0.5%	−4.0%	0.5%	3.5%

In the early 1980s the low level of initial yields for shop investments was severely questioned, and most analyses centred on the excessive rental growth expectation that appeared to push initial yields so low. More attention is now being paid to the risk premium component of the equation, with the downside risk of property investments now the dominant factor and the tenant's covenant, length of lease and presence of upward-only rent reviews having emerged as the important factors. Cash flow now rivals growth prospects as the key factor in the appraisal of property investments.

Whatever the lessons to be learned from such a process, two clear conclusions can be drawn:

a. In the estimation of the most likely selling price, or market valuation, the estimation of adjustments in the normative process of yield construction is difficult, and in practice has been neglected in favour of the positive process of yield analysis. Part Two of this book shows how yield analysis has been used, and how the technique performs in the current property investment market.

b. In the estimation of investment value/worth to an individual investor the yield construction process is more promising. The opportunity exists to agree adjustments with the client, but the quantum of adjustment is difficult to judge and the result is sensitive to changes.

Appraisal by initial yield analysis (empiricism) is the market standard. That is not to say that it provides a satisfactory methodology. The implications of initial yield (implicit) appraisals are considered later.

2.5   Comparing investment opportunities: NPV and IRR

Valuation involves the estimation of worth to an individual. Given the price of the investment, it can be expressed in either of two ways: first as a NPV of the cash flow over the price and second as an (internal) rate of return. In this section, we compare three investments to illustrate these means of comparison. More detail is to be found in Chapter 9. Each investment is to be held for 5 years. The price is known in each case. The NPV and IRR of each is to be estimated.

Investment A is a stock. It is priced at £5. The last dividend, just paid, was £0.50, where

g_1 is the expected growth in dividend in year 1 plus 1;
g_2 is the expected growth in dividend in year 2 plus 1;
g_3 is the expected growth in dividend in year 3 plus 1;
g_4 is the expected growth in dividend in year 4 plus 1;
g_5 is the expected growth in dividend in year 5 plus 1;

and
d_1 is the dividend in year 1;
d_2 is the dividend in year 2;
d_3 is the dividend in year 3;
d_4 is the dividend in year 4;
d_5 is the dividend in year 5;

and
k_5 is the expected dividend yield at the end of year 5.

The expected cash flow is as follows.

Year	Income	Capital	Total
0		−£5.00	− £5.00
1	$0.5 \times g_1$		$0.5 \times g_1$
2	$d_1 \times g_2$		$d_1 \times g_2$
3	$d_2 \times g_3$		$d_2 \times g_3$
4	$d_3 \times g_4$		$d_3 \times g_4$
5	$d_4 \times g_5$	d_5 / k_5	$[d_4 \times g_5] \times [d_5 / k_5]$

Investment B is a property. It is priced at £5m. The rental value, just agreed under a new lease, is £500,000, where

g_1 is the expected net growth in rental value in year 1 plus 1;
g_2 is the expected net growth in rental value in year 2 plus 1;
g_3 is the expected net growth in rental value in year 3 plus 1;
g_4 is the expected net growth in rental value in year 4 plus 1;
g_5 is the expected net growth in rental value in year 5 plus 1;

and

k_5 is the expected yield at the end of year 5.

The expected cash flow is as follows:

Year	Income	Capital	Total
0		−£5m	−£5m
1	500,000		
2	500,000		
3	500,000		
4	500,000		
5	500,000	$[500{,}000 \times g_1 \times g_2 \times g_3 \times g_4 \times g_5]/k_5$	$500{,}000 + [500{,}000 \times g_1 \times g_2 \times g_3 \times g_4 \times g_5]/k_5$

Investment C is a bond. It is priced at £80. The coupon is £5. Redemption in five years' time is at par, £100.
The expected cash flow is as follows:

Year	Income	Capital	Total
0		−80	−80
1	5		5
2	5		5
3	5		5
4	5		5
5	5	100	105

One immediate conclusion can be drawn from these cash flows. No risk attaches to the cash flow in investment C, because both income and capital flows are known with certainty. More risk attaches to investment B. The income over 5 years is known with certainty, but the capital value in year 5 is subject to the values of g_1, g_2, g_3, g_4, g_5 and k_5. The greatest risk attaches to investment A. Neither the income stream nor the capital value is known with certainty; both are subject to future income growth and the future dividend yield. So bonds are less risky in nominal terms than property; and property is less risky than stocks.

What is the value? The value of the gilt can be estimated without further inputs.

The NPV is the summated present value of all cash inflows less the summated present value of all cash outflows. To calculate the NPV requires the estimation of the correct discount rate or required return, E, given in the simplified Fisher equation as (RFR + R). The (internal) rate of return is that discount rate which equates the present values of all inflows and the present values of all outflows. The discount rate appropriate to gilts is the RFR. Assuming investment C is a gilt, the NPV must be nil, and the IRR is the RFR for the purposes of our other valuations.

NPV and IRR routines are standard on financial calculators and spreadsheet programs. For a fuller description of the calculation method underlying these routines, see Baum, Mackmin and Nunnington (2006). The IRR for investment C is 10.32%. This establishes a RFR for the valuation of the other assets. To value investment B, what risk premium is appropriate? Following the preceding text, the property is certainly riskier in nominal terms than the gilt; a 4% risk margin may be appropriate for a retail property. The appropriate discount rate is then 14.32%.

Next, what future value should be assumed? Let us assume no depreciation and growth at 7% p.a., as earlier. Finally, let us assume that yields do not change and that the current initial yield of 10% will apply in 5 years' time. The resale value will then be £701,276/0.10 = £7.01m.

At a discount rate of 14.32%, the NPV is £37,454, meaning that the investment is marginally attractive in comparison with the gilt, the return more than compensating for the risk. At a price of £5,037,454 the property would be fairly priced; its value is the current price plus the NPV. The IRR is 14.52%, again showing that the investment is attractive in comparison with the gilt.

To value investment A, what risk premium is appropriate? Investment A is riskier than investment B because more uncertainty attaches to the cash flow. Assume 6% is appropriate, producing a discount rate of 16.32%. What dividend growth should be assumed? Let us assume 8% p.a., producing a dividend stream as follows: in year 1, £0.5 × 1.08 = £0.54; in year 2, £0.5 × $(1.08)^2$ = £0.58; in year 3, £0.5 × $(1.08)^3$ = £0.63; in year 4, £0.5 × $(1.08)^4$ = £0.68; in year 5, £0.5 × $(1.08)^5$ = £0.73. What will the future dividend yield be? Currently, it is 10%; assume it falls to 8%. The resale value would then be £0.73/.08 = £9.18.

At a discount rate of 16.32%, the NPV is £1.31, meaning that the investment is attractive in comparison with the gilt, the return more than compensating for the risk. At a price of £6.31 the stock would be fairly priced; its value is the current price plus the NPV.

The IRR is 22.87%, again showing that the investment is attractive in comparison with gilt, but also comfortably the most attractive of the three.

This type of analysis is developed in more detail in Part three. The reasons for the divergence between this type of valuation process and the conventional valuation technique are the subject of Part Two.

Chapter 3
The DCF Appraisal Model

3.1   The cash-flow model

The appraisal of all investments is predicated on the assumption that the current value is equal to the net present value (NPV) of the future benefits (see, for example, Damodaran, 2001). This requires us to determine the most likely cash flow that the investment will produce and discount rate we can then use to find the NPV of that cash flow. Chapter 2 introduced the concept of the required return, which is the discount rate for this purpose.

This chapter focuses on the issues that arise when constructing a cash flow. The inputs can be categorised as (a) income/value inputs and (b) cost inputs. The generation of some of these inputs can be challenging and complex, and a full menu of issues to consider would be very long and very detailed. This chapter sets out to introduce the basic structure only. Chapters 8 and 9 provide more examples.

3.1.1   The inputs

In a market valuation the information or inputs into the model should be market-based, while in an investment valuation they could be a mixture of market- and client-specific information.

Market data can be broken down into (a) current and (b) forecast data. It should not be affected by the specific criteria of clients. Current data includes the rent currently payable, the current estimated rental value (ERV), the lease structure and the mechanism for future rental value changes, management, rent review, purchase and sale costs, and any contractually agreed income or outgoings known with some certainty. Forecast data includes ERV changes, depreciation rates, redevelopment or refurbishment costs and exit sale price forecasts.

Certain factors could be subjective to a potential purchaser. These include the precise nature of a proposed redevelopment or refurbishment, the holding period, the extent and costs of loan facilities, taxation and the required return. Nonetheless, in a market valuation they will need to be estimated as market variables, meaning the values that will be assumed by the most likely purchaser (or group of purchasers). For example, the assumed holding period for an appraisal might be determined by the current lease structure, by redevelopment options or by a standard approach to market valuation (say 5 or 10 years). In an investment appraisal, the holding period may be determined by the client's need or intention to sell or refinance the property at a specific future date.

Owing to the range of information that can be included in an explicit appraisal, there is no accepted layout for this kind of valuation, with investors and advisors developing their own approaches and such standardisation as there is being driven largely by software providers. Any model needs to begin with an attempt to create a forecast of the most likely cash flow to be produced by the property, and approximations are to be discouraged. For example, it is typical in market valuations for an assumption to be made that rental income is paid annually in arrears, even though normal rent payment takes place quarterly in advance. In a cash-flow valuation, there is no need to make this simplification.

The return from a property investment is a function of income and capital return, and for shorter leaseholds we may not expect a capital return. Thus, our gross cash flow will be made up of income and (perhaps) capital. The income may increase at reviews. Estimation of a capital return depends upon the timing of a sale; therefore, we need to estimate a likely holding period. Holding costs will be incurred during the period of ownership, and these will need to be estimated. Purchase and sale transfer costs will be payable; at each rent review a fee will be payable; letting or re-letting costs may have to be faced; and management fees may be incurred. Taxes on income and capital gain will be charged. Leaseholders may be faced with dilapidations claims. The income may be inclusive, so that the investor pays any property taxes (business rates in the UK) out of the rent received; and a service charge may not cover the cost of service provision. Properties have to be repaired and refurbished, even then the impact of building depreciation may have to be faced.

The estimation of each of these factors will help us to reach an explicit net cash-flow projection. The target rate has to be added to the preceding list of independent variables, the capital value being the dependent variable.

All variables will now be briefly considered. The general headings under which information needs to be collected are set out in Table 3.1. We also provide broad indicators of the type of information that needs to be considered under each heading.

Part One

Table 3.1 Typical information requirements for discounted-cash-flow (DCF) appraisals.

Type of information	Current information	Forecast information
Value	ERVs of both existing building and any prospective changes to the building in the future Rents passing	Rental value forecasts Rental depreciation rates Exit capitalisation rate forecasts for existing or replacement buildings
Building	Size Costs of maintenance Nature of prospective redevelopment or refurbishment and costs	Changes in building costs Timing of redevelopment or refurbishment
Current leases	Number of tenants Lease expiry or break dates Rent revision dates and type Renewal rights/options	Incidences of future break and renewals Void and future lease incentives
Holding costs	Management costs Rent revision costs Purchase and sale costs	
Other information	Discount rate Taxation Loans: interest and repayment Holding period	

3.1.2 The holding period

For purely technical reasons – that is, to avoid an infinitely long cash-flow projection in a freehold analysis – a finite holding period must be utilised in the analysis model. For freeholds, this implies the assumption of a resale. For leaseholds, the holding period will usually equate with the remaining term.

The overriding concern in the choice of holding period must be the intentions of the investor. Discussions with the investor might reveal the investor's likely or intended period of ownership. Where no intention to sell is apparent, the holding period becomes arbitrary.

In either case, there are reasons for coinciding the resale date with the end of an occupation lease or a rent review-period. This reflects likely practice, as a suspicion that fuller and fairer prices are achieved immediately after review or with a tenant under a new lease in harness appears to be common. (It will be clear from subsequent chapters that conventional valuation techniques may contribute to this policy, although risk aversion is also a mighty influence.)

While the holding period has no effect upon a market valuation in explicit discounted cash flow (DCF) form (see Chapter 5 for an explanation of this point) the introduction of costs, taxes and depreciation allowances in investment analysis will destroy this consistency. Consequently, while periods of 10 or 15 years are often settled on for convenience, it should be noted that slight changes in holding period return may be achieved by shortening or lengthening the holding period, and this type of exercise is one of several uses of the model. Our analyses utilise holding periods that coincide with rent reviews or lease ends and usually fall in the 5–20 year range (in UK practice, these holding periods are typical for DCF analyses).

3.1.3   The lease

Cash flows from investment property are generated by the lease contract and, since the previous editions of this text, lease reform has developed as a major policy issue in the UK. For this reason, we have introduced an extended examination of the impact of lease terms in Chapter 9, page 263.

The major changes in market practice are founded upon the gradual demise of the institutional lease, which had a number of characteristics designed to place major long-term rights and responsibilities onto tenants, thereby securing the cash flow for the landlord. This lease was often for 20 or 25 years, with full repairing and insuring (FRI) responsibility placed on the tenant, and with upward-only rent revisions to market rent every 5 years. In addition, privity of contract existed whereby, upon assignment of the lease, previous tenants remained responsible for rent if the new tenant defaulted. In return, tenants were given a statutory right to renew their lease under the 1954 Landlord and Tenant Act (Baum and Sams, 2007).

As a result, the lease in effect gave rights to perpetual occupation for the tenant during the life of the existing building, and landlords then passed property market risks to the tenant. If the rental market collapsed, as it did in 1990–1992, the landlord's cash flow was (subject to tenant default) immune, and the long lease, the tenant's covenant strength and the upward-only review became the most important issues in valuation (see Chapter 9 for an extended example of this). As a result, valuation is partly an appraisal of the value of a lease contract, and partly an appraisal of a property.

Lease terms can in certain circumstances dominate the property valuation, while in other cases (where there is a short lease and where the parties have agreed to contract out of the 1954 Act) they are of lesser weight. Rarely are they peripheral to the valuation of investment property. In addition, the initial rent is affected by lease terms (Crosby *et al.*, 2005). Lease pricing has become a major valuation issue in the UK since the demise of the standard institutional lease and its replacement with a wide variety of lease lengths, break options, renewal rights and repairing obligations. Not only are existing lease terms central to the valuation process, but 'lease events' – what might happen at a break, or a lease end, when tenants have the right to leave – are now also vital. An assessment of what might happen at the expiry of a lease is often important in assessing the most likely cash flow, and uncertainty surrounding future lease events also contributes to the risk profile of the investment, thereby influencing the discount rate. This is especially so in buildings let to single or few tenants where assumptions surrounding the operation of breaks or renewals can lead to significant differences in valuations.

Also important is the process by which rents are determined. Although the basis of rent upon new lettings at lease renewals and at rent reviews is theoretically the same or similar, practice has shown that the mechanisms create different outcomes (see Baum and Sams, 2007). A rent at renewal or at review has to be agreed between the parties or at a third-party determination if the parties do not agree. Landlords cannot bring in new tenants, and so the determination is often based on ageing comparable evidence that, at different times in the market cycle, can under- or over-estimate the rent that would be achieved at a new letting. Where there is no right to renew a lease, existing tenants have been shown to pay more to retain a lease upon renewal than the rent obtained from new lettings (Fisher and Lentz, 1990). This is not only true in the UK, as in Australia there has been a running battle between large shopping centre owners and small speciality retailers, whose representative bodies complain that they are held to ransom at lease expiry (Crosby, 2006c).

3.2   The cash flow

3.2.1   The gross income

The gross income flow is termed gross effective income in North American texts (see, for example, Greer et al. 1996; Geltner et al. (2007), to distinguish between maximum potential income when the property is fully let and the actual income likely to remain after voids. If voids in a multi-let building are expected, the gross income flow should be reduced to a gross effective income flow by deducting an allowance for voids.

3.2.2   Forecasting: the challenge

The information required for a DCF appraisal set out in Table 3.1 is at the individual property level. This creates problems relating to the need to forecast such factors as: rental growth, the capitalisation rate to be applied to the rent received from the property at the end of the holding period to determine the terminal capital value, rates of depreciation and obsolescence, and redevelopment cost increases, all at the local level, with limited data.

Generally, forecasts of property market rents and values are undertaken at a national, regional and local level. They are normally based upon econometric modelling of the economy and the property market, identifying relationships that have occurred in the past and using leading indicators or forecasts to produce an estimate of each variable in the future. There are inadequacies/deficiencies in both the quality and quantity of data at all levels, but national demand-side data is generally more comprehensive than regional-level data, which in turn is more accessible than local economy data. The better-quality data, coupled with the increased importance of supply side influences and the difficulties of defining coherent local areas, mean that national and regional forecasts are easier to undertake than those at a town or city level.

Forecasts of property market movements, therefore, need informed qualitative adjustment at the individual property level, derived from the available information at the local/town or (more likely) regional level. Value movements within cities and towns can vary substantially from location to location over time, with retail property being the most locationally volatile (with improvements in one part of a town often happening at the expense of another part). Some of these variations are caused by new development changing the relative quality of locations, and very few owners have large enough portfolios to diversify at town centre level. Appraisals can therefore be subject to much uncertainty.

The level and complexity of information required to undertake DCF analysis has raised the following questions: is the valuer, familiar with market valuation, equipped to take on investment appraisal? It is difficult to see why not. Forecasts can be purchased from specialist analysts. The market valuation and investment processes are very closely connected; and valuers are professional experts. The European real estate education system has been researching and teaching the mechanics of DCF for many years, and more recently has added the mechanics of forecasting through econometric modelling, to a level where real estate graduates and students are capable of setting up and discounting cash flows, carrying out risk appraisals, and understanding the basis and limitations of property market forecasts. By working in the market at the local level, they should be more equipped than most to adjust regional- and town-level forecasts to the particular property investment.

3.2.3   The resale price

In the cases of freeholds and long leaseholds the selection of a holding period will trigger the assumption of a resale at that date. The resale price has to be projected as the most likely selling price at that date. If the most common method of market pricing is the years' purchase method, and given that the sale will usually coincide with a review, the freehold resale price is given by:

$$\text{Estimated rental value (ERV)} \times \text{YP in perpetuity}$$

or

$$\frac{\text{ERV}}{\text{Capitalisation rate } (k)}$$

This requires the projection of two variables: ERV at the resale and k at resale.

3.2.4   ERV at resale

A projection of rental value to the point of resale in market valuation could be based on a market-implied growth rate (see Chapter 5). While this may be a guide, it should be remembered that the implied growth rate is an average rate in perpetuity; it is also net of depreciation. It is also a function of the price that is being analysed. In an investment appraisal an attempt has to be made to forecast rental growth year by year, and depreciation should be explicitly accounted for.

Forecasting rental growth over the holding period is important both in the estimation of the rental flow and in the prediction of the resale price. Again, a two-tier approach is necessary.

First, the rental value of the frozen property over time is to be forecast. Forecasting a variable such as this might be based on any of the following three methods:

a. Extrapolation of time series data. A time series is a series of figures, for example, rental values, over time. From the time series it may be possible to identify a long-term trend in rental values, but a cyclical pattern will almost certainly obscure this to some extent. In addition there may be non-recurring influences – rent freezes, for example – that need to be smoothed away. Extrapolation involves continuation of the time series line into the future, reflecting both cyclical variations and the long-term trend.

b. Identifying causal relationships. Analysis of past relationships can often give a clue to the future. Forecasting future economic variables by statistical analysis of these relationships (econometrics) is an integral forecasting tool used, for example, by economists (see, for example, Ball *et al.*, 2000). The analyst forms a hypothesis relating to causal relationships and tests that hypothesis by using statistical tests of data. For example, the lagged impact of interest rates (the independent variable) upon property yields (the dependent variable) might be tested by regressing one factor against the other over time and measuring the strength and significance of the relationship between the two. If correlation is high, a simple prediction may be made.

The ideal situation for the forecaster would be where the independent variables are seen to move in advance of the dependent variable. Analysis of the business cycle is often undertaken to find indicators which lead the economy and those leading indicators form the basis of models which predict changes in the economy.

c. A combined approach. The most common method of forecasting utilised in the property market is an approach that combines extrapolation with a causal analysis, almost certainly in an informal framework. Gilt yields might be used as an indicator of prime property yields: when they fall, property yields might follow. However, this is not always the case. At the time of writing the second edition of this book, falling gilt yields coincided with rising prime property yields, so that an extrapolated forecast would conflict with a simple causal forecast based only on gilt yields.

In such circumstances the analyst is likely to base projections primarily on extrapolation coloured by causal influences (the forthcoming supply of new property in the sector, for example). If such an approach is used, the cyclical and long-term trends in a time series should be differentiated.

There have been rapid strides in forecasting since the first edition of this book was published. Forecasting services, of which several are now available by subscription, form the foundation of the strategies and property investment decisions of many institutional investors.

3.2.5   Capitalisation rate

The prediction of a capitalisation rate for the subject property 10 or 15 years hence requires the estimation of two distinct trend lines. First, yields for the type of property under consideration may be expected to change over the period. If so, the extent to which the market yield will change must be estimated. However, it may be hypothesised that the expectations of the property investment market over the past century have been of generally stable prime yields (Chapter 4), and so this may not be as large a task as it appears. Second, the movement in yield of the subject property against an index of yields for such properties in a frozen state over the holding period needs to be estimated. In other words, the extent of depreciation likely to be suffered by an ageing building (see also Section 3.2.6) needs to be estimated.

A cross-section analysis may facilitate this process: if the subject property is 10 years old and the appropriate capitalisation rate is 7%, given an expectation of stable yields over time, the best estimate of the resale capitalisation rate after a 10-year holding period is the current yield on similar but 20-year-old buildings. This leads us to the subject of depreciation.

3.2.6 Depreciation

Rises and falls in property values (in relative terms) are a function of changes in the value of land and depreciation in the value of buildings. The building will be affected by deterioration (physical wearing out) and by obsolescence caused by technological or fashion changes that render the physical characteristics of the building less useful. In the office and industrial markets, there are numerous examples where changes in practice or space requirements have rendered particular types of building useless for their original purpose (floor to ceiling heights in offices, equipment circulation space in factories), with the result that they have been demolished even though they were physically sound.

Deterioration can to some extent be forecast, but obsolescence, caused by technological and fashion changes cannot always be foreseen within an investment time horizon. Forecasts of this kind of change over the life of a new building are particularly difficult. Nonetheless, some studies exist that examine age-related falls in rental values over time relative to new property values (Baum, 1991; Baum *et al.*, 2005). These can be used as a basis for assessing the likely reduction in rental growth relative to an index of rents for new buildings. In addition to the rent impact, the exit capitalisation rate may rise as a building ages, and regular capital expenditure, refurbishment, or redevelopment may be required.

As a result of depreciation, rental values may be rising as a combined result of market rental growth tempered by depreciation, at a rate of $(1+g)/(1+d)$, where g is the annual rate of rental growth for new buildings and d is the annual rate of depreciation.

Depreciation rates have been studied for a variety of property types, mainly office and industrial, in a variety of locations, but London has been used more than most. The results have suggested a rental value depreciation rate of less than 1% p.a. to more than 3% p.a. More recently, the authors took part in a longitudinal study of depreciation rates over the last 10 and 19 years in the UK (to the end of 2003), and the results of this suggest that the lower end of the range has been more appropriate for UK industrial and office property over this period (Baum *et al.*, 2005).

Two simple methods of measuring or anticipating depreciation are: (i) an empirical approach, assessing the current rental value of the building and comparing it to the rental value of a new building in the same location, with the annualised difference being an indicator of depreciation; and (ii) a theoretical approach, in which the building proportion of property value (found directly from building costs, or by deducing land value for property value) is depreciated over the building life (Baum, 1991).

Allowances for depreciation have been referred to earlier. Both rental value and resale capitalisation rate are adjusted in the example used to effect a loss of value caused by ageing.

Note that the complexity of property depreciation is illustrated by an ageing building producing a rising rental income. This may be explained by the split of investment into site and building (see Chapter 2): while the site may appreciate or depreciate in value in real terms, the building must depreciate. It is, however, impossible to test this effect accurately without abundant evidence of the rental value of bare sites, which is rare in the UK.

Thus, while the depreciation in real terms of a property investment may be attributable to site or building factors, typically it is the latter that is primarily responsible for the income pattern declining in comparison with a 'frozen' index of values.

Acceptance of differential building and site value performance over time leads to a necessary check in the analysis of a property investment. Given an ageing and declining building on an inflation-proof or improving site, the time will come when the net value of the site (after demolition and clearance) exceeds the value of the developed property. This may happen within the holding period, and if so the analysis must reflect that fact, subject to legal considerations (the tenant may not be removable until the lease end).

The estimation of gross income flow requires the estimation of rental values for the subject property as it ages in comparison with the projected value of the 'frozen' property. Again, this allows for building depreciation resulting from the ageing process.

As suggested at 3.2.5 above, this can be achieved by means of a cross-sectional analysis, comparing the current rental values of the existing building and the current rental value of a hypothetical new building in the same location, with the difference then annualised by reference to the age of the building. (Methodological issues to do with the measurement of depreciation are fully discussed in Baum *et al.*, 2005).

As an illustration, assume that the current ERV of the subject 10-year-old building is £25/ft^2. A rental growth estimate of 6% p.a. over the 10-year holding period is projected for the location. 15-year-old similar buildings currently let at £22/ft^2: 20-year-old buildings currently let at £18/ft^2. The capitalisation rate for the 10-year-old building is currently estimated at 7% and the projected resale capitalisation rate is 8% in 10 years' time when the building will be 20 years old.

The projected rental values are as follows:

Years 1–5:		= £25.00
Years 6–10:	£22 × (1.06)^5	= £29.44
Year 10 (resale):	£18 × (1.06)^{10}	= £32.24

The growth rate in the actual property is from £25 to £32.24 over 10 years, which represents a growth rate of 2.57% p.a. (The depreciation rate is given by (1+ location growth)/(1+ property growth) – 1 = 3.34% p.a.)

As the resale capitalisation rate is predicted as 8%, the resale price is therefore:

$$\frac{\text{Rent}}{\text{Yield}} = \frac{\pounds 32.24}{0.08} \quad \text{per square foot}$$

$$= \underline{\pounds 402.94} \quad \text{per square foot}$$

Current valuation

$$= \frac{\pounds 25}{0.07} = \pounds 357.14 \text{ per square foot}$$

The gross cash flow is therefore:

Year	Outlay (£)	Income (£)	Realisation (£)
0	(357.14)		
1–5		25.00	
6–10		29.44	
10		402.94	402.94

The internal rate of return (IRR) of this investment – gross of all costs – is 8.37%.

As a check or alternative, the exit site value may be compared to the exit building value.

In the example, assume the net site value is initially 50% of the total value and is expected to grow at the same rate as the 'frozen' rent index (6%). At the resale date it is worth $\pounds 12.50 \ (1.06)^{10} = \pounds 319.79$. This is exceeded by the property resale value (£403); but in different circumstances, especially where a longer holding period is used, this may not be the case, and where the site value increased at the location growth rate exceeds the existing property resale value less the demolition costs, site value exceeds existing use value and either redevelopment or major refurbishment should be undertaken. Estimates of the current net site value and the rate at which it will increase are therefore needed. The latter should equate with the rate at which newly prime property rental values are expected to increase: the former requires comparable evidence.

3.2.7 Expenses

Implicit within the gross cash flow from a property investment is a series of regularly recurring expenses. These include management costs, either fees charged by an agent or the time of staff. In the former case they may be based upon a percentage of gross rents; in the latter, they need more careful estimation, and may have to be increased over time. Repairs and maintenance will normally be covered, like insurance, by the tenant's obligations under a FRI lease; if not, they must be accounted for, as must the exceptional burden of rates or other property taxes if payable by the investor.

While the investor who provides services, for example, to the common parts of a multi-tenanted office building or shopping centre, will usually expect to recover these expenses in a service charge, the amount received may not quite match the cost of provision through a lagging effect or other causes, in which case an allowance needs to be made.

All expenses not tied to rent must be subject to an allowance for anticipated cost inflation.

3.2.7.1   Periodic expenses

While FRI leases place the burden of normal repairs upon tenants, dilapidations claims are not always met with the required response; in addition to this, improvements may be necessary to make the property marketable.

Thus, at the end of an occupation lease, the investor will be faced with the prospect of redeveloping, refurbishing, repairing or redecorating the property. If the lease end falls within the building period, the prospect must be allowed for, again with an inflation factor.

3.2.7.2   Fees

To strip out all costs to leave a net return estimate, acquisition fees and sale fees at the end of the holding period need to be removed from the cash flow. These will normally be based upon purchase and sale prices.

Rent review fees, based upon the new agreed rent, need to be allowed for at each review, and re-leasing fees, again based on the new agreed rent, have to be provided for at the lease end. Advertising costs may be additional to both sale and re-leasing fees. Value added tax (VAT) should be added to all expenses where appropriate.

3.2.7.3   Taxes

Property investment appraisal for the individual investor or fund can, and should, be absolutely specific regarding the tax implications of the purchase. Thus, capital and writing-down allowances should be taken into account where appropriate. Income or corporation tax should be removed from the income flow. Capital gains tax payable upon resale can be precisely projected by the model's insistence upon estimation of purchase price, sale price, intervening expenditure, holding period and intervening inflation. The effect of tax upon return is illustrated by Example 3.1 at page 78.

3.2.7.4   Debt finance (interest)

The majority of property investments are debt-financed. Private individuals, property companies and private equity funds all use borrowed cash (debt) to purchase property. The reasons for this are as follows.

There are usually limitations on the availability of equity capital. Even if equity finance is available, it is neither limitless nor cheap, as shareholders are demanding and (if a single equity provider is involved) the opportunity costs may be considerable. In any case, why not increase the diversification of a portfolio by using 50% debt finance to buy two buildings of similar cost rather than use all equity to buy one?

Using debt introduces gearing or leverage into the investment. As long as the interest rate is less than the expected return, the return will be enhanced by leverage. A commensurate increase in financial risk also results, but this can be offset by greater diversification.

Debt may increase the tax efficiency of a property investment, especially for a foreign buyer subject to withholding tax, a form of income tax. Interest payments are set off against net rents before income tax is assessed on rent or corporation tax is levied on profits. Increasing leverage can reduce tax and improve after tax returns on equity (see Example 3.5 at page 85).

3.3   The discount rate

The principal purpose of property investment analysis in the form discussed in this chapter is the facilitation of decision making. The basic criterion for decision making in investment, risk considerations apart, is the expected or required rate of return. This is termed the *target rate* (sometimes the *hurdle rate*) of return.

The target rate has already appeared in Chapter 2 as r. It was seen from Fisher's work (see Chapter 2) that the rate of return r can be built up from three factors: expected inflation (i), risk (rp) and time preference (l). $r = (1 + l)(1 + i)(1 + rp) - 1$; r is a compensation for these three factors, these three deterrents to the setting aside of capital for a period. $(1 + l)(1 + i) - 1$ forms the nominal risk-free rate (RFR), so that:

$$r = (1 + \text{RFR})(1 + rp) - 1$$

The target rate, r, should be based upon the return required by the investor to compensate him for the loss of capital employed in the project that could have been employed elsewhere, that is, the opportunity cost of capital (e.g., the redemption yield on similar maturity gilts), plus a risk premium.

3.3.1   The RFR

The determination of the RFR should not present huge challenges. The redemption yield on medium- or long-dated government bonds is often adopted as a proxy for a RFR as these securities produce a guaranteed income flow secured on the government plus a guaranteed sum upon redemption. Nonetheless, although risk free in nominal terms, they suffer from inflation risk (inflation will reduce the nominal return by a different amount to that expected on purchase). Hence, some appraisals adopt the real RFR of return, the proxy for this being the return on index-linked government bonds – but now there is a risk that the nominal return is uncertain. These measures also assume that the bond is held to redemption (bonds are usually traded and their annual performance is subject to variation).

In practice, the nominal cash flow is the relevant income to be analysed and the nominal RFR is therefore appropriate. The life of the bond and the life of the property investment (the proposed holding period) should coincide.

3.3.2   The risk premium

The key challenge involved in estimating the required return is the estimation of the risk premium. While there is a rigorous theoretical basis for estimating the risk premium through capital asset pricing model (CAPM; see Chapter 2 and the following), there are practical problems involved.

In standard finance theory the risk premium can be further split into an asset-class risk premium and an additional risk premium to account for the risk differential between the specific asset's risk and the asset-class risk. This latter factor can be positive or negative. How should appraisers and investors adjust their discount rates to reflect the different levels of risk attached to different investment opportunities? We present three alternatives: CAPM, Weighted-Average Cost of Capital (WACC) and an intuitive approach.

3.3.2.1   Capital asset pricing model

The use of the CAPM to establish the appropriate discount for pricing assets has been the source of much discussion in the real estate literature (see for example, Ball et al., 1998; Brown and Matysiak, 2000b; Hoesli and Macgregor, 2000; and Geltner et al., 2007). The key problem is that the beta of an individual asset is very difficult to estimate because of data limitations. For this reason we cannot at this time recommend this approach, although this may provide a way forward in future. We discuss CAPM in further detail in Chapter 9.

3.3.2.2   Weighted-average cost of capital

In certain circumstances the cost of borrowing may be taken into account by using the WACC. For a fuller discussion of WACC (see the following Brigham and Ehrhardt, 2005; Brealey et al., 2005; Brown and Matysiak,

2000b; and Geltner *et al.*, 2007). A number of companies in the property sector have a target rate of return that is equivalent to their WACC, as this is the overall rate of return required to satisfy all suppliers of capital (both debt providers, meaning lenders, and equity providers or shareholders).

Only when an investment provides a return greater than the investor's cost of capital does an investment increase the firm's value. Hence, WACC establishes the required rate of return, but at the portfolio level. For WACC to be the required return for an asset requires that the proposed investment has the same risk as the average of all existing assets. So the problem remains: what discount rate applies to non-average investments? Should a company apply the same discount rate to cash flows that have different risk profiles? If not, how are adjustments made? The WACC literature has little to add on this point.

In addition, this method of estimating the risk-adjusted discount rate may be unsuitable for many major real estate investors in the UK. For many investing institutions (for instance, pension funds) it is impossible to estimate WACC as they do not normally issue equity and do not normally borrow.

3.3.2.3 An intuitive approach

In current property investment appraisal practice, the assessment of the discount rate is usually based on either the nominal or real RFR of return with a subjective additional premium for property risk. Although there should be a generalised risk margin for property, each individual property should generate its own particular risk premium, some more and some less than the average market rate.

The risk premium may be built up from the following components (Baum, 2003):

- The property market risk premium
- The sector risk premium
- The location premium
- The asset premium

Given adequate data, CAPM should be of assistance in assessing the first three of these components, but not the last.

For an investor who is not fully diversified, which defines the vast majority, the asset premium needs to be assessed by considering the factors that create specific risk. We suggest the following based on Baum (2002):

- Tenant risk
- Lease risk
- Location risk
- Building risk

Properties where the cash flow is more certain should have lower risk margins. For example, a heavily over-rented property (let at more than its full rental value) let on a long lease with upward-only rent reviews to a high-quality tenant is a low-risk investment, as the level of cash flow is virtually guaranteed over a long time period. A property let on a short lease with frequent upward and downward market rent reviews to an unstable tenant has uncertainty attached to the cash flow and should attract a higher risk factor.

One way of identifying the risk premium is to use surveys of investors, and such research is used in a number of countries. In Sweden, for example, periodic performance measurement valuations are undertaken by using DCF approaches, and these valuations are analysed to identify sector and segment target rates of return. In the UK, some ad hoc surveys have been undertaken; they have produced varying rates dependent upon different market conditions and also vary between different sectors and segments. For the major property types (retail and offices) these premiums appear to have been as high as 4% in 1999 but have since reduced, and in 2003 and 2004 were closer to an average of 3% (DTZ, 1999, 2004).

Finally, in discussing appraisals at the individual property level, it is necessary to consider the portfolio aspects of property investment. Many of the factors and risks within the appraisal are specific to the property being appraised and, as such, can be substantially diversified away by holding a portfolio of properties. This book concentrates on the appraisal of individual properties, but it is the portfolio effect that impacts on the risk premium – and property investment pricing – in the market.

3.4   Examples

Example 3.1   The basic discounted-cash-flow model

An office block in a provincial UK city was built and let 17 years ago. It is currently let to a single tenant on a 25-year FRI lease with 5-yearly upward-only rent reviews at a rent of £80,000 p.a. collected quarterly in advance. It now has 8 years unexpired, with the next review in 3 years. It is for sale at £1,250,000. The target rate of return is 9%.
   You estimate the following information:

- The current rental value of the existing building is £100,000 p.a.
- Forecasts of rental growth rates *in the location* are an average 4% p.a.
- The capitalisation rate of the existing building at resale is estimated at 7.5%

The rental depreciation rate of the existing building over the next 8 years is estimated at 1% p.a., with no capital expenditure expected between now and at the end of the lease.
   Other costs are rent reviews costs at 4% of the new rent, purchase costs at 5.75% including UK stamp duty, sale costs at 2.5% and annual management charges at 1% of rent collected.
   What would be the expected cash flow if there were no refurbishment planned assuming a holding period of 8 years?

The full cash flow, quarter by quarter, is set out in Table 3.2. The total outlay including purchase costs is £1,321,875 at the beginning of quarter 1 (point zero), and immediately the first quarter's rent is received in advance for the first quarter of ownership (also point zero). At the end of quarter 1 (point 1) the next quarter's rent is received in advance, and this is repeated every quarter until the rent for the last quarter of the first 3 years is received at point 11. After 3 years, or 12 quarters, a rent review is undertaken and (assuming the rent grows by 4% p.a. in the location less 1% p.a. for depreciation of the building) the expected net growth rate is 2.9703% ((1.04/1.01) − 1). The rental value grows from £100,000 p.a. to £109,178 p.a., which is just under £27,295 per quarter. At the rent review the rent changes from £20,000 per quarter to the new amount. Because there are no more rent reviews this rent remains static for the remainder of the 8-year unexpired term. At quarter 12 the negotiations for the rent review generate a fee of £4,367, which can be deducted from the cash flow at that point. The new rent is collected in advance as from point 12. The cash flow is discounted at the quarterly equivalent of 9% p.a. $= (1.09^{0.25})-1$.

Table 3.2 The quarterly cash flow (lease only).

Period	Gross Income (£)	Annual mainte- nance costs (£)	Rent review, lease, pur- chase, sale costs (£)	Net income (£)	PV @ 9% p.a.	Present value (£)
0	−1,250,000		−71,875	−1,321,875	1.0000	−1,321,1875
0	20,000	200		19,800	1.0000	19,800
1	20,000	200		19,800	0.9787	19,378
2	20,000	200		19,800	0.9578	18,965
3	20,000	200		19,800	0.9374	18,561
4	20,000	200		19,800	0.9174	18,165
5	20,000	200		19,800	0.8979	17,778
6	20,000	200		19,800	0.8787	17,399
7	20,000	200		19,800	0.8600	17,028
8	20,000	200		19,800	0.8417	16,665
9	20,000	200		19,800	0.8237	16,310
10	20,000	200		19,800	0.8062	15,962
11	20,000	200		19,800	0.7890	15,622
12	27,295	273	4,367	22,654	0.7722	17,493
13	27,295	273		27,022	0.7557	20,421
14	27,295	273		27,022	0.7396	19,986
15	27,295	273		27,022	0.7239	19,560
16	27,295	273		27,022	0.7084	19,143
17	27,295	273		27,022	0.6933	18,735
18	27,295	273		27,022	0.6785	18,335
19	27,295	273		27,022	0.6641	17,945
20	27,295	273		27,022	0.6499	17,562
21	27,295	273		27,022	0.6361	17,188

Example 3.1   (Continued)

Table 3.2   (Continued)

Period	Gross Income (£)	Annual mainte- nance costs (£)	Rent review, lease, pur- chase, sale costs (£)	Net income (£)	PV @ 9% p.a.	Present value (£)
22	27,295	273		27,022	0.6225	16,822
23	27,295	273		27,022	0.6093	16,463
24	27,295	273		27,022	0.5963	16,112
25	27,295	273		27,022	0.5836	15,769
26	27,295	273		27,022	0.5711	15,433
27	27,295	273		27,022	0.5589	15,104
28	27,295	273		27,022	0.5470	14,782
29	27,295	273		27,022	0.5354	14,467
30	27,295	273		27,022	0.5240	14,158
31	27,295	273		27,022	0.5128	13,857

The sum of the last column is the NPV of the lease income less the original outlay and produces a total deficit of £770,909 (Table 3.3).

However, at the end of the holding period the property can be sold. The sale price can be forecast as a function of the future rental value at the time of sale capitalised at the exit yield at that point. The existing rental value is £100,000 and it is growing at a net rate of 2.97% p.a. after depreciation. After 8 years it will have grown to £126,385.

The all risks yield will be a function of the market's expectations for income and growth beyond the sale date and the return requirements of the investors at that time. It is therefore not necessarily the same as it is now both because market conditions may have changed but also because, upon sale, the property will be 8 years older than it is now. Even in a market where market yield levels have remained static since the purchase, the expectation for the exit yield would be different simply because the building is less attractive. Assume the older building will sell at an exit yield of 7.5%.

Table 3.3   Exit sale price and NPV calculation.

NPV of cash flow			−£770,909
Exit value	Rental value	£126,385	
	YP perpetuity @ 7.5%	13.3333	
	Estimated sale price	£1,685,134	
	Net of sale costs	£1,643,008	
	PV 8 years @ 9%	0.5019	
	Present exit value	£824,569	£824,569
NPV			+£53,660

Because a positive NPV results, this suggests that the investment will produce a higher return than the target of 9%.

Other inputs that might be considered in a DCF appraisal include the costs of debt financing of the cash flow, taxes on the net income and the sale price, and potential developments such as enhancing the existing building, changing the use and a full redevelopment (potentially for different uses).

Example 3.2 Refurbishment

Assume the aforementioned building is expected to be refurbished at the end of the lease and refurbishment costs are currently £500,000. The refurbishment would take 1 year to complete.

The rental value of a refurbished building is currently estimated at £115,000 p.a.
The capitalisation rate of a refurbished building in 9 years is estimated at 6.5%
Inflation in building costs is forecast to be an average of 4% p.a.

The exit value assuming a refurbishment which takes a year to complete and is undertaken at the end of the lease is as detailed in Table 3.4:

Table 3.4 NPV calculation: Refurbishment option.

NPV of cash flow			**−£770,909**
Exit value	Rental value	£163,681	
	YP perpetuity @ 6.5%	15.3846	
	Estimated sale price	£2,518,167	
	Less sale costs	£2,455,213	
	PV 9 years @ 9%	0.4604	
	Present exit value	£1,130,448	£1,130,448
Less refurbishment costs	Cost of refurbishment	£500,000	
	Inflated at 4%	£711,656	
	PV 9 years @ 9%	0.4604	
	PV of refurbishment	£327,666	−£327,666
NPV			+ £31,873

The calculation allows one year for the refurbishment after which the building is sold at its new rental value capitalised at an exit capitalisation rate. Market levels of capitalisation rates may have changed in the intervening period. But the property has been improved and the exit yield will reflect this. Hence, 6.5% rather than 7.5% is used.

The rental level will also be enhanced, and to a certain extent the impact of rental depreciation will be cured. The rental growth rate will be free of depreciation for a redevelopment and virtually free of it for a high-quality refurbishment. (For example, the value of a 30-year-old newly refurbished building may be no higher than the value of a 40-year-old newly refurbished building.) In this case, the full rental growth rate of 4% p.a. for the location is applied to the £115,000 rental value for a refurbished property. Because of the higher starting rent and higher growth rate, the projected rental value in 9 years is different by over £35,000.

Example 3.2 (Continued)

However, because the refurbishment takes a year to complete, during which period no rent is received, the result suggests that the projected refurbishment will not add value to the premises (it will cost virtually the same amount as it adds to the value), but the difference is marginal.

The preceding example sets out the basic DCF model with income collected as per the UK norm of quarterly rent in advance. However, from now on, the examples will assume rents paid annually in arrears to more concisely illustrate the different issues raised by DCF models.

Leasehold interests are also common in the UK, with the ownership of the interest in land ceasing after a certain term (see Chapter 7 for a detailed discussion). Example 3.3 is a basic leasehold example, with values assessed on both gross and net of tax bases.

Example 3.3   Leasehold property

A leasehold investment property has just been sold for £750,000. It is held from the freeholder on a lease with 10 years unexpired at a fixed rent of £47,500 p.a. The property has just been sub-let on a lease, which expires at the same time as the head lease, at a rent of £200,000 p.a. with one review in 5 years' time. The analysis of similar freehold properties implies a future rental growth rate of 8.71% p.a.

Analysis for gross of tax IRR

Cost:	£750,000	
Income:	Years 0–5	£152,500 p.a. (i.e. £200,000 – £47,500)
	Years 6–10	£200,000 p.a. × $(1.0871)^5$
		= £303,653
	Less	£47,500
		= £256,153

The IRR of this investment gross of tax is 20.48%.

Analysis for net of tax IRR (assuming the investor pays tax on income at 40%)

Cost:	£750 000	
Income:	Years 0–5	£152,500 × 0.6 = £ 91,500
	Years 6–10	£256,153 × 0.6 = £153,692

The IRR of this investment net of tax is 8.85%. A 40% tax rate has resulted in a 57% reduction in return. The use of debt finance may mitigate this: see Example 3.5.

Multi-tenanted property presents an additional set of challenges. These include voids, outgoings and tax.

Example 3.4   Freehold multi-let property

A property is on sale for £25m. An immediate outlay of £100m is essential (for, let us say, repairs). A further outlay of £50m at the end of the 10-year holding period, for improvements prior to a sale, is allowed for and made subject to an inflation allowance. Income tax of 30% of the net income is payable. Capital gains tax of 30% on the net *real* (after inflation) gain produced by the sale price (less fees and the outlay in year 10) over the initial outlay, fees and initial improvement expenditure is provided for. The client's net of tax target rate of return is 6.5% p.a.

The current rental value is £25m, but a void of 20% through the life of the investment is expected. At the next review in 5 years' time the rent is forecast to increase at a gross rate of 10% to £35.43m gross of voids and net of depreciation. After 10 years the net rental value is forecast to have grown to £46.69m and the resale value is calculated to be £583.59m, a function of the rental value in year 10 capitalised at the forecast capitalisation rate for the building, which is 8%.

The inputs into the cash flow and the resulting cash flow are as detailed in Table 3.5:

Table 3.5   Property investment analysis: 10-year model.

Price	£250m
Capitalisation rate (year 0)	7%
Capitalisation rate (year 10)	8%
ERV (year 0)	£ 25m p.s.f.
ERV assuming 5 years older	£ 22m p.s.f.
ERV assuming 10 years older	£ 18m p.s.f.
Rental growth	10% p.a.
Resale property value	£583.59m
Management	10%
Voids	20%
Periodic expenses	See Schedule
Inflation	5% p.a.
Purchase fees	3%
Review fees	7%
Letting fees	15%
Sales fees	2.75%
Income tax	30%
Capital gains tax	30%
Target rate net of tax	6.5%

The 10 year explicit cash flow is set on the next page

Example 3.4   (Continued)

Table 3.5 (Continued) 10 year explicit cash flow

Year	Rent (£m)	Voids (£m)	Gross estimated income (£m)	Outlay resale (£m)	Expenses (£m)	Fees (£m)	Periodic outlays (£m)	Net cash (£m)	Income Tax (£m)	Capital gains tax (£m)	ATCF[a] (£m)
0	0	0	0	−250	0	7.50	100	−357.50			−357.50
1	25	5	20		2		0	18	5.4		12.6
2	25	5	20		2		0	18	5.4		12.6
3	25	5	20		2		0	18	5.4		12.6
4	25	5	20		2		0	18	5.4		12.6
5	25	5	20		2	2.48	0	15.52	4.66		10.86
6	35.43	7.09	28.34		2.83		0	25.51	7.65		17.86
7	35.43	7.09	28.34		2.83		0	25.51	7.65		17.86
8	35.43	7.09	28.34		2.83		0	25.51	7.65		17.86
9	35.43	7.09	28.34		2.83		0	25.51	7.65		17.86
10	35.43	7.09	28.34	583.59	2.83	16.05	81.44	511.61	7.65	−28.86	540.48

[a] After-tax cash flow.

Analysis

Price plus initial works	£ 357.50m
Target rate	6.5%
NPV	£26.17m
IRR	7.36%

The gross of tax IRR is 8.26%, despite the 30% tax rate. The property produces a significantly higher return than the hurdle rate and the gross to net of tax IRR reduction is less than 1%.

Most property investments are financed by using a combination of debt and equity. This has interesting implications for returns, but also for risk, and additionally for tax effects, as using debt may increase the tax efficiency of the deal.

Example 3.5   Debt finance and tax

A property is available for a purchase price including fees of £12,590,350. The current passing rent is £500,000, and the estimated market rental value is £1,000,000. Rental growth of 5% is forecast after depreciation. The property is multi-tenanted and a 10% vacancy rate is your best estimate. Annual operating expenses are expected to be £100,000. The exit capitalisation rate is forecast to be 7.5% and inflation in costs will run at 3%. The required return (assuming 100% equity) is 12%.

Given the preceding, you have estimated the most likely cash flow as follows:

Year	Best-guess income (£)	Best-guess operating expenditure (£)	Net cash flow (£)
1	500,000	103,000	397,000
2	1,102,500	106,100	886,160
3	1,157,625	109,300	932,590
4	1,215,506	112,600	981,405
5	18,293,369	115,900	18,049,813

Here, 70% loan finance is available providing £8,813,245. The remaining 30% equity requirement is £3,777,105. The fixed-interest rate on debt is 8%, and the annual interest-only annual repayment is £705,060.

Example 3.5   (Continued)

The return on equity is 12% – see the following:

Year	Capital	Rent	Outflow	Net cash
0	–£12,590,350	£0	£0	–£12,590,350
1	£0	£500,000	£103,000	£397,000
2	£0	£992,250	£106,090	£886,160
3	£0	£1,041,863	£109,273	£932,590
4	£0	£1,093,956	£112,551	£981,405
5	£17,017,088	£1,148,653	£115,927	£18,049,813
			IRR	12.00%

What is the return on equity using debt finance? Assuming that spare cash is used to reduce debt (the declining balance approach), the IRR rises to nearly 19%.

Year	Project cash flow	Interest	Net cash flow	Cash to equity	Debt outstanding
0	–£12,590,350	£0		–£3,777,105	£8,813,245
1	£397,000	£705,060	–£308,060		£9,121,305
2	£886,160	£729 704	£156,456		£8,964,849
3	£932,590	£717,188	£215,402		£8,749,447
4	£981,405	£699,956	£281,449		£8,467,998
5	£18,049,813	£677,440	£17,372,373	£8,904,376	
IRR	12.00%			18.71%	

Note that the calculation can also be undertaken assuming that debt is not reduced as the net cash flow comes in (the constant balance approach). This reduces the IRR to equity very slightly.

Year	Project cash flow	Interest	Net cash flow	Debt outstanding
0	–£12,590,350		–£3,777 105	–£8,813,245
1	£397,000	–£705,060	–£308,060	–£8,813,245
2	£886,160	–£705,060	£181,100	–£8,813,245
3	£932,590	–£705,060	£227,530	–£8,813,245
4	£981,405	–£705,060	£276,345	–£8,813,245
5	£18,049,813	–£705,060	£8,531,508	
IRR	12.00%		18.62%	

Note also that the increase in return comes at the cost of higher risk. If exit yields were to be higher than forecast (by, respectively, 1% and 3%), the IRR falls from 12% to 9.7% and then to 6% if the large increase in exit yield occurs; but if the property is 70% debt financed, the IRR collapses from 9.7% to 12.8% at a 1% increase in exit yield, but from 6% to only 1.4% if the 3% increase in exit yield occurs.

Exit yield (%)	IRR: 100% equity	IRR on equity: 70% debt
7.50	12.00%	18.60%
8.50	9.70%	12.80%
10.50	6.00%	1.40%

Now let us assume that tax is payable on income and capital gains at 30%. What is the return on 100% equity after tax?

Year	Capital	Income	Tax	Net cash after tax
0	-£12,590,350			-£12,590,350
1	£0	£397,000	£119,100	£277,900
2	£0	£886,160	£265,848	£620,312
3	£0	£932,590	£279,777	£652,813
4	£0	£981,405	£294,422	£686,984
5	£17,017,088	£1,032,726	£1,637,839	£16,411,975
			IRR	8.71%

The IRR falls from 12% to 8.71%. What is the return on 30% equity after tax? Assuming the constant balance approach:

Year	Project cash flow	Interest	Net cash flow	Tax	After tax cash
0	-£12,590,350	£0	-£12,590,350	£0	-£3,777,105
1	£397,000	-£705,060	-£308,060	-£92,418	-£215,642
2	£886,160	-£705,060	£181,100	£54,330	£126,770
3	£932,590	-£705,060	£227,530	£68,259	£159,271
4	£981,405	-£705,060	£276,345	£82,904	£193,442
5	£18,049,813	-£705,060	£17,344,753	£932,780	£7,598,729
IRR	12.00%				15.74%

Summary:

IRR on 100% equity pre-tax	12.00%
IRR on 100 % equity after tax	8.71%
IRR on 30% equity pre-tax	18.62%
IRR on 30 % equity after tax	15.74%
100% equity pre-tax/post-tax return ratio	73.00%
30% equity pre-tax/post-tax return ratio	85.00%

The use of debt increases the tax efficiency of the investment.

If the cost of borrowing is lower than the expected total return on the investment, the use of debt finance can increase return at the cost of higher risk. If tax is payable on income, the use of debt can increase the tax efficiency of the investment, because interest is a deduction to be offset against net rental income before tax is assessed.

Hence, if the market is dominated by tax payers, the market value will probably be determined by reference to the costs and availability of debt. The appraisal model and the appraiser must be prepared to take this into account.

More examples of DCF appraisals are discussed and exemplified in Chapters 8 and 9.

Part Two
Market Valuation Models

Chapter 4
The Theory and Practice of Conventional Appraisal Techniques

4.1 Introduction

The basis of accepted techniques for the appraisal of property investments evolves from the attitudes and perceptions of those who carry out the appraisals and those who own and occupy the properties being appraised. Their influences range from the concepts and techniques taught to them in the formative years of their careers to the market conditions that apply at the time of the valuation and their perceptions of future changes in those conditions.

They will also be influenced by the role of the appraisal. In the UK, valuation usually requires the assessment of an exchange value or market value. Valuations are used in place of the pricing mechanism present in securities markets; and it is only relatively recently that other types of value – and valuation – have been discussed in detail. Part Two of this book therefore deals exclusively with the assessment of market value and critically reviews the approach that has evolved in the UK over a considerable number of years. Valuation has been the principal focus of the main professional institution dealing with real estate in the UK, the Royal Institution of Chartered Surveyors (RICS). However, for a long time valuation was seen as a technical subject to be learnt and passed on from practitioner to practitioner. Although there were a few full-time educational courses in the UK, it was only from the 1970s onwards that real estate became a mainstream degree subject in a number of universities and more academic principles were brought to bear upon the topic.

The original interest in valuation as a more theoretical discipline was initiated by the property crash of 1973. The more violent falls in value in 1990 gave renewed impetus to the call for valuers to modernise their methods and create a defensible, rational approach. This chapter reviews the evolution of the conventional valuation technique (examined in greater detail in the first and second editions of this book), sets out the basic approaches currently adopted by practitioners and critically examines their usefulness.

4.2   The evolution of conventional techniques

4.2.1   The changing perception of investors

The conventional techniques for assessing market value have evolved over a significant time period and have been adapted and amended as circumstances change. Although Trott (1980: 1) suggested that 'for many decades the conventional methods of investment valuation were accepted as logical, practical and seemingly immutable', this was re-examined and shown to be untrue, in the UK at least, in the years that followed, with our first edition detailing the criticisms in book form for the first time.

Techniques can be seen to bend and change as markets evolve. It is therefore virtually impossible to understand the details of valuation methods without an examination of how these methods evolved, and without considering the context within which the changes took place. In the first edition, a detailed examination of how valuation techniques evolved during the twentieth century was undertaken. This examination was based upon primary research into the behaviour of property values in central Nottingham, a major urban centre in the UK (Crosby, 1985), and a review of the basic textbooks of the era.

The economic context of the model remained virtually unchanged until the 1960s. The key issue explaining this was the absence of inflation and more importantly expectations of inflation (and therefore rental growth) until the late 1950s. In the first edition, we showed that basic economic indicators suggested that there was no or little perception of the damage inflation could cause to investment returns, if it was not specifically included in pricing models; and as a result it was not explicitly included in those models.

Table 4.1 sets out a number of local property market indicators for Nottingham City Centre retail, a provincial city situated in the East Midlands region of the UK. This shows that rental values grew by about 2.5 times between 1910 and 1946 and that inflation was also almost exactly the same, growing by 2.51 times in the same period. This represents an annual growth rate of 3.65%. The average yield on government bonds was 3.8%, giving a real return of virtually zero. At the same time property capitalisation rates for retail properties, which were also growing in value at approximately the inflation rate, averaged 5.8% (a 2% risk premium over gilts). An annual rent review structure would have enabled property investors to obtain returns of over 9%, a risk premium above gilts of 6.5%. But this

Table 4.1 Nottingham City Centre, retail property, rents, inflation and initial yields, 1910–1960.

Years	Prime rent		Average rent index (2)		Retail prices index (RPI) (3)	Prime initial	Gilts (5)
	1910 = 100	1946 = 100	1910 = 100	1946 = 100	1913 = 100	yields (4)	
1910	100.0	43.3	100.0	38.2	94	5.0	3.1
1911	96.9		96.0		95	5.0	3.2
1912	95.4		92.9		98	5.0	3.3
1913	95.4		91.6		100	4.5	3.4
1914	95.4		91.6		101	6.5	3.3
1915	95.4		91.6		121	—	3.8
1916	95.4		91.6		143	—	4.3
1917	96.9		94.6		173	—	4.6
1918	99.2		99.3		199	6.75	4.4
1919	101.5		104.4		211	5.0	4.6
1920	104.6		109.8		244	5.0	5.3
1921	106.9		114.8		222	4.5	5.2
1922	109.2		120.5		179	5.5	4.4
1923	111.5		125.6		171	6.0	4.3
1924	118.5		132.5		172	6.25	4.4
1925	123.1		138.7		173	6.0	4.4
1926	127.7		148.8		169	5.5	4.6
1927	133.8		157.6		164	5.0	4.6
1928	140.0		168.4		163	4.0	4.5
1929	147.7		180.1		161	5.0	4.6
1930	153.8		198.7		155	6.0	4.5
1931	135.4		159.9		145	9.0	4.4
1932	135.4		158.9		141	8.0	3.7
1933	135.4		158.2		137	6.5	3.4
1934	135.4		160.3		138	6.5	3.1
1935	135.4		161.9		140	6.0	2.9
1936	135.4		166.7		144	6.0	2.9
1937	143.8		177.8		152	5.5	3.3
1938	152.3		187.2		153	5.0	3.4
1939	146.2		181.5		158	5.0	3.7
1940	140.0		172.1		179	7.5	3.4
1941	140.0		170.0		197	—	3.1
1942	140.0		170.0		210	—	3.0
1943	140.0		170.0		217	—	3.1
1944	140.0		170.4		222	7.0	3.1
1945	161.5		192.8		226	6.0	2.9
1946	230.8	100	262.0	100	236	5.0	2.6

Continued

Table 4.1   (Continued)

Years	Prime rent 1910 = 100	Prime rent 1946 = 100	Average rent index (2) 1910 = 100	Average rent index (2) 1946 = 100	Retail prices index (RPI) (3) 1913 = 100	Prime initial yields (4)	Gilts (5)
1947		105.6		108.9	249	4.5	2.8
1948		110.2		116.0	268	4.4	3.2
1949		111.9		124.1	275	4.5	3.3
1950		114.1		131.4	283	4.5	3.5
1951		116.7		138.0	311	4.5	3.8
1952		123.3		146.3	338	5.0	3.2
1953		139.8		160.9	349	5.5	4.1
1954		158.6		170.0	355	5.25	3.8
1955		179.8		198.3	371	5.0	4.2
1956		200.0		224.5	389	5.5	4.7
1957		212.0		253.7	404	5.5	5.0
1958		222.6		276.5	416	5.5	5.0
1959		233.4		293.3	418	6.0	4.8
1960		242.7		308.3	422	6.0	6.4

opportunity was spurned by property investors, whose fixation with security of income appeared to override their desire for return, as they attempted to tie tenants to very long leases without rent revision. Leases of 21, 42 and 63 years with no or very infrequent rent reviews were not uncommon for good-quality retail tenants in good locations, and this practice turned property into a fixed-income bond investment with a 2% risk premium over gilts.

The obvious question to ask is: why, in the face of such basic evidence, did investors still invest in bonds, which were giving no real returns, and turn property investments – an opportunity to hedge against inflation – into another form of fixed-income bond?

Crosby (1985) concluded that investors had not recognised the harmful effects of inflation on fixed incomes because of the cyclical nature of the inflation and the numerous shocks that had occurred in the first half of the twentieth century. These shocks may have been seen as the only cause of inflation, and investors assumed that it was not the 'natural' state of affairs. The great war of 1914–1918 had seen prices double, while in the 1920s they fell by well over one-third. During World War II prices again rose by over a third. So inflation appeared to be shock-related.

It was only towards the end of the 1950s that bond yields started to increase above their long-term average, and more significantly above the yields on equities, reaching levels of around 5% in the late 1950s and 6.4% by 1960. This suggests that the effects of inflation were beginning to be taken seriously. Ironically, inflation, having peaked in 1951 at 9.9%, fell back through the 1960s and in 1959 and 1960 price rises were as weak as 0.5% and 1%, respectively. But the key point, as always in investment, was to do with expectations. If investors had begun to think that inflation (and rental and dividend growth) was the norm, then they would pay less for fixed-interest investments like bonds and more for property and equities – and they did with the introduction of the reverse yield gap in 1960. In property markets, yields remained close to long-term averages and fluctuated between 4.4% and 6% in the period 1946–1960. However, retail rents in Nottingham rose by between 2.5 and 3 times in the same period. In hindsight, 1960 may be seen as a watershed in the perception of investors in the UK. After 1960, yields in bond and equity markets and other interest rates, as well as lease structures in property, started to reflect anticipated inflation. From Table 4.1 we can see that prime property yields fell below gilt yields for the first time in 1960, and from other empirical evidence we can observe the shortening of the period between rent reviews from 21 to 14 years, then to 7 years, and finally to 5 years in the early 1970s, where (despite being subjected to occasional pressure to move to 3 years) it has remained to the present day (Crosby, 1985).

Between 1960 and 1990, bond yields and short-term fixed-interest rates continued to rise as a result of inflation. Nonetheless, apart from a number of years in the 1970s when inflation peaked at 25% in 1974 and rose again to above 15% in 1979 and 1980, interest rates and bond yields have been above inflation, reflecting (as they should) an expected real return.

In addition to the reduction in the rent-review patterns indicated earlier, the post-1960 era saw the development of the institutional lease in the UK. This lease comprised a 20–25 year term with no breaks, imposed the liability for all repairs and insurance upon the tenant, had periodic rent reviews to market rent every 5 years and reviews were upwards only. This created a secure long-term cash flow, but also gave the landlord the ability to participate in any market increases and protect the income against falls in real value caused by inflation. Despite increasing flexibility in leases since 1990 with shortening lease terms and the introduction of tenant breaks, UK leases are still some of the longest in the world (Crosby *et al.*, 2005).

As property investments could now allow participation in growth while fixed-income investments such as bonds could not, interest rates and bond yields rose above property yields in 1960, and this reversal of the yield gap between fixed income and property's equity-type cash flows (those which can participate in value change) became a fixture of interest rate structures during the high inflationary period of the 1970s and 1980s, and continued into the 1990s.

Part Two

To summarise, in the post-1960 era the pricing of investment assets appeared to reflect the impact of inflation, and the initial yields of investments which could adjust their cash flow remained fairly constant, while those that could not (fixed-income assets) rose significantly to counter the inflation rate. Unfortunately, valuation techniques did not change, and the approaches that had served valuers in the pre-1960 era continued to be used – and are still used – in practice.

The next section of this chapter sets out the conventional model and critically examines it in the light of modern economic conditions.

4.2.2   Historical application of the basic valuation model

We now consider the valuation of three main property 'types': a freehold interest let at its market ('rack') rental value; a freehold interest let at a rent which is below market rental value (a 'reversionary freehold'); and a leasehold interest. The approach to these standard types can be identified from historical texts and cases as follows.

Example 4.1   Rack-rented freehold

We assume a long gilt redemption yield of 4.25%. The net rent passing and estimated rental value (ERV) is £21,000 p.a.; the 'all-risks yield' (capitalisation rate) is estimated to be 6.25% from comparable property sales and reflects a 2% risk premium above bonds.

ERV	£21,000	
YP perp. @ 6.25%	16.0000	
Valuation		£336,000

Example 4.2   Reversionary freehold

As Example 4.1, but the rent passing is £10,000 p.a. and there are 2 years to go to the end of the lease.

Rent passing	£10,000	
YP 2 years @ 6.25%	1.8270	
		£18,270
Reversion to ERV	£21,000	
YP perp. @ 6.25%	16.0000	
PV 2 years @ 6.25%	0.8858	
		£297,633
Valuation		£315,903

Example 4.3   Leasehold

This is the leasehold interest that derives from Example 4.2.

Rent received or rental value	£21,000
Less rent paid	£10,000
Profit rent	£11 000
YP 2 years @ 6.25%	1.8270
Valuation	£20,097

This represents the simplest forms of the approach. Norris (1884) suggests that (as in the preceding examples) the value of the reversionary freehold and lease-hold interests are 'such that the sum of the two is always equal to the total value of the freehold in perpetuity'. In this case £336,000 = £315,903 + £20,907.

This basic model was adapted and refined during the first part of the twentieth century. The development that took place was fully set out in the first and second editions of this text, and we do not propose to repeat that material here. However, we illustrated that at a particular point valuers started to apply different yields or capitalisation rates within the two parts of the basic reversionary model (known as 'term' and 'reversion') because of notions of different levels of risk. Where the rent was contracted under the lease, valuers assumed it had less risk attached, and this was often on account of the rent being below rental value due to growth since the last rent revision date. With over 3% average inflation and long terms between rent revisions, these gaps could become substantial, and valuers applied lower rates to the secure term income than to the fuller reversionary income, which was based on the full or rack rental value. As further justification, the rental value was an estimate that could prove to be inaccurate, while rent was a known and contracted figure with no variations or uncertainties apart from the possibility of default.

From the 1970s onwards, with the virtually universal introduction of upward-only rent reviews within long leases, valuers also began to consider the difference in security of the contracted rent over the entire lease period and the expected uplift at rent review. This resulted in valuers slicing up the reversionary property cash flow horizontally rather than vertically, and applying lower capitalisation rates to the hardcore, layer or bottom slice than were applied to the top slice of income. This practice was also the product of government intervention in the property market in the early 1970s when, as an anti-inflationary measure, a rent freeze was imposed upon commercial property owners, with the result that rent increases could not be applied. The right to receive the existing rent became much less risky than any potential value from future increases, even if those expected increases were based on existing rather than future rental values.

Part Two

The introduction of horizontal as well as vertical slicing of cash flows and the use of different yields within the different parts of the valuation introduces a number of variations within the general conventional theme set out in the preceding text, and these will be examined later in this chapter.

Leaseholds were subject to greater changes in the techniques applied. Leasehold interests are perceived as wasting assets, as all value is normally extinguished at the end of the lease. To take account of this, valuers quite reasonably felt the need to down-value leaseholds relative to freeholds. The discounting process includes an element for replacement of capital, and so simple capitalisation of a finite cash flow is enough to reflect the wasting nature of the leasehold asset (Baum *et al.*, 2006), but valuation practice evolved to go further than this, first by adding an additional risk premium to the capitalisation rate and second by introducing the concept of a sinking fund invested at rates of interest available from banks to replace the asset value, thereby producing a 'dual-rate' approach. As this theory and practice progressed, the sinking-fund element was assumed to be paid for out of taxed income, and so profit rents were valued assuming that a chunk of the profit rent would have to be invested in a risk-free investment out of taxed income. The dual-rate approach, using capitalisation rates at 1% or 2% above those applied to freeholds of the same property type and in similar locations, became the mainstay of leasehold valuations throughout the twentieth century, and in the 1960s tax adjustment also became the norm.

Example 4.3 would therefore be amended to the following:

Rent received or rental value	£21,000
Less rent paid	£10,000
Profit rent	£11,000
YP 2 years @ 7.25/2.5% tax at 40%	1.1166
Valuation	£12,283

The valuation is reduced from £20,097 to £12,283, instantly creating a gap between the value of the freehold in possession and the sum of the values of the freehold subject to the lease and the leasehold interest, or marriage values. Whether marriage values actually do or should exist on this basis is open to debate, but there is no doubt that shrewd property investors of the 1980s and 1990s exploited this poor application of technique to their advantage.

4.3   Rationale of the pre-1960 appraisal approach

Before 1960, valuers could be excused for assuming that commercial property was fundamentally a bond investment offering security of income. Negotiations for new leases with tenants were focused on securing their occupation at the market rent for as long as possible with no reviews and tenants were even offered options to renew at the same rent. There appeared to be little concern that a fixed income would decline in real value in an inflationary environment.

If we consider the valuation of three main property 'types', the logical approach in the pre-inflation perception era would be to assume no value changes in value in the future. Therefore, any increases in cash flow in the future would be caused by differences between the rent passing and current market rental values with no consideration given to whether rental values might change in the future. The discount rate would be based on the risk-free rate of return, given by yields on UK government gilt-edged bonds, plus a risk premium for the additional default risk of tenants compared with the government, plus any perceived generic property risks. In the period up to 1960 a positive yield gap between gilt yields and property existed, in the order of 1.5–2%. It was this comparison that led to 2% being widely and misleadingly quoted as the property risk premium in the 1980s and 1990s, despite the nature (relative risk) of the two investments having changed as soon as property capitalisation rates moved below those of gilts in the 1960s.

To illustrate, the valuation of a rack-rented freehold shop property in (for example) 1950 would have been undertaken on the basis of a capitalisation of the rent at the appropriate yield. For example, the prime shop yield in Nottingham was estimated to be 4.5% at that time (Table 4.1). Assuming a rent of £4,000 p.a., the calculation based on direct comparable analysis would be as shown in Example 4.4.

Example 4.4   Fully let freehold

ERV	£4,000	
YP perp. at 4.5%	22.2222	
Valuation		£88,889

The landlord would expect the rent to be fixed for 21 years at least, possibly 35 or 42 years, if the tenant represented a very good covenant. The valuation has a logical basis if viewed in the light of the following propositions:

a. Property is more risky and less liquid than fixed-interest government securities (2.5% Consols), which yielded around 3.5% to redemption at that time.

b. There is no assumption of an upward trend in rents. The likelihood of a fall in rents is just as possible as an increase, and therefore the objective of fixing a rent for as long as possible is seen as a positive advantage to minimise the risk of a fall in income. An increase in rent is not necessary, as the initial yield is already 1% above the yield on fixed-interest stock.

Part Two

Example 4.4   (Continued)

These assumptions are consistent with the previous analysis of investors' perceptions prior to the movement towards the reverse yield gap which took place later in the decade. The valuation is a simple discounted-cash-flow (DCF) valuation (albeit conveniently presented) as developed in Chapter 3.

To make this comparison clearer, the prospective explicit cash flow can be constructed. Assume that the rent is fixed for 21 years (and that the market would expect another 21-year lease to be granted at the end of the current lease) and that rental values are not expected to show a long-term upward or downward trend. Gilts yields are at 3.5%. A DCF valuation with a 1% risk premium would be as shown in Table 4.2.

Table 4.2   Fully let freehold cash flow.

Years	Rent (£)	YP 21 years @ 4.5%	PV @ 4.5%	Present value (£)
1–21	4,000	13.4047	1.0000	53,619
22–42	4,000	13.4047	0.3968	21,275
43–63	4,000	13.4047	0.1574	8,442
64–84	4,000	13.4047	0.0625	3,350
85–105	4,000	13.4047	0.0248	1,329
106–126	4,000	13.4047	0.0098	527
127–147	4,000	13.4047	0.0039	209
148–168	4,000	13.4047	0.0015	83
169–189	4,000	13.4047	0.0006	33
190–perpetuity	4,000	22.222[a]	0.0002	22
				88,889

[a]YP perp. @ 4.5%.

Note that the result is the same, but the three-line valuation is somewhat easier to produce, especially in the absence of valuation software, spread-sheets or even pocket calculators. A reversionary valuation would be as follows.

Example 4.5   Reversionary freehold

A shop property was let on a 21-year lease, with 6 years unexpired in 1950. The rent under the lease fixed in 1935 would be in the region of 50% of the rental value in 1950 (Nottingham average index 1910 = 100, 1935 = 161.9, 1950 = 344.3). Assuming the rental value of £4,000 p.a. in 1950, the rent under the lease is £2,000 p.a.

The approach at that time would be a capitalisation of the reversion at a yield higher than the term. Adopting a deduction for the additional security of the term income of, say, 1%, the term yield would be at 3.5% with the reversion capitalised at 4.5%.

Current rent	£ 2,000	
YP 6 years at 3.5%	5.3286	
		£ 10,657
Reversion to ERV	£ 4,000 p.a.	
YP perp. at 4.5%	22.2222	
PV 6 years at 4.5%	0.7679	
	£68,257	
Valuation		£78,914

Comments:

a. The term yield is now level with the yield on gilt-edged stock. The term rent is seen as secure, the tenant occupying property worth twice as much as the rent payment. The income is fixed under a contract and the risk of default or fluctuation is minimal. Whether the term is as risk free as a gilt is open to question – and generic property risks such as illiquidity are ignored – but a yield of 3.5% is arguably the correct yield for the very best property, which would additionally presume a letting to an impeccable tenant.

b. The rent on reversion is estimated to be the rental value at the time of the valuation. Considering the perceptions of investors, this would have represented a valuer's best estimate of what the current market rental value would be. There is no implication of growth within the capitalisation rate, and the valuer had no reason to expect an increase in values being any more likely than the review taking place in a trough, such as what happened after 1930. The reversion would have taken place in 1956, 11 years after the war ended, and a sustained period of rental growth had only been evidenced longer than 11 years once since 1910 (in 1918–1930). The more recent history of depression, recovery, war, recovery, was a shorter-term cycle (3 years down, 6 years up, 6 years depressed, 6 years up) up to 1950.

c. The rent on reversion would have been assumed to be fixed on a long lease of either 21, 35 or 42 years in order to stabilise any possibility of fluctuating returns.

d. The yield for the capitalisation of the reversion would have been selected on the basis of comparisons with similar or fully let property investments and represented a level of return that would be sufficient if it was the internal rate of return (IRR) from the investment. Again, this is a DCF valuation. The margin above gilts represented the extra risks attached to property and had no inherent growth implied within it. The investor's willingness to accept a lease with no rent reviews is a testimony to that fact.

Part Two

Example 4.5 (Continued)

Given these assumptions and perceptions, the approach represents a logical, defensible technique to both the capitalisation and prediction of income
flow. The valuation assumes a fixed rent to reversion, a reversion to a rental
level consistent with the valuer's estimate of future rental level and a sustaining
of this level into the distant future.

The income profile shown in Figure 4.1 is consistent with expectations.

The full-cash-flow version would be as shown in Table 4.3, adopting the
same assumptions of a succession of 21-year leases at the expiry of the existing
lease in 6 years' time.

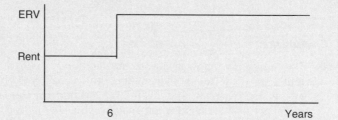

Figure 4.1   Reversionary income profile.

Table 4.3   Reversionary cash flow.

Years	Rent £	YP 21 @ 3.5%/4.5%	PV @ 4.5%	Present value (£)
0–6	2,000	5.3286	1	10,657
7–27	4,000	13.4047	0.7679	41,173
28–48	4,000	13.4047	0.3047	16,337
49–69	4,000	13.4047	0.1209	6,482
70–90	4,000	13.4047	0.0480	2,572
91–111	4,000	13.4047	0.0190	1,020
112–132	4,000	13.4047	0.0076	404
133–153	4,000	13.4047	0.0030	160
154–174	4,000	13.4047	0.0012	63
175–perp	4,000	22.2221	0.0005	41
				78,914

The approach to leasehold investment valuation is based on the same
expectations regarding maintenance of rental values and the fixing of rents
on long review patterns.

By 1950 the use of dual-rate tables was accepted. The development of the
tax adjustment is well documented, and would become the normal approach
after 1960.

Example 4.6   Leasehold

The valuation of the leasehold interest in the previous property (rental value £4,000 p.a., rent paid £2,000 p.a.; unexpired term 6 years) illustrates the process.

ERV	£ 4,000 p.a.
Rent paid	£ 2,000 p.a.
Profit rent	£ 2,000 p.a.
YP 6 years at 5.5% and 2½% adj. tax at 40%	3.1654
Valuation	£6,331

Comments:

a. The profit rent remains at the same level for the whole term and expires in 6 years' time. Because the pre-reverse yield gap perception is that rental values fluctuate rather than continually rise or fall, the leaseholder could be expected to sublet the property for the whole of the remaining term with no reviews. The net income would therefore remain constant.

b. The interest expires in 6 years' time, and upon expiry the lessee has no further interest in the property. Therefore, no value attaches to the interest after 6 years. It is an investment that terminates, and all the return is in the form of income. The investor must recoup his capital invested out of income, while a freeholder owns the interest in perpetuity, meaning that the value of the asset can be expected to be maintained in the long run. To compare the investment in a leasehold interest with a freehold, the leasehold investment is converted into something that can be equally perpetual, by enabling the investor to recoup his initial capital investment at the end of the lease and reinvest in an identical investment for the same price, and so on. The dual-rate approach was evolved to make this comparison, with a tax adjustment justified by the fact that, for the taxpaying investor, the sinking fund would be taken out of a taxed profit rent.

c. Having made the investment comparable with a freehold and in the absence of rental growth expectations, it remains to be considered whether a leasehold is more risky than a freehold. The perceptions were that it was, and so a higher return was used. In practice the valuer would have looked for other leasehold comparisons in accordance with his training (to look for similar comparisons), but in the absence of such comparisons a margin was adopted over and above the freehold yield for similar property. This was of course justified by the notional conversion of the wasting leasehold into a perpetual freehold. In the textbook examples we examined, 1% higher was a typical margin from freehold to leasehold capitalisation rate

d. The sinking-fund rates adopted were justified because sinking-fund investment plans were available at yield levels in the order of 2 to 3% net of tax.

e. The sinking-fund element of net income was not treated differently from the rest of the income for income tax purposes, and so a tax adjustment was made to the element of the income that was going into the sinking fund before it was invested. This ensured that it was then clear how much of the net-of-tax income was left to the investor as 'spendable income'.

The major conclusion from the foregoing analysis is that, in the context of the future expectations of investors and valuers, conventional techniques had a logical and defensible basis in 1950 and by analogy at other times prior to a change in investors' perceptions that occurred in the later 1950s. Whether these valuation models continued to be defensible after the change in perception will be considered in the next section.

4.4   The current conventional market valuation model

In the post-1960 economic conditions, the conventional model came under increasing pressure due to a change in investors' perceptions. In the 1970s and 1980s the reverse yield gap was significant, and growth potential began to dominate property prices. Later, the major property crash in the UK in 1989/1990 created the opposite possibility in investors' minds. These changes posed some interesting questions for any technique that has to maintain its credibility in rising, falling and relatively static markets.

The remaining part of this chapter sets out the conventional valuation approach and how it has been adapted to these challenges. It addresses the different variations on the major conventional theme and how they are applied to both reversionary and over-rented situations, and critically examines their performance.

In the pre-1960 era, the typical valuation could be related directly to other fixed-income investments such as bonds. After the appearance of the reverse yield gap, the model became a comparison model based on a capitalisation rate/all-risks yield, and the capitalisation rate was no longer the required return. For the first time, the yield used in the valuation was not based on a straight comparison with other investment markets. It therefore ceased to be a rate of return and became purely a unit of comparison. It was found by directly comparing deals done for other similar property investments in the same location, with similar physical characteristics and similar lease structures. In effect, the model ceased to be an investment approach and became a comparable approach based upon the capitalisation rate.

This section assesses the model as a market valuation or pricing technique that attempts to make the best use of market comparables; it no longer has a place as an investment appraisal technique or in a detailed analysis of prices.

It is clear that the best pricing technique, meaning an accurate one, must be based on the best evidence of market prices derived from other transactions in the same sub-market. The model's efficiency in its use and adaptation of market evidence is therefore the main criterion to be adopted in assessing its quality. This test is now applied by examining the conventional (pricing) valuation solutions to standard valuation problems.

4.4.1   The fully let freehold

Of all three categories of property investment, the fully let freehold is least prone to variation and hence to inaccurate valuation. The valuation approach is still as it was set out in Example 4.1. The normal approach to a fully let freehold interest for market value purposes is simply the rent passing (which is also the ERV) divided by the capitalisation rate/all-risks yield. As there are no major differences in the application of the model by different practitioners, the chances of different valuers coming up with different valuations based upon the same information base are small. However, the valuation relies upon the strength of the comparable, but comparables may be sparse in a slack market dominated by reversionary freeholds. The quantity and quality of comparable transactions is the key to all comparable valuations; in fully let freeholds methodological factors are less important.

However, when comparables cannot be applied directly, all adaptations are intuitive. For example, if a reversionary freehold comparable shows a yield of 6%, how should this information be applied to a fully let property? What if the comparable is let on 5-year reviews but the subject property is let on 3-year reviews? As the model is based upon rent and capitalisation rate only the capitalisation rate can be adjusted to cope with differences between subject and comparable (hence the term 'all-risks yield', which is also used and suggests that all risks are wrapped up or hidden in the yield).

4.4.2   The reversionary freehold

Three conventional techniques for valuing reversionary freeholds are recognised. These are the term and reversion, the equivalent yield and the layer (or hardcore) approaches.

The basic texts on valuation tend to suggest that the term and reversion approach is the most commonly used method, and the other two are lesser used variations. Research into valuation practice carried out by one of the authors just around the time of the property crash (Crosby, 1991) showed that, although the majority (60%) of valuers questioned used term and reversion 'usually or always', they tended to be valuers who were not specialists in the investment valuation field. They worked for provincial private practices and local authorities and did few valuations of this sort each year. They tended to rely upon traditional training, which continued to support the term and reversion method.

Horizontally sliced layer and equivalent-yield methods were at the time adopted mainly by valuers in London and the larger metropolitan areas specialising in this type of work. The term and reversion method was no longer the standard approach of specialist investment valuers (Crosby, 1991).

In order to set out and compare the three approaches, a single example is used as follows.

Part Two

Example 4.7   Reversionary freehold

Value a good-quality freehold office investment let at a net fixed rent of £150,000 p.a. with the final 6 years of a historic lease still to run. The net ERV of the building is £300,000 p.a. An identical building next door has recently been let on 5-yearly reviews at its ERV and subsequently sold for £5,000,000.

Analysis

$$\text{Capitalisation rate } (k) = \frac{£300,000}{£5,000,000} = 6\%$$

(Note: In the UK, purchaser's costs are usually deducted from valuations after the capitalisation rate has been applied. Because of that, when analysing property transactions for capitalisation rates, these costs have to be added to the contract price to determine the full outlay. Purchaser's costs in the UK at the time of writing are about 5.75%, made up of 4% stamp duty tax and another 1.75% for professional fees. However, to keep examples simple, purchaser's costs will be ignored for the purposes of building and comparing solutions in this section of the book.)

If the valuation had been of a fully let property, the capitalisation rate could have been applied directly. If perfect comparables exist, arguments over technique are redundant and direct capital comparisons are all that is required. However, the subject property is a reversionary property and an adjustment technique is required in order to reconcile imperfect comparables.

Term and reversion

Term rent	£150,000		
YP 6 years @ 5%	5.0757		
		£761,350	
Reversion to ERV	£300,000		
YP perp. @ 6%	16.6667		
PV 6 years @ 6%	0.7050		
		£3,524,800	
Valuation			£4,286,160

Analysis

$$\text{Initial yield} = \frac{£150,000}{£4,286,160} = 3.50\%$$

$$\text{Reversionary yield} = \frac{£300,000}{£4,286,160} = 7.00\%$$

The equivalent yield is the single yield applied to both parts of the valuation to get the same answer. In this case it is 5.97%.

Notes:

a.   The term yield is derived from the fully let comparable and then adjusted downwards to represent the security of the term income. This security is supposed to come from the fact that the default risk is less as the tenant is less likely to leave the premises while paying less than ERV.

b. The capitalisation rate of the reversion is based on the fact that the property becomes fully let in 6 years' time and the comparison is a fully let property, and so the yield can be applied directly.

c. An alternative application of the technique adopts the same 1% differential between the term and reversion yield, but instead of adopting $(k - 1)$ for the term and k for the reversion, it adopts yields which straddle the capitalisation rate, that is, $(k - 0.5\%) \times 5.5\%$ on the term and $(k + 0.5) \times 6.5\%$ on the reversion. The reason for this is explained in what follows.

d. The model makes no attempt to identify the nature of the rent change and whether it is caused by a rent review or a lease expiry. However, if a void period is required, it can be accommodated relatively easily in this vertically sliced model.

Criticisms

i. The term represents a fixed income for the next 6 years. The capitalisation rate represents a growth implicit yield, and so, if the yield choice within the valuation is going to distinguish between the different parts of the valuation (term and reversion), it should take account of the fixed-income nature by applying a yield appropriate to a 'safe' income in default terms, but an extremely poor income in real terms if inflation expectations are positive.

ii. The term yield is often lower than the yield used on the reversion by the 'normal' amount of 1%, but it is not always an advantage to have a lower rent. In a rising market where rent review settlements lag behind open-market lettings, it may be an advantage to lose a tenant and obtain a higher rent from a better-quality tenant. In a falling market, the covenant of the tenant becomes crucial to value, and rules of thumb regarding the value of a secure tenant again appear simplistic.

iii. A reversionary property may not have the same qualities as fully let properties. The capitalisation rate of 6% implies growth that is realisable every 5 years. Theoretically, the growth potential of reversionary properties (let with unexpired terms less than the normal review pattern) is greater than for the fully let property, and so the combined effect of valuing the reversion at the fully let capitalisation rate and the term at 1% less creates a 'correct' valuation. However, the market does not perceive reversions in this light, and it is rare for a reversionary property to be valued at an equivalent or average yield lower than the capitalisation rate of the fully let property. The market tends to adopt a philosophy that discounts the reversionary property value because of the fact that the ERV has been obtained when fully let but is only an estimate in the reversionary valuation. This uncertainty regarding the ERV estimate creates additional risk in the reversionary valuation, and the value is therefore discounted as indicated in note (c).

Part Two

> **Example 4.7** (Continued)
>
> iv. There is a problem with the yield choice for the reversion: the 6% yield implies rental growth that is participated in every 5 years. However, the PV factor relates to the behaviour of the ERV in the 6-year term period. The ERV grows continually, and therefore the reversion should be deferred at a lower yield to imply a better growth potential. This point is illustrated in Chapter 6.
>
> The final result is a valuation that is logically incorrect and practically difficult to understand. It must be incomprehensible to most independent observers, as it isolates one aspect of the investment (security of term income) while keeping all others hidden within the yield. It is, of course, a product of an age that has long since departed, and the traditional application of the method should be laid to rest immediately.

However, it does perform one useful purpose that applications which have replaced it find very difficult to perform, specifically the valuation of properties let on long fixed terms without rent reviews prior to the final reversion. If our example had an unexpired term of 16 years rather than 6 with no rent revisions, the valuation could be approached by a term and reversion method but adopting a yield on the term to reflect the fixed income. This yield could be based on fixed-income government securities adjusted for a few of the additional risks of property investment, mainly concerned with tenant quality and illiquidity, but ignoring those property risks that will only impact on the long distance reversion. In effect, it is a property bond based on the tenant covenant strength. These issues will be returned to later in the chapter.

Layer

The horizontally sliced layer technique came into constant use in the 1970s in response to the early 1970s rent freeze discussed earlier. In the Crosby 1991 research into practice, the age profile of valuers using layer methods indicated a bulge in the age group who entered practice in the early 1970s.

However, in the 1960s, Capital Gains Tax legislation led to the initial use of layer techniques, as valuers sought a method that could identify the prospective capital gain element of the reversion. This technique is illustrated as follows.

Term rent	£150,000	
YP perp. @ 6%	16.6667	
		£2,500,000
Reversion to ERV	£300,000	
Less bottom slice	£150,000	
Top slice	£150,000	
YP perp. @ 7%	14.2857	

PV 6 years @ 7% $\underline{0.6663}$

$\underline{£1,427,876}$

Valuation $\underline{£3,927,876}$

Analysis

$$\text{Initial yield} \quad = \frac{£150,000}{£3,927,876} = 3.82\%$$

$$\text{Reversionary yield} = \frac{£300\ 000}{£3,927,876} = 7.64\%$$

$$\text{Equivalent yield} \quad = 6.44\%$$

Notes

a. The bottom-slice income is perceived to extend into perpetuity on the basis that there is little likelihood of the rent falling below the passing rent, because of the combined effect of upward-only rent reviews and perceived rental growth prospects.

b. The top slice is much more risky. It is based on an estimate of ERV about which it is difficult to be precise. In addition, because of the top-slice nature of the increase, an error in the ERV estimate would create a correspondingly greater error in the value of the top slice. For example, had the ERV only been £270,000 p.a. (a 10% error), the top-slice rental would have been £120,000 p.a. rather than £150,000 p.a. (a 20% fall). The geared nature of the increase is therefore very sensitive to errors in estimation of rental value and is therefore the risky part of the investment.

c. The layer technique more closely aligns with the perceptions of the modern valuer and is therefore more easily adapted for specific circumstances. If the valuer feels that the ERV estimate is very suspect then he or she can amend the top-slice yield by more than 1% (in practice 2% is often used).

Criticisms

i. It is difficult to accept the split of the income into two parts, as the risk of non-receipt attaches to the whole income.

ii. It is more difficult to incorporate breaks into the cash flow than if vertically sliced.

iii. The application of the layer method uses a growth-implicit yield on the bottom slice, which is fixed in nominal terms. As all the growth is in the top slice, and the top slice is highly geared, it might be expected to adopt a fixed-income yield on the bottom slice and a very low yield on the top slice to imply very highly geared growth potential. The valuation is unstable and suffers from the same problems as the term and reversion approach outlined in criticism (iv), but magnified because of the gearing problem.

Part Two

iv. The choice of the yield split between top and bottom slices is very arbitrary and cannot be undertaken other than intuitively.

v.   It is almost impossible to intuitively increase the yield on both top and bottom slices for a property that is let on a long fixed term before reversion. In the Crosby 1991 survey, valuers using this method (and the equivalent-yield method) discarded it in favour of term and reversion for that problem.

Although mathematically and conceptually fraught with problems, the layer technique does have two major advantages for practice. These are the concentration on the important variable of ERV and the lack of downside risk caused by upward-only rent reviews (assuming long unexpired terms and good covenants).

Equivalent yield

The equivalent-yield method differs from the other two approaches simply by failing to differentiate between the yields used on top and bottom slice or term and reversion components. As it applies the same yield to both parts of the income flow, it does not matter whether a horizontally or vertically sliced approach is adopted. In the practice survey, the horizontally sliced equivalent yield is more prevalent than its vertically sliced alternative.

Term rent	£150,000	
YP perp. @ 6.5%	15.3846	
		£2,307,692
Reversion to ERV	£300,000	
Less bottom slice	£150,000	
Top slice	£150,000	
YP perp. @ 6.5%	15.3846	
PV 6 years @ 6.5%	0.6853	
	£1,581,540	
Valuation		£3,889,232

Analysis

Initial yield $= \dfrac{£150,000}{£3,889,232} = 3.86\%$

Reversionary yield $= \dfrac{£300,000}{£3,889,232} = 7.71\%$

Equivalent yield $= 6.50\%$

Notes

a. The equivalent yield represents the IRR of the cash flow assuming a reversion to no more than current rental value. Future rental value growth is still excluded.

b. The equivalent-yield method is supposed to be particularly useful in the analysis of transactions. Another reversionary transaction can be analysed by determining the IRR of the conventional cash flow, which can then be applied to the subject property with suitable adjustments for differences between the comparable and subject property.

c. Criticisms of the two previous models based upon mathematical problems and arbitrary adjustments of the two yields within the valuation are eliminated as there is only one yield.

d. Criticisms of the other two models based on the choice of a growth-implicit yield on the term (or bottom slice) are also eliminated. The single capitalisation rate is the true all-risks yield of the investment. It represents the growth potential of the investment as a whole and the other risks applied to the property as a whole (not to parts of the income profile).

e. Practitioners tend to adopt slightly higher equivalent yields than capitalisation rates from fully let properties for the reasons discussed in note (c) and criticism (iv) of the term and reversion approach. The extent of this increase (we have used 0.5%) is arbitrary.

Criticisms

i. Being a true capitalisation rate technique, the valuer is left to intuitively adjust for every difference between the subject and comparable property. These differences include physical and locational differences as well as tenure (fully let to reversionary freehold) and, if both comparable and subject property are reversionary, differences in lease structures including the unexpired term and ratio of rent passing to ERV (see Chapter 6).

ii. The model is only as good as the comparables on which it is based. As indicated in the previous paragraph, a perfect comparable for a reversionary property is one that has the same locational qualities, is physically similar, and also has the same unexpired term and the same rent passing to ERV ratio. As the subject and comparable property diverge, the quality of the valuation diminishes. This is not exceptional to the equivalent-yield model. But if the subject property has a long fixed term, there is a wide intuitive leap necessary to adapt the yield. In this case, as for the layer approach, valuers often revert to the term and reversion approach using a fixed-income yield on the term to reflect the lack of growth potential.

Conclusions

The criticisms of conventional approaches for market valuation are based on two criteria.

a. Rationality: There is little evidence to suggest that the models as currently used reflect the perceptions of the owners of property investments.

Part Two

Even in the midst of the recession of 1992–1993, prime property yields implied a long-term growth rate in rental values. Even in a low-inflation era such as that of the late 1990s and the new millennium, valuing fixed elements of the cash flow at growth-implicit yields and assuming reversions to no more or less than the current ERV are now obviously devoid of reality.

b. Comparables: As there is no longer a rational basis for these models, the reason they have survived is because of the perceived role of the valuation in fixing price levels. Comparison with identical or similar assets has long been accepted as the best basis for assessing likely selling price. The argument boils down to which conventional technique makes the best use of comparables and whether there is a better way of utilising comparable information. Of the three alternatives, only the equivalent-yield model is totally objective in its analysis of transactions, as it calculates the IRR of the current cash flow assuming a reversion to current ERV only. It does not subjectively amend term or bottom-slice yields as compared to reversion or top-slice yields. By removing these arbitrary adjustments to yields, it is the only true capitalisation rate approach. The equivalent yield is a measure of the qualities of the comparable and needs to be adjusted for the differences inherent in the lease structure of the subject property and for any other differences. All differences are encompassed within the yield, and this is the only thing that can be changed.

Nonetheless, problems arise when comparable and subject properties start to differ, and one or other of them becomes 'abnormal'. In the property market of the 1990s some of these abnormal problems became the norm, and the inadequacies of the techniques set out in this chapter have become more obvious. Particular examples are leaseholds and over-rented properties, which are examined in the following sections.

4.4.3 Leaseholds

A single example is used to illustrate the conventional approach to leaseholds.

Example 4.8   Leasehold

A leasehold interest has 20 years to run, subject to a fixed head rent of £100,000 p.a. The current rental value is £200,000 p.a., subject to 5-yearly reviews. Market evidence suggests a freehold capitalisation rate (k) of 6% for this type of property.

Much criticised, the tax-adjusted dual-rate valuation appears to remain in limited use, but the tax exempt status of pension fund has prompted the use of unadjusted dual-rate valuations. Single-rate valuations have also been suggested (see, for example, Enever, 1981; Baum *et al.*, 2006). These three approaches will be taken as the available conventional techniques.

The three share a common feature, leading to a problem requiring immediate consideration. The capitalisation rate (k) is traditionally settled by reference to the initial yields obtained by purchasers of freehold investments in similar property with a small upward adjustment to account for the so-called extra risk of leasehold investment. This may be said to be the result of several inter-related factors: the top-slice nature of a leasehold, making the profit rent considerably more sensitive to changes in full rental value than the net freehold income; the dual contractual burden suffered by the leaseholder; the risk of a dilapidations expense inherited from previous leaseholders; and others.

The adjustment to k is often accepted as an additional 1% or 2% over the freehold capitalisation rate, which would lead in this case to a rate of 7% or 8%.

The logic of such adjustment is not questioned here (Chapter 7). Investors are generally said to be risk-averse (Chapter 2); so greater volatility in the net income, even if equal chances were applied to increases and decreases, would be sufficient to justify a higher yield.

However, the quantum of the adjustment is in the hands of the valuer. In the usual case, where market evidence is slight or imperfect, a considerable burden settles itself upon the valuer's intuition. This problem must be borne in mind for later reference: but, for the purposes of the examples, a capitalisation rate of 6% is used to isolate other errors and to reduce variations in an area where the valuer's inspiration is in danger of influencing his or her logic.

Dual rate, tax-adjusted

Rent received	£200,000 p.a.
Less rent paid	£100,000 p.a.
Profit rent	£100,000 p.a.
YP 20 years at 6% + 3% tax 40p	8.1950
Valuation	£819,500

Analysis

Required yield (spendable income) = 6% × £819,500	= £ 49,170 p.a.
Left for sinking fund (gross) = £100,000 − £ 49,170	= £50,830
Sinking fund (net) = £50,830 * (0.6)	= £30,498
Accumulation of sinking fund = × Amount £1 p.a., 20 years at 3%	= 26.8704
Capital recouped	= £819,500

Notes

a. As noted, the 6% capitalisation rate would normally be derived from sales of comparable freehold properties and adjusted upwards to account for extra risk.

b. The sinking-fund accumulative rate of 3% is supposed to represent the net-of-tax return available on a guaranteed sinking-fund policy taken out

> ## Example 4.8   (Continued)
>
> with an assurance company, which would provide risk-free return of capital. The sinking fund is designed to replace the initial capital outlay on what is a wasting asset. The historical organisation of the profession demanded that a property-wide means of comparison be evolved. While leaseholds might best be compared with redeemable stock, reality required that they be comparable with property investments and that leaves freeholds. The wasting nature of the asset had, then, to be countered by the replacement of capital over the period of the lease so that an interest similar to a freehold can be shown to exist. Provided the right steps are taken with the sinking fund, the right price is paid.
>
> c.   The tax adjustment of say 40% counters the fact that any higher rate 40% taxpayer would lose a portion of his profit rent in tax. While the effect on the remunerative rate or yield is not regarded as important (all, or most, investment opportunities are quoted on a gross-of-tax basis), its effect on the sinking-fund payment is vital. Without adjustment, the sinking fund would become inadequate as a result of income tax reducing the whole profit rent, including the amount destined for the sinking fund. As it has to accurately recoup capital, a 'grossing-up' factor is applied to cancel out the effect of tax (see, for example, Baum *et al.*, 2006): this grossing-up factor, in this case $1/(1-0.4)$, is the tax adjustment.
>
> d.   A 'true net' valuation (using a net-of-tax profit rent, a net capitalisation rate and no tax adjustment) would produce an identical result.
>
> ### Criticisms
>
> The criticisms set out here question some of the technical issues created when trying to apply conventional capitalisation rate techniques to leaseholds. There are some more fundamental criticisms with leasehold valuations that are critical, but they are dealt with later.
>
> i.   Why use such a consistently low accumulative rate? It is only in the most recent years that risk-free interest rates have dropped to the level that have been used consistently throughout the last 40 years. Bank deposits or building society accounts have earned considerably more in almost every year between 1960 and 2000, and yet are regarded as safe. It is true that they do not provide a guaranteed accumulation, but there is probably an equal risk of increases and decreases in the rates offered. Even risk-averse investors until very recently would be unlikely to discount the yield they would accept on guaranteed accumulations by as much as is necessary to produce 3%. Borrowers would certainly not set up 3% sinking funds when the cost of the capital they have employed to purchase the interest has been significantly more, even in the early 2000s with base rates at sub-5%.
>
> ii.   Why adjust for tax? Valuations are usually estimates of market value. Hence, the purchaser's tax rate is unlikely to be known and a guess, or average, has to be made or a corporation tax rate adopted. The current higher rate of income tax has often been used, but this is rarely the marginal rate of tax even where the small-scale investor is involved, and this ignores the

common case where a tax exempt fund is likely to buy, or where a company paying corporation tax is likely to purchase, either for occupation or investment. The considerable interest of gross funds in this market may be explained by the use of tax-adjusted valuations leading to low asking prices and resulting in high IRRs for purchasers (Baum, 1982; Baum and Butler, 1986).

iii. As noted in the RICS research report (Trott, 1980), the combination of three variables in the tax-adjusted, dual-rate valuation (capitalisation rate, sinking-fund accumulation rate and tax rate) makes a full analysis of transactions hazardous.

These criticisms may be countered by an untaxed approach that is often used to reflect the interest of the gross funds and more realistic accumulative rates.

Dual rate, unadjusted for tax

Rent received	£200,000 p.a.
Less rent paid	£100,000 p.a.
Profit rent	£100,000 p.a.
YP 20 years at 6% + 4%	10.6858
Valuation	£1,068,580

Analysis

Yield = 6% × £1,068,580	=	£64,115
Sinking fund = £100,000 − £64,115	=	£35,885
Sinking-fund accumulations × A £1 p.a., 20 years at 4%		29.7781
		£1,068,593

Notes

a. The sinking-fund accumulative rate used here should be the risk-free rate allied to the unexpired term.

b. A tax adjustment is superfluous in this case as the income of a gross fund is not reduced by tax. If, however, this represented a market valuation, any bidding taxpayer would have to accept a very low rate of return so as to compete if they allowed for a risk-free recoupment of capital.

Criticisms

i. It is easily proven that a single-rate years' purchase figure allows for recoupment of capital at the capitalisation rate (see, for example, Baum et al., 2006). The justification for a dual-rate approach is the argument that, *if a sinking fund were actually taken out in practice*, there would be no reason for the accumulative rate offered by an assurance company coinciding with the capitalisation rate attainable upon purchasing the investment, thus necessitating a dual-rate approach. But are sinking funds actually taken out in practice? There are sound reasons for concluding that few investors would arrange for recoupment of capital in this way:

- *Occupiers* can usually be regarded as long-term (more than the profit rent period) tenants. The initial capital outlay, or regarded as an investment of cash `in the business', is recouped out of profits, which (hopefully) outlive the profit rent.

Example 4.8 (Continued)

- *Investors* are likely to be holders of a number of property interests. In such a case, recoupment of capital from a wasting asset like a leasehold is unlikely to be by means of a sinking fund: it can be so by investing profit rents in similar investments. Income will be reinvested in the business in various ways, so it is difficult to conceive any investor actually behaving in a way assumed by the model.
- *Borrowers* in either category will have a cost of capital well in excess of the 3% or 4% accumulative rate. Consequently, no purchaser would set up a sinking fund to recoup capital at low accumulative rate when, as an alternative, they could reduce a debt costing much more.
- Even if there were some investors who took out sinking funds, it has been well illustrated (Fraser, 1977) that, while the concept of the sinking fund in leasehold valuations is designed as an attempt to reconcile the differences between the freehold and the wasting leasehold asset, the recoupment of capital in times of inflation becomes inadequate. Freeholds are likely to increase in capital and rental value over time. If the sinking fund replaces the initial capital cost of the leasehold, then the leasehold fails to keep pace with the freehold, and the rationale of the dual-rate concept is not put into practice. In the past various methods of adjusting the sinking fund to cope with inflation have been suggested by various writers including Fraser, Greaves and Rose. But the effect is to increase the sinking-fund element and reduce valuations still further. It will be shown later that more rational approaches to leaseholds suggest that they have been undervalued by conventional approaches, not over-valued, and any 'improvements' which make valuations even less accurate must be flying in the face of logic.

ii. There is a mathematical error in applying dual-rate valuations to reversionary leasehold situations. There are corrections that can be made, but they do not remotely address the more fundamental conceptual issues with leasehold conventional valuations.

Single rate

Rent received	£200,000 p.a.	
Less rent paid	£100,000 p.a.	
Profit rent	£100,000 p.a.	
YP 20 years at 6%	11.4699	
Valuation		£1,146,990

Analysis

Yield = 6% × £1,146,990		= £68,820
Sinking fund		= £100,000 − £68,820
		= £31,180
× A £1 p.a., 20 years at 6%		36.7856
		£1,146,975

Notes

a. As demonstrated by the analysis, the single-rate valuation allows for the recoupment of capital at the remunerative rate. Whether such a rate could be earned in practice is not necessarily important for the reasons stated within criticism (i) of the dual-rate unadjusted-for-tax approach (see also Colam, 1983).

b. However, recoupment of capital would have to be out of taxed income, as profit rents are subject to income tax and reinvestment in any medium would only be possible with the after-tax income. Hence, a net-of-tax valuation may be required. The example used is a net-of-tax valuation for a gross fund: if the potential purchaser is a taxpayer competing with taxpayers, then a tax adjustment will be needed. In such a case the net profit rent should be capitalised by a years' purchase factor at a net-of-tax yield, otherwise a dual-rate valuation will be the result. However, net-of-tax adjustments within conventional models are more complex than might be supposed. It is not enough to reduce both income and yield by the tax rate as the yield is a function of both future growth and target rate, and growth rates are the same net or gross of tax. This point is picked up when applying more rational techniques to leasehold valuations.

c. All foregoing criticisms appear to be met. The accumulative rate is no longer critically low; the problem of average tax adjustment can be avoided by investigating the market; there is no artificial assumption that a sinking fund is actually taken out, as reinvestment is at the remunerative rate, thereby obviating the problems of recoupment in times of inflation; and there is no mathematical error when valuing varying profit rents at a single rate of interest. Unfortunately, more fundamental problems with valuing leaseholds exist.

Conclusions: Leasehold valuations
Leasehold investment valuations are relatively rare compared with the more common freehold. However, the complexity of the leasehold problem is far greater than for freeholds, and the margin for error is much greater.

Part Two

The basic approach is the same as for freeholds. The prospective cash flow of the leasehold investment is set out on the assumption that rents are reviewed up to current rental levels, but future increases in rental value are ignored. The cash flow is capitalised at the capitalisation rate, found by comparison.

In the preceding critique, it was concluded that the dual-rate approach should be laid to rest and single-rate valuations would be a preferred alternative. However, a fundamental problem remains. This is examined in detail in Chapter 6 and is summarised here. All conventional approaches to leasehold valuations, whether single rate or dual rate, rely on a comparison technique. The perfect comparison, in addition to physical and locational qualities, would be leasehold, of the same unexpired lease term and with the same reversionary date and the same ratio of rent to ERV.

It is impossible to envisage such a catalogue of similar qualities. The market's solution is therefore to use freehold comparables because they are more plentiful. But freeholds are not the same; in fact, apart from both being based upon properties, they could not be more dissimilar. In an effort to compensate for some of these differences, valuers using conventional techniques are encouraged to add a risk margin to the freehold capitalisation rate. Using the capitalisation rate from a freehold, which incorporates an implicit expectation of future growth in rental values, a depreciation rate and a risk premium (Chapter 2), as the value measure for a shorter term and differently structured cash flow, is so simplistic that valuations carried out by that method are, in our opinion, virtually useless. We hope to show that the individuality of leasehold cash flows makes simplistic comparable valuations based on ill-considered relationships with other property assets a prime case for negligent valuations, and a large number of leaseholders have sold substantial assets for a lot less than they were worth over the last 30–40 years.

4.4.4   Over-rented properties

So far we have looked at the conventional approach to the market valuation of properties let either at their ERV or at rents less than ERV. Starting in early 1990, the UK experienced a deep recession, and rental values fell in nominal terms in many locations, especially those that showed the major growth in the 1980s boom. This includes the City of London and the southeast region of the UK. According to Investment Property Databank, in May, 1992, 70% of Central London offices were over-rented, and by an average of over 35%. The degree of over-renting increased over the following year to May 1993. Also, at the same time, over 60% by value of the Investment Property Databank was let on leases with over 15 years unexpired, virtually all with upward-only rent reviews every 5 years (Crosby *et al.*, 1998).

Given a low-inflation and low-growth outlook for the UK economy, periods of over-renting are now expected to reappear at regular intervals in the future. A further example was provided by the period 2000–2003, when falls in rents for Central London offices again took place and many aging office properties built in the late 1980s had not regained their 1989/1990 rental levels well into the 2000s because of a combination of low growth and depreciation.

UK valuers had not experienced any prolonged period of over-renting in the past before 1990. In 1973–1974, property values fell, but in most locations they had recovered their previous values within 5 years, a normal rent revision period, owing to high inflation rates. Valuers therefore had to adapt to the changing circumstances with little help from past experience, and they attempted to adjust the existing conventional models to the task. The staple diet of mainstream practice was the horizontally sliced equivalent-yield or layer model; so this was the main focus of their attempts.

We set out the conventional approach and its limitations in the following example.

Example 4.9   Over-rented freehold

A Central London office building is to be valued in June 1992. It was let on a 20-year full repairing and insuring lease in March 1990 with 5-year reviews at a passing rent of £2m p.a. The ERV has now fallen to £1m p.a. The fully let rack-rented capitalisation rate is estimated to be 8%. Gilt yields are approximately 10%.

Valuers in practice started to approach the challenge of over-rented properties by adapting the layer method and 'top-slicing' the portion of the contractual rent they considered to be in excess of the current rental value. They capitalised the core income as if the property was fully let at the appropriate capitalisation rate. They then capitalised the top-slice income for the unexpired term of the lease at a rate that reflected the fact that it was a fixed income and that it was dependent on the tenant's ability to continue to pay the rent. The approach is shown diagrammatically in Figure 4.2.

Core Income		
ERV	£1,000,000	
YP perp. @ 8% (all risk yield)	12.5000	
Value of term		£12,500,000
Top slice		
Passing rent	£2,000,000	
ERV	£1,000,000	
Overage	£1,000,000	
YP 17.75 years @ 13%	6.8135	
Value of reversion		£6,813,459
Valuation		£19,313,459

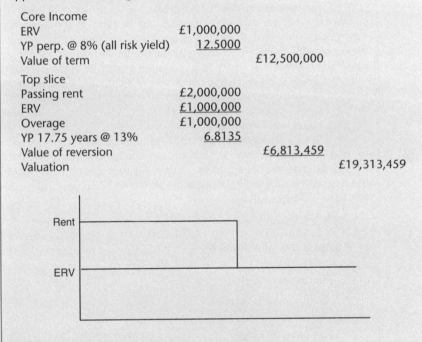

Figure 4.2   Over-rented property income profile.

Example 4.9   (Continued)

This approach is logical to valuers because, given that the layer method is standard, they are used to dividing a rising income between the passing rent and the ERV. With an over-rented property, valuers merely reverse the layers. In this approach, valuers capitalise the top-slice income for the whole period for which the tenant is contracted to pay the higher rent as, at each rent review, the upward-only provision would keep rents at no less than the contract rent.

Some valuers at the time considered that a sinking fund should be applied to the top-slice income because it is a wasting asset. Our views on dual-rate valuations are clearly set out earlier; following this, we cannot justify adopting a dual-rate solution to this problem.

There are two main problems with the conventional approach:

a. If the capitalisation rate implies long-term rental growth (which is the still the case with a rate of 8%), then the ERV may rise to exceed the passing rent before the lease expires. Therefore, it may be incorrect to capitalise the top-slice income for the whole of the unexpired term.
b. Capitalising the top slice as a fixed sum ignores the rental growth implied by the capitalisation rate (and the implied decline in the amount of the top slice) so that part of the overage is double counted.

To compensate for the fact that the overage might be eliminated before the end of the lease, the term of the overage can be taken to an earlier review only. However, the only realistic or rational approach is to forecast the review at which the overage is eliminated. As conventional models hide growth in the yield, they have no mechanism by which to incorporate growth in to the calculation.

Valuers advocating and using conventional techniques have resisted the challenge of models that explicitly incorporate rental growth for the past 30 years. In the case of over-rented properties, there appears to be no choice; see Chapter 10 for a full example.

Even if the necessity to forecast the point at which the rent will be reviewed to more than the current rent is accepted, the core and top-slice method will still not be a defensible approach. This is illustrated here. If it is assumed that the rent will rise above £2m p.a. by the review in 12.75 years' time (2005), the valuation will be as follows:

Core income.

ERV	£1,000,000	
YP perp. @ 8% (all risk yield)	12.5000	
	£12,500,000	
Top slice		
Passing rent	£2,000,000	
Less ERV	£1,000,000	
Overage	£1,000,000	
YP 12.75 years @ 13%	6.0731	
	£6,073 085	
Valuation		£18,573,085

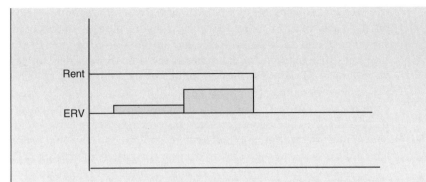

Figure 4.3 Double counting in over-rented property valuation.

The valuation is lower than the previous solution by 4%. However, this is still an over-valuation because there is double counting of the notional rent increases at the reviews in 1995 and 2000 (those included by the use of 8% on the bottom slice). This is illustrated in Figure 4.3, where the hatching represents that part of the income flow that is effectively valued twice, once within the yield of 8% and once explicitly in the top-slice capitalisation.

To help overcome this problem, valuers must now explicitly consider growth. The best solution to this problem using conventional models would be to shelve the popular layer method and to adopt a term and reversion approach. Having anticipated when the overage is eliminated, the term of 12.75 years could be valued at a risk-free rate subject to a risk premium to reflect weakness in the covenant of the tenant paying attention to the additional risk of any default while paying excessive rent, with the reversion valued as usual at the capitalisation rate. In this valuation 13% reflects a risk premium of 3% above government bonds, which suggests an illiquid bond with quite significant default risk. If the tenant does default, the overage is lost and the best the investor can hope for is a letting at rental value. If the tenant is believed to be very secure at the level of over-rent, then a small risk premium above bonds would be warranted.

Term rent	£2,000,000	
YP 12.75 years @ 13%	6.0731	
		£12,146,170
Reversion to ERV	£1,000,000	
YP perp. @ 8%	12.5000	
PV 12.75 years @ 8%	0.3748	
		£4,685,513
Valuation		£16,831,68

This valuation remains subject to a single remaining error in the way that the reversion is discounted in a term and reversion valuation. This is referred to in the preceding text and is further discussed in Chapters 5 and 6.

In the absence of a DCF approach, there is a simple alternative to adopting either a core and top slice or a term and reversion approach to the

Part Two

over-rented problem. Many valuers reverted to a fully let initial-yield approach on the basis that, in many markets, the core data of rack-rented capitalisation rate and rack rental value are impossible to gauge. In the Central London office market, for example, at the time of the crash, all new lettings were subject to significant rental inducements, and almost all other properties were over-rented. There was virtually no direct evidence of 'real' rents or capitalisation rates. Properties let on long leases with no prospect of a rent increase before the lease expires had become fixed-cash flows secured on the covenant of the tenant, and had little to do with conventional property risks. The initial yield can then be based upon the gilt yield with a margin for illiquidity and default risk, or have reference to the level of return on debenture stock secured on the tenant company (Chapter 10).

For properties let on shorter leases, valuers have to pay more regard to the property risks inherent in the reversion, making an initial-yield approach hazardous in the extreme.

4.5   Conclusions

Conventional techniques have been under attack for over 30 years. Around 1960, they changed from DCFs at required rates of return to comparison techniques using the yield as the unit of comparison. Investment rationality ceased to be a criterion, and objectivity and accuracy in the use of transaction evidence became the key to their acceptance.

Few problems have been seen in the valuation of fully let properties, where comparables can be directly applied. Problems only emerge in thin markets as with all comparable approaches. As the UK market is heavily transacted relative to many other property markets, valuers have been able to survive using comparables-based techniques for the major property types

For reversionary freeholds, however, the method has more problems as lease structure has an influence on the quality of the comparable. If plenty of comparables with similar lease structures exist, the method produces solutions that are reasonably based on the criterion of accuracy, if not that of rationality. However, as the quality of comparables diminishes, the lack of rationality leads to valuations that are not soundly based and leave too much to the intuition of the valuer. These problems become extreme as the differences between the comparable and the subject property become wider and conventional techniques have increasing difficulty with unusual lease structures.

The market of the early 1990s made a large number of properties unusual. It is ironic that the true limitations of the conventional techniques have been exposed by falls in rental value even though it was the new perception of growth in the 1960s that precipitated the debate. Over-rented properties therefore represent a very significant valuation problem, but have served a very valuable purpose in making the UK valuation profession increasingly aware of the limitations of the tools of their trade.

Conventional leasehold valuation has always been the most discredited aspect of conventional valuation methodology. Not only are there a multitude of detailed criticisms, there are a number of fundamental flaws that the conventional model cannot compensate for. A comparison technique relies upon the quality and quantity of comparables. There is not sufficient quantity in the leasehold market, and, even if there were, quality would be unlikely to exist because of the individuality of each interest based upon complex lease arrangements. The recessionary market of the early 1990s has only reinforced the view that the conventional approach is impossible for a professional to defend.

There are alternatives to conventional approaches that pass the tests of objectivity in the use of market evidence while retaining some underpinning of rationality. These alternatives to the conventional approaches are set out in Chapter 5.

Part Two

Chapter 5
Contemporary Growth-Explicit Market Valuation Models

5.1 Introduction

During the 1970s, numerous techniques were suggested as alternatives to the conventional growth-implicit approach for the valuation of property investments. Conspicuously missing from the debate was an examination of the function the models were supposed to perform. This changed in the 1980s (see Chapter 1) and the distinction between assessing market value and investment worth or value has culminated in separate definitions for market value and investment value in international valuation standards.

In Chapter 4 we set out and criticised the standard methods applied in UK practice for the assessment of market value. However, in judging the quality of models for estimating market price we do not dispute that the most important criterion is that market information and behaviour is observed and applied. To carry out a successful market valuation, therefore, the valuer must attempt to collect information on prices, and the valuation outcome is the product of the interpretation of transaction evidence.

If the market relies on conventional techniques to interpret market evidence, then it is to be expected that these techniques will influence price in the short term. Valuers will apply these techniques to be in synchronisation with others operating in the same field. However, although this is entirely rational behaviour, there are dangers in using valuation techniques that stray from the underlying logic of how actual investors price their purchases. Irrational pricing models will ultimately fail to deliver optimum results for clients, will lead valuers to lack understanding of the true drivers of the markets in which they operate and may lead to erroneous and negligent valuations. Valuers will fail to spot fundamental market changes, and pricing valuations will in certain circumstances fail to indicate sale prices in the short term.

Short-leasehold investments in the early 1980s and over-rented property investments in the early 1990s are both examples of the pricing process failing to keep in step with rationality. This led not only to significant mismatches between price and underlying value but also to valuers being subject to criticism. Worse, in many respects, is the possibility that investors might restrict and distort the information flow made available to valuers in order to influence valuations. For example, one of the drivers for producing complex lease agreements in the property recession of the early 1990s and again in 2000–2003 (using rent-free periods to defend headline rents, for example) was to provide a basis for the overvaluation of property assets in order to give comfort to lenders in marginal cases.

We have discussed in Chapter 4 how valuation models are not static, and the history of valuation techniques set out more fully in the first two editions of this text indicates a constant realignment to changing economic and other circumstances. The current demise of the conventional leasehold model and the questioning of the relevance of the reversionary freehold model for over-rented properties indicate that change is still taking place.

In this part of the book we will set out and test alternative approaches to the market valuation of freehold and leasehold investments. The basis of the pricing valuation is the analysis of transactions; the basis of a rational pricing model, as set out in Chapter 2, is

$$k = \text{RFR} + rp - g + d$$

where
k = the capitalisation rate (or initial yield of a fully let property)
RFR = the risk-free rate
rp = the risk premium
g = the expected rate of rental growth
d = expected depreciation

RFR and rp together make up a required or target rate of return (r); g and d together produce net expected rental growth. None of these drivers of capitalisation rate appear in conventional techniques, which rely solely on direct comparable evidence on which to base their assessment of the capitalisation rate. Even if we accept for the moment that the best evidence of exchange price is comparable evidence from similar properties, a rational model should have some direct linkage to the main drivers of price if the valuation is to properly reflect investor expectations. So, to develop an alternative approach, the required return and net rental growth will form the foundation of a fuller analysis of transactions.

5.2   Analysing transactions

5.2.1   Implied rental growth rate analysis

Let us assume a fully let prime property investment has just been bought at a capitalisation rate of 5%. In a conventional valuation this capitalisation rate of 5% would be applied to the subject property, adjusted slightly according to the differences between subject property and comparable.

But the investor did not buy the property in the expectation of receiving a fixed income into perpetuity and a total return of 5% p.a. The investor expected rents to be reviewed in an upward direction. From these rent increases (and related capital value increases) comes an increase in the total return. Five per cent is not an acceptable level of total return. What is the required return?

a. **The required rate of return.** The investor would have to consider the returns available from other investments in the same risk class as property. If we assume for the moment that we are taking a portfolio view of property, the required or target rate of return should be based upon the rate of return for a risk-free asset plus a premium for the added risk and illiquidity associated with investing in property.

In nominal terms, gilts or bonds produce a risk-free return over a range of different time periods. The income and capital repayments are at a known level (if the investment is held to redemption) and default risk is at a minimum. The returns are subject to inflation risk, which creates problems for investors with real liabilities, but we assume that nominal risk is dominant and will use dated gilts as a surrogate for the nominal risk-free rate of return. In the 1970s and 1980s, the gap between dated gilts and property yields was high because of the high level of expected inflation built into the gilt yield. In both the first and second editions of the book we used a gilt rate of 11%, consistent with that period of time. Since the mid-1990s, the UK government economic policy has identified low inflation and had succeeded, up to the time of writing, in keeping rates at under 3% for most of the new millennium.

At the time of writing (in 2006) UK dated government bond rates were in the region of 4.5–5%, dependent upon time to redemption, and property capitalisation rates had fallen to their lowest levels since serious observation of UK property markets had begun in the 1970s. The CB Richard Ellis (CBRE) average yield series shows retail yields of around 4.5% in 2006.

The next stage is to estimate the risk premium. Property is undoubtedly riskier in nominal terms than gilts, because the cash flow is less certain (see Chapter 2). Surveys of investor target rates (DTZ, 1999; 2004) indicate a risk premium of around 4% around the end of the 1990s falling to around 2–3% in the mid-2000s. We have assumed a 3% premium for the purposes of this exercise, giving a target rate of around 7.75%.

b. **The level and timing of rental growth.** Another major input into the appraisal model is the expected level and timing of rental growth. If a purchaser accepts a particular initial yield for an investment, the yield implies that a particular level of rental growth will be necessary to provide the required rate of return. Alternatively, if a level of rental growth is assumed, the investor's prospective rate of return (IRR, see Chapter 2) can be calculated. An assumption of one major input leads to the calculation of the other.

The time at which the rental growth can be realised is also relevant. The implied rental growth rate can be found from the assumption of a target rate of return only if the rent review pattern of the transaction property is known or assumed. The result represents the long-term average rate of rental growth expected by the market. This is an interpretation of the expectations of the investor and the amount of growth necessary to make the purchase reasonable. In the UK, 10–15-year leases with upward-only periodic market reviews every 5 years are common (see Crosby *et al.*, 2005, for an extensive review of the Landlord and Tenant system in the UK).

The limitations of these assumptions are investigated in Chapter 6.

5.2.2 Calculation of the implied rental growth rate

Example 5.1

A freehold shop property has just been let on a 25-year lease with 5-year rent reviews at a net rent of £200,000 p.a. and subsequently sold for £4,000,000.

$$\text{Capitalisation rate}\,(k) = \frac{£200,000}{£4,000,000} = 0.05 = 5\%$$

Capitalisation rate	$(k) = 5\%$
Assumed target rate of return	$(r) = 7.75\%$
Timing of rent reviews	$(t) = 5$ years
Implied annual rental value growth rate	$(g) = ?$

There are a number of formulae that can be used to calculate the implied constant annual rental value growth rate. They all reconcile, as they are based upon identical assumptions (and therefore limitations), and two approaches are set out in the following text.

a. The basis of the calculation is an equation in which the target rate is made up of the capitalisation rate plus the annual sinking fund required to replace the expected capital gain over the review period. Effectively, where the target rate $r = \text{RFR} + rp$, we have $k = r - g + d$ and (ignoring depreciation) $r = k + g$. Because this formula assumes annual growth, the sinking fund is necessary to convert a one-off increase in rents at the rent review to an annualised value.
If the original sum is £1, the capital gain is equal to

$$(1+g)^t - 1$$

The annual sinking fund formula incorporating r and the review term t is

$$\frac{r}{(1+r)^t - 1}$$

Example 5.1   (Continued)

The formula is therefore

$$r = k + \frac{r}{(1+r)^t - 1} \times \left((1+g)^t - 1 \right)$$

Rearranging,

$$k = r - \frac{r}{(1+r)^t - 1} \times \left((1+g)^t - 1 \right)$$

Let p = rental growth over the review period (t) and SF = annual sinking fund to replace £1 over the review period at r.
Then $k = r - (\text{SF} \times p)$.
g may then be derived from p, as $(1 + p) = (1 + g)^t$.

To find the implied rental growth rate to get a 5% initial return up to a 7.75% total return based upon 5-yearly rent revisions:

$$k = r - (\text{SF} \times p)$$

$$0.05 = 0.0775 - \frac{r}{(1+r)^t - 1} \times p$$

$$0.05 = 0.775 - 0.17131 \times p$$

$$p = \frac{0.0775 - 0.05}{0.17131}$$

$p = 0.16053$ (16.05% increase in rental value every 5 years)
$1 + p = (1 + g)^t$
$1.16053 = (1 + g)^5$
$g = ((1.16053)^{1/5}) - 1$
$g = 0.0302$ (3.02% p.a.)

b. A second formula is based on a discounted-cash-flow (DCF) net present value approach to the problem. The outlay is the capital value ($1/k$); the inflows represent the value of the term income until the first review; the property is then assumed to be sold at the first review. The rental value on review is capitalised at the same capitalisation rate as represented by the current purchase and the capital value obtained is then entered as an inflow at the first review. The equation for an income of £1 is

$$\frac{1}{k} = \frac{1 - (1+r)^t}{(r)} + (1+g)^t \times \frac{1}{k(1+r)^t}$$

The formula can be rewritten in conventional UK valuation format to enable a valuer to solve implied growth rate calculations with the aid of familiar formulae.

$$(1+g)^t = \frac{\text{YP perp.} @k - \text{YP } t \text{ years} @r}{\text{YP perp.} @k \times \text{PV } t \text{ years} @r}$$

$$(1+g)^5 = \frac{\text{YP perp.} @5\% - \text{YP } 5 \text{ years} @7.75\%}{\text{YP perp.} @5\% \times \text{PV } 5 \text{ years} @7.75\%}$$

$$(1+g)^5 = \frac{20 - 4.0192}{20 \times 0.06885} = \frac{15.9808}{13.7703} = 1.16053$$

$$g = \left[(1.16053)^{1/5}\right] - 1 = 0.03021 = 3.02\% \text{ p.a.}$$

The solutions reconcile and indicate that the rent must increase by a factor of 1.16053 at each review in the future if the required return from the property is to be achieved. This simple model enables us to develop a more explicit DCF approach to market valuation.

5.3   Short-cut DCF valuation models

5.3.1   Introduction

In simple terms, the major criticism of conventional appraisal models as applied to the post-reverse yield gap property market is the implicit nature of the capitalisation rate employed. Specifically, we noted in Chapter 4 the failure of the capitalisation rate to perform as a target rate or expected internal rate of return, as it had been prior to the appearance of the reverse yield gap. A DCF appraisal model that is explicit regarding the anticipated cash flow can now be developed employing a discount rate which represents the investor's target rate.

Discounted-cash-flow appraisals in this format, but recommended for analysis rather than market valuation, were first suggested in the 1970s (e.g. the Marshall, 1976 'equated yield analysis'). This term was used to draw attention to the internal rate of return/redemption yield nature of the discount rate employed to distinguish it from the all-risks yield or growth-implicit capitalisation rate used in conventional appraisals, now called the equivalent yield. This terminology is now past its sell-by date and the yield should simply be called the target rate, hurdle rate or required rate to align property terminology with other markets.

We presented a full version of the cash-flow model that can be used for either market valuation or investment value/analysis in Chapter 3, but the development of the cash-flow model for market valuation is undertaken in the following sections using a more simplified structure. For example, all costs of management, purchase, sale and review are ignored, and explicit references to depreciation in rental growth rates, recurrent capital expenditure and any need for redevelopment/refurbishment are implied within capitalisation and target rates.

5.3.2   An explicit cash-flow model

In developing a cash-flow model for market valuation, a number of problems must be faced. The first is that the underlying basis of the valuation is the level of prices in the market place as evidenced by market transactions. The inputs into the model must be market based, and hence we must use implied growth rate analysis rather than forecasts for deriving the rental growth projections. The key problem is that, to derive a rental growth figure from a market, an assumption of the target rate must be made. Although these can be based on survey work, estimates for individual properties are far from unarguable. But, as we show in Chapter 6, in the market valuation model the choice of target rate is surprisingly unimportant to the outcome.

Because freeholds are perpetual in nature, we also need to limit the length of the calculations and decide upon a holding period (see Chapter 3). Even if no sale is envisaged by a purchaser, the discounting process will reduce the value of tranches of income received a long way into the future to a nominal amount. If a long enough holding period were adopted, the assumption made about a future notional sale date would be inconsequential to the valuation obtained.

For the period of the cash flow, a constant growth rate is applied, causing the rental flow to be increased at the same rate at each expected review date in the future. The yield used to discount the cash flows is the target rate.

After a reasonable period (Marshall adopted 30 years), the property would be notionally sold by capitalising the rental value into infinity at that point. Implied rental growth analysis is based on a presumption of perpetual growth in a freehold: if implied growth is used this must be reflected in the resale price projection. The resale price is therefore arrived at by capitalisation of the then rental value at a rate that implies future growth; the implied rate of growth is derived from the current market capitalisation rate; so the same rate should be used at the point of resale.

Thus a simple valuation by an explicit cash-flow model requires four major inputs:

a.   Target rate (r)
b.   Market capitalisation rate (k)
c.   Rent review period (t)
d.   From r, k and t, implied growth (g) can be calculated

Example 5.2

Value the freehold interest in a shop property (similar to that in Example 5.1) just let on a 25-year lease with 5-year reviews at its current net rental value of £100,000 p.a. Use a target rate of 7.75%; market capitalisation rates are around 5%. Assume a holding period of 30 years. The implied rental growth rate is 3.02% (from the previous analysis).

Valuation:

Years	Current ERV £ p.a.	A £1 @ 3.02%	Forecast income (£)	YP 5 years @ 7.75%	PV @ 7.75%	Present value (£)
1–5	100,000	1.0000	100000	4.0192	1.0000	401,916
6–10	100,000	1.160529	116052	4.0192	0.6885	321,147
11–15	100,000	1.346828	134682	4.0192	0.4741	256,610
16–20	100,000	1.563033	156303	4.0192	0.3264	205,042
21–25	100,000	1.813946	181394	4.0192	0.2247	163,837
26–30	100,000	2.105137	210513	4.0192	0.1547	130,913
30	100,000	2.443073	244307	20.0000[a]	0.1065	520,532
						2,000,000

ERV = estimated rental value.
[a]YP perp. at 5%.

A different holding period does not change the result. Assume a sale after 15 years.

Years	Current ERV £ p.a.	A £1 @ 3.02%	Forecast income (£)	YP 5 years @ 7.75%	PV @ 7.75%	Present value (£)
1–5	100,000	1.0000	100,000	4.0192	1.0000	401,916
6–10	100,000	1.160529	116,052	4.0192	0.6885	321,147
11–15	100,000	1.346828	134,682	4.0192	0.4741	256,610
15	100,000	1.563033	156,303	20.0000[a]	0.3264	1,020,326
						2,000,000

ERV = estimated rental value.
[a]YP perp. at 5%.

Note that both valuations reconcile with the conventional valuation:

ERV/k   Valuation: £100,000/0.05 = £2,000,000

As stated in Chapter 4, the fully let freehold (of all investment types) is least prone to inaccurate valuation by the implicit conventional technique. The advantage offered by a DCF valuation in the preceding format is not that (as long as growth forecasts are linked to the market by an implied rental growth formula) a more accurate valuation will result, but that:

a.   More information is provided for future analysis purposes.
b.   The market valuation model is more readily compared with an invest-ment appraisal (see Chapter 3).
c.   The yield used enables cross-investment comparisons.
d.   Specific problems affecting the cash flow of the investment can be more easily incorporated.

The fact that conventional and modern approaches reconcile is proof of the assertion that contemporary *market* valuations are based on transactions and not forecasts. The perpetual capitalisation rate of the comparison is broken down into the required return or target rate, the review pattern and the growth rate. If the property income is then projected forward at that growth rate, reviewed every 5 years and discounted at the target rate, the solution will be the same as that produced by a simple capitalisation in per-petuity at 5%. As the comparable in Example 5.1 is identical to the subject property, a direct capital comparison can be made. The comparable has a rent that is double that of the subject property, so the valuation must be half as much, that is, £2,000,000 against £4,000,000.

The long version of the DCF can be shortened by assuming a resale at the capitalisation rate at any time when the property is fully let, that is, at any future review date. If, however, the capitalisation rate for the property needs to be adjusted (e.g., if the property was let on 3-yearly reviews while the 5% capitalisation rate derived from comparables is based on 5-yearly reviews) the calculation can only be shortened by use of DCF formulae (in particular, a summation of the perpetual geometric progression).

5.3.3   DCF by Formula

The capital value of an income flow is the summation of the discounted value of each block of income. If it is assumed that the rents grow every 5 (t) years at a constant rate and the discount rate also remains constant, the income flow represents a geometric progression. An examination of the solution for the explicit cash flow indicates that the YP for 5 years at 7.75% is used in the capitalisation of each block of income. In addition, every 5 (t) years, the previous rent is increased by the factor $(1 + g)^t$ and each block is discounted by $(1 + r)^{-m}$ where m increases by 5 years for every tranche of income. The common ratio is therefore:

$$\frac{(1 + g)^t}{(1 + r)^t}$$

and the formula summates to

$$YP\ n\ \text{years} = YP\ t\ \text{years} @\ r \times \left(\frac{1 - \left((1+g)^n / (1+r)^n \right)}{1 - \left((1+g)^t / (1+r)^t \right)} \right)$$

where

income	=	£1 p.a.
total term	=	n years
term of review	=	t years
target rate	=	r %
growth rate	=	g % p.a.

This formula represents the summation of the DCF model to create a multiplier for use with the current rental value. (A fuller explanation of the mathematics involved in creating these formulae is included later in this chapter when real value models are considered.) The solution to the example is as follows:

To value Example 5.2 assuming a perpetual holding period:
ERV £100,000 p.a.; $r = 7.75\%$; $g = 3.02\%$; $t = 5$ years; $n = $ perpetuity.
As $n = $ perpetuity,

$$YP\ \text{perp.} = YP\ 5\ \text{years} @\ 7.75\% \times \left(\frac{1 - \left((1.0302)^n / (1.0775)^n \right)}{1 - \left((1.0302)^t / (1.0775)^t \right)} \right)$$

as $n = $ perpetuity, $\dfrac{1 - (1.0302)^n}{(1.0775)^n} = 1 - 0 = 1$

$$YP\ \text{perp.} = 4.019157 \times \frac{1}{0.200958} = 20$$

YP perp. $= 20.00$: $\underline{k = 5\%}$

The solution is

ERV	£100,000 p.a.
YP whole term	20.00
Valuation	£2,000,000

Thus, both shortened DCF and DCF by formula valuations are straightforward and reconcile with conventional techniques in the case of the fully let freehold. This is not, however, necessarily true of reversionary freeholds or of leaseholds (see Chapters 6 and 7).

5.3.4   The rational model

A variation on the shortened DCF approach is the 'rational model' of Sykes (1981), the basis of which Greaves had already established (Greaves, 1972a,b). The approach of the model mirrors the approach of Norris (1884) noted in Chapter 4 and is best illustrated using a reversionary freehold. The capitalisation of a rack-rented property let on a normal review pattern is undertaken at the appropriate capitalisation rate (k) found from market analysis. This capitalisation rate is a surrogate for an increasing rental value (at each review date) discounted at the opportunity cost of capital (risk adjusted), that is the target rate (because $k = r - g$). The key advance is that the capitalisation of a current rent fixed under a lease is at the target rate. However, the model suffers from a variety of limitations, which create problems in all but the most elementary of appraisals, and attempts to suggest solutions to various applications (Sykes and McIntosh, 1983; McIntosh, 1983) have only served to highlight these problems, which are well documented. (Any reader wishing to investigate this model further should refer to Bowcock, 1983b; Baum, 1984a; Baum and Yu, 1985; Crosby, 1985; Fraser, 1985a; and Greaves, 1985 – all consolidated in Crosby, 1987.)

As a result of the criticisms made by these authors we pay no further attention to this work as published, although we recognise its contribution to a wholly desirable progress towards DCF-based market valuations.

An alternative to DCF or rational models – all of which are expressions of the same explicit cash-flow projection and capitalisation process – is the real value model of Wood (Wood, 1972), which can be amended and reconciled with the short-cut DCF approach (Mason, 1978; Crosby, 1983).

5.4   Real value models

5.4.1   Real value theory

The real value model was formed by Wood as part of his Ph.D. research (Wood, 1972) and subsequently published (Wood, 1973). It has gained little acceptance in its published form and was dismissed as impractical by the Royal Institution of Chartered Surveyors (RICS) valuation research project interim report: 'It is considered that Wood's "real-value" approach is too complex for most practitioners to use in their day to day work' (Trott, 1980). Nonetheless, it is our view that it offers considerable insight.

The real value approach of Wood starts from the simplifying premise that an income will be reviewed at each rent payment date to a new rental that matches inflation over the intervening period. The investor has as a result an inflation-proof investment. A rent paid annually in arrears, however, would always be worth less than an inflation-proof rent and would decline in real value over each year, while the inflation-proof rent would have a static real value profile into perpetuity.

The rate of return required on such an income is the interest rate required for giving up capital, taking into account all risks attached to the investment but excluding any extra return for the effects of future inflation. Wood termed this real return the inflation-risk-free yield (IRFY).

Fisher (1930) broke this down into a reward for three factors (see Chapter 2): time preference or impatience (l), expected inflation (i) and risk (rp). Wood's IRFY is a combination of l and rp such that IRFY $= (1 + l)(1 + rp) - 1$.

The valuation of an income fixed in nominal terms should not be carried out by discounting at the IRFY. The rate of return must reflect the fact that on each rent payment date the same sum of money would be paid, regardless of the fact that, if inflation was present, the purchasing power of the last payment would be less than the previous payment. This inflation-prone income would not have the ability to retain its purchasing power and the real value of the income would decline. The investor would require not only a real return to match his inflation-proofed counterpart but also an added return to make up for the decline in purchasing power, that is, $(1 + l)(1 + i)(1 + rp) - 1$.

The yield differential between fixed-interest and index-linked gilts illustrates the difference between an inflation-prone yield and an inflation-risk-free yield. The valuation of an inflation-proofed income would be undertaken at the IRFY (q). If the income was receivable in 1 year's time, the valuation would be

$$\text{PV £1 in 1 year at } q = 1/(1 + q)$$

The valuation of an inflation-prone income receivable at the end of the year would be at a higher rate of return. The IRFY would be supplemented by the inflation rate: the two incomes differ only insofar as in one case the income can rise with inflation, while the fixed income cannot. The real value income profile is set out in Figure 5.1.

The real return is adjusted for the inflation rate (i), and the fixed income is discounted in the usual way:

$$\text{PV £1 in 1 year at } (1 + l)(1 + i)(1 + rp) = 1/(1 + l)(1 + i)(1 + rp)$$

Assuming that inflation and growth are the same, the different profiles of the target rate and real value approaches can be compared for an inflation-proofed and a more normal property income, subject to a periodic review.

The periodically reviewed income compounds downwards in real terms until a review where the purchasing power is returned. In actual money or nominal terms the rent is reviewed to a higher level and can be used to purchase goods that have also increased in value. In money terms the income is increased to $(1 + i)$ at the review while it remains static between reviews. In real terms the income is static at each review, but between reviews the income declines by $(1 + i)$; see Figure 5.1.

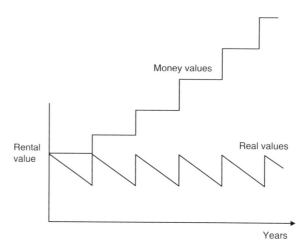

Figure 5.1   Real value income profile.

In valuation terms, the term rent between reviews is capitalised as follows:

$$\text{Income} \times 1/(1 + q) = \text{Real value of year 1 rent}$$

This rent has now been adjusted for inflation and is equivalent to an inflation-proofed rent, and can now be discounted at the IRFY (q):

$$\text{Income} \times \frac{1}{(1+i)} \times \frac{1}{(1+q)} = \text{Income} \times \frac{1}{(1+i)(1+q)}$$

The valuation of a proofed income $= 1/(1 + q)$
The valuation of a prone income $\ = 1/(1 + i)(1 + q)$

The determination of yields for the proofed and prone incomes are then incorporated into the valuation of a periodic rental flow. Assuming t is the rent review term and n the whole term (assume perpetuity for a freehold), the valuation can be built up in blocks of the review pattern term. The present value of £1 p.a. formula is

$$\frac{1 - PV}{r}$$

This can be substituted for the PV £1 formula when the rent is to remain static in money terms, but declining in real value. When the rent is assumed static (even though it is declining in real terms) the yield is adjusted as for the PV of £1.

$$\text{Thus, PV of £1 p.a. at } q \text{ adjusted for } i = \frac{1 - (1/(1+q)(1+i))}{(1+q)(1+i) - 1}$$

The rent is assumed to remain static at each review in real terms and the capital value of each block is discounted at the IRFY. The valuation of a periodically reviewed rent is undertaken by constructing a series and summating to obtain the real value formula of Wood for the YP of a rising income.

1st t years rent:	£R p.a.
YP t years (prone):	$\dfrac{1 - \left(1 \big/ \left((1+q)(1+i)^t\right)\right)}{(1+q)(1+i)-1}$
2nd t years rent:	£R p.a.
YP t years (prone):	as above
PV t years (proofed):	$1/(1+q)^t$
3rd t years rent:	£R p.a.
YP t years (prone):	As above
PV $2t$ years (proofed):	$1/(1+q)^{2t}$
Up to and including	
Last t years rent:	£R p.a.
YP t years (prone)	as before
PV $n-t$ years (proofed):	$1/(1+q)^{n-t}$

Summating this progression leads to a YP formula as follows:

$$\text{YP of whole term } (n) = \text{ YP } t \text{ years (prone) } \times \frac{(1-(1+q)^{-n})}{(1-(1+q)^{-t})}$$

The valuation of a rising income can be undertaken using the preceding formula. The valuer needs to determine q, i, t and n. Trott (1980) comments,

> The method has suffered from its complexity. A valuation technique, if it is to be accepted by the profession, must be easily understood and easy to use. Its theoretical soundness must be matched by a practical application. Unlike the later, and theoretically similar, target rate analysis, Dr Wood's method is difficult to use. For instance, to obtain the years' purchase in perpetuity from Wood's tables the valuer must know: (i) the inflation risk-free yield (q), (ii) the inflation risk rate per cent (i) and (iii) the rent review period (t).

These criticisms can be countered. Index-linked investments could provide suitable measures of comparative real returns. The typical rent review period is something all valuers are aware of. The analysis of future inflation rates would be the necessary subject of research; the distinction between real and inflationary growth would become a consideration.

As an analysis model, the extra inputs necessary can be subjectively assessed. However, the static real value assumption could usefully be dropped in favour of separate assessments of inflation and rental growth. For example,

Part Two

the long-term Investment Property Databank (IPD) rental growth indices show that real retail rental growth has been positive over the long term but office rents have declined significantly in real terms over the same period.

Using the model for valuations, it would be necessary to make assumptions about expected inflation rates to assess implied real growth or falls in rental value. The model instigated by Wood therefore appears to have more use in the determination of real returns, as opposed to fixed-income returns, for comparative investment appraisal. The real value model is better equipped in this respect than the short-cut DCF approach.

At present, most investment portfolio performance measurements concentrate on the use of total nominal returns rather than real returns for comparison purposes (property performance measurement is no exception). This may change in the future as pension funds are increasingly driven by the need to match real liabilities. If the evaluation of real returns and real and inflationary growth or loss is demanded in the future, Wood's real value model may yet be shown to be of greater significance.

Although the criticisms of complexity when compared with short-cut DCF models for investment appraisal seem unfounded, difficulties in applying this method to market valuations are apparent. These difficulties can be overcome by simplifying the real value model and reconciling it to the short-cut DCF model. When both methods are reconciled in this way, it is immaterial which one is adopted, but further insights are revealed.

5.4.2 A real-value/short-cut DCF hybrid

The main discrepancy between real value theory and short-cut DCF techniques is the definition of growth. The short-cut DCF models define the growth in rents in money terms as g, while the real value theory discounts the fixed-income by a yield made up of real return (IRFY, or q) and inflation (i). If a static real value profile is assumed, then i and g are the same: the level of rental growth (g) is equal to the level of inflation (i). In these circumstances the two models can be reconciled by substituting g for i in the real value formula. The short-cut DCF model requires a choice of target rate (r), while the real value model relies on a choice of inflation risk-free yield (q).

Real value theory suggests that a fixed income and a reviewable income can be distinguished by the rate of inflation, the fixed income being less attractive and its real value compounded downwards by the inflation rate. The difference between the two types of income could be viewed as being the rental growth that the reviewable income can exploit, or the rate of rental growth forgone by the fixed-income recipient. The effect of this view would be to discount the fixed income by an additional factor of g or to increase the reviewable income by a factor of g. These two alternatives represent the two different methods. The additional discount by g represents the basis of approach for a real value hybrid; the increase in the reviewable rent by g has already been shown to be the basis of the short-cut DCF technique.

The real value hybrid starts from the basis of discounting a proofed income at a real return (IRFY). The valuation of a proofed income of £1 at the end of 1 year is given by:

$$£1 \times \text{PV } £1 \text{ in 1 year at } q = \frac{1}{(1+q)}$$

The valuation of a fixed income of £1 at the end of 1 year is again undertaken on the basis that it is declining in real value by the rate of rental growth. The rent can be discounted at g before being discounted at l, or the discount rate can be made up of both l and g:

Either

$$£1 \times \frac{1}{(1+g)} \times \text{PV } £1 \text{ in 1 year at } q = \frac{1}{(1+g)} \times \frac{1}{(1+q)}$$

$$£1 \times \text{PV } £1 \text{ in 1 year at } q \text{ (adj.}g) = \frac{1}{(1+q)(1+g)}$$

The reconciliation of the real value and short-cut DCF models can now be undertaken. The short-cut DCF model requires a choice of r, while the real value model requires a choice of q. They both use g. Consider the valuation of a fixed income of £1 for 1 year by both techniques.

Method (a): short-cut DCF

$$£1 \times \text{PV of } £1 \text{ in 1 year at } r = \frac{1}{(1+r)}$$

Method (b): real value

$$£1 \times \text{PV of } £1 \text{ in 1 year at } q \text{ (adj.}g) = \frac{1}{(1+q)(1+g)}$$

On the assumption that the same valuation should be found by either method, the inflation prone capital value of £1 is

$$\frac{1}{(1+r)} \ or \ \frac{1}{(1+q)(1+g)}$$

Therefore,

$$\frac{1}{(1+r)} = \frac{1}{(1+q)(1+g)}$$

Part Two

Solving the equation gives

$$\text{(i)} \quad q = \frac{(1+r)-1}{(1+g)}$$

$$\text{(ii)} \quad g = \frac{(1+r)-1}{(1+q)}$$

$$\text{(iii)} \quad r = (1+q)(1+g)-1$$

This mathematical relationship has already been noted in Chapter 2 in the context of fixed-income and index-linked gilts.

To reconcile the methods, the short-cut DCF approach requires a choice of r and g. The real value approach requires q but q can be a product of r and g. So, given r and g, q can be calculated. The reverse is true (r from q and g), but as the widest acceptance of contemporary techniques has been for methods based on an assumption of r, the former is taken as a basis for the application of the model. If future trends move the emphasis to the selection of real returns for property investment, the real value model can change to the latter basis.

The valuation, by both techniques, of a proofed income of £1 for 1 year illustrates the reconciliation. The short-cut DCF technique increases the rent by rental growth before discounting at the target rate. The real value approach assumes a reinstatement of the rent at the end of the year, and discounts the real value of the rent at a real return.

Method (a): short-cut DCF

$$£1 \times (1 + q) \times \text{PV £1 in 1 year at } r = \frac{(1+q)}{(1+r)}$$

Method (b): real value

$$£1 \times \text{PV £1 in 1 year at } q = \frac{1}{(1+q)}$$

To reconcile, the assumption of the same valuation by both methods is taken:

$$\frac{(1+g)}{(1+r)} = \frac{1}{(1+q)}$$

This equation solves exactly as in the previous example.

The criticisms of Wood's approach made by Trott concerned the choice of inputs. The valuer must know:

a. The inflation risk-free yield
b. The inflation risk rate percent
c. The rent-review period

The discrepancy between Wood's inflation risk rate and rental growth has been countered in the real value hybrid. Any new approach based on explicit future value changes must either assume or know the review pattern; and the inflation-risk-free yield can be calculated from the target rate and growth. The real value hybrid, therefore, enables the same inputs that are required in the short-cut DCF model to be used.

On the basis of these assumptions, the model can be formulated. Using Example 5.2 (target rate 7.75%, rental growth 3.02% p.a., reviews every 5 years) the capital value of the right to receive an estimated rental value of £100,00 p.a. with these inputs can be determined.

The valuation of the first 5 years must discount the rent at an inflation-prone yield $((1 + l)(1 + i)(1 + rp) - 1)$. This can be represented by the target rate, r.

Year 1–5	ERV	£100,000 p.a.
	YP 5 years at 7.75%	4.0192
Valuation		£401,916

(This part of the valuation is the same as in the short-cut DCF approach.)

The rent review is not treated as an increase in rent, but as a reinstatement of the real value of the rent. In real terms the rent will be returned to its existing value of £100,000 p.a.; but it will still be fixed for the next 5 years, and as it is inflation prone, it is valued at the target rate.

Year 6–10	ERV	100,000 p.a.
	YP 5 years at 7.75%	4.0192
Valuation		£401,916

The progression can be built up to form an infinite number of capital values of £401,916 for each 5-year block, at the start of each block. Figure 5.2 illustrates this.

To complete the valuation, the capital value of each block must be discounted to present values. The yield at which we need to discount can be

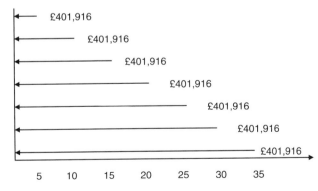

Figure 5.2 Capital values in real terms.

selected by determining whether the capital value is prone or proofed. The block of income from years 6 to 10 has a capital value of £401,916 at the end of year 5. The purchasing power of that value must be ascertained. As the capital value has been assessed by capitalising a rent in real terms, not money terms, the capital value is also in real terms. It is apparent that, if rents rose by 3.02% p.a. then the rent on review would be £116,053 (the amount of £1 in 5 years at 3.02% = 1.16053 from the formula $(1+q)^5$), not £100,000. The capital value in year 5 of the right to receive £116,053 p.a. for years 6–10 (in year 5) would also be higher, at £466,435.

The amount stated in the valuation (£401,916) represents the purchasing power of the right to receive the next 5 years' rent, not the nominal value (£466,435). The capital value of £401,916 is proofed against inflation and can rise continuously during the waiting period if inflation is present. It must therefore be discounted at an inflation risk-free yield.

$$\text{IRFY } (q) = \frac{(1+r)}{(1+g)} - 1 = \frac{1.0775}{1.0302} - 1 = 0.0459$$

$$= \underline{4.59\%}$$

The valuation of the interest therefore uses a succession of rents of £100 000 p.a., capitalised every 5 years at a target rate, and then discounted at the inflation risk-free yield for the appropriate number of years.

Years	1–5	£100,000 p.a.	
	YP 5 years at 7.75%	4.0192	
			£401,916

Years	6–10	£100,000 p.a.	
	YP 5 years at 7.75%	4.0192	
	PV 5 years at 4.59%	0.7990	
			£321,148

Years	11–15	£100,000 p.a.	
	YP 5 years at 7.75%	4.0192	
	PV 10 years at 4.59%	0.6385	
			£256,611

These form a geometric progression that can be summated into a formula. The constants are rent and the YP 5 years at 7.75%; the only change is the number of years for the discounting of each block.

Assuming rent = £1, then capital value = years' purchase. The last term will have a PV of the number of years less 1 term. Thus, the value of the last tranche is PV

$$\text{(whole term } -t \text{ years)} = \frac{1}{(1+q)^{n-t}}$$

The summation (S) is:

(1)
$$S = \text{YP } t \text{ @ } r\left[1 + \frac{1}{(1+q)^t} + \cdots + \frac{1}{(1+q)^{n-t}}\right]$$

Multiplying both sides by $\dfrac{1}{(1+q)^t}$

(2)
$$S\left(1/(1+q)^t\right) = \text{YP } t \text{ @ } r\left[\frac{1}{(1+q)^{2t}} + \cdots + \frac{1}{(1+q)^{n}}\right]$$

Deducting (2) from (1)

$$S - S(1/(1+q)^t) = \text{YP } t \text{ @ } r\,[\,1 - (1/(1+q)^n)\,]$$
$$S[1 - (1/(1+q)^t)] = \text{YP } t \text{ @ } r\,[\,1 - (1/(1+q)^n)\,]$$

$$S = \text{YP } t \text{ @ } r\left[\frac{1 - \left(1/(1+q)^n\right)}{1 - \left(1/(1+q)^t\right)}\right]$$

One advantage of the real value approach is that the latter term can be amended from:

$$\frac{[1 - (1/(1+q)^n)]}{[1 - (1/(1+q)^t)]}$$

to

$$\frac{[\{1 - (1/(1+q)^n)\}/q]}{[\{1 - (1/(1+q)^t)\}/q]}$$

which constitutes

$$\frac{\text{YP } n \text{ @ } q}{\text{YP } t \text{ @ } q}$$

Including the first term, the formula becomes

$$\text{YP of the whole} = \text{YP } t \text{ @ } r \times \frac{\text{YP } n \text{ @ } q}{\text{YP } t \text{ @ } q}$$

To determine the capital value of the right to receive a rent of £100,000 p.a. in perpetuity growing at 3.02% p.a. reviewable every 5 years (see Example 5.2), and to obtain a target rate of 7.75%, the valuation proceeds as follows:

$$\text{Preliminary calculation: } q = \frac{(1+r)}{(1+g)} - 1$$

$$q = \frac{1.0775}{1.0302} - 1 = 0.0459 = 4.59\%$$

Valuation: ERV   £100,000 p.a.

$$\text{YP} = \text{YP 5 years @ 7.75\%} \times \frac{\text{YP perp. @ 4.59\%}}{\text{YP 5 years @ 4.59\%}}$$

$$\text{YP} = 4.0192 \times \frac{21.7912}{4.3791} = \qquad \underline{20.0000}$$

Valuation   £2,000,000

The underlying assumptions have been reconciled and the answer is consistent with previous results.

5.5   Arbitrage model

In the mid-1990s, French and Ward developed a model (the Arbitrage Model) and joined with Crosby to develop applications of this approach (French and Ward, 1995, 1996; Crosby *et al.*, 1997). French and Ward (1995) attacked the reliance of all of the other contemporary applications on the 'all encompassing' target rate of return and suggested that the financial analysis known as arbitrage lends itself to segregating the capital value of the cash flows 'which is more appropriate for financial investors...' .

This led them to take a different view of the contracted cash flow, suggesting that the value of the fixed term income under the lease would be determined by the security of that fixed income, based on the same principles as valuing repayments under a loan secured on the tenant's covenant strength. As a result, the discount rate would be of the same order as that applied to such repayments. They suggested that the risk premium might be in the order of 1–2% above the risk-free rate, which is lower than the traditional view of the property risk premium of 2–3%. Because of this they termed the discount rate the 'low-risk yield'.

The adoption of lower yields for the element of the fixed income had already been introduced within the debate over over-rented property in the early 1990s (see, for example, the sliced-income approach in the second edition

Part Two

of this text and Chapter 10) but had not been proposed for the more standard rack-rented and reversionary property valuations which had adopted an average target rate across the whole of the cash flow.

Having valued the term income at this low-risk yield, the arbitrage method developed the valuation of each subsequent tranche of income between rent reviews by using a summation formula. This effectively capitalised the reversion at the all-risks yield, but deferred the value at a discount rate termed the deferred capital yield (DCY). This yield was applied to the reversion value based on the current estimated rental value, not the expected rental value including growth, in effect adopting the same approach as for the real value hybrid.

Because the low-risk yield values the term more highly, it must be the case that (in order to justify and analyse comparable evidence) the market DCY is higher than the IRFY used in the real value hybrid approach. The method suggests that the contract rent has been undervalued by a DCF approach, and implies that the risk of achieving the estimated market rent upon reversion has been underestimated and therefore the reversion overvalued.

This DCY rate can be derived from the formula:

$$(1 + \text{DCY})^t = \frac{1}{1 - (k \times ((1-(1+r)^{-t})/r))}$$

Using the same Example 5.2 as for the other approaches and adopting the same target rate, the arbitrage DCY calculation becomes:

$$(1 + \text{DCY})^5 = \frac{1}{1-\left(0.05 \times \left(1-(1+0.0775)^{-5}\right)/0.0775\right)}$$

$$(1 + \text{DCY})^5 = \frac{1}{1-\left(0.05 \times 4.0192\right)}$$

$$\text{DCY} = 0.04589 = 4.59\%$$

The valuation for Example 5.2 proceeds as follows:

Rent	£100,000	
YP 5 years @ 7.75%	4.0192	
Value of term		£401,916
Reversion to ERV	£100,000	
YP Perp @ 5%	20.0000	
PV 5 years @ 4.59%	0.7790	
Value of reversion		£1,598,084
Valuation		£2,000,000

The DCY is the same as the IRFY in the real value approach. But as the Arbitrage model was established to adopt tenant-based yields rather than the more conventional property-based target rates, assuming a low-risk yield of 5.75%, the DCY becomes 4.8821%, confirming that it would increase the value of the term but reduce the value of the reversion.

Rent	£100,000	
YP 5 years @ 5.75%	4.2412	
Value of term		£424,117
Reversion to ERV	£100,000	
YP Perp @ 5%	20.0000	
PV 5 years @ 4.88%	0.7879	
Value of reversion		£1,575,883
Valuation		£2,000,000

Where the target rate is the same in all methods, Crosby (1996b) showed that they all reconcile. Real value and short-cut DCF reconcile as IRFY = $(1+r)/(1+g) -1$. Arbitrage and real value also reconcile, as the valuation is identical apart from the deferment where arbitrage uses PV at DCY, while real value uses PV at IRFY. IRFY equals DCY where i and g are the same.

Arbitrage

$$V = \text{CRP} \times \frac{1-(1+r)^{-t}}{r} + \frac{\text{CRV}}{k(1+\text{DCY})^t}$$

Real value

$$V = \text{CRP} \times \frac{1-(1+r)^{-t}}{r} + \frac{\text{CRV}}{k(1+q)^t}$$

Short-cut DCF

$$V = \text{CRP} \times \frac{1-(1+r)^{-t}}{r} + \frac{\text{CRV}(1+g)^t}{k(1+r)^t}$$

where
- V = capital value
- CRP = current rent passing
- CRV = current rental value
- k = capitalisation rate
- r = target rate
- DCY = deferred capital yield
- q = inflation risk-free yield
- t = unexpired term to next rent change
- g = Annual rental growth rate

Note: in a rack-rented property, CRP = CRV.

5.6   Summary

Real value approaches were criticised in the 1980s and have not gained any acceptance within the property valuation profession. Nothing has changed in the 19 years since our first edition, and as explicit cash flows conducted on computers take over from calculators and formulae, the aforementioned short cuts are less likely to be incorporated into professional practice.

However, real value does focus attention on the basic concepts, and illustrates that theoretically both nominal and real returns can be incorporated into market valuation practice. They isolate the behaviour of the different parts of the valuation and what is implied behind the use of different yields in the different parts. In particular, the deferment and discounting of reversionary values can imply many things about the expected behaviour of the reversion over the period of the term. The real-value method focuses attention on real absolute returns, which is increasingly important for pension funds. Arbitrage in application has the same structure as real value and therefore requires similar inputs.

DCF by formula, short-cut DCF, real value hybrid and arbitrage methods all reconcile as they are summations of identical geometric progressions as long as inflation and growth are assumed equal and the same target rate and all-risks yields are used. Crosby (1996b) comments:

> No one model appears "better" than the others, as they provide a raft of identical technique to which valuers can apply their expertise. They should, however, focus the valuer's attention on the important issues surrounding the valuation, and the different levels of risk of contracted rents and uncertain reversions is definitely one of them.

The models fall into two camps. Arbitrage and real value utilise current rental values only although growth rates can be included in the determination of yields. Explicit DCF and short-cut DCF are more explicit concerning future value changes. In the next two chapters, real value/arbitrage models are combined as are explicit/short-cut DCF to illustrate applications of the market valuation models. We now explore a range of practical problems in the valuation of freehold (Chapter 6) and leasehold (Chapter 7) investment properties using these two approaches.

Part Two

Chapter 6
Contemporary Freehold Market Valuations

6.1 Introduction

In this chapter, we investigate and exemplify the market valuation of freehold investments by contemporary approaches.

It should be remembered in reading the examples used in this chapter that, as we demonstrated in Chapter 5, all contemporary models reconcile, given the use of the same target rate and capitalisation rate. We therefore concentrate on the fundamental issues raised by the previous chapters, which are mainly to do with the selection of inputs, especially the target rates used and the respective risk premium inputs. For example, in what circumstances should the risk premium be based on the tenant and lease risk (the arbitrage approach; see Chapter 5) rather than property risk (Chapter 2)?

In the second part of the chapter we move on to compare the solutions provided by the contemporary models with those produced by a conventional approach.

Before setting up a number of examples to illustrate the application of these models, a short discussion is necessary to put the models in context. First, because in this part of the book we focus on pricing or market valuations, valuations must be based upon transaction evidence. For simplicity, the same comparable will be used in most of the examples. This comparable is assumed to be a fully let (rack-rented) property that has just been let on a 5-year review pattern and sold to show a capitalisation rate of 5%.

Second, the analysis of the transaction requires an assumption of target-rate choice. We will assume, as in the previous chapter, that the required return or target rate is 7.75% (derived from a risk-free rate of 4.75% plus a property risk premium of 3%). Later in this chapter we undertake a detailed critique of this subjective assumption.

Once that assumption has been made, the implied rental growth rate can be calculated. The analysis of the transaction is set out as follows:

$$(1+g)^t = \frac{\text{YP perp. @ } k - \text{YP } t \text{ years @} r}{\text{YP perp. @ } k \times \text{PV } t \text{ years @} r}$$

$$(1+g)^5 = \frac{\text{YP perp. @ } 5\% - \text{YP } 5 \text{ years @} 7.75\%}{\text{YP perp. @ } 5\% \times \text{PV } 5 \text{ years @} 7.75\%}$$

$$(1+g)^5 = \frac{20.0000 - 4.0192}{20.0000 \times 0.6885}$$

$$(1+g)^5 = \frac{15.98}{13.77} = 1.1605$$

$$g = (1.1605)^{1/5} - 1 = 0.030223 = 3.0223\% \text{ p.a.}$$

where YP perp. =YP perpetuity, g = annual rental value growth and t = period between rent reviews.

As the comparison is a freehold investment fully let on 5-year reviews, any valuation of a property let at its rack rental value that is expected to grow with reviews every 5 years does not require the application of a more complex model than the capitalisation rate approach, that is, specifically, multiplying the rental value by the appropriate multiplier. For a rack-rented property let on 5-year reviews for which the correct capitalisation rate is 5%, the years' purchase in perpetuity factor is 20.000. Multiplying the rental value by 20 takes full account of the risk premium, the expected rental growth rate and the 5-year review pattern. Any DCF (discounted-cash-flow)-based model using these inputs will produce the same result. Example 6.1 falls into this category.

The various contemporary valuation models will be applied using the usual market valuation assumption of income payable annually in arrears, even though the UK market collects rents (generally) quarterly in advance. This considerably helps in reconciling the underlying arithmetic. Both conventional and contemporary models can be amended to deal with quarterly in advance payments of rent or any other payment structure.

6.2   Rack-rented freeholds

We investigate two different problems:

a.   The valuation of property let subject to a review pattern where evidence of capitalisation rates is available for the same review pattern (Example 6.1).

b.   The valuation of property let subject to a review pattern where evidence is only available for property let on a different review pattern (Example 6.2).

Part Two

6.2.1 Perfect comparable evidence

Example 6.1

Value the freehold interest in a property just let at its rental value of £200,000 p.a. on a 5-year review pattern. A similar property, also just let on a 5-year review pattern recently sold for a price based on a 5% capitalisation rate.

In both models no resort would need to be made to an analysis for the implied growth rate, as a direct and simple initial-yield capitalisation would be undertaken (£200,000/.05 = £4m). If, however, a full analysis and valuation were undertaken, assuming $r = 7.75\%$ (target rate of return) and given that $k = 5\%$ (capitalisation rate), and $t = 5$ years, the analysis for implied growth produces implied growth of 3.0223% p.a. (see preceding text), and the valuations would proceed as follows:

Explicit DCF
Assume a 10-year holding period.

$r = 7.75\%$
$t = 5$ years
$g = 3.0223\%$ p.a.
$k = 5\%$

Year	Current rent p.a. (£)	Amount of £1 in 5 years @ 3.0223 p.a.	Projected rent p.a. (£)	YP 5 years @ 7.75%	PV @ 7.75%	Present value (£)
1–5	200,000	1.0000	200,000	4.0192	1.0000	803,831
6–10	200,000	1.1605	232,106	4.0192	0.6885	642,295
10	200,000	1.3468	269,366	20.0000[a]	0.4741	2,553,873
						4,000,000

[a]YP perp. at 5%.

The projected rental increases are discounted at the target rate until the deemed resale, when the property is assumed to be sold at the capitalisation rate for a fully let property (k).

Arbitrage/real value
If we assume the same capitalisation rate and target rate, we know that DCF and real value/arbitrage approaches reconcile. The arbitrage valuation could proceed as follows:

$$\text{irfy/dcy} = ((1+r)/(1+g)) - 1 = (1.0775/1.030223) - 1$$
$$\text{irfy/dcy} = 0.0458913 = 4.5891\%$$

For a fully let freehold, the real value formula is

$$\text{YP of the whole income} = \text{YP } t \ @ \ r \times \frac{\text{YP perp. } @ \ q}{\text{YP } t \ @ \ q}$$

and the calculation becomes

Estimated rental value (ERV)   £200,000 p.a.

$$\frac{\text{YP 5 years}@7.75\%\times\text{YP perp.}@4.5891\%}{\text{YP 5 years}@4.5891\%}$$

$$=\frac{4.0912\times21.7912}{4.3792}=20.000$$

Valuation   £4,000,000

In this case, both methods reconcile to the conventional valuation based on a 5% capitalisation rate. However, if a different target rate is used to discount the contracted lease rent at a rate determined by the tenant's covenant strength, then the target rate could reflect a smaller risk margin above government bonds. Assuming a 4.75% risk-free rate, a 1–1.5% risk premium would generate a target rate of around 6% in the UK.

Using a lower required return and the same market capitalisation rate means that implied growth would be amended downwards to 1.1028% p.a., and the irfy/dcy in that case would be a function of 1.06/1.01028 −1 = 4.8438. The valuation becomes

ERV   £200,000 p.a.

$$\frac{\text{YP 5 years}@6\%\times\text{YP perp.}@4.8438\%}{\text{YP 5 years}@4.8438\%}$$

$$=\frac{4.2124\times20.6451}{4.3482}=20.0000$$

Valuation   £4,000,000

The reduced risk rate on the fixed income between now and the first review is compensated exactly by the implied increase in risk of the reversion, represented by an increased irfy/dcy (4.84% rather than 4.59%) to capitalise and discount the reversion.

This raises some interesting points about the comparable evidence. The valuation uses market evidence derived from a comparable sold for a 5% capitalisation rate. If this is a good comparable, it is good in all respects – including the relative covenant strength of the two tenants. The arbitrage approach simply differs in the estimation of the relative values of the first 5 years of the lease term (for which the rent is known with certainty) and what is effectively treated as a reversion in both the comparable and the very similar subject. As comparable and subject begin to diverge in quality, especially covenant strength and lease security, more fundamental issues will arise. This is the case in the following examples.

Part Two

6.2.2   Imperfect comparable evidence

Example 6.2

Value a rack-rented freehold let on a different review pattern. Assume the same comparisons as before, but the subject property is let on a 3-year review pattern at £200,000 p.a.

The analysis for the target rate and the implied growth rate is as before at 7.75% and 3.0223% p.a., respectively; target rate and irfy/dcy are 6% and 4.8438% for the arbitrage/real value approach.

DCF by formula
Assume a 9-year holding period.

$r = 7.75\%$
$t = 3$ years
$g = 3.0223\%$
$k = 5\%$

Note, however, that k is the relevant capitalisation rate where reviews are 5-yearly. Where reviews are 3-yearly, the potential for growth is enhanced and market capitalisation rates would be forced down. A new capitalisation rate must be derived, and this can be done by using the DCF formula developed in Chapter 5.

$$k = r - (\text{SF} \times p) \text{ (see Chapter 5, Section 5.2.2)}$$

where

k = capitalisation rate
r = target rate
SF = annual sinking fund over rent review period t at r
p = percentage rental growth over the review period t such that $p = (1 + g)^t - 1$ where g = annual rental growth

$$k = 0.0775 - \left[\frac{(0.0775)}{(1.0775)^3 - 1} \times \left((1.030223)^3 - 1 \right) \right]$$

$k = 0.0775 - (0.308784 \times 0.093437)$
$k = 0.048648 = 4.8648\%$

The valuation is
Rental value	£200,000	
YP perp. @ 4.8648%	20.5557	
Valuation		£4,111,148

Explicit DCF

Year	Current rent p.a. (£)	Amount of £1 in 3 years @ 3.0223%	Projected rent p.a. (£)	YP 3 years @ 7.75%	PV @ 7.75%	PV (£)
1–3	200,000	1.0000	200,000	2.5888	1.0000	517,753
4–6	200,000	1.0934	218,687	2.5888	0.7994	452,548
7–9	200,000	1.1956	239,121	2.5888	0.63900	395,555
9	200,000	1.3073	261,463	20.5557[a]	0.5108	2,745,292
						£4,111,148

[a]YP perp. at 4.8648%.

The solution using both DCF approaches is nearly £111,148, or 2.8%, higher than in Example 6.1, reflecting the advantage of 3-yearly reviews in a rising market. But note the detail revealed in the explicit DCF approach; what is assumed about the lease and the rent review pattern? The 9-year holding period is used for convenience, and the capitalisation of the rent in perpetuity is undertaken using a rate of 4.8648%, implying a 3-yearly review pattern *in perpetuity*, rather than 5%, which is appropriate for a 5-yearly review pattern.

Which is most sensible? If we were dealing with a 9-year lease remainder, we would then have to ask: what will happen at the lease end? Will the property be re-let on 3- or 5-yearly reviews? And what assumption has to be made about the comparable from which the capitalisation rate evidence is derived? If the standard review length is 5 years, then at some point in the future we would assume that the subject property will be re-let on a 5-yearly reviews, at which point the correct capitalisation rate becomes 5%. However, a change in review pattern would have an impact on the rental value, which is based on the lease terms. If the lease terms change, then the rent should change. In the preceding example the rental value was based on 3-year reviews. If the rental value was assumed to alter by exactly the right amount to compensate the landlord for the change to a 5-year review pattern, the outcome remains the same. In reality, tenants do not always compensate the landlord for the changes in lease terms.

Arbitrage/real value
The inputs into the model (r = 6%, g = 1.1028% p.a. and q = 4.8438%) are as calculated in Example 6.1. They are inserted into the '3 YP formula' incorporating a change of review pattern from 5 years to 3 years.

Part Two

Example 6.2   *(Continued)*

ERV   £200,000 p.a.

$$\frac{\text{YP 3 years @ } 6\% \times \text{YP perp. @} 4.8438\%}{\text{YP 3 years @} 4.8438\%}$$

$$= \frac{2.6730 \times 20.6451}{2.7312} = \qquad\qquad 20.2050$$

Valuation   £4,040,997

The capitalisation rate is now 4.95% and the increase in value only just over 1%, reflecting the increased risk attached to the reversion implied within the target-rate choice. Why is the result different from the DCF result?

The reduced target rate for the lease and the implied higher discount rate for the reversion have an impact upon the result caused by the shorter review period. The philosophy underlying the arbitrage/real value approach is different from the philosophy underlying the DCF method. The former applies more value to the certain initial rent and less to the uncertain rent to be received following the first rent review. If the comparable has a 5-year review pattern and the subject a 3-year review pattern, the potential cash flow from the subject is more attractive – but this is tempered by the increased risk attaching to the rent received following the review. The differences in DCF and arbitrage/real value approaches will increase as the review pattern becomes more dissimilar from the comparison.

As in all cases, the four models would all give the same answer if the target rate were the same. Differences are caused by the subtle difference in philosophy of the arbitrage/real value approach – which may, in many situations, offer a more insightful approach to estimating the value of the subject investment given imperfect comparable evidence.

6.3   Two-stage reversionary freeholds

6.3.1   Short reversions

Example 6.3

Value the freehold interest in a shop property that is let on a lease with 4 years unexpired at a rent of £100,000 p.a. The ERV is £200,000 p.a. based on a 5-year review pattern and a similar property has just been sold at a capitalisation rate of 5%.

Explicit DCF
To reflect investors' implied expectations of future growth, an explicit DCF approach would entail increasing the rent by the implied growth rate at each

lease renewal or review and discounting the total income flow at the target rate as shown in the following table:

Years	Current rent p.a. (£)	Amount of £1 @ 3.0223%	Projected rent p.a. (£)	YP at 7.75%	PV at 7.75%	Present value (£)
1–4	100,000	1.0000	100,000	3.3306	1.0000	333,064
5–9	200,000	1.1265	225,297	4.0192	0.7419	671,770
10–14	200,000	1.3073	261,463	4.0192	0.5108	536,773
15–19	200,000	1.517	303,436	4.0192	0.3517	428,904
20–24	200,000	1.7607	352,146	4.0192	0.2421	342,712
25–29	200,000	2.0434	408,676	4.0192	0.1667	273,842
29	200,000	2.3714	474,280	20.0000[a]	0.1148	1,088,840

[a]YP perp. @ 5%.

Valuation £3,675,905.

Short-cut DCF

In market valuation, it is essential to be rational in interpreting one type of transaction for use in valuing another. When dealing with a reversionary situation, the prospect of a lack of similarity between comparables and the subject property increases, and in Example 6.3 we have an example of a lack of similarity.

So far we have been choosing arbitrary notional resale dates to illustrate the operation of the DCF technique. We can improve upon this and eliminate unnecessary work. The comparable gives us the YP multiplier for a rack-rented property. In the short-cut DCF model this is assumed to produce the resale value at the point where the property becomes rack rented on 5-year reviews (and therefore becomes the same as the comparable). From that point onwards, there is no need to discount the cash flows further into the future, because this will produce the same result as capitalising in perpetuity at the capitalisation rate (5%).

Because of this, the DCF technique for market valuation can be short-cut. The short-cut growth-explicit DCF approach is undertaken by assuming that the investor receives a fixed income (the rent passing) from the property until the next rent review or lease renewal (whichever is sooner) plus a notional sale price based upon the rental value at that time capitalised at the all-risks yield (ARY)/capitalisation rate. This cash flow is then discounted at the target rate of return. This would have the effect in Example 6.3 of reducing the notional resale date to 4 years' time, thus turning the reversionary valuation into a two-stage calculation, in other words, a term and reversion valuation.

The short-cut DCF valuation in the following is set out in conventional format as the number of separate parts to the valuation has been reduced to two,

Example 6.3   *(Continued)*

producing the same valuation as the seven-stage explicit DCF approach illustrated earlier.

Term rent	£100,000	
YP 4 years @ 7.75%	3.3306	
		£333,064
Reversion to ERV	£200,000	
Amount of £1 in 4 years @ 3.0223%	1.1265	
Inflated rental value	£225,297	
YP perp. @ 5%	20.0000	
PV 4 years @ 7.75%	0.7419	
		£3,342,841
Valuation		£3,675,905

In undertaking *market valuations* such as this, there is no need to extend the cash flow beyond the date at which the full rental value on a normal review pattern is obtained if the same target rate and the average long-term growth rate analysed from comparables is used. In all further freehold examples, therefore, we shall use this short-cut version of the growth-explicit DCF model, but as ever, we need to bear in mind the potential complications caused by imperfect comparable evidence.

Arbitrage/real value

In the arbitrage approach the target rate applied to the known initial rent is a function of the risk-free rate plus a tenant-based risk premium, assumed to be 6% as before. The 3 YP formula, which forms the basis of the arbitrage–real-value hybrid, produces a 5% capitalisation rate in perpetuity (which is more easily derived in this case from the market) and the reversion is capitalised at this rate. The discount rate applied to the reversion – the irfy – is again 4.8438%, reflecting 5-yearly rent reviews, a target rate of 6% and a market capitalisation rate of 5%. Using these inputs, the valuation is as follows:

Current rent	£100,000 p.a.	
YP 4 years @ 6%	3.4651	
		£346,511
Reversion to ERV	£200,000	
YP perp. @ 5%	20.0000	
PV 4 years @ 4.8438%	0.8276	
		£3,310,470
Valuation		£3,656,981

Because of the use of different target rates in the arbitrage and DCF valuations they do not equate. Is the difference significant? What causes the difference? Given this, which approach is best, that is, which is most rational?

The difference is small – the DCF valuation is only 0.5% higher – because the difference between the term in the subject property and the normal rent review pattern is small. The difference is caused by the 4-year term in the subject property, which brings forward by 1 year the point at which a risky event – the rent review – occurs, and a different target rate applied to the initial rent. This reduces the value of the property below the DCF result to reflect the earlier occurrence of the risk event (which is ignored by the DCF approach).

As suggested earlier, if the same target rate was used in both approaches, there would be no difference. As the two-stage reversionary model is the basic diet of UK valuation practice, the real value/arbitrage model is applied to this example to show that they do indeed all reconcile when capitalisation rate and target rate are the same.

Using a target rate of 7.75% and an ARY of 5% produces an implied growth rate of 3.0223% p.a. and an irfy/dcy of 4.589%. The valuation becomes

Current rent	£100,000 p.a.	
YP 4 years @ 7.75%	3.3306	
		£333,064
Reversion to ERV	£200,000	
YP perp. @ 5%	20.0000	
PV 4 years @ 4.589%	0.8357	
		£3,342,841
Valuation		£3,675,905

Now the final result and the respective values of term and reversion are the same in all models. So, how are the valuation approaches different? And which is best?

The main difference between DCF and arbitrage/real value methods are that arbitrage and real value rely on a real interest rate approach to deferring the reversion. Both real value and DCF models are explicit about the growth rate required to obtain the target rate, but the real value approach reflects this in the discount rate, while DCF reflects growth explicitly in the cash flow itself.

A return to the original summation of the model in Chapter 5 will illustrate that real value and DCF models are doing the same thing in a different way. The real value approach views income profiles in real terms, while the DCF model views the rental flows in absolute money terms. The reversion to a rental value of £200,000 p.a. in the real value model is the expected real value of the rent on reversion, while the rent of £225,297 p.a. in the DCF model represents the expected nominal value of the rent on reversion.

The deferments are at two different discount rates. The real value approach recognises the rent of £200,000 as having the ability to rise as rental values rise, and so the deferment is at a growth-implicit yield. The explicit-DCF approach estimates rent in nominal terms in the future and discounts on the basis that the purchasing power of the estimated rent will decline as inflation arises in the 4-year period before receipt of that income.

The two approaches reconcile as follows. The term valuations are common; the reversions differ.

Part Two

Example 6.3   *(Continued)*

$$\text{DCF: revision = rent } (1 + g)^4 \times \frac{1}{(1+r)^4}$$

$$\text{Real value: reversion = rent } \times \frac{1}{(1+q)^4}$$

As $(1 + r) = (1 + q)(1 + g)$, the DCF approach becomes:

$$\text{rent } (1 + g)^4 \times \frac{1}{(1+q)^4 (1+g)^4}$$

which reduces to:

$$\text{rent} \times \frac{1}{(1+q)^4}$$

The short-cut DCF and the real value/arbitrage models are therefore the same and should give identical solutions. Any difference in result is therefore to do with the choice of discount rates applied to different tranches of income. But this is an important issue – and the lessons revealed by the arbitrage approach are instructive. So far the choice of either a property target rate or a tenant-based target rate has had little impact on the solutions. As we shall see in the following set of examples, this is not always the case.

6.3.2   Long reversions

In Chapter 4 we identified problems connected with the use of conventional models when the lease structure of the comparable and subject properties are very different. We also suggested that an example of a challenging problem is when the term of a reversionary valuation is very long.

Contemporary techniques should be able to deal accurately with this problem. As they recognise that the term value is fixed and is therefore prone to falls in value in real terms, they should value the term at the appropriate required return (i.e., they do not use a growth-implicit yield to value the fixed income) regardless of the length of the term. Example 6.4 illustrates.

Example 6.4

Value the freehold interest in a similar shop property to the one valued in Example 6.3. However, in this case the lease has 24 years unexpired at a net rent of £100,000 p.a. and the estimated current rental value is £200,000 p.a. based on 5-yearly rent reviews.

This example may seem extreme. However, a number of old leases let for very long periods without review (or with very long reviews) are still in existence and significant over-renting exists within the UK lease regime, where in 2007 upward-only rent reviews were still standard practice.

Assuming the same facts as before

r = 7.75%
g = 3.0223% p.a.
k = 5% (based upon 5-year reviews)

Growth-explicit DCF

Term rent	£100,000	
YP 24 years @ 7.75%	10.7520	
		£1,075,201
Reversion to ERV	£200,000	
A £1 24 years @ 3.0223%	2.0434	
Inflated rental value	£408,676	
YP perp. @ 5%	20.0000	
PV 24 years @ 7.75%	0.1667	
	£1,362,682	
Valuation		£2,437,883

The valuation assumes a fixed income of £100,000 p.a. for the next 24 years followed by a notional sale of the property newly leased at the rental value at the time (£408,676 p.a.) capitalised (sold) at 5%. The cash flow of £100,000 for 24 years and the sale proceeds are both discounted at the target rate of return, 7.75%.

Arbitrage/real value

Term rent	£100,000	
YP 24 years @ 6%	12.5504	
		£1,255,036
Reversion to ERV	£200,000	
YP perp. @ 5%	20.0000	
PV 24 years @ 4.8438%	0.3213	
	£1,285,400	
Valuation		£2,540,435

In Example 6.3, the DCF valuation was marginally higher. In this valuation the real value/arbitrage is higher by over 4%. As far more of the value is based on the fixed term, the use of a lower discount rate in the real value/arbitrage approach has more effect and is not cancelled out by the fall in the reversion value. If the appropriate discount rate for this tenant is 6% rather than 7.75%, the arbitrage/real value approach is clearly better – more logical – in this case.

This situation has even greater relevance when over-renting is considered. By definition, over-renting implies even more concentration of the value in the contract rent passing under the lease.

Part Two

6.3.3   Over-rented properties

In our second edition of this text, written during 1993 and 1994, we identified the valuation of properties let at more than their current rental value as a major problem facing practitioners in the UK.

In 1990 the market had crashed. Even though inflation was relatively high, very significant falls in the real value of rents led to significant falls in nominal rental values and the recovery was slow. This 'over-renting' problem still exists. Falling inflation has meant that over the last 10 years a number of market segments have experienced nominal falls in rental value on the back of relatively (compared with 1990) minor falls in the real value of rents. In addition, some individual properties subject to depreciation have struggled to regain their 1989 levels of rental value and many of these buildings were subject to 20- and 25-year leases with upward-only reviews. Despite at least three 5-yearly reviews having passed, landlords have often enjoyed no increases, and in some cases tenants are still paying the 1989 rent (for a fuller example of this problem, see Chapter 9).

Example 6.5

A secondary property suffering depreciation is let on a lease that has 14 years unexpired, with upward-only market rent reviews in 4 years' time and 9 years' time. The passing rent is £250,000 p.a. The ERV is now only £200,000 p.a.

Similar properties have been selling for relatively high yields of 8%. A higher risk premium for property is also required, and increasing the target rate from 7.75% to 9% is suggested. Both rates assume an 'average'-quality tenant for the quality of the property.

The valuation is to be carried out under two alternative assumptions. The first is that we have an average tenant in place; the second is that the tenant is a very strong financial institution.

Figures 6.1 and 6.2 illustrate the problem faced by the valuer. Rental values might be expected to grow in the long term. However, as the passing rent is higher than the rental value, the valuer has to determine the point at which the rental value will rise above the rent passing (the 'cross-over point'). The rent is not expected to fall at any future review on account of the upward-only rent reviews, and so once the estimate of the cross-over point is made, the valuation involves the discounting of a fixed term at the rent passing until the next review after the cross-over point, with a reversion to a notional sale price at that review. If the cross-over point does not occur before a rent review that takes place within the term of the lease, or before a break clause, the reversion date is the lease renewal date or the break-clause date.

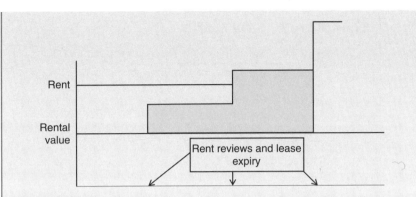

Figure 6.1   Over-rented income profile assuming breakthrough between first and second review.

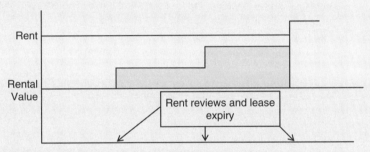

Figure 6.2   Over-rented income profile assuming no breakthrough before last review in the lease.

Average tenant

i. **Growth-explicit short-cut DCF** Analysis for implied growth in rents:

$$(1+g)^t = \frac{\text{YP perp. @ } k - \text{YP } t \text{ years@} r}{\text{YP perp. @} k - \text{PV } t \text{ years@} r}$$

where

   g = implied annual rental growth rate
   t = term of the rent review pattern of the rack-rented property
      (5 years)
   k = capitalisation rate of rack-rented property (8%)
   r = target rate of return (9%)

Example 6.5   *(Continued)*

$$(1+g)^5 = \frac{\text{YP perp. @ 8\% } - \text{YP 5 years @ 9\%}}{\text{YP perp. @ 8\% } - \text{PV 5 years @ 9\%}}$$

$$(1+g)^5 = \frac{12.5000 - 3.8897}{12.5000 - 0.6499} = \frac{8.61}{8.12} = 1.0598$$

Implied growth $= (1.0598)^{1/5} - 1 = 1.1693\%$ p.a.

When does this suggest that the ERV will overtake the rent passing?

At first review: $200,000 \times (1.011693)^4 = £209,520$
At second review: $200,000 \times (1.011693)^9 = £222,059$

This suggests that rental growth will not overtake the rent passing by the last review in 9 years' time. The implied growth rate is not high enough for the rent to catch up with the current passing rent by the end of the lease, and the valuation for the average tenant is as follows:

Rent passing	£250,000	
YP 14 years @ 9%	7.7862	
		£1, 946,538
Reversion to ERV	£200,000	
Amount of £1 in 14 years @ 1.1693%	1.1767	
	£235,348	
YP perp. @ 8%	12.5000	
PV 14 years @ 9%	0.2992	
		£880,339
Valuation		£2,826,877

ii. **Arbitrage/real value** The valuation starts from an assessment of the additional default risk attached to the tenant where the property is over-rented. If we assume that the average tenant is more vulnerable to default given this situation, the target rate used for the term should reflect this risk. The target rate of 9% assumes a tenant of this quality, but also includes the normal property risks. For the arbitrage approach we are interested in a risk premium for the tenant ignoring normal property risks, and we could add to that an additional risk premium for the increased likelihood of default caused by over-renting.

If the default risk is so great as to expect a tenant default in the near future, the valuation should revert to the value of the property vacant and to let (the core of a 'core and top-slice' approach set out in Chapter 4, or the rack-rented approach set out in this chapter).

The target rate for the arbitrage approach should be the tenant's target rate assuming a normal tenant and a normal lease structure; let us assume 7.5%. If we assume over-renting increases the possibility of tenant default, then a rate of 8% might be appropriate for the term while it is over-rented.

The reversion becomes more interesting. The 8% target rate is a tenant-based yield taking into account some over-renting. The arbitrage reversion is a function of a standard tenant target rate of 7.5%. As the capitalisation rate is 8%, the implied growth is negative (−0.0587%) and the dcy/irfy is higher than 8% (8.136%).

Current rent	£250,000	
YP 14 years @ 8%	8.2442	
Value of term		£2,061,050
Reversion to current rental value	£200,000	
YP in perp. @ 8%	12.5	
PV 14 years @ 8.136%	0.3345	
		£836,340
Valuation		£2,897,390

The result is a slightly higher valuation than the DCF approach (2.5% higher). The 8% on the term represents a normal tenant's yield of 7.5% with 0.5% added for the additional risk of the over-rented income during the term. The 8% capitalisation rate is the normal capitalisation rate observed for similar fully let properties let to average tenants. As the target rate is 7.5%, the dcy/irfy has ended up higher than the capitalisation rate.

Strong tenant

What will happen to the valuations if the tenant is a very strong financial institution? The benefit of having a better tenant in place will have a relatively greater impact on over-rented properties than any other. Reducing the tenant's risk rate even further to accommodate the reduced likelihood of a tenant default will increase the value even further, as the property income for the first 14 years has become a fixed-income bond secured on the tenant covenant strength. Where the risk-free rate is 4.75% and corporate bond margins above government bonds are unlikely to be very significant, there is a case for valuing this (albeit still illiquid) cash flow at a target rate close to the corporate bond rate. Let us assume 6.5%. The arbitrage/real value valuation is set out first as follows:

i. Arbitrage/real value

Current rent	£250,000	
YP 14 years @ 6.5%	9.0138	
		£2,253,461

What must be assumed on reversion? We cannot expect the high-quality tenant to stay in place after 14 years have elapsed; so we have the same reversion as before (which uses comparable market evidence and assumes an average quality tenant for the building).

Reversion to current rental value	£200,000	
YP in perp. @ 8%	12.5	
PV 14 years @ 8.136%	0.3345	
		£836,340
Valuation		£3,089,801

Example 6.5 *(Continued)*

The valuation is now 6.6% higher to reflect the additional covenant strength. This must make good sense and appears to confirm the superiority of the arbitrage/real value model. But the insight offered by the arbitrage/real value model can easily be applied within the DCF model. All we need to change is the discount rate for the term income, as follows.

ii. Growth-explicit short-cut DCF

Rent passing	£250,000	
YP 14 years @ 6.5%	9.0138	
		£2,253,461
Reversion to ERV	£200,000	
Amount of £1 in 14 years @ 1.1693%	1.1767	
	£235,348	
YP perp. @ 8%	12.5000	
PV 14 years @ 9%	0.2992	
	£880,339	
Valuation		£3,133,803

The only difference between the arbitrage/real value and DCF approaches as applied above is the reversion. The cause of the difference is the property-adjusted target rate of 9%: the resulting implied growth rate is an average obtained from the whole of a perpetral cash flow from the comparison. The comparison included a first term of 5 years let to an average tenant, which should have had a discount rate of less than 9%. Using 9% on the reversion overvalues it slightly to compensate for the undervaluation of the term. If we adjust the term value, we should adjust the reversion value, and this happens in arbitrage but not in short-cut DCF. This application of the short-cut DCF or any approach based on property risk rates loses its consistency if adjustments are made to one part of the valuation but not the other part or parts, given that the comparable was analysed over its whole term.

The development of the arbitrage/real value method has therefore offered an insight regarding the discounting of low-risk fixed incomes, which should be imported into all contemporary valuations.

The major difference between the valuation of a rising market and the valuation of an over-rented property is the added importance attached to tenant strength in the latter. The ability of the tenant to pay a rent that is, in our example, expected to last for a number of years is crucial to the maintenance of the income stream. The income stream from an over-rented property let to a sound tenant is basically a bond investment, and the quality of the investment has ceased to be based upon traditional property risks. It is now based upon the ability of the tenant to continue to pay the rent for the unexpired term of the lease. In the early- to mid-1990s in the Central London office market, virtually all of the value resided in long leases with upward-only rent reviews coupled with significant over-rents. Understanding the different nature of fixed-lease rents and property-based reversions became crucial to rational valuation.

6.4   More complex reversionary freeholds

As valuations become more complex, the conventional valuation approach becomes more subjective. Contemporary models have less difficulty in adapting to these complex situations as they give more help to the valuer in interpreting transaction evidence. In the previous edition of this text we introduced examples in which more complex cash flows might need to be considered, and in this edition we address a new set of issues.

In the 10 years since the publication of the previous edition, one of the most important property market issues to emerge is that of commercial lease reform. From a situation where the physical and leasing environment tended to focus on long uniform institutional leases with many buildings let to single tenants, weak letting markets backed up with government pressure for reform has led to a situation where a greater variety of lease lengths and forms are now available. In addition, more high-rise multi-let buildings are being built in the major commercial centres. We have therefore addressed the valuation issues raised by these changes.

The two issues addressed are

a. The approach to different leasing outcomes or events such as rent reviews, lease expiries and break clauses. Coupled with this is the treatment of multi-let properties.

b. The approach to valuing different forms of rent review, other than the standard market review.

The issues are addressed within the context of two hypothetical examples, Examples 6.6 and 6.7.

6.4.1   Lease events

The move towards more flexible leasing in the UK has raised a number of questions for valuers concerning their attitude to lease expiries and break clauses. This has been coupled with the increasing use of lease incentives, which has made the identification of rental values at lease renewal, rent review or new lettings more difficult.

The nature of any future rent determination, the nature of actual and prospective tenants by number and quality, and the relevant lease terms all play a vital role in the market valuation of a building. While these issues lend themselves to more sophisticated modelling in an investment appraisal of the

Part Two

type undertaken later in this book (Chapter 9), their impact on market value estimates using comparable evidence also has to be faced.

A key issue that has arisen has been the tension between valuers' typically conservative views of cash-flow prospects compared with the empirical evidence produced by recent works such as the OPRent Research Reports (Baum, 2003b onwards) and the IPD Lease Events study (Strutt and Parker/IPD, 2006). These reports have shown that the incidence of break clauses being operated and leases not renewed is much lower than valuers had typically built into their valuations. For example, in the UK in 2005, around 75% of breaks by number and 60% by value were not exercised and 40% by number and 30% by value of leases were renewed (Strutt and Parker/IPD, 2006); yet valuations had typically assumed that all breaks were exercised in single-tenant properties (Baum, 2003b).

In the following example a comparison is drawn between the impact of this difference of opinion on valuations of a lease. For simplicity, we use the DCF approach in isolation.

Example 6.6

Value a three-storey office block let in three equal-value units, each with a rental value of £200,000 p.a., on the leases described here. Assume an average target rate of 8.5% and an average capitalisation rate of 6% for properties let on 15-year leases to tenants of the same calibre as the tenant of Units 1–3. By calculation, the rate of rental growth implied by this target rate and capitalisation rate is 2.8013%.

a. Unit 1 is let on a 15-year lease with 5-year upward-only rent reviews at a rent of £150,000 p.a. and has 12 years unexpired.
b. Unit 2 is let on a 15-year lease with 5-year upward-only reviews with 12 years unexpired at £150,000 p.a. but is subject to a break clause at the next review, with a penalty clause of 6 months' rent if the break is exercised.
c. Unit 3 is also let at £150,000 p.a. but the lease expires in 2 years' time.

The DCF valuation of Unit 1 would be as follows:

Term rent	£150,000	
YP 2 years @ 8.5%	1.7711	
Value of term		£265,667
Reversion to ERV	£200,000	
Amount of £1 in 2 years @ 2.8013%	1.0568	
Inflated rent	£211,362	
YP in perp. @ 6%	16.6667	
PV 2 years @ 8.5%	0.8495	
Value of reversion		£2,992,377
Valuation		£3,258,044

If it were assumed that both of the other tenants stayed (at the upcoming break in 2 years' time for Unit 2 and at the lease expiry in 2 years' time for Unit 3), then these valuations would be identical to Unit 1. However, since the 1990 property crash, properties with long leases without any breaks have been perceived as a lower risk than where the tenant has the ability to leave. Some valuers habitually made the conservative assumption that all breaks are operated and all tenants leave at the lease expiry. In making this assumption and making further assumptions concerning void periods between lettings and the length of rent-free periods and other incentives to be given to incoming tenants, valuations of short unexpired terms and leases with breaks have been lower than valuations of such leases as applies to Unit 1.

In addition, as seen in Example 6.5, the quality of the tenant has also become more important since the property crash of the early 1990s, when the economic situation led to an increase in company failures. A strong tenant that could weather a storm became increasingly desirable, and so covenant strength began to materially affect market value.

If we want to make the assumption that all tenants leave at the earliest opportunity and that tenant quality affects prices, then the models can be adapted for these assumptions. Chapter 8 introduces more sophisticated techniques for modelling the options inherent in different lease events.

For Unit 2, let us assume that the tenant breaks and pays a penalty of half the current annual rent in 2 years' time. The property takes 1 year to re-let with no rent-free period (i.e., the ERV is the effective rental value, not the headline rent after incentives have been paid). The term is therefore capitalised for 2 years, but the reversion is deferred 3 years.

Term rent capitalised as before for Unit 1		£265,667
Reversion to ERV	£200,000	
Amount of £1 in 3 years @ 2.8013%	1.0864	
Inflated rent	£217,283	
YP in perp. @ 6%	16.6667	
PV 3 years @ 8.5%	0.7829	
Value of reversion		£2,835,209
Valuation		£3,100,876
Plus break penalty	£75,000	
PV 2 years @ 8.5%	0.8495	
Value of break penalty		£63,713
Valuation		£3,164,589

The break operation assumption has deducted nearly £100,000 from the valuation.

For Unit 3, the valuation would be as before but with no break penalty being payable.

Term rent capitalised as before for Unit 1	£265,667
Value of reversion as before for unit 2	£2,835,209
Valuation	£3,100,876

Example 6.6   *(Continued)*

The valuation has fallen again because of the lack of a penalty payment.

If these units formed part of a portfolio of properties, even one multi-let business park, and the valuer were to make the aforementioned assumption that all leases are not renewed and all breaks operated, then a clear error would result. Assuming the portfolio valuation were the sum of the values of the individual properties, the portfolio valuation would assume the same outcome across the portfolio as a whole. All leases would not be renewed and all breaks would be operated. But evidence suggests otherwise, meaning that an undervaluation would result. In all cases, the assumption that all leases are not renewed by tenants is illogical, and valuers should be applying some form of probability adjustment to the valuation. At its simplest level this could be achieved by carrying out two market valuations, assuming in one case that the tenant stays and in the other case that he or she leaves. The two outcomes can then be weighted for the final valuation.

For example, Unit 2 would be valued at the same value as Unit 1 if the tenant is assumed not to break. If it was felt that the probability of the break being operated was 30%, the valuation would be the 70% of the Unit 1 value and 30% of the Unit 2 valuation.

Value assuming tenant stays	£3,258,044 × 70% =	£2,280,631
Value assuming tenant goes	£3,164,589 × 30% =	£949,377
Valuation		£3,230,008

Unit 3 would be valued at the same value as Unit 1 if the tenant is assumed to renew the lease. If it was felt that the probability of the lease being renewed was 40%, the valuation would be the 40% of the Unit 1 value and 60% of the Unit 3 valuation.

Value assuming tenant renews	£3,258,044 × 40% =	£1,303,218
Value assuming tenant goes	£3,100,876 × 60% =	£1,860,526
Valuation		£3,163,763

This example raises another issue relevant to the use of contemporary models with multi-let property. Valuing lease by lease could raise issues of differing tenant covenant strength and therefore different capitalisation rates. A movement in the capitalisation rate should be matched by a corresponding movement in the target rate. In the short-cut DCF it would be inappropriate to have different implied rental growth rates for different tenants in the same location as rental growth is a product of the location, not the occupier.

6.4.2   *Alternative review forms: indexation and fixed increases*

Commercial lease reform in the UK has not yet led to the widespread introduction of alternative forms of rent review. If the government does carry out its long-standing threat to outlaw upward-only rent reviews, there is some evidence from overseas that the UK would quickly revert to alternative forms of lease to include indexation and fixed rent increases. Those operating in the UK suggest that the market has already manufactured more of these forms of lease although this does not show up in the 2005 Investment Property Databank (IPD) lease data. In many cases these new forms of review suit both landlords and tenants. The capitalisation of rents produced by these alternative lease forms poses new problems for UK valuers.

Example 6.7

Assume the same property as in Examples 6.1–6.4. Assume a target rate of return of 7.75% for the property and 6.25% for the tenant and assume a property let on a 15-year full repairing and insuring lease with 5-year upward-only reviews. The capitalisation rate is 5%. The rental value under these terms is £200,000 p.a.

The property has been let on the following leases:

Lease 1: A 10-year lease with annual reviews based on the consumer price index at an initial rent of £200,000 p.a. (an indexed lease).

Lease 2: A 10-year lease with annual fixed increases of 2.5% p.a. compound (a stepped lease).

These forms of rent revision divorce the property income from the property market and convert the lease income into either an index-linked or a conventional bond-like income stream based on the covenant strength of the tenant. They appear to have become increasingly popular, and given that the UK government's inflation target is 2.5%, both of these leases appear to produce the same investment, worth the same amount. The expected cash flows look the same, and if we use the same target rates, the DCF and arbitrage methods must produce the same result. But the investments may not have the same value because the risks may be perceived to be different.

Explicit DCF

Indexed lease So far we have discounted the explicit cash flow at the property risk rate but this example indicates why we believe that approach is limited. The whole of the lease income is based on non-property issues with reviews based on inflation rates not property rental values. The income is risk free in real terms, but the risk attached to the nominal cash flow is that inflation does not perform as anticipated, and so our forecast of nominal cash flow is incorrect. All inflation-proofed returns, such as the first 10 years' income produced by this investment, are subject to the risk that nominal income will be different to that expected. What, then, is an appropriate risk rate? The property target rate of 7.75% (using a risk premium of 3%) is inappropriate for this income, as it takes account of the greater uncertainty of nominal rental growth rates, and not simply the uncertainty of inflation rates. We will therefore use a lower risk premium of 1.5%.

The expected cash flow for the first 10 years is as shown in Table 6.1. Value of first 10 years' income is £1,650,110.

Part Two

Example 6.7   *(Continued)*

Table 6.1   Indexed-lease cash flow.

Year	Inflated rent @ 2.5% p.a. (£)	PV @ 6.25%	Present value (£)
1	205,000	0.9412	192,941
2	210,125	0.8858	186,131
3	215,378	0.8337	179,562
4	220,763	0.7847	173,225
5	226,282	0.7385	167,111
6	231,939	0.6951	161,213
7	237,737	0.6542	155,523
8	243,681	0.6157	150,034
9	249,773	0.5795	144,739
10	256,017	0.5454	139,630

Year 10 exit valuation As we have now decided that tenant's yield discount rates are superior to property target rates, there is an argument here for a reversion using the arbitrage approach to analysis of comparisons and application to the subject property, in this case the reversion. However, as we have used property target rates for all the explicit-DCF applications, we retain it for this reversion.

The valuation therefore reverts to a property market assessment of the reversionary value based on a forecast of rental growth (in this case the implied growth rate), the capitalisation of the forecast rental value at the capitalisation rate and a deferment of the reversion at the target rate of 7.75%.

Value of 1st 10 years	£1,650,110	
Reversion to rental value	£200,000	
Amount of £1 in 10 years @ 3.0223%	1.3468	
Inflated rental value	£269,366	
YP in perp. @ 5%	20.0000	
PV 10 years @ 7.75%	0.4741	
Value of reversion		£2,553,873
Valuation		£4,203,984

But, as already indicated, adopting target rates and growth rates for the reversion only when they are derived from an analysis of perpetual capitalisation rates (which also include the assumption that the term income is valued at the same target rate) is inconsistent.

Stepped lease This is a 10-year lease with annual fixed increases of 2.5% p.a. compound. The nominal cash flow is risk free in nominal terms, other than due to tenant default, but it is also subject to inflation risk, in that, if inflation is not as expected, the real value of the income will be different. This opens up the debate as to whether a nominal cash flow is more risky than an index-linked cash flow. If inflation is more than expected the index-linked bond will give a higher income, while the fixed income will do better if inflation is lower than expected. In simple terms, and in the context of market valuation, the expected cash flows and discount rate are identical and so are the valuations. A different approach might be taken to an investment appraisal of these cash flows for investors who may have a specific preference for either risk-free nominal or real cash flows.

Arbitrage/real value
The real value approach is set up in real terms and particularly suited to dealing with the indexed lease and to any case where rent is pre-agreed in real terms.

Indexed lease The property income for the first 10 years has been constructed as if it were an index-linked bond secured on the covenant strength of the tenant. The discount rate is therefore the index-linked risk-free return plus a risk premium for the tenant default risk. If risk-free real returns are assumed to be 2.25% (4.75% less expected inflation at 2.5%) and a risk premium of 1.5% is applied, a discount rate based on a real required return of 3.75% is suggested. In nominal terms, because the increase is delivered annually in arrears, the net of growth discount rate can also be approximated by a simple deduction of the growth rate from the target rate, that is, 6.25% − 2.5% = 3.5%. Because these relationships are geometric and not additive, the accurate discount rate to be used is given by the inflation risk-free-yield/defered capital yield (irfy/dcy), in this case, $(1 + r)/(1 + g) - 1 = 1.0625/1.025 - 1 = 3.6585\%$.

The valuation of the first 10 years is therefore

First 10 years	£200,000	
YP 10 years at 3.6585%	8.2506	
Value of first 10 years		£1,650,110

The reversion valuation would follow the format for other real value/arbitrage reversions to ERV, capitalisation rate and deferment at the irfy/dcy. This would not necessarily be the same rate as that used to discount the indexed-linked cash flow, as this is the tenant's yield based on an analysis of the comparable, which was a standard UK lease with periodic upward-only reviews. However, 6.25% was based on the tenant's covenant strength and bond yields, as well as expected inflation; so we have used this rate for the reversion as well as for the capitalisation of the index-linked rent. The calculation for the reversion discount rate is therefore $(1.0625/1.01378) - 1 = 4.806\%$.

Reversion to ERV	£200,000	
YP in perp. @ 5%	20.0000	
PV 10 years @ 4.806%	0.6254	
Value of reversion		£2,501,500
Valuation		£4,151,610

Stepped lease Assuming the same target rate and as the fixed increases are the same as those assumed for the indexed-linked lease, the discount rate to apply to the initial income is again 3.6585%. The same applies to the reversion, which is the same investment after 10 years regardless of the lease term, and so the valuations are identical to the aforementioned ones.

Table 6.2 indicates that the two properties are worth more when appraised by DCF than by real value/arbitrage. The difference is in the reversion. We submit that again the use of tenants' yields more accurately interprets the comparable evidence. Undervaluation of term incomes leads to overvaluation of the reversion, and in this case the undervaluation

---

Example 6.7   *(Continued)*

of the term income has been rectified in the DCF model with no balancing reduction in the valuation of the term. The arbitrage approach does that and so the reversion values are more rational.

Table 6.2   DCF and arbitrage valuation, indexed and stepped leases.

	DCF term	DCF revn.	DCF total	Arb. term	Arb. revn.	Arb. total
Indexed	£1,650,110	£2,553,873	£4,203,984	£1,650,110	2,501,500	4,151,610
Stepped	£1,650,110	£2,553,873	£4,203,984	£1,650,110	2,501,500	4,151,610

revn. = reversion; Arb. = Arbitrage.

6.4.3   Summary

These examples are not comprehensive and we could have developed many others. But they are sufficient to illustrate that market valuations can be successfully carried out by models that more closely mimic the perceptions and expectations of purchasers. The comparison of the models, especially those dealing with different forms of rent review and over-renting, also illustrates that models that fail to distinguish between the lease income and the property reversion can be misleading. UK practice has learnt a lot from the experiences of the 1990s – and there are still circumstances when contemporary market valuation models can hide fundamental issues. More attention on tenant-based discount rate choice is another step forward in our understanding of valuations for pricing. We therefore commend the real value/arbitrage method using tenant-based discount rates.

These contemporary approaches as applied to freehold valuations have now been fully compared. The second half of this chapter examines the new models in comparison with the old. As the equivalent-yield method is the most defensible conventional approach (Chapter 4) and real value/arbitrage is the most similar to the conventional approach (in that it has an identical layout, uses current rental values and only differs on yield choice on the term and on the deferment of reversions), these two models will be used to undertake the comparison.

6.5   Comparing conventional and contemporary techniques

6.5.1   Defending conventional techniques

The change in the perceptions of investors outlined in Chapter 4 should naturally and logically have led to a change in the standard form of valuation model. As we have shown, there are several alternative models available that take a more rational view of investor expectations based on an explicit-DCF format employing required rates of return compatible with other forms of investment. Why then, over 40 years after the appearance of the reverse yield gap, has the technique of choice used by valuers remained largely unchanged?

The simple answer to this question is as follows: the alternative models incorporate three extra variables (the target rate, the growth rate and the timing of rent increases in the future). Although the timing of future rent increases is based on current or actual lease patterns, the target rate and growth rate are not so simple to calculate. Although we showed in Chapter 5 that if the target rate is assumed the growth rate can be calculated using market analysis, this still leaves the problem of subjective target-rate choice. It is this challenge that has been side-stepped.

DCF models that rely on the calculation of implied growth also rely upon comparable evidence. Logic has been suggested as a major criterion for acceptability in a valuation model (Chapter 1); objectivity in the use of comparable evidence is another. Conventional techniques now rely on objectivity rather than logic, and a defence of the use traditional models in practice relies on the argument that objectivity is not present in the contemporary models' choice of target rate, while objectivity is present in the conventional models' use of comparisons. This argument can now be examined.

6.5.2   Target-Rate Choice

The first part of the argument relates to the subjective choice of target rate in DCF-based models. In property markets, use is made of some finance market theory and practice, such as the weighted-average cost of capital and capital asset pricing models, but calculations are imprecise and (as discussed in Chapter 2) the determination of the risk-free rate of return plus a subjective risk premium is often adopted.

The reasons for using conventional gilts are a natural consequence of a supposition that gilts are a substitute for a risk-free investment (ignoring interest rate and inflation risks). The proposed 2–4% risk margin has little other basis than the historical relationship between prime property yields and gilt yields prior to the reverse yield gap (Table 3.1). A detailed investigation of the historical relationship (Crosby, 1985) confirmed that a margin of 2% was the investor's perception of the risk differential between shop property and gilts prior to the reverse yield gap. However, an historical analysis of yield choice would suggest a different margin for different sectors (industrials, offices) and classes (prime, secondary) of property (Table 6.3).

Table 6.3   Gilt and property yield differentials, 1929–1955.

	Prime shops	Secondary shops	Prime offices	Ground rents
Yield gap (%)	2.25	3.03	3.03	0.73

If a historical basis is valid for target-rate choice, then target rates will vary for each type of property. But target-rate choice in modern times should not be based on historical analysis: a more rational *ex ante* basis must be found. This basis should be founded upon the qualitative differences between the benchmark risk-free asset (gilts) and property. The risks of property have been examined in Chapter 2. In a valuation context, the difficulty of quantifying risk factors for an individual property (and tenant) is dealt with happily in the choice of a capitalisation rate. Target rates in practice should in theory be no exception.

Survey work used to derive of investors' target rates of return undertaken between 1999 and 2006 show differences between different property types, and also that the margin fluctuates through different market conditions (DTZ, various years). In 1999, for example, the required return was roughly 4% above government bond rates for shops and offices, although since then the margin has reduced. But such quantitative evidence is in very short supply and has hardly been attempted at the individual property level. As a result, to assess risk premiums for individual properties within each valuation is not, we suggest, a realistic proposition. The problems of identifying and quantifying target rates in the market valuation context leaves the valuer open to charges of inadequate analysis and of subjectivity. Although an attempt to quantify the 'risk' of property investments is a relevant area of study in the context of the investment appraisal (Chapter 9), we feel that, without much more empirical work aimed at identifying market target rates, it is not realistic to expect valuers to volunteer to attack this problem in the market valuation context.

Target-rate choice is therefore a subjective element in the DCF-based valuation process, and to that extent the defence of conventional techniques is sound. However, is the valuation sensitive to target-rate choice? To investigate this, an analysis of fully let freehold and reversionary freehold valuations follows.

6.5.3   Fully let freeholds: contemporary versus conventional valuations

Subjective target-rate choice is inevitable, and this impacts upon implied growth rates. But is this important? We have examined the effect of varying the target rate by undertaking an analysis of valuation ranges produced by a wide variation in target rates. In the following example, target rates of 7.75% and 15% are utilised and the resulting valuations compared.

Example 6.8

This is the same example as used in Example 6.1. Value the freehold interest in a property just let at its rental value of £200,000 p.a. on a 5-year review pattern. A similar property also just let on a 5-year review pattern recently sold for a price based on a 5% capitalisation rate.

Conventional valuation

ERV	£200,000 p.a.
YP perp. @ 5%	20.0000
Valuation	£4,000,000

Contemporary valuation using an explicit-DCF format

Analysis

$$(1 + g)^t = \frac{\text{YP perp. @ } k - \text{YP } t \text{ years @ } r}{\text{YP perp. @ } k \times \text{PV } t \text{ years @ } r}$$

a. At $r = 7.75\%$, $g = 3.0223\%$ p.a.
b. At $r = 15\%$, $g = 10.857\%$ p.a.
  i. Assume a target rate of 7.75% and a growth rate of 3.0223% p.a.: the expected cash flow is as shown in Table 6.4.

Table 6.4   Cash flow, Example 6.8, target rate 7.75%.

Years	Income growth @ 3.0223% p.a. (£)	YP @ 7.75%	PV @ 7.75%	PV (£)
1–5	200,000	4.0192	1.0000	803,831
6–10	232,106	4.0192	0.6885	642,295
11–15	269,366	4.0192	0.4741	513,221
16–20	312,607	4.0192	0.3264	410,085
21–25	362,789	4.0192	0.2247	327,675
26–30	421,027	4.0192	0.1547	261,826
31–35	488,615	4.0192	0.1065	209,210
36–40	567,052	4.0192	0.0733	167,168
41–45	658,080	4.0192	0.0505	133,574
46–50	763,721	4.0192	0.0348	106,731
51–55	886,320	4.0192	0.0239	85,283
Present value				£3,660,901

Part Two

Example 6.8   *(Continued)*

Rental value in year 55	£1,028,601 p.a.	
YP in perp. @ 5%	20.0000	
PV 55 years @ 7.75%	0.016484	
Present value of reversion		£339,099
Valuation		£4,000,000

ii. Assume target rate 15%; implied growth is now 10.857% p.a. The expected cash flow is shown in Table 6.5.

Table 6.5   Cash flow, Example 6.8, target rate 15%.

Years	Income growth @ 10.857% p.a. (£)	YP @ 15%	PV @ 15%	PV (£)
1–5	200,000	3.3522	1.0000	670,431
6–10	334,848	3.3522	0.4972	558,062
11–15	560,615	3.3522	0.2472	464,526
16–20	938,602	3.3522	0.1229	386,668
21–25	1,571,444	3.3522	0.0611	321,859
26–30	2,630,971	3.3522	0.0304	267,913
31–35	4,404,873	3.3522	0.0151	223,009
36–40	7,374,806	3.3522	0.0075	185,631
41–45	12,347,181	3.3522	0.0037	154,518
46–50	20,672,121	3.3522	0.0019	128,619
51–55	34,610,053	3.3522	0.0009	107,062

Present value		£3,468,298

Rental value in year 55	£57,945,471 p.a.	
YP in perp. @ 5%	20.0000	
PV 55 years @ 15%	0.0004588	
Present value of reversion		£531,702
Valuation		£4,000,000

Despite the huge divergence in target-rate choice, there is no difference in the valuations.

The use of the explicit-DCF approach reveals a number of interesting points. Although the valuations reconcile, the variables are extremely diverse. The increase in the target rate from 7.75% to 15% means that a much higher growth rate is required to justify the initial return of 5%. But the influence of this variation is nil when perfect comparables are present. The results confirm that the driver of the valuation is the comparable evidence; where that evidence is applied to a standard lease structure identical to that from which the comparable yield was obtained, the results conform perfectly to one another. But of course in such a case the required valuation is much easier to obtain through conventional techniques.

Part Two

6.5.4   Reversionary freeholds contemporary versus conventional valuations

The valuation of reversionary freeholds is more complex than the valuation of fully let freeholds. The perfect comparison (in the same or very similar location with the same or similar physical characteristics) becomes harder to find because of the effect of the existing lease. For reversionary freehold investments, the property is let on an existing lease at a rent that is often at less than the ERV (but can be more). The perfect comparable is a property that has not only a similar quality of tenant and the right physical and locational characteristics, but also the same unexpired term and the same rent received–rental value ratio. Differences in these latter factors will cause properties to have different growth prospects, regardless of future growth in rental values.

It would be useful at this stage to reiterate the defence of conventional techniques:

a. The need for subjective target-rate choice is an inherent flaw in contemporary models.
b. The objectivity of conventional models is ensured by their use of comparables.

The availability and use of comparables and the effect of target-rate choice in the valuation of reversionary freeholds can now be examined to determine whether any of the models pass the tests of rationality and objectivity. The availability and analysis of comparables is examined first.

6.5.4.1   The availability and analysis of transaction evidence

The availability of transaction evidence depends on the amount of activity in the market place and the amount of disclosure of that activity. Until the early 1980s, both of these factors contrived to make comparables hard to find. However, the quantity of transactions has increased during the 1980s in the UK property investment market. IPD (1991) suggested that in the peak years of property trading in 1987 and 1988 the institutions were selling nearly 10% of their portfolios and turning over capital sums equivalent to 25% of portfolio value, while at the beginning of the 1980s sales were less than 1% of value. This increased level of activity has continued into the new millennium, and IPD (2004) suggests that portfolio turnover is typically above 10% p.a. in the UK. However, secrecy and the nature of the market place still make property transaction information difficult to acquire and interpret.

Where evidence is available we suggest contemporary techniques make better use of the available evidence; and where evidence is thin, contemporary techniques are better able to produce rational valuations. To illustrate the point, we use Example 6.9 to illustrate how both methods approach the analysis of a reversionary property transaction.

Part Two

Example 6.9

A property is let at a current rent of £150,000 p.a. with 3 years unexpired. The ERV is £200,000 p.a., and the property has just been sold for £3,750,000. Finding yields and growth rates from transaction evidence includes an element of trial and error. This has been made simple by the use of spreadsheet and other computer applications. For example, 'goal seek' in Microsoft Excel instructs the computer to iteratively find an unknown input into the valuation in order to produce a particular output. This approach has been utilised in the analyses set out here.

For a conventional valuation, all that is required is the discount rate that, when applied to the rent until the next rent change and to the current rental value thereafter, would produce an output of £3.75m. The unknown internal rate of return (IRR) of the conventional cash flow – and hence the appropriate equivalent yield – is 5.147%. The valuation is set out as follows:

Current rent	£150,000 p.a.	
YP 3 years @ 5.147%	2.7158	
		£407,365
ERV	£200,000 p.a.	
YP perp. @ 5.147%	19.4289	
PV 3 years @ 5.147%	0.8602	
		£3,342,635
Valuation		£3,750,000

A contemporary analysis requires a subjective assumption to be made regarding the target rate. Once this has been decided the implied growth rate and capitalisation rate can be computed by iteration. If a different target rate is decided upon, a different set of growth rates and capitalisation rates are computed. Using target rates of 7.75% and 15%, the following valuations are produced, both valuing the comparable at the correct price of £3.75m.

a. Assuming a target rate of 7.75%:

Current rent	£150,000 p.a.	
YP 3 years @ 7.75%	2.5888	
		£388,315
Reversion to ERV	£200,000	
Amount of £1 in 3 years @ 2.8424%	1.0877	
Inflated rent	£217,544	
YP in perp. @ 5.1729%	19.3313	
PV 3 years @ 7.75%	0.7994	
Value of reversion		£3,361,685
Valuation		£3,750,000

Using a target rate of 7.75%, the capitalisation rate is 5.1729% and the implied growth rate 2.8424%.

b. Using a target rate of 15%:

Term rent	£150,000	
YP 3 years @ 15%	<u>2.2832</u>	
Value of term		£342,484
Reversion to ERV	£200,000	
Amount of £1 in 3 years @ 10.6523% p.a.	<u>1.3548</u>	
Inflated rent	£270,964	
YP in perp. @ 5.2285%	19.1258	
PV 3 years @ 15%	<u>0.6575</u>	
Value of reversion		<u>£3,407,516</u>
Valuation		£3,750,000

Using a target rate of 15%, the capitalisation rate is 5.2285% and the implied growth rate is 10.6523%.

It would appear from these analyses that the conventional technique requires no subjective assumptions in the analysis of comparables, whereas the contemporary analysis requires an assumption of target rate before the capitalisation rate and implied growth rate can be calculated. But it can be seen that there is no problem or error in either contemporary or conventional analysis/valuation where the perfect comparable exists. The comparable illustrated would be perfect for a property let at, say, £225,000 p.a. on a lease with 3 years unexpired and a rental value of £300,000 (i.e. with the same rent–rental value ratio of 75%) . In fact the only difference between the comparable and the subject property in this case would be that the subject property has at any one time an extra 50% of income, so it should have a capital value of 50% more than the comparable. The value has to be 50% more than £3,750,000, that is, £5,625,000.

If we now carry out a conventional valuation of the subject property at a capitalisation rate of 5.147% and two contemporary valuations at 7.75%, a capitalisation rate of 5.1729% and at a 15% target rate, and a capitalisation rate of 5.2285%, they will both produce a valuation of £5,625,000. Perfect comparables produce 'perfect' answers whatever the technique. Hence, criticisms of subjectivity concerning target-rate choice in contemporary techniques are erroneous. The debate regarding investment valuation techniques must therefore focus on situations where valuers are forced to use imperfect comparables.

The following section of this chapter looks at how the two approaches apply comparable information to the valuation of other properties that are not identical in lease structure to the comparable.

6.5.4.2 Applying comparable evidence

To look at the relative performance of the conventional (equivalent yield) and contemporary (DCF) models, two reversionary properties will be valued based on the evidence from a third reversionary property

Part Two

Example 6.10

A shop property has just been sold for £2,000,000. The current rental value is estimated to be £150,000 and the rent passing is £100,000. The lease has 3 years unexpired. (Differences from £2,000,000 in the following valuations are the result of rounding errors.) Analyse this comparable.

a. Equivalent yield

Rent passing	£100,000	
YP 3 years @ 7.0385%	2.6225	
		£262,247
Reversion to ERV	£150,000	
YP perp. @ 7.0385%	14.2075	
PV 3 years @ 7.0385%	0.8154	
		£1,737,754
Valuation		£2,000,001

This valuation shows that the equivalent yield of the transaction is 7.0385%. No subjectivity has been required.

b. Short-cut DCF

Target rate: Assume (a) 7.75% and (b) 15%.

i. 7.75% target rate: The analysis is undertaken by determining which capitalisation rate reconciles with the growth rate and target rate (and irfy/dcy in real value/arbitrage). This analysis cannot be undertaken by assessing the equivalent yield and then inserting it into the implied rental growth rate formula as the capitalisation rate (k).

A capitalisation rate of 7.05336% implies a growth rate of 0.8004% p.a. at a 7.75% target rate. These inputs generate a valuation of £2m. The following illustrates that it is correct:

Term	£100,000	
YP 3 years @ 7.75%	2.5888	
Term value		£258,877
Reversion to ERV	£150,000	
Amount of £1 in 3 years @ 0.8004% p.a.	1.0242	
Inflated rent	£153,631	
YP perp. @ 7.05336%	14.1776	
PV 3 years @ 7.75%	0.7994	
Reversion value		£1,741,126
Valuation		£2,000,002

ii. 15% target rate: The solution to provide a valuation of £2,000,000 is

Target rate	15%
Implied growth	8.8406% p.a.
Capitalisation rate	7.1777%

Example 6.11

This concerns the valuation of a property with similar but not identical lease characteristics. A similar shop property is let on a lease at a rent of £75,000 p.a. The lease has 4 years unexpired and the ERV is £150,000 p.a.

In this case the unexpired term is 1 year longer and the rent passing is at a lower percentage of ERV than in the comparable property. The comparison is not perfect, but it is close.

a.   Equivalent yield

Rent passing	£75,000	
YP 4 years @ 7.0385%	3.3843	
		£253,820
Reversion to ERV	£150,000	
YP perp. @ 7.0385%	14.2075	
PV 4 years @ 7.0385%	0.7618	
	£1,623,495	
Valuation		£1,877,315

No subjective adjustments have been made to the valuation, so the solution has been objective throughout the analysis and valuation stages. However, the slightly longer unexpired term and the lower rent passing may have induced some valuers to consider changing the equivalent-yield subjectively. If those differences had been more marked, most valuers would start to consider amendments to the yield, based entirely upon their intuition.

b.   Short-cut DCF
   i.   7.75% target rate:

Term rent	£75,000	
YP 4 years @ 7.75%	3.3306	
Value of term		£249,798
Reversion to ERV	£150,000	
Amount of £1 in 4 years @ 0.8004% p.a.	1.0324	
Inflated rent	£154,860	
YP in perp. @ 7.0534%	14.1776	
PV 4 years @7.75%	0.7419	
Value of reversion		£1,628,828
Valuation		£1,878,626

The difference in the conventional and contemporary valuations is minute, at just over £1,300 (0.07%).

   ii.   15% target rate

Term at 15% (r) = £214,123

Example 6.11   *(Continued)*

Reversion value:
Growth at 8.8406%, rent capitalised @ 7.1777% and deferred at
15% = £1,676,789
Valuation   £1,890,912

The 15% valuation is now approximately £12,000 (or just over 0.5%) above
the 7.75% valuation. The target-rate choice is not a significant factor in this
valuation and does not produce any major divergence between the DCF
solutions. What of poor-quality comparisons? Will conventional or contemporary techniques fall apart?

Example 6.12

A shop property similar to the comparable shown in Example 6.10 is let on an
historic lease that has no further rent reviews. The rent passing is £75,000 p.a.
and the lease has 20 years unexpired. The ERV is £150,000.

The only difference between this property and the previous one is that
the unexpired term is 20 years, not 4. If the equivalent yield is assumed to
be the same as the comparable (as it is a perfect comparison in terms of
physical and locational characteristics), the objective valuation would be as
follows:

a. Equivalent yield

Rent passing	£75,000	
YP 20 years @ 7.0385%	10.5624	
		£792,179
Reversion to ERV	£150,000	
YP perp. @ 7.0385%	14.2075	
PV 20 years @ 7.0385%	0.2566	
	£546 778	
Valuation		£1,338,957

This valuation takes no account of the differences between the comparable and the subject property. It assumes that the only difference is that one
property will generate an income of £75,000 p.a. more than the other
between years 4 and 20. The yield adopted suggests that the income flows
have the same growth potential, even though one reverts to a 5-year review
pattern in 4 years' time while the other will provide no income growth for
20 years.

The growth potential cannot be reflected automatically in the valuation,
and so the valuer is now forced to amend the yield intuitively (subjectively)
to make up for the limitations of the technique. The adjustment is totally

intuitive and has no boundaries. If the valuer adjusts the capitalisation rate to 7.5% approximately, it reduces the valuation by 7.7%; if the adjustment is 1%, the resulting 8% capitalisation rate reduces the valuation by 15%.

b.   Short-cut DCF

   i.   7.75% target rate

Term rent	£75,000	
YP 20 years @ 7.75%	10.0035	
Value of term		£750,265
Reversion to ERV	£150,000	
Amount of £1 in 20 years @ 0.8004%	1.1729	
Inflated rent	£175,929	
YP in perp. @ 7.0534%	14.1776	
PV 20 years@ 7.75%	0.2247	
Value of reversion		£560,525
Valuation		£1,310,789

   ii.   15% target rate

Term 20 years at 15% (r) = £469,450
Reversion value:
Growth at 8.8406%, rent capitalised @ 7.1777%, deferred 20 years at 15% = £694,978
Valuation   £1,164,428

The subjective choice of target rate at the beginning of the analysis stage is now significant. The 7.75% DCF valuation is now higher than the 15% valuation and by a significant amount (nearly £150,000 or over 10%). However, the equivalent-yield valuation is higher than both DCF valuations, although it is quite close to the DCF at 7.75%.

However, while the DCF valuations do appear to be variable, this point was illustrated over a very great range of target rates. There is, in addition, an inbuilt constraint on the impact of the target-rate choice – a doubling of the target rate does not produce a halving of the valuation. Meanwhile, as we have seen, there are no available boundaries suggesting appropriate adjustments to be made to the equivalent yield within the conventional approach. The range of valuations that is the result of adjusting the equivalent yield by 1% is higher than the range of valuations caused by the full increase of target rate from 7.75% to 15% within the contemporary model. A 1% change in the equivalent yield seems far more likely to occur in practice than a doubling of the target rate.

The constraint within the contemporary model exists because a higher target rate reduces the value of the term income but increases the value of the reversion. In the preceding valuations, the 7.75% target rate generates a term value of £750,265, while at 15% it reduces to £469,450. However, the implied

Part Two

Example 6.12   *(Continued)*

growth rate applied to the reversion increases by more than the target rate (to compensate for the delaying effect of the rent review pattern) and this causes the reversion to be more highly valued at the higher target rate (£560,525 at an r of 7.75% against £694,973 at an r of 15%). There is a cancelling-out effect. The resulting difference in the valuation is smaller than expected, and in situations where the reversion value dominates the capital value, a higher target-rate choice can often produce a higher total valuation.

The extent of the cancelling-out process is dependent on the relative ratios of values in the term and reversion, which in turn are dependent on the ratio of the term rent to ERV and the unexpired term of the lease. To study this effect, an examination of a number of different capitalisation rates and ratios of ERV to current rent received was undertaken using the following ranges:

Capitalisation rates: 3.5–7% (step 0.5%)
ERV–rent ratios: 25%, 50%, 75%, 100%
Review pattern: 5 years
Unexpired term: 1–10, 15, 20, 25, 50
Target rates: 10–20% (step 1%)

We tested 560 permutations and 11 valuations were carried out for each permutation, making a total of 6,160 valuations. The results were then analysed to show the excess of the highest valuation in each case over the lowest valuation in each case. These results are illustrated in Tables 6.6–6.9.

A further analysis was undertaken to assess at what unexpired term the higher target-rate choice did not exhibit the highest valuation for each situation. This represented the point at which the increase in value in the reversion caused by a higher target-rate choice was compensated by the reduction in the term value. At this changeover point the range in values is at a minimum and the choice of target rate practically irrelevant (Table 6.10).

For unexpired terms of 10 years and less, the range in valuation solutions is very low at 2.2187%. The range increases both as the unexpired term increases and as the capitalisation rate increases. Therefore, the valuation of prime property would appear to be more objective by contemporary techniques than would be valuations of higher yielding secondary property.

The smallest ranges in value are when the rent passing to ERV ratio is high. As the unexpired term increases beyond 10 years, the ranges increase, except where the changeover points illustrated in Table 6.10 are reached. The values for the 160 permutations analysed for over 10 years unexpired show an average range of 15%. (For a more detailed explanation and analysis of Table 6.10, see Crosby, 1985.)

Table 6.6 Range of valuations: EY 10–20%, rent received–ERV ratio 25%.

Unexpired term (years)	Capitalisation rate (%)										Average	SD
	3.5	4.0	4.5	5.0	5.5	6.0	6.5	7.0	7.5	8.0		
1	0.54	0.66	0.79	0.88	0.96	1.06	1.15	1.32	1.42	1.52	1.030	0.309
2	1.09	1.26	1.47	1.65	1.82	2.00	2.26	2.53	2.73	3.02	1.983	0.611
3	1.53	1.80	2.05	2.30	2.62	2.89	3.24	3.52	3.90	4.21	2.806	0.859
4	1.94	2.25	2.56	2.94	3.28	3.69	4.06	4.43	4.82	5.32	3.529	1.073
5	2.34	2.71	3.10	3.50	3.91	4.34	4.78	5.24	5.72	6.21	4.184	1.236
6	2.70	3.15	3.61	4.03	4.52	4.95	5.24	5.93	6.49	6.96	4.782	1.360
7	3.05	3.51	3.98	4.47	5.02	5.53	6.05	6.58	7.11	7.77	5.307	1.497
8	3.36	3.89	4.38	4.93	5.50	6.07	6.56	7.06	7.66	8.14	5.755	1.537
9	3.69	4.24	4.79	5.35	5.83	6.47	6.92	7.57	8.12	8.67	6.165	1.589
10	3.99	4.61	5.17	5.73	6.26	6.88	7.40	7.89	8.36	8.94	6.523	1.568
15	5.50	6.17	6.79	7.33	7.78	8.24	8.48	8.72	8.84	8.81	7.666	1.123
20	6.99	7.69	8.23	8.55	8.86	8.67	8.60	8.11	7.28	6.51	7.949	0.758
25	8.47	9.05	9.37	9.50	9.09	8.45	7.49	6.60	5.51	4.49	7.802	1.649
50	14.42	12.72	10.75	8.32	5.71	9.04	14.53	20.38	28.26	36.89	16.102	9.285
Average (first 10 years)	2.422	2.808	3.190	3.578	3.972	4.379	4.790	5.207	5.633	6.076		
SD	1.085	1.242	1.383	1.537	1.686	1.861	1.987	2.106	2.247	2.387		
Average (total)	4.257	4.551	4.788	4.963	5.083	5.585	6.214	6.849	7.587	8.384		
SD	3.540	3.221	2.891	2.579	2.372	2.477	3.174	4.306	6.106	8.179		

Part Two

Table 6.7 Range of valuations: EY 10–20%, rent received–ERV ratio 50%.

Unexpired term (years)	Capitalisation rate (%)										Average	SD
	3.5	4.0	4.5	5.0	5.5	6.0	6.5	7.0	7.5	8.01		
1	0.50	0.57	0.69	0.76	0.84	0.98	1.06	1.15	1.24	1.41	0.920	0.283
2	0.86	0.99	1.16	1.30	1.43	1.64	1.78	2.00	2.24	2.40	1.58	0.497
3	1.13	1.34	1.52	1.75	1.94	2.19	2.39	2.59	2.88	3.09	2.082	0.626
4	1.37	1.57	1.79	2.00	2.28	2.51	2.82	2.98	3.31	3.56	2.419	0.706
5	1.50	1.73	1.97	2.21	2.46	2.71	2.97	3.23	3.50	3.77	2.605	0.725
6	1.60	1.85	2.11	2.31	2.58	2.78	3.05	3.32	3.51	3.79	2.690	0.693
7	1.70	1.93	2.10	2.31	2.57	2.78	2.97	3.16	3.43	3.61	2.656	0.613
8	1.73	1.97	2.14	2.30	2.57	2.63	2.89	2.99	3.15	3.20	2.557	0.483
9	1.76	1.96	2.13	2.29	2.36	2.55	2.56	2.71	2.75	2.77	2.384	0.330
10	1.75	1.90	2.07	2.16	2.28	2.30	2.29	2.32	2.22	2.08	2.137	0.180
15	1.78	1.73	1.64	1.53	1.33	1.23	1.07	1.50	2.12	2.82	1.675	0.475
20	1.96	1.81	1.57	1.34	1.88	2.82	3.95	5.38	6.90	8.76	3.638	2.439
25	2.32	2.08	1.69	2.76	4.09	5.92	7.95	10.47	13.18	16.43	6.689	4.909
50	3.90	5.72	9.69	14.91	21.78	29.31	37.47	45.34	52.96	59.82	28.090	19.105
Average (first 10 years)	1.390	1.581	1.768	1.939	2.131	2.307	2.478	2.645	2.823	2.968		
SD	0.409	0.452	0.471	0.499	0.546	0.551	0.604	0.637	0.697	0.757		
Average (total)	1.704	1.939	2.305	2.852	3.599	4.454	5.373	6.367	7.385	8.394		
SD	0.753	1.124	2.087	3.383	5.095	6.980	9.043	11.029	12.960	14.737		

Table 6.8 Range of valuations: EY 10–20%, rent received–ERV ratio 75%.

Unexpired term (years)	Capitalisation rate (%)										Average	SD
	3.5	4.0	4.5	5.0	5.5	6.0	6.5	7.0	7.5	8.0		
1	0.42	0.52	0.54	0.65	0.72	0.85	0.92	1.06	1.14	1.22	0.804	0.264
2	0.67	0.77	0.91	1.02	1.18	1.29	1.46	1.58	1.70	1.90	1.248	0.389
3	0.78	0.90	1.06	1.18	1.30	1.49	1.62	1.82	2.04	2.18	1.437	0.452
4	0.79	0.91	1.07	1.19	1.32	1.44	1.57	1.77	1.91	2.13	1.410	0.416
5	0.72	0.83	0.94	1.05	1.16	1.27	1.39	1.50	1.61	1.73	1.220	0.322
6	0.62	0.67	0.76	0.80	0.88	0.97	0.98	1.07	1.07	1.14	0.896	0.169
7	0.44	0.47	0.48	0.54	0.48	0.52	0.50	0.46	0.42	0.36	0.467	0.049
8	0.26	0.26	0.20	0.16	0.18	0.20	0.22	0.32	0.51	0.55	0.286	0.129
9	0.15	0.17	0.30	0.39	0.56	0.68	0.82	1.13	1.40	1.69	0.729	0.502
10	0.31	0.44	0.61	0.80	1.07	1.32	1.68	2.07	2.42	2.89	1.461	0.836
15	1.46	1.99	2.62	3.42	4.32	5.27	6.41	7.57	8.84	10.21	5.211	2.834
20	2.55	3.64	4.84	6.30	7.99	9.90	12.04	14.18	16.51	19.01	9.696	5.334
25	3.63	5.14	7.10	9.44	12.15	14.93	18.14	21.43	24.80	28.41	14.517	8.079
50	9.15	14.26	20.80	28.15	35.95	43.56	51.09	58.32	64.79	70.39	36.23	18.552
Average (first 10 years)	0.516	0.594	0.687	0.778	0.885	1.003	1.116	1.278	1.422	1.579		
SD	0.218	0.249	0.293	0.327	0.367	0.411	0.479	0.548	0.614	0.734		
Average (total)	1.568	2.212	3.016	3.935	4.947	5.978	7.060	8.163	9.226	10.272		
SD	2.303	3.612	5.288	7.187	9.216	11.205	13.208	15.131	16.894	18.479		

Part Two

Part Two

Table 6.9 Range of valuations: EY 10–20%, rent received–ERV ratio 100%.

Unexpired term (years)	Capitalisation rate (%)										Average	SD
	3.5	4.0	4.5	5.0	5.5	6.0	6.5	7.0	7.5	8.0		
1	0.35	0.40	0.45	0.55	0.60	0.66	0.78	0.84	0.97	1.04	0.664	0.225
2	0.45	0.60	0.63	0.76	0.87	0.95	1.10	1.18	1.27	1.43	0.924	0.303
3	0.42	0.52	0.58	0.65	0.77	0.89	0.97	1.04	1.12	1.27	0.823	0.266
4	0.24	0.32	0.36	0.45	0.49	0.54	0.58	0.70	0.75	0.80	0.523	0.178
5	0	0	0	0	0	0	0	0	0	0	0	0
6	0.32	0.40	0.45	0.56	0.61	0.67	0.79	0.85	0.91	1.05	0.661	0.225
7	0.71	0.86	0.97	1.13	1.30	1.48	1.67	1.80	2.08	2.31	1.431	0.505
8	1.12	1.32	1.58	1.82	2.06	2.38	2.72	3.00	3.30	3.69	2.299	0.822
9	1.53	1.84	2.22	2.58	2.91	3.31	3.37	4.26	4.73	5.23	3.234	1.180
10	1.99	2.24	2.83	3.32	3.85	4.41	4.94	5.56	6.22	6.82	4.236	1.555
15	4.25	5.25	6.29	7.48	8.70	10.16	11.56	13.03	14.59	16.21	9.752	3.848
20	6.24	7.89	9.81	11.81	13.98	16.25	18.68	21.24	23.81	26.49	15.62	6.521
25	8.04	10.40	13.16	16.03	19.19	22.51	26.06	29.59	33.26	36.90	21.51	9.337
50	16.18	22.94	30.27	37.95	45.69	52.94	59.82	66.19	71.57	76.42	48.00	19.80
Average (first 10 years) SD	0.713	0.868	1.007	1.182	1.346	1.529	1.728	1.923	2.135	2.364		
	0.603	0.724	0.866	1.006	1.159	1.332	1.495	1.694	1.894	2.083		
Average (total)	2.989	3.940	4.971	6.078	7.216	8.368	9.529	10.66	11.76	12.83		
SD	4.368	6.092	8.004	9.998	12.04	13.983	15.86	17.63	19.19	20.63		

Table 6.10 Unexpired term (in years) at which highest target rate does not produce highest value.

Capitalisation rate (%)	Rent received/ERV ratio			
	25%	50%	75%	100%
3.5	50+	50+	10	5
4.0	50+	25/50	9	5
4.5	50+	25	9	5
5.0	50+	20	9	5
5.5	50+	15/20	9	5
6.0	25/50	15/20	8	5
6.5	25/50	10/15	8	5
7.0	25/50	10/15	8	5
7.5	25/50	10/15	8	5
8.0	25/50	10/15	8	5

6.6   Taxation and market valuation

The effects of taxation on the future flows of income and/or capital are mainly ignored in the market valuation of freehold interests. Yet the structure of leases within the property investment market can produce a wide variety of taxation implications. The market is made up of a variety of groups or individuals and institutions, many having an exposure to taxation. No two groups of purchasers will be exactly alike, so it is beyond dispute that taxation is a crucial part of an investment appraisal for an individual purchaser (Chapter 9). But, what of market valuation?

The two main taxes relevant to property investments are those on income (income and corporation tax) and capital gains (capital gains tax, CGT). Each is taxed at an individual or corporate's marginal rate, but CGT is payable only on real gains made in excess of inflation. This can make a difference to the way property investors think about certain investments.

Conventional appraisal techniques assume that investors make a gross-of-tax comparison with other investment opportunities, and returns on capital are therefore assessed on that basis. Using the conventional model for a rack-rented freehold investment, and the pre-1960 assumptions of no growth, a gross-of-tax or net-of-tax comparison becomes immaterial, as Example 6.13 shows.

Part Two

Example 6.13

Capitalisation rate   6%
Tax rate   40%
ERV   £6,000 p.a.

a. Valuation (1): gross-of-tax

ERV	£6,000 p.a.	
YP perp. at 6%	16.6667	
Valuation		£100,000

On a net-of-tax basis, the required return (based on the opportunity cost, given that all investments are subject to the same tax) falls by 40% to 3.6%. The income after tax also falls by 40% to £3,600 p.a.

b. Valuation (2): net-of-tax

Net ERV	£3,600 p.a.	
YP perp. at 3.6%	27.7778	
Valuation		£100,000

In times of growth, this conventional approach can become misleading. It suggests that the investor's return is reduced by the tax rate, but this is not the case.

A contemporary technique can be used to illustrate that the delivered return is not reduced by 40%. Assume a target rate of 11%. A 6% capitalisation rate implies a growth rate of 5.57142% p.a. to achieve a return of 11%, assuming 5-year reviews. If a net-of-tax return of 6.6% (11% × 0.6) is required and the growth rate of 5.57142% p.a. is achieved, the irfy/dcy (or real return if inflation and rental growth are the same) is calculated as

$$\text{Irfy/dcy} = (1 + r)/(1 + g) - 1 = 1.066/1.0557142 - 1 = 0.97\%$$

The 3 YP formula generates a capitalisation rate of 1.14%, which in turn generates a YP in perpetuity of 87.579. This YP applied to the net-of-tax cash flow of £3,600 p.a. produces a valuation of over £300,000!

ERV (net)	£3,600 p.a.	
YP in perp.	87.579	
Valuation		£315,286

This seemingly ridiculous solution (compare £100,000) is produced by a calculation that increases the rents at the same growth rate as for the gross-of-tax valuation, but discounts the future flows at a net-of-tax discount rate.

The 40% reduction in the target rate has produced a relatively much greater proportional reduction in the real return, and the real values of the future flow are discounted at over 5% gross (irfy $= (1 + r)/(1 + g) - 1 = 1.11/1.0557142 - 1 = 5.14\%$) but at less than 1% net (0.9743%).

The valuation is nonetheless logical. Assume that the gross rent of £6,000 does increase by 5.57% p.a. up to the first review in 5 years' time. The rent at review will be:

£6,000 × $(1.0557)^5$ = £7,868 p.a.
After deducting 40% for tax the net ERV at year 5 is

ERV	£7,868 p.a.
less 40%	£3,147 p.a.
net ERV	£4,721 p.a.

The current net-of-tax income is £3,600 p.a. The increase in rent also represents 5.57% p.a.

$$£3,600 \times (1.0557)^5 = £4,721 \text{ p.a.}$$

The net-of-tax ERV grows at the same rate as the gross-of-tax ERV: so it is not the assumption of rental growth that creates the problem. The problem lies in the choice of the net-of-tax target rate. The target rate does not fall by the tax rate; it can, however, be correctly assessed by using a real value approach. Tax should be deducted from the real return rather than the fixed-income return, that is, from the irfy rather than from the target rate.

$$\text{Net-of-tax irfy} = 5.14\% \times 0.6 = 3.0853\%$$

The target-rate net-of-tax can be found by a rearrangement of the formula irfy $(q) = (1 + r) / (1 + g)-1$ to $r = (1 + q) (1 + g)-1$. As the growth rate is held at its original level of 5.57% p.a., the equation becomes

$r = (1.03085) \times (1.0557)-1 = 8.8286\%$

The 3 YP formula can now be used to calculate a net-of-tax capitalisation rate.

$$\text{YP} = \text{YP 5 years @ 8.8286\%} \times \frac{\text{YP perp. @ 3.085\%}}{\text{YP 5 years @ 3.085\%}}$$

YP = 3.90760 × (32.4121/4.5686) = 27.7187

ERV (net)	£3,600 p.a.
YP perp.	27.7187
Valuation	£99,787

$$k = \frac{£3,600}{£99,787} = 3.61\%$$

This approach can therefore be used to appraise the net-of-tax target rate for an individual by

a. Analysing the implied growth rate from the gross-of-tax capitalisation rate
b. Calculating the gross-of-tax real return (irfy/dcy)

Example 6.13   *(Continued)*

c.   Reducing the real return by the investor's rate of tax
d.   Calculating the net-of-tax target rate using $r = (1 + g)(1 + net\ irfy/dcy) - 1$

This valuation assumes a perpetual holding period, but if the investor sells the property after, say, 10 years, it can be shown that the investor does achieve a net-of-tax return of 8.8286%, a marginal tax rate of only 20% on the gross-of-tax return of 11%. This assumes that any growth in capital value should be exempt from tax on account of the capital gains tax indexing provisions (this assumes a static real value; inflation and growth being equal). Only if rental growth does not match inflation will the holding period materially affect the net-of-tax returns.

An explicit-DCF valuation is used here to show how the return will be achieved and to illustrate that the real value approach has correctly appraised the situation. The two valuations – one perpetual, one for 10 years – equate. On the basis of a 10-year holding period the purchase price of £100,000 will produce a fixed rent of £3,600 net for the next 5 years, a reversion to £4,721 net in years 5–10 and a sale price of £171,951 in year 10 (assuming the growth rate of 5.57% p.a. is achieved and capitalisation rates remain static). Table 6.11 shows the DCF valuation.

Table 6.11   Explicit-DCF net-of-tax valuation.

Years	Outflow (£)	Inflow (£)	PV @ 8.8286%	PV (£)
0	(100,000)		1.0000	(100,000)
1		3,600	0.9189	3,308
2		3,600	0.8444	3,040
3		3,600	0.7759	2,794
4		3,600	0.7130	2,567
5		3,600	0.6552	2,359
6		4,721	0.6020	2,843
7		4,721	0.5532	2,612
8		4,721	0.5084	2,401
9		4,721	0.4671	2,206
10		4,721 + 171,951	0.4293	75,854

Net present value = £0.

Reversionary freehold investments are more difficult to value on a net-of-tax basis, because they enjoy inherent real growth produced by the lease structure. As the reversion to a higher rent gets closer, the capital value increases even if the ERV does not. In a rising market, therefore, a CGT liability will arise even if the growth in rents only matches inflation.

Example 6.14

Value a property where the current rent is £10,000 p.a., the unexpired term is 10 years, the ERV is £100,000 p.a., and the purchaser pays tax at 40%.

The conventional valuation of the reversionary freehold at a 6% equivalent yield is as follows:

Current rent	£10,000 p.a.	
YP 10 years at 6%	7.3601	
		£73,601
Reversion to ERV	£100,000 p.a.	
YP perp. at 6%	16.6667	
PV 10 years at 6%	0.5584	
		£930,660
Valuation		£1,004,261

In 1 year's time the capital value will have risen to £1,054,520 simply because of the approach of the reversion. In 10 years' time the capital value will have risen £1,666,667 (ERV × YP perp. @ 6%) on the reversion to the ERV of £100,000 p.a. This assumes no rental growth. The increase in value would be subject to capital gains tax, as it is a real rather than an inflationary gain.

Net-of-tax flows		
Income, years 1–10	£10,000 p.a.	
less tax at 40%	£4,000 p.a.	
Net-of-tax income	£6,000 p.a.	

Sale price on lease renewal in year 10	£1,666,667
Less purchase price	£1,000,000
Gain	£666,667
Tax at 40%	£266 667
Sale price	£1,666,667
Less tax	£266,667
Net proceeds of disposal	£1,400,000

Inflows	
Years 1–10	£6,000 p.a.
Year 10	£1,400,000

The net-of-tax internal rate of return on this cash flow is 3.38%.

A 40% reduction from the gross-of-tax yield of 6% would give a net-of-tax yield of 3.6%. However, a conventional valuation carried out on the net-of-tax basis using this net yield as a capitalisation rate would give a different result to the gross-of-tax valuation.

Current rent	£6,000 p.a.	
YP 10 years at 3.6%	8.2748	
		£ 49,649

> **Example 6.14** *(Continued)*
>
> | | |
> |---|---|
> | ERV | £60,000 p.a. |
> | YP perp. at 3.6% | 27.7778 |
> | PV 10 years at 3.6% | 0.7021 |
> | | £117,176 |
> | Valuation | £1,219,825 |
>
> Introducing the growth element implicit in current market conditions complicates the valuation process still further. A real value or target-rate valuation to show a target rate of 11% and a rack-rented capitalisation rate of 6% would have produced a slightly different gross-of-tax solution.
>
> $k = 6\%$, $r = 11\%$, $g = 5.57\%$ p.a., irfy/dcy = 5.14%
>
> | | |
> |---|---|
> | Current rent | £10,000 p.a |
> | YP 10 years at 11% | 5.8892 |
> | | £58,890 |
> | ERV | £100,000 p.a |
> | YP perp. at 6% | 16.6667 |
> | PV 10 years at 5.14% | 0.6068 |
> | | £1,009,440 |
> | Valuation | £1,068,330 |
>
> Adopting a real value net-of-tax approach, the irfy is reduced to 3.0853%, assuming a 40% tax rate. The target rate can be assessed by $r = (1 + q)(1 + g) - 1$, that is $((1.03085 \times 1.0557) - 1) = 0.088292$ or 8.8292. The valuation becomes (at a net-of-tax target rate of 8.8286% and a net-of-tax irfy of 3.0853%):
>
> | | |
> |---|---|
> | Current rent (net-of-tax) | £6,000 p.a. |
> | YP 10 years at 8.8286% | 6.4664 |
> | | £38,798 |
> | ERV (net) | £60,000 p.a. |
> | YP perp. at 3.0853% × YP 5 years at 8.8286% | |
> | YP 5 years at 3.0853% | 27.7187 |
> | PV 10 years at 3.0853% | 0.73796 |
> | | £1,227,318 |
> | Valuation | £1,266,116 |

The solution is not clear. The different capital gains tax treatment of real and inflationary gains makes the use of 'short-cut' valuation models extremely dangerous when the complexities of taxation are involved. Even the growth-explicit models as applied in the preceding discussion ignore the capital gains tax liability inherent in reversionary investments. Practices such as assessing a gross-of-tax redemption yield (target rate) and then reducing this to a net-of-tax redemption yield by deducting the income tax rate are fraught with danger.

The danger becomes extreme in certain cases. For example, growth-explicit models that discount at net-of-tax target rates based on a simplistic reduction from gross target rates will produce valuations that suggest investments have infinite values when the net-of-tax target rate is lower than the growth rate.

Given the difficulties of carrying out market valuations on a net-of-tax basis, it is not surprising that gross-of-tax comparisons are commonplace. If all income flows were taxed similarly, then the problem would be a minor one. But they are not. In essence, initial incomes are taxed at the investor's own marginal income tax rate, inflationary capital gains are exempt from tax, and real capital gains are not. A gross target rate is made up of real return and growth, and growth can be made up of real growth/loss and inflationary growth. The initial return can be made up of all ranges of these elements; so generalising on the taxation incidence of a particular investment property for the typical purchaser is dangerous. This is not to say that an individual purchaser should not consider the taxation implications of a purchase: this is the role of investment appraisal, covered in Chapter 9. At this point, let it suffice to say that explicit DCF models are of infinitely greater value than conventional models or short-cut contemporary techniques in assessing tax implications.

It has already been established that, when using the conventional basis, comparisons should have similar lease structures, locational and physical similarities, similar unexpired terms and ERV–rent received ratios. Added to this list are similar taxation profiles (although the last factor flows from the preceding). A consideration of the effect of tax reinforces the need for high-quality comparable evidence.

Contemporary models, on the other hand, require a subjective target-rate choice based on other investments (probably conventional gilts). Part of the yield differential should be the product of different taxation implications. Freehold property has advantages over gilts. Although the capital gain from gilts is exempt from tax, prime properties invariably produce lower initial returns than gilts except where the expected risk premium is greater than the expected growth rate. This normally implies greater capital gains for prime property, and (given that such gains may be largely or wholly exempt from capital gains tax as a result of index-linking) net-of-tax prime property returns may be relatively higher for the same gross-of-tax return. This problem is mitigated by the influence of non-tax-paying institutions on both gilt and property prices.

Our suggested approach to tax in freehold market valuations is to ignore taxation and to make comparisons on a gross-of-tax basis, undertaking the valuation using a DCF approach. If tax effects clearly begin to dominate market value for a dominate group of buyers, an explicit DCF net-of-tax valuation is necessary.

Part Two

6.7   Conclusions

The material presented in this chapter examines the limitations and flaws present in both conventional and contemporary freehold valuation methodology. We conclude that, while the basis of market value is the interpretation of transaction evidence derived from comparable properties, property investments are heterogeneous and valuers require a logical approach that helps them in their use of imperfect comparable evidence.

We believe that the advantages of the growth-explicit methods are undeniable, and markets will work irresistibly toward their adoption. It was notable that valuers began to adopt these kinds of approaches in their day-to-day work in the aftermath of the 1990 recession, when the need for change was heavily influenced by the inadequacies of existing conventional techniques for dealing with over-renting. However, it is slightly ironic that models developed to address issues raised by inflationary markets in the 1960s, 1970s and 1980s should come into their own when values were falling. The time at which these alternative models show least advantage is in low inflationary markets when implied growth falls to very low levels. This is because there is virtual parity between capitalisation rates and target rates, there is no implied growth, conventional assumptions concerning cash flow become the expected reality and the models merge. While this may be a feature of property markets from time to time, a robust valuation methodology needs to be defensible in all economic conditions.

Contemporary techniques are criticised for the subjectivity involved in the choice of target rate, but the effect of the subjectivity is minimal for reversionary property with under 10 years unexpired. The charge of subjectivity should be more eagerly aimed at the standard conventional equivalent-yield model, which requires an unbridled degree of manipulation in the valuation stage. The popular valuer's claim of the objectivity and superior of conventional techniques is simply unfounded unless the number of transactions in the market is enough to give close-to-perfect comparisons every time.

A logical market valuation model that helps the valuer interpret the non-perfect comparison but retains as much objectivity as possible is essential. The equivalent-yield model does not pass the test, while the short-cut DCF and the other contemporary models can suffice especially if a more rigorous basis for target-rate choice is agreed upon. Even if a more rigorous basis is not available, the compensating effects inherent within freehold reversionary valuation by contemporary techniques would lead to more consistent valuations in practice.

We do not suggest that contemporary models are perfect. Being more sophisticated than the conventional techniques by introducing more variables involves inevitable subjectivity in the analysis of transactions. This analysis can be as simple as extracting an implied constant growth rate for the location assuming a constant target rate, but as we illustrate in our demonstration of the arbitrage/real value model, can be extended to applying different target rates for different parts of the cash flow based on the relative certainty of the contracted rent and the relative uncertainty of a reversion. In our view, this is an improvement on the normal approach to contemporary valuation and analysis, and despite the difficulties introduced to the process, is a very welcome addition to our understanding of the market. This is particularly apparent from the problems that have arisen with valuations subject to long leases in falling or fallen markets.

The use of constant growth rates and average target rates is a simplification of what drives prices, and we can introduce more and more subjectivity and variation into the analysis of transactions by varying these factors. If we attempt to mimic perfectly investors' perceptions and assumptions when purchasing property interests, we are moving into the realms of a full explicit cash flow as set out in Chapter 3. We will extend our discussion of these fully explicit models in the context of assessing investment value in Chapter 8, but suggest there is a natural limit to the use of explicit models in a market valuation context.

However, despite this limit, our overriding conclusion is that conventional models are not built upon on the logic of the market in which they operate. They cannot, therefore, adapt to changes in that market. The 1990s in the UK, for example, exposed them to new problems, which they did not adequately handle. Meanwhile, growth-explicit models are based on logic and can adapt to changing circumstances. It is no accident, therefore, that the growth-explicit models have been able to adapt to over-renting with minimal adjustment, while the conventional models collapsed. Who knows what new shock lies around the corner?

Part Two

Chapter 7
Contemporary Leasehold Market Valuations

7.1 Introduction

In this chapter we examine the valuation of leasehold interests. As in the previous chapter, we use examples to illustrate the application of contemporary market valuation models before comparing and contrasting conventional and contemporary approaches.

One of the fundamental concepts underlying the conventional model was the sinking fund. This concept assumed that the reinvestment of income through the sinking-fund mechanism provided enough capital upon expiry of the leasehold interest to buy another leasehold interest of equal length. A constant repetition of this purchase at the subsequent expiry dates into infinity turned the terminable leasehold into a perpetual interest. The reason for this approach, which on the surface appeared to make a leasehold look like a freehold, was to enable comparisons to be made with the freehold market simply because fewer leasehold interests are sold.

This was a worthy endeavour: the quality of a valuation depends largely upon the quality of comparable evidence, but the quantity of available information concerning leasehold transactions is likely to be less than the information concerning freeholds. The sinking-fund concept is, however, fatally flawed (see Chapter 4); so it is a significant test of contemporary techniques to examine how they cope with the problem of comparables derived from freeholds. So in this chapter we will look at freehold comparables and apply them to contemporary valuations of the leasehold interest.

Contemporary transaction analysis goes further than determining the capitalisation rate of the interest. It relies on the estimation of a rack-rented perpetual capitalisation rate, an implied rental growth rate and a required return for the freehold interest. For many of the examples used in this chapter, we will assume that a freehold rack-rented property, in the same location as the leasehold interest to be valued, will sell for a capitalisation rate/all-risks yield of 6% if let on 5-year reviews. Target rates of return for freehold interests in this location let to similar tenants are assumed to be 9%.

Assuming a fully let property from which the capitalisation rate is observed, the implied growth can be found as follows:

$$(1 + g)^t = \frac{\text{YP perp. @ } k\% - \text{YP } t \text{ years @ } r\%}{\text{YP perp. @ } k\% \times \text{PV } t \text{ years @ } r\%}$$

$$(1 + g)^5 = \frac{\text{YP perp. @ } 6\% - \text{YP } 5 \text{ years @ } 9\%}{\text{YP perp. @ } 6\% \times \text{PV } 5 \text{ years @ } 9\%}$$

$$(1 + g)^5 = \frac{16.6667 - 3.8897}{16.6667 \times 0.6499}$$

$$(1 + g)^5 = \frac{12.78}{10.83} = 1.1795$$

$$g = (1.1795)^{1/5} - 1 = 0.0335765 = 3.35765\%$$

The growth rate, subject to the limitation of being a constant average, represents the freeholder's need for growth to obtain the required rate of return. As such it identifies the implied rate of growth in the rental value of all similar property in the particular location and can therefore be used in the valuation of other interests in that location, including leaseholds.

However, the required return for a leasehold interest will usually be different from that of a freehold. (This will be discussed in greater detail later in this chapter.) In the previous chapter we distinguished between short-cut DCF (discounted-cash-flow) approaches using property-based discount rates and real value/arbitrage model utilising tenant-based discount rates, and the same distinction can be made for leaseholds, but there is a market perception that leaseholds are inherently riskier than freeholds, and in conventional approaches an arbitrary addition of 1–2% is often adopted to represent this perception. However, the discussion in Part Two will illustrate the fact that different leasehold structures demand different yields, dependent upon how much of the cash flow is generated by future growth. The risk attached to certain leasehold cash flows would suggest extremely high discount rates, while other leasehold cash flows have more in common with fixed-income bonds than any other property investment.

For the purposes of examining the contemporary model, we will undertake all leasehold valuations using a target rate of 15%. The implied growth rate will be derived from an analysis of the freehold capitalisation rate and target return.

7.2   Fixed leasehold profit rents

Example 7.1

A property has 6 years unexpired at a ground rent of £20,000 p.a. The head-lessee has sub-let the property for the remainder of the term at £300,000 p.a. with no further reviews. Assuming a target rate of 9% for a freehold, we assume a target rate of 15% for the leasehold to reflect increased risk.

However, the risk of this particular investment is almost solely dependent upon the covenant strength of the sub-lessee. If the sub-lessee is very strong or the market for this type of property is very active, then the cash flow is similar to a fixed-income bond. If the tenant was weak and the market poor, the income could turn into a liability very easily and is a high-risk investment, because a void would create a negative cash flow as the ground rent still has to be paid.

a.   Explicit DCF

Year	Rent received (£)	Rent paid (£)	Profit rent (£)
1	300,000	20,000	280,000
2	300,000	20,000	280,000
3	300,000	20,000	280,000
4	300,000	20,000	280,000
5	300,000	20,000	280,000
6	300,000	20,000	280,000

Given that fixed rents are received and paid, there is no advantage in a tabular layout. Capitalisation of the profit rent is possible by using a simple YP multiplier, in this case for 6 years at 15%. A conventional layout is illustrated as follows:

Profit rent	£280,000 p.a.	
YP 6 years at 15%	3.78448	
Valuation		£1,059,655

b.   Short-cut DCF, real value/arbitrage

Although this is not the case in this example, where the two leases that go together to make up a profit rent are not synchronised in terms of changes to any profit rent (e.g. where reviews are timed differently), contemporary approaches require that the two elements of the profit rent are capitalised separately. DCF by formulae, real value or arbitrage approaches will therefore be applied by capitalising the rents received and the rents paid separately in all examples. This approach is illustrated here.

Rent received	£300,000 p.a.	
YP 6 years at 15%	3.78448	
Value of rent received		£1,135,344
Less: rent paid	£20 000 p.a.	
YP 6 years at 15%	3.78448	
Cost of rent paid		£75,690
Valuation		£1,059,655

7.3   Geared leasehold profit rents

7.3.1   *Reviewable rent received, fixed rent paid*

> ### Example 7.2
>
> A shop property is let on a ground lease with 50 years unexpired at a fixed rent of £50,000 p.a. The property has just been sub-let at its estimated rental value (ERV) of £300,000 p.a. on 5-year reviews. Similar freehold properties sell for 6% capitalisation rates when let on 5-year review patterns.
>
> A fixed rent, paid coupled with expectations of future rental growth in the sub-lease, creates an interesting situation that the valuers who originally applied conventional techniques did not envisage. The expectation in the pre-1960 reverse yield gap environment was of no growth. The ability of the rent to grow was no advantage over the fixed ground rent; indeed, the lack of an ability to change was seen as secure and less risky (the yield on fixed ground rents being lower than the yield on rack rents). The conventional valuation technique (assessing the profit rent and capitalising this over the unexpired term) fitted these perceptions, so that the expected income flow was as shown in Figure 7.1. The obvious solution was to assess the difference in rents and capitalise at the appropriate rate, assessed as more risky (or, more accurately, less attractive) than a freehold. But the expected income profile takes on a different shape given expectations of growth (Figure 7.2).
>
>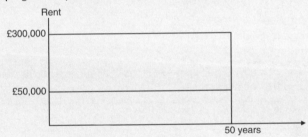
>
> **Figure 7.1**   Fixed profit rent income profile.
>
>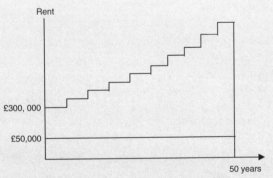
>
> **Figure 7.2**   Geared profit rent growth income profile.

Example 7.2   *(Continued)*

The income is expected to grow as rents received increase and the liability to pay rent does not increase. More subtly, *the rate at which the profit rent grows is not the same as the rate at which the sub-rent grows.*

The growth rate received by the leasehold investor is geared and is not the same as the rate of growth in the equivalent freehold. The growth in profit rent will be different depending on the ratio of rent received to the rent paid. The problem can be illustrated by two identical profit rents based on different rents.

Case (1)	Rent received	£10,000	Case (2)	Rent received	£100,000
	Rent paid	£1,000		Rent paid	£91,000
	Profit rent	£9,000		Profit rent	£9,000

Assuming 10% p.a. growth, in case (1) a rent review in year 5 will increase the rent received to

£10,000 × A £1 5 years at 10% (1.61051) = £16,105 p.a.
Less rent paid   £1,000 p.a.
Profit rent   £15,105 p.a.

In case (1), the profit rent increase from £9,000 to £15,105 represents an increase of 67.8% over 5 years or *10.9% p.a.* In case (2) the same assumptions produce a review rent of:

£100,000 × A £1 5 years at 10% (1.6105) = £161,051 p.a.
Less rent paid   £91,000 p.a.
Profit rent   £70,051 p.a.

The increase from £9,000 to £70,051 represents an increase of 678% or 50.7% p.a. In the following 5 years, the increases are

	Freehold	Leasehold (1)	Leasehold (2)
Growth in ERV (%)	61.05	61.05	61.05
Growth in net income (%)	61.05	65.09	140.36
Increase p.a. (%)	10.00	10.55	19.17

The gearing effects where head rents are fixed are as follows:

i.   Except where the rent paid is a peppercorn (a nominal amount) rental growth will be greater for a leasehold than for an equivalent freehold.
ii. The rate of growth is dependent on the ratio of the rent received to the rent paid.
iii. The rate of growth diminishes at each subsequent review and tends towards the rate of growth in the ERV in perpetuity.

How do contemporary models cope with this issue?

a. **Explicit DCF**

In an explicit-DCF approach all future rent changes are incorporated into the income flow so that the gearing effects are taken into account. Assuming the same freehold analysis as before ($r = 9\%$, $k = 6\%$), this leads to a growth rate of 3.35765% p.a. Assuming the same risk adjustment (+6%), the DCF yield model is based on the following inputs.

$r = 15\%$
$g = 3.35765\%$ p.a.

The valuation is set out in cash flow form below:

Years	Income (£)	Rent paid (£)	Profit rent (£)	YP @ 15%	PV @ 15%	PV (£)
1–5	300,000	50,000	250,000	3.3522	1.0000	838,039
6–10	353,862	50,000	303,862	3.3522	0.4972	506,421
11–15	417,395	50,000	367,395	3.3522	0.2472	304,424
16–20	492,335	50,000	442,335	3.3522	0.1229	182,225
21–25	580,730	50,000	530,730	3.3522	0.0611	108,703
26–30	684,994	50,000	634,994	3.3522	0.0304	64,662
31–35	807,979	50,000	757,979	3.3522	0.0151	38,375
36–40	953,045	50,000	903,045	3.3522	0.0075	22,731
41–45	1,124,156	50,000	1,074,156	3.3522	0.0037	13,442
46–50	1,325,988	50,000	1,275,988	3.3522	0.0019	7,939

Valuation   £2,086,961

b. Real value/arbitrage

The income flow is capitalised in two parts. The capital value of the right to receive the rent from the sub-lessee is found and the capital value of the liability to pay the ground rent is then deducted. The remainder is the capital value of the net income to the head-lessee. The risk rate used in both parts of the calculation should be the risk rate relevant to the head-lessee's net income; so in this case the whole of the rental value is capitalised at 15%, and the liability to pay the ground rent is also capitalised at 15%, to leave a residue of the head-lessee's interest, by implication valued at a 15% yield.

$\text{irfy} = (1.15/1.0335765 - 1) = 11.2641\%$

Valuation
Rent received   £300,000

$$\text{YP 5 years @ 15\%} \times \frac{\text{YP 50 years @ 11.2641\%}}{\text{YP 5 years @ 11.2641\%}}$$

3.3522 × 8.8350/3.6715   = 8.0666
                                                                            £ 2,419,986
Less rent paid   £50,000 p.a.
YP 50 years @ 15%   6.6605
                                                                            £333,026
Valuation   £2,086,960

7.4   Synchronised reviews in head- and sub-leases

Example 7.3

A shop property similar to that examined in the previous example is held from the free-holder on a lease with 20 years unexpired. The rent is geared (meaning the rent for the head-lease is agreed as a fixed percentage of rental value, or rents received or receivable), and the sub-lease is for the remainder of the term with 5-year reviews. The rent has just been agreed at the ERV of £300,000 p.a. and the head-lease specifies that the rent pay-able to the freeholder is to be 50% of ERV. Assume the same target rate (15%), growth rate (3.35765% p.a.) and irfy (11.2641%) as before.

In this case, the profit rent will behave in exactly the same way as the rent received from the sub-letting. If the rental value grows by the implied growth rate, so will the profit rent.

a. Explicit DCF

Years	Income (£)	Rent paid (£)	Profit rent (£)	YP @ 15%	PV @ 15%	PV (£)
1–5	300,000	150,000	150,000	3.3522	1.0000	502,823
6–10	353,862	176,931	176,931	3.3522	0.4972	294,876
11–15	417,395	208,697	208,698	3.3522	0.2472	172,927
16–20	492,335	246,167	246,168	3.3522	0.1229	101,412

Valuation   £1,072,038

b. Real value.

In this case there is no need to separate the capitalisation of the rent received from the capitalisation of the rent paid. However, this is the only occasion on which this is the case, apart from situations where both rents are fixed for the term of the head-lease or the rent paid is a peppercorn and the profit rent can be directly capitalised. For simplicity the valu-ation is set out below in the same form as before, a form which will suit all situations.

Rent received   £300,000

$$\text{YP 5 years @ 15\%} \times \frac{\text{YP 20 years @ 11.2461\%}}{\text{YP 5 years @ 11.2461\%}}$$

$$\frac{3.5216 \times 7.82771}{3.67147} \qquad\qquad \frac{7.14692}{\qquad} $$
                                                                        £2,144,076

Less rent paid   £150,000

$$\text{YP 5 years @ 15\%} \times \frac{\text{YP 20 years @ 11.2461\%}}{\text{YP 5 years @ 11.2461\%}}$$

$$\frac{3.5216 \times 7.82771}{3.67147} \qquad\qquad \frac{7.14692}{\qquad}$$
                                                                        £1,072,038

Valuation   £1,072,038

7.5   Reversionary leaseholds

7.5.1   Reviewable rent received, fixed rent paid

Example 7.4

A similar shop property as that used in the previous examples is held from the freeholder on a lease with 23 years unexpired. The rent was fixed at the beginning of the lease 40 years ago at a rent of £4,000 p.a. and has no further reviews. The property is now sub-let on a modern lease with 5-yearly rent reviews at £200,000 p.a. The ERV is £225,000 p.a. and the next review is in 3 years' time.

a. Explicit DCF

The income is £200,000 until the review in 3 years' time. At that point the rental income will increase to the rental value based upon the current rental value of £225,000 grown at the implied growth rate of 3.35765% p.a. The rent paid is a fixed sum for the whole of the lease.

Years	Income (£)	Rent paid (£)	Profit rent (£)	YP @ 15%	PV @ 15%	Present value (£)
1–3	200,000	4,000	196,000	2.283225	1	447,512
4–8	248,434	4,000	244,434	3.3522	0.6575	538,755
9–13	293,038	4,000	289,038	3.3522	0.3269	316,735
14–18	345,650	4,000	341,650	3.3522	0.1625	186,137

Valuation   £1,598,493

b. Real value

The real value approach to reversionary leaseholds is consistent with its approach to reversionary freeholds. The valuation of the rent received consists of a term income that is fixed for the next 3 years as in the explicit-DCF approach. This income is therefore valued at the required return. Upon review, the income reverts to rental value and is then reviewed every 5 years over the next 20 years.

As the income has a 20-year term and 5-year reviews, it is valued using the 3 YP formula which incorporates the total term, the review pattern and the rental growth rate implied by the use of the irfy. The fact that the rental value is also expected to grow over the interim period while the valuation reverts to ERV is taken into account by deferring the reversion at the irfy.

Term rent	£200,000
YP 3 years @ 15%	2.28323
Value of term	£456,645
Reversion to ERV	£225,000

$$\text{YP}^5 \text{ years @ 15\%} \times \frac{\text{YP 20 years @ 11.2461\%}}{\text{YP 5 years @ 11.2461\%}}$$

Example 7.4 *(Continued)*

$\dfrac{3.5216 \times 7.82771}{3.67147}$	7.14692	
	£1,608,057	
PV 3 years @ 11.2461%	0.7260	
Value of reversion		£1,167,443
Value of rent received		£1,624 088
Less rent paid	£4,000	
YP 23 years @ 15%	6.3988	
Value of reversion		£25,595
Valuation		£1,598,493

7.6   Reviewable rent received, unsynchronised reviewable rent paid

Example 7.5

Assume a similar property and location as used in all the previous examples. The shop property is held from the freeholder on a 63-year lease with rent reviews every 21 years. There are now 30 years unexpired and the current net rent passing is £100,000 p.a. The ERV based upon 5-year reviews is £200,000 p.a. The property is sub-let on a 15-year lease with 5-year reviews that now has 13 years unexpired and the rent passing is £175,000 p.a.

It is unreasonable to expect that all rent reviews in the leases that make up a leasehold investment will be synchronised or even on the same review pattern. In this example the sub-letting is subject to a normal modern lease, but the property is held from the freeholder on an old lease subject to what is now an abnormal review pattern. The result is that the unexpired term does not fit easily into the review pattern of the sub-lease. If the head-lessee continues to sub-let the property on leases with 5-year reviews after the current sub-lease expires, eventually there will be a 'fag-end' of 2 years.

This example raises a number of problems concerning rental values as well as capitalisation. Properties let on long review patterns have long been the subject of discussion between landlord and tenant at rent review, and rules of thumb have emerged whereby the rent paid by the tenant is increased to reflect this advantage to the tenant. The most common rule is to use a factor based on the number of years by which a review term exceeds the normal period of 5 years. A 21-year review period would (depending upon the quality of the location and the property) warrant an uplift of around 15% above that obtainable under a normal 5-year review. In current rental value terms this produces a rent of £230,000 instead of £200,000.

The last review is only 2 years from the expiry of the lease. This rent may well be discounted for that fact at that point in time. However, this will have little

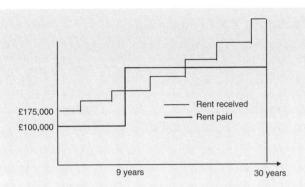

Figure 7.3 Unsynchronised reviews – income profile.

bearing on the valuation as it is for a short period of time and 28 years into the future.

Figure 7.3 illustrates the complexity of the cash flow to the head-lessee.

a. Explicit DCF

The profit rent has periods of being both positive (years 1– 9 and 14–30) and negative (years 10–13 and possibly up to 18 years).

Years	Income	Rent paid (£)	Profit rent (£)	YP @ 15%	PV @ 15%	PV (£)
1–3	175,000	100,000	75,000	2.2832	1.0000	171,242
4–8	220,830	100,000	120,830	3.3522	0.6575	266,318
9	260,478	100,000	160,478	0.86957	0.3269	45,618
10–13	260,478	309,608	–49,130	2.85498	0.28426	–39,872
14–18	307,245	309,608	–2,363	3.3522	0.1625	–1,287
19–23	362,408	309,608	52,800	3.3522	0.0808	14,302
24–28	427,475	309,608	117,867	3.3522	0.0402	15,873
29–30	504,224	309,608	194,616	1.6257	0.0200	6,319

Valuation   £478,513

b. Real value

Rent received	
Term rent	£175,000
YP 3 years @ 15%	2.28323
	£399,564
Reversion to ERV	£200,000

$$\text{YP 5 years @ } 15\% \times \frac{\text{YP 27yrs @ } 11.2461\%}{\text{YP 5 years @ } 11.2461\%}$$

$$= 3.35216 \times \frac{8.38033}{3.671473} = \qquad 7.65147$$

Example 7.5   *(Continued)*

PV 3 years @ 11.2461%	0.725996	
	£1,110,988	
Value of rent received		£1,510,552
Less rent paid		
Rent passing	£100,000	
YP 9 years @ 15%	4.77158	
		£477,158
Reversion to ERV (21 years reviews)	£230,000	
YP 21 years @ 15%	6.31246	
PV 9 years @ 11.2461%	0.38265	
		£555,558
		£1,032,716
Valuation		£477,836

For the first time there is a difference in the two approaches, even though it is only £677. This difference relates to the treatment of the 2-year unexpired term after the last rent review in year 28. The explicit-DCF approach has used the rent based upon 5-year rent reviews to value the last 2 years. Theoretically, this rent should be reduced for the shorter period between rent revision in the last 2 years (in the same way as it would be increased if the review pattern was longer than 5 years). The real value approach builds the reduced rental value of the last two years into its calculation and is therefore more theoretically accurate.

Using the implied rental growth rate and the leasehold target rate, the reduced rental value can be calculated by comparing the capital value of a 5-year review pattern with the capital value of the 2-year review pattern. Using real value principles, the value of a 5-year review pattern is

Rental value on a 5-year review		£200,000
$\text{YP 5 years @ }15\% \times \dfrac{\text{YP perp. @ }11.2461\%}{\text{YP 5 years @ }11.2461\%}$	8.10562	
		£1,621,123

The capital value of a 2-year review pattern let at an unknown rent is

Rental value on a 2-year review		£x
$\text{YP 2 years @ }15\% \times \dfrac{\text{YP perp.@ }11.2461\%}{\text{YP 2 years @ }11.2461\%}$	8.45726	
		£8.45726x

Assuming that the capital value should remain the same for a property let under 2-year reviews at a lower rent as it is for the property let on 5-year reviews:

£8.45726x = £1,621,123
x = £191,684 p.a.

If this new rental value is now plugged into the DCF approach for years 29 to 30, the value of those last 2 years falls to £5,639 from £6,319, a fall of £690 and within £13 of the £677 difference between DCF and real value approaches (a rounding error).

7.7   Over-rented leaseholds

In Chapter 6 we looked at a valuation of a freehold over-rented property. We complete our examination of the application of contemporary growth-explicit models to leasehold valuation by valuing a head-leasehold interest in a similar property.

Example 7.6

An office block in Central London is held on a long ground lease with 22 years unexpired at a rent passing of £625,000 fixed 3 years ago. The lease provides for upward-only rent reviews as and when the sub-lease is reviewed, to 50% of rental value. The property is sub-let to a good covenant tenant for the remainder of the term with a review in 2 years' time and every 5 years thereafter. The rent passing is £1,250,000 p.a. The rental value is now estimated to be only £1,000,000 p.a., and similar freehold properties sell for capitalisation rates of 7%. Value the head-leasehold interest.

As the lease rents are geared to each other, this is a relatively straightforward case. The first step in either the short-cut DCF or the real-value approach is to calculate the implied rental growth rate from the freehold transaction evidence. At a 7% capitalisation rate and a 9% target rate, the implied rental growth rate is 2.28687% p.a.

The next step is to assess when the ERV will overtake the rent passing.

At the first review: $£1,000,000 \times (1.0228687)^2 = £1,046,260$
At the second review: $£1,000,000 \times (1.0228687)^7 = £1,171,492$
At the third review: $£1,000,000 \times (1.0228687)^{12} = £1,311,712$
At the fourth review: $£1,000,000 \times (1.0228687)^{17} = £1,468,717$

As the rent passing is £1.25m, this suggests the overage (or froth, as it is sometimes called) will be eliminated by the third review in 12 years' time.

a. Explicit DCF

Years	Income (£)	Rent paid (£)	Profit rent (£)	YP @ 15%	PV @ 15%	Present value (£)
1–12	1,250,000	625,000	625,000	5.4206	1	3,387,887
13–17	1,311,712	655,856	655,856	3.3522	0.1869	410,921
18–22	1,468,717	734,358	734,358	3.3522	0.0929	228,754

Valuation   £4,027, 562

b. Real value

Calculate irfy: irfy = (1.15/1.02286869)–1 = 12.429%

Rent received   £1,250,000
YP 12 years @ 15%   5.4206
                                                 £6,775,774

Example 7.6 *(Continued)*

Reversion to ERV	£1,000,000	
YP 5 years @ 15% $\times \dfrac{\text{YP 10 years @ 12.429\%}}{\text{YP 5 years @12.429\%}}$	5.21825	
PV 12 years @ 12.429%	0.24517	
		£1,279,351
Value of rents receivable		£8,055,124
Less rent paid	£625,000	
YP 12 years @ 15%	5.4206	
		£3,387,887
Reversion to ERV (50%)	£500,000	
YP 5 years @ 15% $\times \dfrac{\text{YP 10 years @ 12.429\%}}{\text{YP 5 years @ 12.429\%}}$	5.21825	
PV 12 years @ 12.429%	0.24517	
		£639,675
Value of rents paid		£4,027,562
Valuation		£4,027,562

In this case of perfectly aligned gearing there is no need to capitalise the two elements separately, but we have adopted this approach to illustrate the real value/arbitrage method as it works in more complex cases.

In Chapter 6, we finished our look at freehold market valuations by comparing the conventional and contemporary models with each other. We complete our examination of market valuations by carrying out a similar exercise for leaseholds.

7.8   Conventional versus contemporary techniques

Our critique of leasehold valuations using conventional techniques in Chapter 4 illustrated that changes in investors' perceptions in the 1950s and 1960s introduced a variety of problems, and we conclude that a rational and logical basis for appraisal had been lost.

Any defence of the continued use of years' purchase dual-rate, tax-adjusted, capitalisation factors applied to current profit rents must, as in a defence of freehold appraisals, be based on the objectivity delivered by analysis of similar transactions.

While a debate exists regarding whether a sufficient quantity and quality of comparables exists for the typical freehold valuation, there is no doubt that good leasehold investment comparisons are usually very hard to find. To provide a perfect comparison, a leasehold investment must be similar in terms of a wide variety of criteria.

These criteria change depending on the nature of the subject leasehold investment. The fixed-income leasehold, where the head-lease and the sub-lease have
no more reviews and expire at the same time, creates a property investment
where the property characteristics (location and so on) are of very little importance compared with the quality of tenant (Baum and Butler, 1986).

The investment comprises a fixed-income stream and can be valued by
direct comparison or by reference to other fixed-income investments. It has
been termed the 'property gilt'. We have already seen that over-renting can
generate a very similar scenario.

When rising or falling rents are introduced into either lease, the criteria
defining a good comparison change. The usual characteristics of a similar tenant, a similar position, a similar physical condition and so on, are necessary,
but similarity in this situation also relates to lease structure. A good comparable requires to be of the same or similar unexpired term, with a similar relationship between rent passing and ERV in the sub-lease, a similar relationship
between rents received and rents paid to the superior landlord, and similar
covenant strength. Because of this the use of intial yields in order to effect a
comparison of highly individual leasehold investments is highly dangerous.

In our investigation of freeholds, we were able to examine in some detail
the criteria of rationality and objectivity and, while coming down on the side
of contemporary models on both counts, conventional and contemporary
models often reach very similar conclusions. Those who still use and defend
leasehold conventional techniques have no such comfort. The valuation
method is both illogical and it produces what are close to random results.

The reason for this is not to do with the usual debate regarding the use of
dual-rate or single-rate valuations, and tax adjustments or no tax adjustments. Solving the mathematical problems of reversionary dual-rate valuations set out in some textbooks is futile.

The real problem is that, since the appearance of the reverse yield gap
around 1960, the conventional approach ceased to be an investment method
and became a comparison model. The core of the valuation is the capitalisation rate. As the cash flow only considers the current levels of rent and rental
value, the yield (and only the yield) has to take full account of what can be
the highly complex future behaviour of the cash flow. There are two major
fundamental constraints to this comparison within leasehold valuation.

The first is the inadequacy of the capitalisation rate in dealing with the
complex structure of the cash flow created by the relationship between the
two leases. This complexity was illustrated in Example 7.2 (Section 7.3)
where it was shown that identical current profit rents could be derived from
very different rental levels within leases and produce very different future
cash flows. Gearing distorts the shape of future cash flows to create complex
interests that are incapable of simplistic comparison.

The second major constraint is the nature of the capitalisation rate as
applied to a finite-income stream. This is often used as a surrogate for a

Part Two

higher target return coupled with an implied rental value growth rate. But the same capitalisation rate can imply different growth rates or required returns if used within YP factors for different finite terms.

Consider the following example.

Example 7.7

Value the leasehold interest in property held at a peppercorn rent for the next 15 years. The property is sub-let for the remainder of the term at the ERV of £100,000 p.a. with rent reviews in year 5 and 10. A similar freehold, fully let on a 5-year review pattern, has just sold on the basis of a 6% capitalisation rate.

It might be assumed, as the profit rent will grow at the same rate as the ERV, that a direct comparison could be made between freehold and lease-hold. Assuming that no risk adjustment is required to distinguish between the freehold and leasehold in this case, and that a 9% target rate is required, the growth rate needed to increase an initial 6% to the target rate of 9%, assuming 5-year reviews, is 3.35765% p.a. in perpetuity.

The conventional application of the comparable to the leasehold using a cap-italisation rate of 6% would produce a gross single-rate valuation as follows:

Profit rent	£100,000 p.a.
YP 15 years at 6%	9.7122
Valuation	£971,220

If, as suggested, the 6% capitalisation rate is a short cut to assuming 3.35765% p.a. rental growth receivable every 5 years, then the internal rate of return (IRR) over the 15 years should be 9%, as it would be for the freehold. Unfortunately, this is not the case. A DCF approach does not produce the same answer. Using the real-value 3 YP formula to illustrate, we have:

$$irfy = (1.09/1.0335765) - 1 = 0.05459 = 5.459\%$$

Profit rent £100,000 p.a.

$$\text{YP 15 years at 5.459\%} \times \frac{\text{YP 5 years at 9\%}}{\text{YP 5 years at 5.459\%}}$$

$$= 10.065 \times \frac{3.8897}{4.2751} \qquad\qquad 9.1575$$

Valuation £915,752

As the direct use of the capitalisation rate gives a solution over 6% higher than the DCF approach (which is explicit regarding the growth rate) the capitalisation rate of 6% must imply a higher growth rate than 3.35765% to produce an IRR of 9%. The growth rate implied by a 6% capitalisation rate for 15 years to produce an IRR of 9% is in fact 4.8% p.a.. To add to the confusion, the capitalisation rate of 6% implies different growth rates for every different unexpired term. Table 7.1 illustrates the implications of a perpetuity capitalisa-tion rate of 6% for terminable incomes on 5-year reviews.

Table 7.1 Capitalisation rates for terminable incomes.

Years	YP @ 6%	DCF multiplier	Required capitalisation rate to equate with DCF solution (%)
5	4.2124	3.8897	9.00
10	7.3601	6.8715	7.47
15	9.7122	9.1575	6.91
20	11.4699	10.9100	6.62
25	12.7834	12.2535	6.45
30	13.7648	13.2834	6.34
35	14.4982	14.0730	6.26
40	15.0463	14.6783	6.20
45	15.4558	15.1424	6.16
50	15.7619	15.4981	6.12
75	16.4558	16.3572	6.04
100	16.6175	16.5847	6.01
Perpetuity	16.6667	16.6667	6.00

Notes: YPs at $k = 6\%$, $r = 9\%$, $g = 3.35765\%$ p.a., $t = 5$ years.

From Table 7.1, it is possible to conclude that the required capitalisation rate on a 15-year term to imply 3.35765% p.a. growth and to deliver a required return of 9% is 6.91%. The valuation of the 15-year income flow required for Example 7.7 should have been as follows:

Profit rent	£100,000 p.a.
YP 15 years at 6.91%	9.1575
Valuation	£915,752

Had the valuation been of a 25-year leasehold, the capitalisation rate would have been 6.45%. A 50-year term, on the other hand, would not need much adjustment from the perpetual capitalisation rate of 6% (to 6.12%). The valuer must either dispose of the capitalisation rate approach or guess the adjustment. The use of comparisons that do not have the same unexpired term invalidates growth-implicit capitalisation rate comparisons.

There remains very little to be said regarding the conventional technique. It is a comparison technique that relies on evidence of transactions. The yield choice should be based upon the evidence of sales of similar properties but, on the assumption that it is unlikely that many of these will be leaseholds, these will be freehold. The 'risks' hidden within the capitalisation rate are different for freeholds and leaseholds, and so different that the investments are likely to have nothing in common except the fact that they are secured on real property. The contemporary alternatives are clearly better, as they are more closely related to the rationale of the property investment market. However, they also suffer from a number of limitations. The remaining part of this chapter isolates these limitations.

7.9   The limitations of the contemporary models for leaseholds

Because real value/arbitrage and short-cut or explicit-DCF techniques all reconcile (or can be reconciled), any limitations in the valuations of leaseholds are common to all of these approaches.

When used as market pricing/valuation models, they utilise evidence of market transactions. Leasehold transactions may be rare, but if they can be found, they must constitute the best evidence of market value. Although it is possible to analyse leasehold transactions by growth-explicit methods, the next section highlights the difficulties inherent in interpreting these transactions if they can be found.

7.9.1   Analysis and valuation using leasehold comparables

To illustrate the possible use of comparisons, it is assumed that a similar property in terms of physical and locational characteristics is available.

Example 7.8

A leasehold interest has sold for £736,000. The rent paid to the freeholder is £100,000 p.a. on a lease with 10 years unexpired and with no further reviews. The lessee had just sub-let the property for the remainder of the term, with a review in 5 years' time, at the ERV of £200,000 p.a.

A conventional analysis (on a single-rate gross-of-tax basis) would simply find the capitalisation rate on the basis of a 10-year term at the current profit rent.

Profit rent	£100,000 p.a.	
YP 10 years at ?%	x	
Sale price		£736,000

£736,000 = £100,000x : x = 7.3600;
YP 10 years at 6% = 7.3600;
Capitalisation rate = 6%.

In practice, this information would then be applied directly to any property of similar locational and physical characteristics, at worst disregarding any lease structure differences, and at best amending the capitalisation rate intuitively to reflect perceived differences.

The contemporary analysis is more complex. To find the target rate of the investment, the valuer must either assume a growth rate or assess an implied growth rate by using freehold comparisons. Adopting the first alternative, an assumed growth rate of 5% p.a. would produce a target rate of just under 10.25%:

Current profit rent	£100,000 p.a.	
YP 5 years at 10.25%	3.7667	
Valuation of term		£376,670
ERV	£200,000 p.a.	
A £1 in 5 years at 5%	1.2763	
Inflated rent	£255,260 p.a.	
Less rent paid	£100,000 p.a.	
Profit rent	£155,260 p.a.	
YP 5 years at 10.25%	3.7667	
PV 5 years at 10.25%	0.6139	
		£359,030
Valuation		£735,700
Sale price		£736,000

The actual IRR is 10.24%.

This analysis is based on pure speculation regarding the anticipated growth rate. It could alternatively have been based on an assumption of a freehold target rate from which a growth rate could have been assessed. This is surely a more promising approach: freeholds provide much more market evidence. For example, assume that the freehold interest in a property similar to the subject in Example 7.8, recently let on a lease with a 5-year reviews at its ERV, has been sold on the basis of a capitalisation rate of 4%.

The analysis for the implied growth rate produces the following growth rates, depending upon the required return selected:

a. Target rate 7%: rental growth 3.23% p.a.
b. Target rate 15%: rental growth 11.74% p.a.

The application of this information to the valuation of a leasehold investment can now be considered.

Example 7.9

The leasehold interest in a property similar to the subject in Example 7.8 (in terms of locational and physical factors) is let on a lease with 20 years unexpired at a fixed rent of £200,000 p.a. The property has just been let at its ERV of £300,000 p.a. on a 20-year lease with 5-year reviews.

Two transactions are now available for analysis. These are the sale of the leasehold interest, which indicated the 6% capitalisation rate for a 10-year term, and a freehold interest sold to show a yield of 4%.

Example 7.9   *(Continued)*

The conventional valuation is likely to be undertaken using the 6% capitalisation rate, supported by the lower freehold yield (perceived to be for a less risky or more attractive investment).

Profit rent	£100,000 p.a.
YP 20 years at 6%	11.4699
Valuation	£1,146,990

An alternative approach is the YP dual rate. Assuming an institutional investment, no adjustment for tax would be made.

Profit rent	£100,000 p.a.
YP 20 years at 6% and 4%	10.6858
Valuation	£1,068,580

Contemporary analysis produces two alternative implied growth rates at the freehold target rates of 7% and 15%. These are 3.23% and 11.74% respectively. These are appropriate indicators, given that what is needed is the market perception of the rate at which the property's ERV is expected to increase, a factor quite independent of tenure. The analysis for the leasehold target rate can therefore be repeated at these two growth rates.

The analysis of the comparison by trial and error produces the following solutions. At a growth rate of 3.23% p.a. the leasehold IRR is 8.8%, and at a growth rate of 11.74% p.a. the IRR is 15.4%.

The valuation of Example 7.9 can now be attempted using each of these sets of results.

a. $r = 8.8\%$, $g = 3.23\%$

Years	Income (£)	Rent paid (£)	Profit rent (£)	YP @ 8.8%	PV @ 8.8%	PV (£)
1–5	300,000	200,000	100,000	3.9099	1.0000	390,992
6–10	351,683	200,000	151,683	3.9099	0.6559	389,009
11–15	412,269	200,000	212,269	3.9099	0.4302	357,080
16–20	483,293	200,000	283,293	3.9099	0.2822	312,586

Valuation	£1,449,667

b. $r = 15.4\%$, $g = 11.74\%$

Years	Income (£)	Rent paid (£)	Profit rent (£)	YP @ 15.4%	PV @ 15.4%	Present value (£)
1–5	300,000	200,000	100,000	3.3207	1.0000	332,065
6–10	522,594	200,000	322,594	3.3207	0.4886	523,421
11–15	910,349	200,000	710,349	3.3207	0.2387	563,167
16–20	1,585,810	200,000	1,385,810	3.3207	0.1167	536,834

Valuation	£1,955,486

Table 7.2 Performance of comparable and subject at different rental growth rates.

Valuations	Rental 0% p.a.	Growth 3.23% p.a.	Rate 11.74% p.a.
Comparison £736,000	6%	8.8%	15.4%
Conventional valuation £1,146,990	6%	11.5%	21.5%
Required return at 8.8% £1,449,667	3.28%	8.8%	18.7%
Required return at 15.4% £1,955,486	0.21%	5.7%	15.4%

Note: Results are expressed as total returns (IRR) over the life of the investment.

The valuation results show a considerable variation between the two contemporary approaches; but note that both the contemporary solutions are well in excess of the conventional approach. To compare the results, the IRRs of the comparable and the property to be valued are assessed for each solution at different prospective growth rates (Table 7.2).

The results indicate that the valuations are true to their assumptions. The conventional valuation reconciles with the comparison given a nil growth assumption (i.e. the subject property purchased at the conventional valuation and the comparable would both give a total return of 6% p.a. if there were no rental growth over the life of the investment). The two contemporary valuations reconcile with the comparable at the growth rates implied from the relevant target rate assumptions for the freehold.

All the valuations are fraught with problems. They indicate how the assumptions made are vital to producing reasonable results. Valuers are more likely to be accurate if they make an attempt to rationalise the target rate and growth rate choice (and therefore make an assumption on the future behaviour of the cash flow) rather than rely on the capitalisation rate. It is only when nil growth assumptions are valid that the simplistic capitalisation rate analysis has any meaning. The contemporary approaches give some help to the valuer in identifying the individual variations wrapped up in the cash flow; the conventional approach gives no help and actively hides the different attributes. Application to leaseholds show they are a menace, and it is a lasting indictment on the valuation profession in the UK that they are still utilised and still passed on uncritically to the next generation of valuers.

Part Two

7.9.2   *Analysis and valuation using freehold comparables*

All the examples in the first part of this chapter were based on valuations of leasehold interests derived from analyses of freehold transactions. This, the more usual approach to the valuation of leaseholds, highlights the two main problems involved in using the contemporary model.

The first is the subjective choice of target rate necessary when assessing the growth rate implied in the price paid for the freehold. In freehold valuation, this has been shown to be an insignificant problem, but this does not hold for leaseholds.

The second problem is the adjustment of the yield upwards for the additional risk of the leasehold interest. This adjustment was arbitrarily chosen at 6% (moving 9–15%) in the examples.

These two yield adjustments combine to create a situation where the subjective inputs made by the valuer are very significant. An example will illustrate.

Example 7.10

A head-leasehold interest is to be valued. The property comprises a shop that is held from the freeholder on a lease with 20 years unexpired at a fixed rent of £100,000 p.a. The property has just been sub-let for the remainder of the term on a lease with 5-year reviews at the ERV of £200,000. There are no leasehold comparables available but similar freehold properties let on 5-year review patterns sell for rack-rented capitalisation rates of 7%.

The first step in the valuation is the analysis for implied rental growth, which is derived from the choice of the target rate for the freehold. In the analysis of freehold interests in Chapter 6, the target rates used for demonstration were 7% and 15%, a wide variation used to prove the relative insignificance of the target rate choice. A more reasonable variation is taken as 5%, from a risk-free return of, say, 5% up to a required return of 10% incorporating a risk premium of 5%.

The implied rental growth rate is calculated as follows:

$$(1 + g)^t = \frac{\text{YP perp. @ } k\% - \text{YP } t \text{ years @ } r\%}{\text{YP perp. @ } k\% \times \text{PV } t \text{ years @ } r\%}$$

$$(1 + g)^5 = \frac{\text{YP perp. @ 7\% } - \text{YP 5 years @ 10\%}}{\text{YP perp. @ 7\% } \times \text{PV 5 years @ 10\%}}$$

$$(1 + g)^5 = \frac{14.285 - 3.7908}{14.2857 \times 0.6209}$$

$$(1 + g)^5 = \frac{10.4949}{8.8700} = 1.1832$$

$$g = (1.1832)^{1/5} - 1 = 0.034209\% = 3.4209\%$$

If the required return is lowered to 5%, the implied rental growth rate becomes a negative 2.315% p.a. The next stage of the valuation is to determine the required return for the leasehold interest. This choice is also subjective in the hands of the valuer. As a result of the individual nature of leasehold interests, the possible range is large.

For the purposes of the example, we will assume a minimum of no risk adjustment over the freehold interest (a capitalisation rate of 5%) to a 10% risk premium (a capitalisation rate of 15%) over the freehold. The matrix shown in Table 7.3 provides the contemporary solutions to Example 7.10 given this range of assumptions of freehold and leasehold required returns.

The range of valuations at first sight looks high, ranging from just over £500,000 to over £1.8m. However, the most dominant factor in the level of the valuation is the risk premium adjustment from freehold to leasehold. If the same risk premium is adopted, the valuations remain reasonably constant, regardless of the target rate choice in the original freehold analysis. This focuses attention on the choice of risk premium from freehold to leasehold. Are leaseholds more risky than freeholds, and if so, by how much?

Table 7.3 Leasehold valuations based upon ranges of freehold and leasehold required returns.

Leasehold target rates	Freehold target rates used to analyse growth rates	
	5%	**10%**
5%	£936,852	£1,856,373
10%	£684,527	£1,173,563
15%	£530,084	£807,316

Risk will be examined in detail in Chapter 9, but a few observations are warranted in the context of market valuation and pricing. It has already been suggested that the problem with leaseholds is their individuality, caused by the presence of two leases and their unique relationship to each other. A risky valuation is one where the possible variation of inputs into the model causes significant differences in the solution. Our two analyses of the variation caused by the valuer's subjective inputs indicate that the leasehold valuation is more sensitive to these inputs, and therefore it is a more risky form of valuation than valuations of typical freeholds.

The individuality of leasehold interests means that there is more variation in the possible required returns from these investments. For example, a short leasehold interest, held on a fixed rent until expiry, and sub-let on a fixed rent until expiry, is a fixed-income investment based upon the covenant of the sub-tenant and may attract very little risk premium above the gilt market. A highly geared interest, on the other hand, would attract a substantial risk premium, especially if most of the value was based upon future rental growth and the current profit rent is very small. The target rate choice in a leasehold valuation is the single most important factor in the valuation, and at present, this is a subjective, qualitative choice in the hands of the valuer. Once an objective approach to this is achieved, a rational valuation based on market transactions can be produced. Without serious debate, achieving this objectivity in required return will continue to be elusive.

There is no doubt that, over the past 30 years or so, the rapid change in lease structures has led to investment opportunities for alert investors in the leasehold market. Geared cash flows, secured on good covenant tenants and purchased from vendors still advised on the basis of traditional valuation methods, have produced enormous annual returns. Anecdotal evidence of 30% and 40% p.a. total returns achieved over long periods by investors in leaseholds are commonplace. This suggests a serious underestimation of the underlying worth of this asset type over a long period – and valuers have to take the blame for this.

On balance, therefore, explicit-DCF approaches and other contemporary forms of valuation are (with the exception of very simple examples, such as very long leases subject to peppercorn rents) the only models appropriate for valuing leasehold interests. However, for valuers and investors to become more comfortable about this, the target rate choice needs more debate. Even subject to this reservation, it is clear that the adoption of more rational pricing models would lead to more rational price levels in the leasehold investment market.

7.10 Taxation and the market valuation of leaseholds

Leasehold capitalisation rates are typically higher than those used to value freeholds to account for the perceived disadvantages of leasehold investments in comparison with freeholds. One of those disadvantages can be the relative incidence of taxation. In particular, there will be no tax-free capital gain to redemption through asset appreciation as a result of inflation.

Given higher initial yields, more income is produced for a given outlay. This extra income is taxed. Freehold property investments, largely free of capital taxes and providing low-income yields, are generally subject to a low tax incidence. In the leasehold market, on the other hand, high-rate taxpayers have to obtain a much higher return gross-of-tax to compensate for its significant reduction by taxation. It is not surprising, therefore, that high-rate taxpayers do not participate to a great extent in the leasehold investment market (especially the short-leasehold market). This reinforces the view that taxation should not generally be a consideration in leasehold market valuations but, as for freeholds, is a crucial element in an investment appraisal.

However, where it is possible to identify a group of potential purchasers who are subject to a common tax incidence the following approach may be utilised.

Example 7.11

Value the head-leasehold interest in a property held on a lease with 20 years unexpired at a fixed rent of £50,000 p.a. The property has just been sub-let for the remaining 20 years, with 5-year reviews, at the ERV of £200,000 p.a. Assume a target rate of 15%, growth of 6% p.a. and income tax at 40%. The real net yield should not be the net-of-tax real required return (see Chapter 6, Section 6.6).

The gross-of-tax real return is $(1 + r)/(1 + g) - 1 : (1.15)/(1.06) - 1 = 8.4906\%$, which at 40% tax gives a net real return of 5.0943%. The net of tax target rate is therefore the product of the net-of-tax irfy/dcy and the growth rate $(1 + g)$ $(1 + q) - 1$.

Net-of-tax target rate = $(1.06 \times 1.050943) - 1 = 11.40\%$
Net-of-tax irfy approach

Rent received (net of tax)	£120,000 p.a.	
YP 20 years @ 5.0934% × YP 5 years @ 11.4%		
YP 5 years @ 5.0934%	10.4758	
		£1,257,100
Less rent paid	£30,000 p.a.	
YP 20 years at 11.4%	7.7594	
		£232,780
Valuation		£1,024,320

Many valuers might argue that the identification of the tax position of a dominant group of purchasers in a submarket is unlikely and difficult unless the group concerned is gross funds (tax-exempt pension funds and charities). The effect of tax upon market-valuation techniques is therefore debatable, irrespective of whether conventional or contemporary methods are employed.

7.11 Conclusions

The valuer must accept that the valuation of leasehold investments is a much more difficult problem than valuing freeholds. Market pricing is a comparative exercise, the quality of the valuation ultimately rests on the quality of the information, and there is likely to be little high-quality evidence available for leasehold valuations.

Leasehold valuations are usually based on freehold transaction evidence, and our analysis of the conventional model shows that it fails to accurately interpret this evidence. This leads to valuations that have little logical basis and should be wholly abandoned. The alternative contemporary approach is preferable. It enables the valuer to make reasoned qualitative decisions and to translate those decisions into a rational quantitative model.

Part Two

Nonetheless, the valuation is subject to variation dependent upon different possible interpretations of market information. This leads us to suggest an obvious progression in practical valuation, which is acceptance of the fact that the valuation is simply a best estimate around a range of possible estimates, and should begin to be reported as such. If the valuer is unsure about certain inputs into the model, information technology makes the production of a number of solutions a simple affair, and an analysis of the risk implicit within a valuation is an easily obtained by-product.

In the same way that the owner of a picture would not expect the art valuer to precisely predict the selling price at auction, clients can readily accept that the individuality of property causes valuation to be an imprecise science, or at best a more precise art. Valuation reports quoting mean and standard deviations for more sophisticated clients, and ranges for other clients, should become the norm.

There are problems with any departure from single-point estimates. In the UK and elsewhere, valuers have been subjected to negligence claims and the concept of margin of error has been established in some courts since 1977. This concept suggests that, if the valuation is perceived by the courts, upon the advice of expert witnesses, to be outside an acceptable range, then it is negligent. If valuers submit a range within a valuation report, they may feel that they are explicitly drawing attention to the margin of error, on the back of which they might feel a negligence case could be supported. This is unfortunate.

Other problems may be the potential misuse of valuation ranges by clients. Lenders, for example, have a variable track record when it comes to their use of valuations in secured lending decisions and a number of negligence cases have backfired on lenders (Crosby *et al.*, 1998c).

Nonetheless, it is true to say that the market valuation of highly individual property assets like leaseholds is very likely to lead to a possible range of values, dependent on the subjective risk premium choice. It is impossible, then, to deny that this produces a halfway house between the desired objective pricing process and the subjective assessment of investment value/worth. The two processes are likely to become less and less separate as property assets become more unique and as pricing models become more rational. But progress is slow.

Part Three
Investment Value and Worth

Chapter 8
Property Investment Value: the Assessment of Worth

8.1   Introduction: a model for analysis

Assessing property investment value or worth was explained in Chapter 1 as an exercise differentiated from pricing or market valuation by its subjectivity. Property investment appraisal in the form of a cash-flow model was introduced in Chapter 3, in which we suggested that the same discounted-cash-flow (DCF) model could be used both for market valuation and for investment value/worth calculations.

This chapter concentrates on the use of cash-flow models for the estimation of investment value/worth to an investor. For our purposes, the investor is likely to be an institutional fund or a property company.

Investment value/worth may be expressed in three forms. Where the price of an investment is known, for example in a retrospective analysis after a sale, or where negotiations for a purchase by private treaty have neared completion, then the worth of the investment must be expressed either as a rate of return or as an excess value over the price (net present value – NPV) at a given target rate (Chapter 2). Where the price is unknown, for example, where an investment is to be sold by auction, the analysis is aimed at an assessment of the capital value of the investment, or the maximum price that can be paid, given a target rate of return.

We utilise a single model for all such appraisals. Such a model may be more explicit than that used in market valuation (Baum, 1984b), because it is no longer necessary to generalise. For example, the tax implications of an investment purchase to a particular investor may be ascertained, while net-of-tax appraisals in market valuation are usually avoided because a market tax rate cannot be generalised. In fact, the model should be absolutely explicit so that the assumptions upon which the NPV or internal rate of return (IRR) are predicated are exposed.

In order to be accurate, the rate of return needs to be an overall rate of return based upon an explicit projection of the cash flow likely to be produced by the investment. This rate of return has appeared throughout this book as the IRR, the required return, target rate or the redemption yield.

We need to be careful to stress, however, that we are aiming at analyses of net returns, that is, returns remaining after all expenses have been stripped away. This is not always the case when terms of overall return are used: for example, redemption yield as used by the *Financial Times* for the analysis of gilts is gross-of-tax and gross-of-transaction costs. Consequently, given that the purpose of property investment analysis is to facilitate investment comparison, and therefore decision making, the analyst must be careful to adjust such measures to the same, absolutely net, terms in pursuit of accurate comparisons.

We do not, however, base our analysis upon the estimation of real returns, that is, returns remaining after the effects of inflation have been stripped away. We recognise that real return analysis (to produce real-return estimates or to estimate capital value given a target real return) is increasingly desirable and possible since the introduction of index-linked gilts and given the practices of several investment management companies. However, for reasons we have already stated in Part One, the focus of this book is upon nominal returns. See also Hoesli and MacGregor (2000).

In the near future this may have to be reconsidered. In pursuit of this, the models presented in this chapter and throughout this book are immediately adaptable to real return analysis, and the analyst can amend the outlines presented herein accordingly.

Property investment appraisal has been particularly aided by the popularisation of spreadsheets and our own work has developed in this way. Consequently, our model has taken shape as an explicit cash-flow projection in nominal terms and in spreadsheet (row and column) format.

The goal of property investment value/worth calculations is an analysis of risk against return. The basic model is exactly as presented in Chapter 3, but the inputs are now subjective.

8.2 Risk/return analysis

8.2.1 Introduction

The focus of this chapter is the analysis of property investment opportunities by means of DCF techniques. While several markets throughout the world exhibit a reluctance to abandon initial-yield-based analysis, consumer-led and computer-aided improvements in service have produced, and continue to produce, widespread refinements in DCF methods. Investors now expect a present value or IRR analysis based upon income and expense projections. This is a first and base level of analysis. Analysts are, as a result, increasingly forced to use market analysis to predict the uncertain or, as stated in the introduction to this chapter, to make an explicit projection of the cash flow likely to be produced by the investment.

This element of uncertainty demands another level of decision-aiding analysis. However, risk analysis, well explored in financial theory, has not yet been the subject of adequate examination in the real estate sector, and empirical tests of real estate risk have not yet been developed to a point that enables risk/return analysis to be widely practised in property markets. There is an absence of reported data regarding the riskiness of individual real estate investments, both in terms of quantum and source.

In addition, the recognition of portfolio risk, spurred by dominance of the real estate market by institutional investors in the UK and by a similar increasing influence in the US, has produced applications of the capital asset pricing model (CAPM) to real estate investment in recent years. The intellectual appeal of CAPM coupled with a well-documented burst of real estate buying by UK institutions aiming towards real estate/fixed-interest security/equity diversification has established risk/return analysis at the portfolio level as the subject of much research interest in the developed property markets of the UK, North America and Australasia.

The intention in this section is to link these levels of decision aids in a logical manner and to establish the interdependence of the underlying techniques. Each succeeding level of analysis subsumes the previous level; deficiencies at any level are therefore compounded. It is important, therefore, to identify both theoretical and practical problems in the application of each level of analysis before proceeding to the next.

All levels of decision technology for real estate investment discussed herein are based on DCF analysis and utilise a return measure. Estimation of return may be by NPV or IRR (see, for example, Geltner *et al.*, 2007). These alternatives, introduced in Chapters 2 and 3, are assessed briefly in the following section.

8.2.2   NPV or IRR?

It appears clear that in the general finance area the debate concerning a theoretical preference for NPV or IRR has been well settled in favour of the former. Brigham and Ehrhardt (2005) are positive enough:

> the NPV method exhibits all the desired decision rule properties and, as such, it is the best method for evaluating projects. Because the NPV method is better than IRR we were tempted to explain NPV only, state that it should be used as the accepted criterion, and go on to the next topic.

Brigham and Ehrhardt's only reason for not doing so is the continued use of IRR in the market. This preference for NPV is dependent, of course, upon the 'desired decision rule properties', which are in essence aimed towards maximisation of shareholder wealth. In real estate terms, this translates simply to maximisation of present asset values, the normal aim of a limited-resource investor.

Part Three

Greer *et al.* (1996) therefore express surprise that in real estate literature IRR continues to find favour:

> While the internal rate of return has little substantive advantage over alternative methods of applying discount rates to projected cash flows, it does have serious weaknesses not found in the alternatives. Persistent support of a favoured technique might be admirable were there no substitutes that possess equal power to discriminate between acceptable and unacceptable opportunities. Such is not the case, however, with the IRR approach. Its continued advocacy is therefore somewhat curious.

IRR continues to find favour because it is simpler to use and because it produces a result that is directly comparable with returns reported on indexes and benchmarks. The intuitive appeal of return expressed in a single-point return measure, with no requirement upon the analyst to assess a target or hurdle rate, is obvious. Nonetheless, Jaffe (as long ago as 1977) considered that IRR remained popular in real estate simply because real estate research and debate lag behind general financial literature. Thirty years later, we can argue that this is an open question.

It is clear that IRR is flawed where reinvestment of returns is likely. Given that IRR incorporates a risk premium (see the following text), the implicit assumption where reinvestment is likely that cash flows of any amount can be reinvested to earn the same rate is unrealistic. Modified IRR and Financial Management Rate of Return techniques (see, for example, Robinson, 1986; Newell, 1986) were proposed as intended solutions of this IRR defect; but as the appeal of the accepted technique is simplicity, such modifications have been found to be superfluous. The prospect of multiple IRR solutions with cash-flow sign changes such as are typical in a real estate investment (which may require refurbishment or repair or fall vacant at any time) is a further restriction.

Comparison of mutually exclusive projects requiring different initial outlays is more logically dealt with by NPV; in this situation incremental analysis (see Baum *et al*, 2006) is another example of a superfluous theoretical advance designed to enable IRR to produce the same result as NPV. In conclusion, NPV is clearly preferable as a decision aid, but IRR has attractions for practitioners.

Both NPV and IRR will be utilised in the following discussion of risk/return analysis, which will be based around the following example.

Example 8.1

The property investment analyst has been appointed advisor to a tax-exempt investment fund that has to make a choice between two alternative property investments which it has been offered. Investment A is a leasehold shop; Investment B is a small freehold office building. Each is for sale at £1,300,000, and the following information is available.

Investment A
The property comprises a single shop unit that is arranged on three floors with a total net floor area of 2,875 ft^2. The current leaseholder holds the property on a net lease for a

term of 35 years expiring 5 years after the purchase is likely to be completed, at a fixed rent of £22,500 p.a. The entire property is let on a net lease to the current occupier for a term expiring 2 days before the head lease at a rent of £450,000 p.a., subject to a review to open-market rent 2 years before the lease expires. The current open-market rental value is £525,000 (net) p.a. Acquisition fees are estimated at 3% of purchase price. Rent review fees are estimated at 7.5% of the revised rent. Management costs are 10% of rent collected p.a. Rents are currently growing in this part of the UK at 5% p.a. and little change is expected in the short term.

Investment B
The property is a small freehold office building with a total area of 3,000 ft^2, let with 5 years (at the likely completion date) of the current lease to run. Last year's rent was £200,000 and around 30% of this rent was lost in outgoings, including management fees. Acquisition and sale fees are estimated at 5% of price. Rents are annually review-able in line with RPI (the retail price index). Current capitalisation rates are between 10% and 12%.

General
RPI increased by 3.5% last year. British government fixed-interest securities, medium-dated, currently yield around 11% if held to maturity. Rents from each property can be assumed to be received annually in arrear. All fees can be regarded as reliable cost estimates.
    A basic NPV/IRR analysis of each transaction might be presented as follows:

Investment A

Current rent received	£ 450,000 p.a.
Head rent paid	£ 22,500 p.a.
Remainder of lease	5 years
Term of review	3 years
Acquisition fees	3%
Rent review fees	7.5%
Management costs	10%
Price	£1,300,000
Target rate	11%
Rental value	£ 525,000 p.a.
Rental growth	5% p.a.

Appraisal

End of year	Rent in (£)	Rent out (£)	Review fees (£)	Management fees (£)	Outlay (£)	Acquisition fees (£)	Net cash (£)
0	0	0	0	0	1,300,000	39,000	(1,339,000)
1	450,000	22,500	0	45,000	0	0	382,500
2	450,000	22,500	0	45,000	0	0	382,500
3	450,000	22,500	45,580	45,000	0	0	336,920
4	607,750	22,500	0	60,775	0	0	524,475
5	607,750	22,500	0	60,775	0	0	524,475
						NPV	£219,130
						IRR (%)	16.9029

Example 8.1   *(Continued)*

Investment B

Current rent received	£200,000
Term to review	1 year
Sale fees	5%
Acquisition fees	5%
Rent review fees	0.00
Management costs, etc.	30%
Price	£1,300,000
Target rate	11%
RPI growth	3.5% p.a.
Resale cap rate	11 % p.a.

Appraisal

End of year	Rent in (£)	Resale (£)	Management fees (£)	Outlay (£)	Acquisition/ sale fees (£)	Net cash (£)
0	0		0	1,300,000	65,000	(1,365,000)
1	207,000		62,100	0	0	144,900
2	214,250		64,275	0	0	149,975
3	221,740		66,522	0	0	155,218
4	229,500		68,850	0	0	160,650
5	237,540	2,159,430	71,260	0	107,970	2,217,730
					NPV	£422,700
					IRR	18.2503%

The results, employing the data and variables as listed, show Investment B to be preferable to Investment A by both NPV and IRR criteria. (It should be noted that NPV and IRR will not always indicate the same decision, referring us back to the conclusion that, when in doubt, NPV should always be followed.)

However, this fails to take account of the risks of these investments. In Chapter 2 risk was defined as 'uncertainty regarding the expected rate of return from an investment'. In this case, each investment suffers from two major uncertainties. For Investment A, these are the estimated current rental value and the anticipated rate of rental growth. For Investment B, they are the resale capitalisation rate and the rate of change in the RPI. The remainder of this chapter is devoted to methods of dealing with these uncertainties.

8.2.3   Sensitivity analysis

Sensitivity analysis was developed as a means of identifying the independent variable which causes the greatest change in the dependent variable. Many other simple explorations of risk are made possible by this technique.

The values of the two uncertain (risky) variables in Investments A and B may not turn out to be as expected and shown in the preceding basic analysis. Given this, it will be useful to know what the effect of likely changes will be upon return. Sensitivity analysis can be used to explore the question: 'what if?'

Let us assume that a reasonable margin of error in each case is determined to be plus or minus 20%. What is the effect of a 20% change in each, and then both, variables?

	NPV (£)	IRR (%)
Investment A		
Rental value		
+20%	349,450	19.86
−20%	88,820	13.56
Rental growth		
+20%	237,930	17.35
−20%	200,690	16.4
Both variables		
+20%	372,000	20.34
−20%	74,060	13.16

Every outcome indicates that the investment is worthwhile at a target rate of 11%.

	NPV (£)	IRR (%)
Investment B		
Resale capitalisation rate		
−20%	727,060	22.48
+20%	219,790	15.02
RPI growth		
+20%	475,560	19.05
−20%	371,150	17.45
Resale capitalisation rate −20% / RPI growth −20%	790,350	23.31
Resale capitalisation rate +20% / RPI growth −20%	175,010	14.24

Again, every outcome indicates that the investment is worthwhile at a target rate of 11%. The worst outcome is better than the worst outcome in A, and the best is also better than the best outcome in A. It continues to appear to be the better buy.

However, this rudimentary form of sensitivity analysis has failed to consider whether a 20% increase or reduction in each variable is equally likely. Let us assume that market research shows that this is patently not the case here. While rental growth variation in the south of England may show a 20% variation from the expected, the estimated market rental may only vary from the expected by up to 5%. On the other hand, RPI changes may vary by 30% from the expected, and a thin market means that the resale capitalisation rate could lie anywhere between 8% and 14%. Revised figures on these more realistic estimates are as follows:

	NPV (£)	IRR (%)
Investment A		
Rental value		
+5%	251,710	17.674
−5%	186,550	16.108
Rental growth		
+20%	237,930	17.351
−20%	200,690	16.456
Best outcome	271,450	18.131
Worst outcome	169,040	15.670

	NPV (£)	IRR (%)
Investment B		
Resale capitalisation rate		
8%	879,240	24.373
14%	161,820	14.018
RPI growth		
+30%	502,490	19.450
−30%	345,850	17.051
Best outcome	982,660	25.630
Worst outcome	97,940	12.861

This more realistic form of sensitivity analysis leaves Investment B as the better choice, but begins to raise questions. The worst outcome of A is now better than the worst outcome of B, which now complicates the decision somewhat. If the target rate were to increase to 13%, the implications are more vital: with some outcomes, Investment B should not be undertaken, while at all outcomes Investment A remains viable. Given this information, some investors would choose A, as they would not be prepared to face the slightest prospect of a loss.

Sensitivity analysis therefore allows a more informed decision to be made. It does, however, fail to address a vital point. What are the chances of the possible variations becoming fact? It may be, for example, that there is only the slightest of chances that RPI growth will be more than 20% in excess of the expected, whereas it is almost impossible to estimate a likely resale capitalisation rate due to a paucity of market evidence. This will surely qualify the preceding analysis. What is now implied is an element of qualitative or subjective judgement. The best outcome in A is less profitable than the best outcome in B, but the latter may be much less likely than the former. This element of risk must be taken into account in a full analysis. It is not enough to say what could happen; it is necessary to qualify such hypotheses by probabilities, and to some extent the next set of techniques – and certainly the mean–variance criterion (see Section 8.2.5) – attempt to do this, leaving sensitivity analysis behind as a somewhat rudimentary (albeit objective) risk analysis technique.

8.2.4   Risk adjustment techniques

Both the potential variation and the chances of variation in the outcome from the expected must be taken into account in a full risk/return analysis. Yet the decision maker will demand as clear a recommendation as possible. Risk adjustment techniques satisfy these demands. Unfortunately, they leave rather large questions unanswered en route. Nonetheless, they are widely practised, both consciously and unconsciously, in both wider investment markets and in real estate.

Three manifestations of risk-adjusted technique will be considered here. They are risk-adjusted discount rates, the certainty-equivalent technique and a hybrid of these, suitable for UK property investment analysis, termed here the sliced-income method.

Risk-adjusted discount rate

Whether by NPV or IRR, the estimation of a single-point return estimate has to cope with varying risks (defined here as variance of possible returns) between alternatives. Choosing on the basis of IRRs alone where risks differ presumes indifference to risk, which undermines a whole stream of accepted finance wisdom (Chapter 2). Given that most investors are risk-averse to a degree, a choice on the basis of IRR involves a risk adjustment.

The adjustment may be to discount rate or to income. The use of the risk-adjusted discount rate is in accord with Fisher's work, as presented in Chapter 2. The interest (or discount) rate r can be constructed from the function $[(1 + l)\ (1 + i)\ (1 + rp) - 1]$, where l represents a return for time preference, i represents a return for expected inflation and rp represents a return for risk. The risk-free rate (RFR), 11% in the sensitivity example, is a function of l and i: $(1 + l)(1 + i) - 1$, so $r = (1 - RFR)(1 + rp) - 1$. This is the risk-adjusted discount rate. The greater the amount of perceived risk, the higher is r.

Note that this is not the way the risk-adjusted discount rate (RADR) is normally constructed in practice. Instead, the RADR is usually found by $RFR + r$. The difference is usually small, and can be shown to be unimportant when the choice of r is non-scientific. For example, suppose $RFR = 0.11$ and $r = 0.05$. $(1 + RFR)(1 + r) - 1 = 16.55\%$; $RFR + r = 16\%$.

The use of RADR implies that more return is required to compensate for greater risk. How much more is impossible to determine objectively: this depends upon the risk–return indifference curve of the investor, a subjective matter. Figure 8.1 illustrates this concept. Most investors – and the market, in accepted finance theory – show behaviour that is risk-averse, where an increase in risk would lead to an increase in required return. In the case of A, the proportionate increase in measured return would exceed the proportionate increase in risk; A is therefore risk-averse.

So solidly entrenched in financial theory is the acceptance of risk aversion that Investor B, who requires more return in exact proportion to the increase in risk, is called in some texts (see, for example, Gitman, 2006) risk-indifferent! This leaves us in some confusion concerning the position of C, typically termed risk-seeking, yet still requiring more return for some more risk. In fact all three are risk-averse.

The subjectivity of the risk–return trade-off makes it difficult for the analyst to rank investments that are subject to risk by IRR alone [while the CAPM can be used to avoid this problem, its application to real estate is in question (see Chapter 2, Section 2.3)]. By practice the analyst may be able to build up helpful experience, but marginal cases will always devalue the reliability of advice. If, on the other hand, NPV techniques, which are to be preferred, are relied upon, what then? The risk adjustment has necessarily to be made to

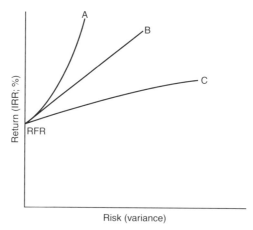

Figure 8.1   Risk/return indifference curves.

the target or hurdle rate. The problem of quantum adjustment to account for risk is exactly the same as for IRR. Hence, the use of RADR in this first level of analysis is subject to charges of subjectivity in discount rate choice.

Nonetheless, Investment B was shown by sensitivity analysis to be riskier than Investment A. Even without the advantage of such an analysis – which does not, it should be remembered, make a decision – the experienced investor or analyst should be capable of discerning such differences and, hence, make reasonable adjustments to the RFR to produce different RADRs.

Assume 12.5% is chosen for A and 17.5% is chosen for B. The results are

Investment A

	NPV	£158,330
	IRR	16.903%

Investment B

	NPV	£37,100
	IRR	18.250%

Note that, on the basis of NPV, A becomes preferable. On the basis of IRR too, A produces a greater yield margin over the target rate. Yet, if RADRs of 12.5% and 15% respectively are used, the results are

Investment A

	NPV	£158,330
	IRR	16.903%

Investment B

	NPV	£170,920
	IRR	18.250%

Now, on the NPV criterion, B should be bought. This brings to light the major problem with the RADR method. There may be no objective criteria for the determination of the RADR, and relatively slight changes may reverse a decision.

Additionally, the use of the RADR implies an increasing discount applied to future returns, and therefore that cash flows become riskier the longer the investor has to wait to receive them. The inappropriateness of such a by-product of the technique is demonstrated by the pre-let development project not subject to a fixed-price building contract. The riskier cash flows are in the earlier, and not the later, years.

Finally, risk premiums have to be determined individually for each project. No two property investments are alike: risk is a complex function of gross incomes, operating expenses and capital returns.

Consequently, RADR is difficult to use reliably in practice. It continues to be used because of its simplicity and ease of application. In property investment analysis the following method, certainty equivalent cash flows, is hardly used at all, but is probably superior.

Part Three

Certainty-equivalent cash flows

Avoiding the subjective adjustment of the discount rate implies facing the adjustment of the income stream. The second vital input into real estate investment appraisal is the projected income flow, a function of a complex relationship of gross rental, operating expenses, financing arrangements, taxation and capital return, all of which are subject to potential variance and hence risk.

The certainty-equivalent technique utilises the concept of risk aversion by theorising a single-point income level that the investor would trade for the variable cash flows actually in prospect. In relation to the expected (average) income flow utilised in risk-adjusted discounting, the certainty-equivalent income flow for a risk-averse investor will be lower. Because risk–return indifference is unique to the investor, the certainty-equivalent cash flow is best determined in a process of dialogue between analyst and investor.

The selection of the certainty-equivalent cash flow by way of the certainty-equivalent inputs (rental growth, initial rental value, resale capitalisation rate and others) is, nonetheless, not ideally performed in this manner as the investor may, avite reasonably, suggest that the onus of analysis should fall not upon the investor but upon the analyst. An objective, analyst-performed selection of a certainty-equivalent income may be produced by use of the CAPM (Brealey *et al.*, 2005); we prefer a simpler route, utilising standard deviation (SD) analysis.

Our use of the SD is designed to replace the best estimate of the cash flows by a certainty-equivalent cash flow of which there is approximately an 84% chance of bettering and only a 16% chance of failing to achieve. Assuming a normal distribution of possible cash flows, 1 SD on either side of the expected (best estimate) cash flow includes 68% of all possible outcomes. The remaining 32% includes 16% that lies below the expected cash flow less 1 SD, and 16% that lies above the expected cash flow plus 1 SD. Consequently, the use of the expected cash flow less 1 SD as the certainty equivalent results in the 84:16 chance of bettering it, thus reflecting a generous (but objectively determined in all cases) degree of risk aversion on behalf of the investor.

In the example, each investment has two variables. Assume that the potential outcomes and associated probabilities for each variable are represented by the following samples from a continuous distribution:

Investment A			
Rental value	£498,750	£525,000	£551,250
Probability	0.2	0.6	0.2
Rental growth	0.04	0.05	0.06
Probability	0.3	0.4	0.3

Investment B			
RPI growth	0.0245	0.035	0.0455
Probability	0.333	0.334	0.333
Resale capitalisation rate	0.08	0.11	0.14
Probability	0.3	0.4	0.3

Calculation of the SD is performed as follows. (This calculation assumes, incorrectly, that the observations are derived from a finite population. See Section 8.2.7 for a discussion of this problem.)

a. Calculate the expected value
   expected value $(\bar{r}) = \Sigma(p \times \hat{r})$

b. Calculate the variance
   variance $(\sigma^2) = \Sigma p(\hat{r} \times \bar{r})^2$

c. Calculate the standard deviation
   SD (population) $= \sqrt{\sigma^2}$

	Expected value	Variance	SD
Investment A			
Rental value	£525,000	£27,562,500	£16,601
Rental growth	0.05	0.00006	0.007745

	Expected value	Variance	SD
Investment B			
RPI growth	0.035	0.000073	0.008568
Resale capitalisation rate	0.11	0.000540	0.023237

We can now calculate the certainty equivalents for these variables.

	Expected value	SD	CE (rounded)
Investment A			
Rental value	£525,000	£16,601	£508,400
Rental growth	0.05	0.007745	0.04225

	Expected	Variance	SD
Investment B			
RPI growth	0.035	0.008568	0.02643
Resale capitalisation rate	0.110	0.023237	0.13324

These values can now be fed back into the analysis model using the risk-free target rate of 11% (remember that the investments are now effectively risk-free: the values of the variables chosen represent certainty, or risk-free, equivalents of their expected values). The results are as follows:

	NPV	IRR
Investment A	£184,670	16.061%
Investment B	£156,060	13.907%

This produces the same decision as the RADR (NPV) method at RADRs of 12.5% and 17.5%, respectively, and suggests that the safer investment, A, should be purchased.

This interpretation of the certainty-equivalent technique has the apparent advantage over RADR of objectivity. While using SDs to compute certainty equivalents of the variables ignores the investor's risk–return indifference function, and is only therefore of use where it is not possible to establish it, this is a major theoretical deficiency that is of little practical importance. The investor's risk–return indifference is extremely difficult to measure. Moreover, the choice of certainty equivalent need not be given by the expected value: ±1 SD any proportion or multiple of 1 SD can be used instead to reflect the investor's risk aversion. Consequently, we favour the use of this technique alongside risk-adjusted discount rates, and suggest it as a more practicable means of general risk analysis.

The sliced-income approach

While the certainty-equivalent technique may represent an improvement over RADRs, particularly when the standardisation allowed by use of SDs is incorporated, the technique lends itself to further rational development in the special case of property investment analysis in the UK and other markets with rents fixed under leases. By combining risk-adjustment and certainty-equivalent methods a 'sliced' view of a property investment can be moulded for use where property investment cash flows lend themselves to differential treatment. (This technique was first published in the first (1988) edition of this text and its basic principles have since been adopted in other approaches such as the arbitrage pricing method, illustrated in Chapter 5.)

Such cases exist wherever a minimum rental is guaranteed (certain) and an extra rental is possible (risky). Examples are (in the US) contractually pre-determined level or stepped rents in shopping malls with extra percentage rents paid subject to retail turnover performance, or (in the UK) property let, as it typically is, subject to 5-yearly rent reviews that are upward only. In effect, a minimum rent equal to the previous contract rent is (ignoring default risk) guaranteed; any overage is a bonus.

The guaranteed income (assuming a quality tenant) should be discounted at (close to) a risk-free rate, in accordance with its certain nature. The overage, or possible bonus, is then calculated by comparing the expected – most likely – income stream (calculated exactly as per RADR techniques) with the certain income and producing a top-slice income, which, owing to its leveraged nature, is extremely sensitive to changes in variables (rental value, rental growth, operating expenses and so on) and is therefore highly risky. Commensurate with this, it is discounted at a highly risk-adjusted rate.

This technique is best illustrated by Investment A. Upward-only rent reviews in the sub-lease will guarantee a rent on reversion equal to the current rent paid by the sub-tenant. This is therefore risk-free.

The certain income is calculated in this example as the cash flow that would be received if the upward-only rent review in year 3 resulted in the same rent being paid. The overage is the difference between this and the expected rent based on the expected values of the two variables of estimated rental value (ERV) and rental growth. The resulting certain income is discounted at the RFR of 11%.

The overage is more risky than the expected income flow. Consequently, where 12.5% was the overall RADR previously used to produce an NPV of £158,330, a higher rate (15% in this example) should be used in the valuation of the overage rent. A total NPV of £142,670 is produced: no IRR can be calculated, as there are two separate cash flows and only one outlay. The result is close to those produced for Investment A by both RADR and CE techniques.

The sliced-income method is inappropriate for Investment B, which is best analysed using CE techniques. The conclusion from these analyses is best based on the preferred NPV technique. Using the sliced-income technique, Investment A produces an NPV of £142,660. Using the certainty-equivalent technique, Investment B produces an NPV of £156,060. The decision is a marginal one.

Ideally, all three first level techniques should produce similar results. This cannot, however, be guaranteed. It will only happen if the subjectivity of the risk-adjusted rates in risk-adjusted discount rate and sliced income analysis coincide in effect with the arbitrariness of the certainty-equivalent income. It is the subjective and arbitrary nature of these techniques that harbours a wealth of criticism.

The major criticism of all techniques that incorporate RADRs, that is, that future returns are increasingly heavily penalised without consistent justification, remains. This first level of analysis, however applied, has the merit of producing a single comparative decision aid: purchase if NPV is positive; where investments are mutually exclusive, purchase the investment with the higher NPV. This is a criticism as well as a merit. The decision maker may not appreciate the analyst's roughshod disregard of his individual risk–return indifference. He or she may therefore prefer separate measures of risk and return, and to base his or her decision on these two results, rather than upon the single NPV measure.

Part Three

Part Three

Appraisal: Investment A, sliced income

End of year	Rent in (£)	Rent out (£)	Review fees (£)	Management fees (£)	Outlay (£)	Acquisition fees (£)	Net cash (£)	Certain (£)	Overage (£)
0	0	0	0	0	1,300,000	39,000	−1,339,000		
1	450,000	22,500	0	45,000	0	0	382,500	382,500	0
2	450,000	22,500	0	45,000	0	0	382,500	382,500	0
3	450,000	22,500	45,580	45,000	0	0	336,920	336,920	0
4	607,750	22,500	0	60,775	0	0	524,475	382,500	141,975
5	607,750	22,500	0	60,775	0	0	524,475	382,500	141,975

PV: £1,329,900   PV: £151,760

Total NPV: £142,660

8.2.5   The mean–variance criterion

The subjectivity of the risk–return indifference function for the investor may render an objective decision-aiding analytical technique dangerous in the hands of the analyst. Risk adjustment techniques encourage the analyst to presume to replace the subjective function by objective experience, but the sophisticated investor may not be satisfied with this. For example, utility (Byrne, 1996) may affect his position. This is largely ignored in this analysis, but further reference to the point should be made by the serious reader. The analyst may wish to judge the merits of two alternative investments against each other by comparing their expected return and their risk in combination, represented graphically as follows. Assume Investment A is low risk, low return, and Investment B is high risk, high return (see Figure 8.2).

Some investors will prefer A while others will prefer B. This will depend on their risk aversion, as represented by risk–return indifference curves (Chapter 2). Suppose investor Z is highly risk-averse, while Y is not risk averse (see Figure 8.3). (It is assumed that all investors will accept the RFR for a risk-free investment.)

Investor Z would buy Investment A, because the expected return is more than enough to compensate for the risk involved. He would not, however, buy B. Investor Y, on the other hand, would probably prefer B to A because the margin of return over the minimum required is higher. If, however, Investment B were riskier than A but produced less return, then any investor would choose A (see Figure 8.4).

This leads directly to the mean–variance criterion. This is a decision rule, which states the following:

Purchase Investment A if, and only if,

the return on A > return on B
and the risk of A ≤ risk of B.

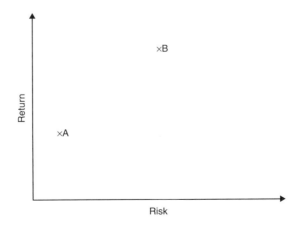

Figure 8.2   The two investment case: 1.

Part Three

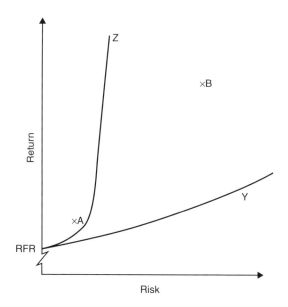

Figure 8.3   The two investment case: 2.

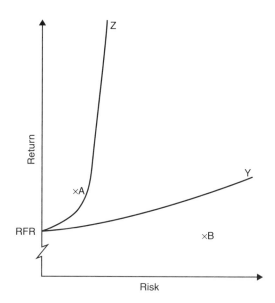

Figure 8.4   The two investment case: 3.

This applies to all risk-averse investors (thought to be the vast majority) and is therefore an objective decision rule, regardless of the risk–return indifference of the investor.

We have already concluded that return may be measured in two ways: NPV or IRR. The rule might therefore be:

Purchase investment A if, and only if,

IRR A > IRR B or   NPV A >   NPV B
                    at RFR   at RFR
and   the risk of A ≤ the risk of B

Given that risk is separately measured, it follows that the NPV must be at the RFR. But how is risk to be measured? It has already been shown that standard deviation (σ or SD) offers a quantitative risk measurement device. It has been applied to variables; but now it must be applied to the return. What is the potential variability of the return from the expected return?

The following discussion continues the unrealistic presumption made to date that the observed values of the variables are part of a discrete, and not continuous, distribution. (This understates risk, and SD, but may not be misleading in a comparison of similar investments.) Given this, there are nine potential IRRs from Investment A. These are as follows (probabilities in parentheses):

	Rental growth		
Rental value	4% (0.3)	5% (0.4)	6% (0.3)
498,750 (0.2)	15.670% (0.06)	16.108% (0.08)	16.547% (0.06)
525,000 (0.6)	16.456% (0.18)	16.903% (0.24)	17.351% (0.18)
551,250 (0.2)	17.219% (0.06)	17.674% (0.08)	18.131% (0.06)

The expected (weighted average) return is given by $\Sigma\,(p \times r)$, which in this case is 16.898%. (Note the difference between this and the result of the most likely rental value in combination with the most likely rental growth, 16.903%. These are not the same.) The SD of these returns is 0.605%.

For NPV, the appropriate figures are as follows:

	Rental growth		
Rental value	4% (0.3)	5% (0.4)	6% (0.3)
498,750 (0.2)	169,040 (0.16)	186,550 (0.08)	204,410 (0.06)
525,000 (0.6)	200,690 (0.18)	219,130 (0.24)	237,930 (0.18)
551,250 (0.2)	232,350 (0.06)	251,710 (0.08)	271,450 (0.06)

$\bar{r} = \Sigma(p \times \bar{r}) = £219,241$; $\sigma = £25,160$. The SD of NPVs is the same as that of total values of the nine possible cash flows. Again, the most likely NPV (£219,130 is not exactly the same as the weighted average (£219,241).

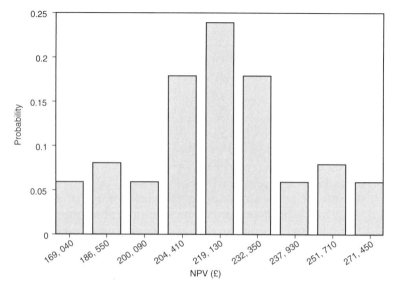

Figure 8.5   Distribution of NPVs.

This computation was relatively straightforward. The assumption of a discrete distribution of cash flows in place of the more probable continuous distribution has cut down the number of possible cash flows from infinite to nine (Figure 8.5). In addition, perfect serial correlation of cash flows in years 3, 4 and 5 simplifies the exercise. The combination of a particular rental growth and a particular rental value (nine in all) predicts the cash flows in each of these years, as it determines the rent review fee to be deducted in year 3 and the level rents received in years 4 and 5. If this were not so the number of possible cash flows would have been 729.

The degree of simplification employed is illustrated by Investment B. There is no serial correlation between cash flows. Even assuming three discrete RPI growth figures – unrealistic, of course – the number of potential cash flows is $3 \times 3 \times 3 \times 3 \times 3$: combining the effect of three discrete resale capitalisation rates produces a total number of possible cash flows of (again, by coincidence) 729. Even a spreadsheet user will take some time to produce estimates of SDs and expected IRR and NPV when the assumption of a discrete distribution is relaxed, and this number approaches infinity.

So, for illustration purposes only, and to aid the completion of the mean–variance analysis, Investment B will be analysed making these two simplifying assumptions:

a.   Cash flows are perfectly serially correlated from year to year. For example, 3% RPI growth in year one pre-determines 3% RPI growth for each year from 1 to 5. This overstates the risk of the investment.

b. The values of variables form a discrete distribution. This slightly understates the risk of the investment.

IRRs Analysis: Investment B

	Resale capitalisation rate		
	0.08	0.11	0.14
IRRs			
0.0245	23.111% (0.06)	17.051% (0.08)	12.861% (0.06)
0.035	24.373% (0.18)	18.250% (0.24)	14.018% (0.18)
0.0455	25.635% (0.06)	19.450% (0.08)	15.175% (0.06)

$\bar{r} = \Sigma(p \times \bar{r}) = 18.817\%; \sigma = 4.109\%$

	NPVs resale capitalisation rate		
	0.08	0.11	0.14
RPI growth			
0.0245	779,700 (0.06)	345,850 (0.08)	97,940 (0.06)
0.035	879,240 (0.18)	422,700 (0.24)	161,820 (0.18)
0.0455	982,660 (0.06)	502,490 (0.08)	228,100 (0.06)

$\bar{r} = \Sigma(p \times \bar{r}) = £482,010; \sigma = £286,870$

Comparative results

	IRR		NPV	
	Expected	SD	Expected	SD
Investment A	16.898%	0.605%	£219,240	£25,160
Investment B	18.817%	4.109%	£482,010	£286,870

The expected return of A is less than that of B: but the risks of B are higher than those of A. This means that a decision using the mean–variance criterion is impossible, and we are referred back to the risk–return indifference of the investor. Risk-averse investor would choose A; while a less risk-averse investor may choose B.

A problem to be tackled in many cases is the difference in size of investments. These are identical. But what if A cost £1,300,000 while B cost £2,200,000? While the return measures may be capable of direct comparison (NPV is preferable in such a case, Brigham and Ehrhardt, 2005), the SD of returns from a large project would inevitably be higher than the SD of returns from a small project of identical risk. Consequently standardisation is necessary and is achieved by using the coefficient of variation, a measure of risk relative to the size of the project. This could be:

$$\frac{\text{SD of PVs}}{\text{Expected PV}} \quad \text{or} \quad \frac{\text{PV}}{\text{PV}}$$

For Investment A, in the preceding analysis,

this is $\qquad \dfrac{£25,160}{£1,558,240} = 0.01615$

For Investment B, it is $\qquad \dfrac{£286,870}{£1,651,870} = 0.17366$

The conclusion to be drawn from these figures is that B is over 10 times riskier per unit of investment size than A.

8.2.6   The coefficient of IRR/NPV variation

Another interpretation of the coefficient of variation proposed by Reilly and Brown (2002) and Brigham and Ehrhardt (2005) has more immediate appeal and more general an application in decision making. The mean–variance criterion will not provide a decision where the project of higher risk produces a higher return: yet this is to be expected in a competitive market for investments. An objective measure of risk per unit of return may be useful for the investor, or analyst, without a clear picture of subjective risk–return indifference.

Either NPV or IRR might be used in a coefficient of variation for measuring risk against return. The IRR version is calculated as follows:

$$\frac{\text{SD of IRR}}{\text{Expected IRR}} \quad \text{or} \quad \frac{\sigma\,\text{IRR}}{\text{IRR}}$$

For Investment A, this is $\qquad \dfrac{0.0605\%}{16.898\%} = 0.03580\%$

For Investment B, it is $\qquad \dfrac{4.109\%}{18.817\%} = 0.21837\%$

It shows that Investment B is much riskier (around six times) than Investment A per unit of return and would prompt all but the least risk-averse investor to choose Investment A. Figures 8.6 and 8.7 illustrate the comparison.

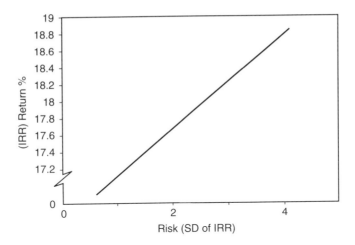

Figure 8.6   Investment A: risk/return: 1.

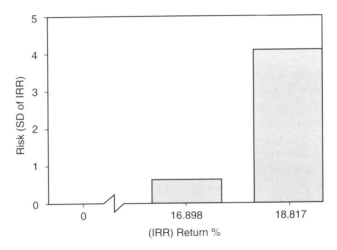

Figure 8.7   Investment A: risk/return: 2.

In NPV terms, the measure is

$$\frac{\text{SD of NPV}}{\text{Expected NPV}} \quad \text{or} \quad \frac{\text{NPV}}{\text{NPV}}$$

For Investment A, this is $\dfrac{4.109\%}{18.817\%} = 0.21837\%$

For Investment B, this is $\dfrac{£286,870}{£482,010} = 59.515\%$

Part Three

This comparison almost exactly repeats the result of the coefficient of IRR variation.

There are again reasons for preferring the NPV measure. The coefficient of IRR variation should only be used where two acceptable investments are being compared: otherwise, an apparently superior (lower risk per unit of return) investment may be preferred when it is expected to fail to produce a return equal to or exceeding the target rate (and would therefore be unacceptable). The coefficient of NPV variation does not suffer from this problem (an unacceptable project would produce a negative coefficient).

8.2.7 SDs in risk analysis: some problems

Reaching this stage has only been possible with the aid of some simplifying assumptions regarding the nature of the probability distributions of the variables employed and, hence, a rather robust use of SDs. In this section we consider further the possible problems we have to date circumnavigated by the use of these assumptions.

Measures of investment risk are more difficult to achieve where the possible values of variables are drawn from a continuous, rather than a discrete, distribution, where the values are drawn from a skewed distribution and where the values of variables from year to year are not perfectly serially correlated. In our property investment appraisal model the first of these problems is exemplified by the fact that rental growth has to be represented as a minimum, expected and maximum value (say, 4%, 5% and 6%) when average rental growth p.a. could theoretically take any value between minus infinity and plus infinity to any number of decimal places. Second, the problem of lack of serial correlation is exemplified by the fact that rental growth achieved over a second rent-review period may have no relationship with the equivalent value of the first review period, and so on, radically complicating the analysis.

a. Sample SD The former problem is easily avoided by use of sample statistics. Use of the sample SD puts into effect the truism that the discrete SD (or SD of a population, σ_p) understates the risk of a variable drawn from a continuous distribution. Given that the population SD = variance^2, the sample SD (σ_s) can be found as follows:

$$\text{variance} = \sigma_p{}^2$$

$$\sigma_s = \sqrt{\left[(\text{variance})\frac{n}{n-1}\right]}$$

where n = the number of samples taken from the population.

For example, assuming maximum, expected and minimum values of rental growth of 4%, 5% and 6% with probabilities of 0.2, 0.6 and 0.2, respectively, variance $= \Sigma \, (\hat{r} - \bar{r})^2 p$

where

$\hat{r}$ = observed value of the variable

$\bar{r}$ = expected value of the variable

p = probability of occurrence of observed value

$V = \sum (0.04 - 0.05)^2 (0.2) + (0.05 - 0.05)^2 (0.6) + (0.06 - 0.05)^2 (0.2)$

$\quad = (0.00002 + 0.00002)$

$\quad = 0.00004$

$$\sigma = \sqrt{\left[(\text{variance}) \frac{n}{n-1}\right]}$$

The use of n, the number of observations, is problematic. Estimates of rental growth are unlikely to be made by sampling a population. Forecasting is more likely to be undertaken by a combination of time series extrapolation and causal analysis (see Ball *et al.*, 1998). However, it is possible to hypothesise that rental growth for each of the last 10 years may be taken as the population from which samples of 4%, 5% and 6% may be drawn. In that case, n is 10.

$\sigma = \sqrt{[(0.00004) \, (10/9)]}$

$\quad = \sqrt{[(0.00004) \times 1.1111)}$

$\quad = \sqrt{0.00004444}$

$\quad = 0.006667$

Note that if the sample were drawn from 100 observations, $\sigma_s = 0.006356$. As the number of samples taken increases, σ_s reduces and approaches σ_p ($\sigma_p = \sqrt{v}$, so that $\sqrt{(0.00004} = 0.006325)$.

Of the variables listed in Example 8.1 (table for Investment B at page 230) only the scale-based fees can be regarded as suitable for this type of sample analysis, and they are unlikely to be of major importance. The major variables are ERV at years 0, 5 and 10, rental growth and the resale capitalisation rate. All samples are drawn from continuous infinite populations. The choice, between the more correct sample SD, hypothesising a number of samples, and the population SD is a marginal one, given the likely small difference in result.

b. Skewness Skewness describes the tendency of a distribution of values of a variable to differ from the normal curve. This occurs where the median value does not equate with the mean or the mode, and the area of the curve to one side of the expected (mean) value does not equate with the area of the curve to the other side; in other words, the value of the subject variable is

Part Three

more likely to be higher than lower, or vice versa, than the mean value. In a normal distribution it is equally likely that a higher or a lower value will be the outcome.

The SD used as a risk measure for much of this chapter may be acceptable as a measure of dispersion in all symmetrical and even moderately skewed distributions. However, it becomes misleading as a measure of risk where the distribution is highly skewed.

This is not likely to be a fatal problem in property investment analysis. Most variables discussed in this chapter are likely to be drawn from relatively normal distributions. However, problems may be encountered at rent reviews, which are typically 'upward-only' in the UK. In a non-inflationary context, upward-only rent reviews may significantly skew the distribution of potential rents at review, and this is a factor that must be considered within a risk–return analysis that relies upon the SD measure. This issue is further developed in the Appendix to this chapter.

c. Serial correlation between cash flows Where a multi-period analytical model is used, many variables have to be estimated at more than one point in time. For example, rent review fees may be 7%, and it would usually be presumed that they would continue at that level. Perfect serial correlation between succeeding levels of rent review fee percentages is thereby assumed. However, average rental growth p.a. between years 0 and 5 is unlikely to predict, except in an extremely complex manner, the average rental growth p.a. between years 6 and 10. In other words, there is unlikely to be strong serial correlation between succeeding values of expected rental growth (for empirical evidence of this, see Brown and Matysiak, 2000b).

Even allowing for the effect of the UK 5-yearly rent review stabiliser, this is a considerable problem. Given a simple model with three major variables (ERV, resale capitalisation rate and rental growth) the extension of the time period for analysis beyond 5 years to a typical 15 increases the number of cash-flow possibilities (even taking only three values of what are continuously distributed variables from infinite ranges) from 27 to 6,561. A mean–variance analysis of the type presented for purposes of comprehension in this chapter is thereby made unworkable.

There are four possible solutions to this problem.

i. Assuming serial correlation. The first is the method adopted to date in this chapter, and that is to assume perfect serial correlation between cash flows. This confines the number of possible cash flows in this case to 27, but overstates the riskiness of the project. Given that the purpose of the analysis may be a relative judgement rather than an absolute measure of risk, this need not be a problem. However, it will be misleading where the shapes of the distributions of the variables in the two projects are considerably different: the riskier project may be excessively penalised. Wider comparisons (e.g. with alternative investments) may also become invalid as a result of this simplification.

ii. Interpolation. Robinson (1987) suggests a simple robust solution: interpolation of the SD or coefficient of variation, measured between the extremes of perfect serial correlation and independence between cash flows [see the example given in point (c), p. 250]. The advantages and disadvantages of such an approach are relatively self-evident: accuracy is not guaranteed, but a solution is attainable within a reasonable time.

iii. Hillier and Sykes. A third solution is the type of algebraic approach adapted from the work of Hillier (1963) to real estate by Sykes (1983b).

As Robinson (1987) shows, a maximum value for a project's risk is given by the SD measure where the values of variables over time are independent of their of their preceding values, and a minimum value of the same project's risk is given by the SD measure where each variable is perfectly serially correlated. See Example 8.2.

Example 8.2

Cost of project: £1,000
Return in year 1:   £50 (.5p) or £75 (.5p)
Return in year 2:   £1,500 (.5p) or £1750 (.5p)

Possible net cash flows: perfectly independent

Year	0	(£1,000)	(£1,000)	(£1,000)	(£1,000)
	1	£50	£50	£75	£75
	2	£1,500	£1,750	£1,500	£1,750
NPV at 10%		£285.12	£491.74	£307.85	£514.46
SD of NPVs		£103.93			

Possible net cash flows: perfectly serially correlated (so that an income of £75 in year 1 predicts the larger return in year 2).

Year	0	(£1,000)	(£1,000)
	1	£50	£75
	2	£1,500	£1,750
NPV at 10%		£285.12	£514.46
SD of NPVs		£114.67	

Within these two extremes lies the possibility that cash flows are partially correlated. The cash flow might represent the result of the interplay of many variables, some of which are independent of their preceding values (repair expenses, for example) and some of which are perfectly serially correlated (gross rent between reviews, for example). If there is partial correlation between these cash flows, the SD of the NPVs lies between £103.93 and £114.67; beyond this it is only possible to say that a precise measure would be extremely difficult, necessitating the estimation of partial correlation coefficients between all the cash flows. (Robinson's approach, however, is simple interpolation: use (say) £109.30 as a mid-point SD measure.)

Sykes suggests that the fortunate aspect of property investment analysis in this respect is the fact that cash flows are either perfectly correlated or independent, and not partially correlated. (This ignores the complex effects of expenses, fees and so on.) Thus, while rents between reviews are perfectly correlated, Sykes posits that rents immediately before and after review are, in an inflationary environment and given normal depreciation, independent.

Hillier's equations for the SD of independent cash flows and perfectly correlated cash flows, respectively, are as follows:

$$\sigma^2 \text{NPV} = \sum_{j=1}^{\hat{}} \frac{\sigma^2 j}{(1+i)^2 j}$$

$$\sigma^2 \text{NPV} = \left[\sum_{j=1}^{\hat{}} \frac{\sigma j}{(1+i)^j} \right]^2$$

Sykes then derives a formula for establishing the SD of a property investment (ignoring outgoings) as follows. Assuming a 10-year holding period, the cash flow is made up of four variables. These are the outlay, the initial rent, the rent paid at the first and second reviews and the resale price.

a. The outlay: The outlay is known and risk-free. The SD of the NPV is identical to that of the total present value of a cash flow. Thus, in estimating the risk of an investment where the outlay is risk-free, the outlay may be ignored.

b. Rent, years 0–5: This will usually already have been negotiated at the time analysis is carried out and is thus risk-free, in the absence of default risk. The SD is nil, and this variable may be ignored in a combined expression of the risk of the investment.

c. Rent, years 6–10 and 11–15: These are perfectly correlated, although the two expressions are independent of each other and of the starting rent. Thus, the expression for the SD of the present value of the rent between years 6 and 10 is

$$\sigma^2 = \sigma \left[\sum_{j=6}^{10} \frac{1}{(1+i)^j} \right]^2$$

where j = number of years and i = target rate.
     The equivalent for years 11–15 is

$$\sigma^2 = \sigma \left[\sum_{j=11}^{15} \frac{1}{(1+i)^j} \right]^2$$

d.   Resale price: This is an independent risky variable (c). The total expression is therefore

$$\sigma^2 \; \text{NPV} = \sigma \left[\sum_{j=6}^{10} \frac{1}{(1+i)^j} \right]^2 + \left\{ \sum_{j=11}^{15} \left[\frac{1}{(1+i)^j} \right] \right\}^2 + \left[\frac{\sigma^c}{(1+i)^{15}} \right]^2$$

This is the expression for total risk of an investment with perfect correlation within reviews and assuming no correlation between different period review rents and resale price.

As Sykes points out, the resale price presents a problem, as it represents the result of resale capitalisation rate (independent) and ERV at the resale date. This complicates the estimation of SD by formula, but Sykes suggests formulae employing partial derivatives (Sykes 1983b).

Sykes' adaptation of Hillier's work to UK property is a useful advance. It is questioned by Brown and Matysiak (2000b), who are critical of its assumption of complete independence of rents between review, ignoring as it does the many complications created by outgoings and upward-only reviews. It is of necessity, therefore, a short cut. The same is only true to a much reduced extent in the case of the following, fourth, solution to the problem of independence cash flows

iv. Simulation. We referred earlier in this Chapter to 6,561 potential cash flows from a simple property investment.

It would be quite possible to program a spreadsheet to estimate the NPV of all 6,561 cash flows and to calculate the SD of the results. It would, however, be difficult to do this in a reasonable amount of time; and, in any event, 6,561 is a small number of potential cash flows.

A solution to this is (Monte Carlo) simulation. Given estimates of the worst, expected and best outcomes of all variables and the associated probabilities, many programs are available to select, at random, combinations of variables, calculating and storing the NPV produced by the resultant cash flow, and repeating the exercise strictly in accordance with the probabilities given. If the analyst specified a 60% chance of repairs being necessary at a cost of £50,000 at the lease end, then 6 times out of 10 the cash flow thrown out by the simulation will include this expense. Simulation programs run this exercise repeatedly, calculate NPVs and may be made to produce the SD of the results. It is to be expected that the shape of the simulated distributions will be identical to the shape of the curve of the population, and so the SD measure will be accurate.

The advantage of the numeric simulation technique is its ability to accurately take into account all variables, unlike the adaptation of the algebraic Hillier technique described above. It can also deal with the problems of serial correlation (or lack of it) within a variable and a divergence between

Part Three

sample and population SD measures. Care must be taken where there is a suspicion of interdependence (correlation) between variables, for example where a
high rate of RPI growth might imply rises in capitalisation rates, in which case
a simple simulation exercise would understate risk to some extent. But this,
too, can be dealt with and simulation is of considerable aid in the decision.

Simulation spreadsheet add-in packages such as @RISK and Crystal Ball are
now commercially available and allow correlations between variables and different types and shapes of distributions to be utilised. Simulation is therefore
now used to compare Investments A and B. Using the mean–variance criterion
for investment decision-making necessitated the estimation of possible values for each of two variables in each case.

For Investment A, the variables were rental value and average rental
growth. Pessimistic, expected and optimistic values for these variables were
as follows, with associated probabilities:

Rental value	p
498,750	0.2
525,000	0.6
551,250	0.2

Rental growth	p
4%	0.3
5%	0.4
6%	0.3

For Investment B, the variables were the average increase in RPI and the
resale capitalisation rate. Pessimistic, expected and optimistic values for
these variables, with probabilities, were as follows:

RPI growth	p
2.45%	0.2
3.5%	0.6
4.55%	0.2

Resale capitalisation rate	p
0.14	0.3
0.11	0.4
0.08	0.3

In a simulation program, the analyst need not be restricted to pessimistic, expected and optimistic values, depending upon the parameters established in the program used. Any number of value bands for each variable may be employed.

In the simulation program we constructed upon a spreadsheet, we chose five value bands for each variable. The value bands used (which are broadly consistent with previous pessimistic, expected and optimistic values for the two variables in Investment A) are as follows:

Investment A

Rental value (p)	
Pessimistic	498,750 (0.2)
Expected	525,000 (0.6)
Optimistic	551,250 (0.2)
Band 1	492,190–505,310 (0.1)
Band 2	505,320–518,440 (0.2)
Band 3	518,450–531,560 (0.4)
Band 4	531,570–544,690 (0.2)
Band 5	544,700–557,810 (0.1)

Rental growth (p)	
Pessimistic	0.04 (0.3)
Expected	0.05 (0.4)
Optimistic	0.06 (0.3)
Band 1	0.0375–0.0425 (0.15)
Band 2	0.0426–0.0475 (0.2)
Band 3	0.0476–0.0525 (0.3)
Band 4	0.0526–0.0575 (0.2)
Band 5	0.0576–0.0625 (0.15)

New subjective probability estimates for these value ranges have been assigned (strictly, the possibilities of rents below £492,190 and above £557,810 should be included in the outlying ranges).

Simulation programs work by generating random numbers within the chosen value bands in a frequency determined by the probability assumptions made. Hence, given sufficient cycles, 40% of all simulated cash flows will be on the basis that the rental value will be between £518,450 and £531,560; 20% of all simulated cash flows will be on the basis of growth of between 4.26% and 4.75%. Random number generation selects any value within these ranges and not a finite central point.

Part Three

The first 10 results in our simulation exercise were as follows:

Cycle	ERV (£)	Growth (%)	NPV (£)	IRR (%)
1	517,700	5.96	227,880	17.11
2	507,360	5.90	213,650	16.77
3	553,810	4.44	243,880	17.49
4	523,550	6.23	240,450	17.41
5	539,620	4.14	220,990	16.95
6	498,280	5.70	198,370	16.40
7	518,540	4.63	204,370	16.55
8	519,770	4.84	209,660	16.67
9	529,580	5.64	236,890	17.33
10	526,500	5.18	224,280	17.03

Already, the probability distribution of variables is being reflected in the random generation of values. The average ERV is £523,470, close to the expected £525,000; the average growth is 5.27%, close to the expected 5%, but likely to become much closer to it over 200 cycles (see p. 257: it becomes 5.06%).

Investment B

For Investment B, the appropriate value bands with new probabilities are as follows:

RPI growth (%) (p)	
Pessimistic	2.45 (0.2)
Expected	3.5 (0.6)
Optimistic	4.55 (0.2)
Band 1	2.1875–2.7125 (0.1)
Band 2	2.7126–3.2375 (0.2)
Band 3	3.2376–3.7625 (0.4)
Band 4	3.7626–4.2875 (0.2)
Band 5	4.2876–4.8125 (0.1)

Resale capitalisation rate (p)	
Pessimistic	0.14 (0.3)
Expected	0.11 (0.4)
Optimistic	0.08 (0.3)
Band 1	13.26–14.75 (0.15)
Band 2	11.76–13.25 (0.2)
Band 3	10.26–11.75 (0.3)
Band 4	8.76–10.25 (0.2)
Band 5	7.26–8.75 (0.15)

The first 10 results were as follows:

Cycle	Capitalisation rate (%)	RPI growth (%)	NPV (£)	IRR (%)
1	12.43	4.19	330,140	16.84
2	11.99	2.50	254,100	15.58
3	9.88	3.53	563,500	20.29
4	11.27	3.52	394,740	17.83
5	11.12	3.18	385,380	17.68
6	12.55	3.39	265,140	15.77
7	10.09	3.22	510,150	19.52
8	10.17	4.51	603,400	20.87
9	8.99	4.45	779,430	23.18
10	14.29	2.91	106,410	13.02

Two hundred cycles of each cash flow were recorded. Arguably, this is insufficient a number to ensure that the simulation is absolutely representative of the totality of possible cash flows, but for purposes of illustration 200 will suffice.

Again the mean–variance criterion can be employed in decision making. This time, however, the problem of choice of sample or population SD is effectively avoided, as a large number of cycles will cause the two to equate. Serial correlation between cash flows can also be easily avoided in the simulation exercise (although our simple simulation exercise was not designed to overcome this problem). The problem of skewness is effectively avoided by the use of realistically normal probability distributions for each variable in each case, resulting in a normal distribution of IRRs and NPVs. Hence, the following results are satisfactory for our purpose:

	Investment A	Investment B
Number of cycles	200	200
Average IRR	16.89%	18.87%
σ of IRR	0.53%	3.39%
Minimum IRR	15.64%	12.51%
Maximum IRR	18.19%	27.12%
Average NPV	£218,790	£478,610
σ of NPV	£21,950	£235,870
Minimum NPV	£167,790	£78,560
Maximum NPV	£274,000	£1,114,460
Average rental growth/RPI growth	5.06%	3.56%
Average rental value/resale capitalisation rate	£523,760	10.89%

The interpretation of the results is as follows:

For Investment A, the average NPV is £218,790. There is a 68.26% probability that the NPV will lie between £218,790 ± £21,950, that is, £196,840 and £240,740; a 95.46% probability that the NPV will lie between £218,790 ± (2 × £21,950), that is, £174,890 and £262,690; and a 99.74% probability that the NPV will lie between £218,790 ± (3 × £21,950), that is, £152,940 and £284,640.

For Investment B, the average NPV is £478,610. There is a 68.26% probability that the NPV will lie between £478,610 ± £235,870, that is, £242,740 and £714,480; a 94.46% probability that the NPV will lie between £478,610 ± (2 × £235,870), that is £6,870 and £950,350; and a 99.74% probability that the NPV will lie between £478,610 ± (3 × £235,870), that is, −£229,000 and £1,186,220.

Comparison of discrete and simulated results:

	Discrete mean–variance	Simulation
Investment A		
Average expected IRR (%)	16.90	16.89
σ IRR (%)	0.61	0.53
Coefficient of IRR variation (%)	3.58	3.12
Average expected NPV (£)	219,240	218,790
σ NPV (£)	25,160	21,950
Coefficient of NPV variation (%)	11.48	10.03
Investment B		
Average expected IRR (%)	18.82	18.87
σ IRR (%)	4.11	3.39
Coefficient of IRR variation (%)	21.84	17.97
Average expected NPV (£)	482,010	478,610
σ NPV (£)	286,870	235,870
Coefficient of NPV	59.52	49.28

Note how the original discrete test overstates risk by a small amount, as a result of the discrete variable values, the effect of the new probabilities, and/or the effect of using the overstated measure of population SD (p) in the original analysis. The nine cash flows analysed earlier will thus inevitably produce a higher population SD than the 200 used in simulation, all other things being equal; hence the simulation results are to be preferred as being more accurate.

In practice, the discrete mean–variance test, using optimistic, expected and pessimistic values, can hardly be said to be inadequate. The above results show a clear decision on the basis of coefficient of variation measures: the differences between the results of the two approaches are hardly significant.

Nonetheless, given that the effort involved in carrying out a simulation need not be greater than alternative less rigorous methods, it is to be recommended.

In conclusion, while the mean–variance criterion allows no clear decision, the coefficient of IRR variation indicates that Investment A is to be preferred by all but the risk-indifferent and risk-seeking investor; while B will probably be more profitable than A, the investor takes on considerably more risk per unit of return.

Figures 8.8 and 8.9 illustrate graphically the relative risks and returns of the two investments. More simulation material is presented in the appendix to this chapter.

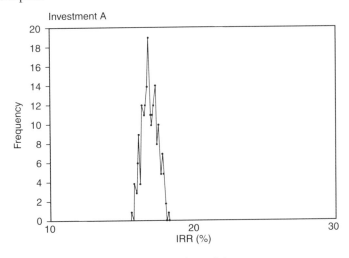

Figure 8.8   Investment A: Distribution of possible returns.

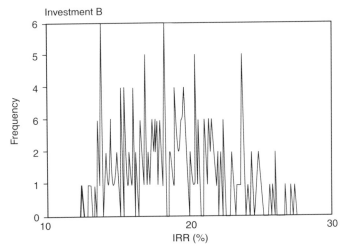

Figure 8.9   Investment B: Distribution of possible returns.

Part Three

8.3   Portfolio risk

In Chapter 2 we discussed the work of Markowitz and Sharpe in developing modern portfolio theory (MPT). They showed how the combination of two or more investments whose returns fluctuate in different conditions but in opposite directions can reduce risk without at the same time reducing return. Further, the conclusion of MPT must be that a riskier investment may be preferred to a safe investment, as the effect of including that investment may, if it shows inverse correlation with the existing portfolio, be to reduce portfolio risk without paying for that benefit in loss of return.

This may be the case if in our example Investment B were a US investment (let us say, Texas) and Investment A is a shop in the south of England. Investment A may be less risky than B. However, if the fund holds only UK real estate, and if US real estate has a tendency to perform well when the UK real estate performs badly, then B may be preferable.

The difficulties of applying this logic are in quantifying the relative attraction of the two investments to the holder of a portfolio and in the assumptions that must be made in order to progress the measurement process.

The CAPM (Chapter 2) requires at least one major assumption to be made. The difficulties of measuring the covariance of a real portfolio and the relative variance of potential new investments are enormous, and the CAPM proceeds by hypothesising that all rational investors hold a market portfolio made up of all investments. This, of course, includes real estate, and must also include all other investment types throughout the world. This need not be an insurmountable objection if it can be shown that relatively small portfolios can be representative of the market. Unfortunately, little or no evidence has been produced to demonstrate this in the context of a portfolio including international real estate.

If, however, we ignore this problem and adduce the return on the market, perhaps by taking the UK stock market as a surrogate market portfolio, then it is necessary to measure β for property investments. The formula

$$r = \text{RFR} + \beta\,(rp)$$

where

r = required return on subject investment
β = measure of relative risk
rp = market risk premium (expected return on the market less RFR)

enables us to decide whether an investment is under- or overpriced (see Chapter 2). β is a measure of covariance of the investment's performance against the market. In the example, would we need measures of the expected return on offices in the US; or in Texas; or in a part of Texas; or in the particular sub-location; or of the particular office?

We also need forecasts of expected returns. Given that reliable forecasts do not exist, we may be tempted (as CAPM requires) to base expectations on past performance. To obtain this, we need records of past performance of offices in Texas, shops in the south of England, and so on. Let us assume that we are able to derive β for shops in the south of England and for offices in Texas, that the investor holds a UK market non-property portfolio, and that returns on the market have been 18% over the last 5 years and that the RFR is 9%. If the performance of Texas offices is negatively correlated with the UK stock market, we may find the following values for β:

Texas office   −0.3
South of England shop   +0.18

The required returns are then (r_s and r_t, for Investments A and B, respectively):

$$r_s = 0.09 + 0.18\,(0.09)$$
$$= 10.62\%$$
$$r_t = 0.09 - 0.3\,(0.09)$$
$$= 6.3\%$$

Given that expected returns are 16.9% and 18.8%, respectively, the probable choice is Investment B, reversing all previous indications.

It is not yet common practice to choose property investments on the basis of beta, but work continues in this field (for early examples, see Baum and Schofield, 1991; Hargitay and Yu, 1992; Brown and Matysiak, 2000b).

8.4   Summary

Sensitivity analysis showed that a realistic choice of variable parameters produced a much wider range of returns for Investment B than for Investment A, although the average for B was higher. The conclusion that may be drawn from this is that a higher return is likely for B but at the cost of a higher risk.

Sensitivity analysis produced no simple decision rule, providing the analyst instead with a range of results. We favour this approach in the majority of circumstances: it allows the investor to retain the decision responsibility with the help of the analyst in determining realistic variable parameters.

Risk adjustment techniques, on the other hand, attempt to provide an objective decision, but only by way of subjective risk adjustment. Three methods were presented. On the basis of the risk-adjusted discount rate technique, Investment A produced a higher NPV and a higher margin of return over the risk adjusted rate, and would be preferred. The certainty-equivalent technique, offered as a preferable risk adjustment method, offered an even clearer decision, as the NPV of Investment B became negative and the profitable Investment A would have been preferred. The sliced-income approach is particularly suited to UK property investment analyses because of the commonality of the upward-only rent review at 5-year intervals and may be

Part Three

an improvement upon the certainty-equivalent technique in some cases. In this case it produces a result which makes a choice between the investments marginal.

The fault of risk adjustment techniques is the probability that the professional analyst will replace the subjective risk–return indifference of the investor by an apparently objective analysis that is in reality subjective to the analyst. This is unlikely to be acceptable to the sophisticated investor, who may wish to base his decision upon separate measures of risk and return. The measures used in the mean–variance criterion are NPV or IRR for return, and SD of NPV or IRR for risk. Investment A would be preferred if

NPV (IRR) A > NPV (IRR) B
and SD A ≤ SD B

In this case, as is typical, the mean–variance criterion produced no clear decision. The return of B exceeded that of A, but so did its risk. It is impossible to say which is better, as a choice depends upon the investor's risk aversion. The mean–variance criterion's strict decision rule makes it of little use in many cases.

An attempt to objectify the risk–return trade-off is the coefficient of IRR variation, which measures the risk of an investment per unit of return. Strictly speaking this does not improve upon the mean–variance criterion as a decision rule, as the subjective risk aversion of the individual investor remains to be interpreted. But investors may have little experience of quantifying their own degree of risk aversion and may prefer to base a decision on a simple comparison of coefficients of IRR variation. A clear decision may emerge for the typical investor (averagely risk-averse): in the comparison of Investments A and B, this was almost certainly true, as B was shown to be around six times as risky per unit of return than was A, and A would therefore have been chosen.

Finally, all of the foregoing analyses may be misleading if the main concern of the investor is the risk of his portfolio, and not of the individual investment. Investment B in the analysis is shown to be much more risky than A; but if it were a US property and US real estate investments can be shown to demonstrate a degree of inverse correlation with the UK property investments, the effect of including B in a UK property-dominated portfolio may be to reduce the overall risk of the portfolio, at the same time improving return by a greater amount than would be expected by buying A. An analysis of this type requires the estimation of betas of individual properties or property types, and there is no clear consensus that this can be achieved in a reliable and useable manner.

Property investment appraisal remains a developing field. Investors will always be concerned about risk and return, about minimising one while maximising the other. How these issues are precisely defined, and how analytical techniques develop in order that they may be measured, will continue to provide rich fields of enquiry for students, academics and investment professionals.

Part Three

8.5   Appendix: pricing the options inherent in leased commercial property – A UK case study

8.5.1   Introduction

This appendix is based on one of a series of papers setting out the findings of a programme of research and development carried out at the Department of Real Estate and Planning at the University of Reading and at OPS (Oxford Property Systems, a software development company) over the period 1999–2006. The programme aims to identify the fundamental drivers of the pricing of different lease terms in the UK property sector, to identify key issues in pricing cash flows derived from leases with different lease lengths and other terms, to develop a model for return estimation and pricing of these cash flows under a variety of lease variations and to use the model to draw conclusions about the market pricing of lease cash flows. Simulation is used as the engine that drives the commercial software programme (OPRent), which resulted.

Although it is possible to quantitatively model both the landlords' and tenants' positions in lease negotiations, the complexity of the legal issues that influence the rental impact of lease terms makes a solution to pricing challenging. The approach of valuers and funding criteria also add complexity to the issue and add an institutional dimension to the problem, impeding the adjustment towards rational pricing. The intricacy of these issues possibly explains the conservatism of many market participants towards flexi-leases. However, it also provides a potential opportunity to market participants with the ability to accurately price flexibility in lease terms.

The research uses data derived from major databases maintained by Investment Property Databank (IPD) and the Valuation Office, interviews and workshops with over 50 market participants (owners, letting and investment agents, valuers and rent review surveyors) and a questionnaire survey carried out in 2006. The OPS software development work was based on the outputs of this research.

From the landlord's perspective, the main factors driving the required 'compensation' for a lease term amendment include expected rental volatility, expected probability of tenant vacation and the expected costs of tenant vacation. These data are used in conjunction with simulation technology to measure the value of options inherent in certain lease types to explore the required rent adjustment. The resulting cash flows have interesting qualities that illustrate the potential importance of option pricing in a non-complex and practical way.

Finally, the introduction of a new variable, rental growth volatility, into systems for modelling and pricing property cash flows has important and perhaps surprising implications.

Part Three

8.5.2   *Factors affecting the value effects of lease variations*

8.5.2.1   *Rental valuation*

The landlord perspective

Flexible leasing creates uncertainty in the cash flow. The long lease with upward-only rent reviews on full repairing and insuring terms has the essential advantage of minimising cash-flow uncertainty. Modelling the impact of flexible leases introduces the need to deal with uncertain cash flows.

Where break clauses are the issue, the key variable is the probability of the tenant exercising the break and vacating. Where short leases are the problem, the key variable is the probability of lease renewal. In each case, void lengths, empty property costs and re-letting costs are relevant. Until recently, data availability has been limited with little empirical evidence of the probability of breaks and lease renewals and void periods. However, even though these data are now available in the UK (Strutt and Parker/IPD, 2006), the value of mean figures will be limited by the fact that individual features of properties and tenants will affect the propensity of the tenant to vacate, as will the economic and business environment.

It is apparent that the probability of tenant vacation will be influenced by the nature of the specific tenant, lease, market sector and building. The main driver for tenants breaking will normally be the needs of the business in a rapidly changing business environment forcing a need to expand or contract. Despite data describing the incidence of breaks and renewals, little work has been done on the drivers for breaking or not renewing leases. However, the property-based factors could be:

- The length of the notice period
- The amount of the financial penalty
- The expected cost of dilapidations
- The estimated amount spent fitting out premises
- The availability of alternative premises
- The estimated costs of relocation
- Expected rental growth

The estimated probability of letting termination is the first key variable used in calculating the expected cost of tenant vacation. The second key variable is the expected length of the void period. The expected costs of a void will be a function of the estimated probability of costs being incurred and the amount of these costs. In addition, there is a possibility of a downward rent review.

The probability of the rent received exceeding rental value at rent review is dependent upon the expected level of rental growth, the time to rent review and the volatility of rental growth. Hence, in the absence of reliable transaction evidence involving comparable leases, investors' pricing adjustments should be based upon

- Expected rental volatility
- Expected probability of tenant vacation
- Expected costs of tenant vacation
- Expected rental growth
- Time to rent review

The tenant perspective

Interviews with practitioners suggest that the economic value put on short leases was variable between tenants. The general impression given was that a majority of retail tenants placed a higher value on securing a trading position than on obtaining flexibility. This is less true of office and industrial tenants.

Tenants who perceive a high degree of risk in a venture or a location will tend to place a high value on a short lease for two main reasons. First, they perceive a need for a certain exit strategy. Second, long leases can decrease the project IRR from the tenant's point of view.

However, fit-out costs can be an important variable. Tenants with substantial fit-out costs place little value on short leases as they may need 10–15-year write-off periods to maximise IRR. It was estimated by interviewees that average required write-off periods were 7–8 years.

8.5.2.2   Capital valuation

The importance of valuers and valuation methodology is illustrated by the fact that the required rent effect of a lease variation is often calculated by reference to the yield (valuation) impact of that variation. Say a property let on standard terms is valued by reference to a rental value of £10 and a yield of 10%. The valuer may be asked to estimate the yield impact of a change from a 15-year lease to a 5-year lease. Assume that the yield moves out to 12%. This leads to a fall in value of 15%. It can be put right by a 15% rent increase, and this is where many will end their analysis.

This is not true value maximisation: it is based on likely selling prices, not on cash flows, and is therefore a mechanism based on very short-term analysis. As a result of similar considerations, it can be difficult to obtain strong views concerning the rent impact of lease variations, as there can be a strong desire to protect the headline rent and to use other lease terms (rent frees, inducements) to compensate for variations. The source of this attitude is again the protection of the short-term valuation rather than the optimisation of the longer-term cash flow. Nonetheless, the valuation process is not wholly ignorant of future cash flows.

Discussions with valuers suggest that for properties with short leases, break clauses and imminent lease expiries the main valuation adjustment is the incorporation of a void allowance in the valuation. Generally this is the case for leases of less than 5 years unexpired. However, it was pointed out that the void allowance did not reflect the 'true' expected costs of a void. Rather it was moderated to reflect the fact that the tenant would probably not break. Where it was certain that the tenant would break, then a full void allowance was included in the valuation.

With regard to break clauses it was stated that the notice period and any penalty would be factored into the valuation so that a long notice period and substantial rent penalty could neutralise the void allowance. For shopping centres with short leases, a valuer would build in a running void assumption into the cash flow based on expected average void rate and expected average void period.

Flexible leasing may lead to faster lettings and less rent-free periods. The rental increase available may easily compensate for the risks of voids and re-letting costs. Valuation methodology does not naturally assist in examining this problem, which is regarded as an investment appraisal challenge left for owners and consultants rather than valuers.

Interviewees noted this tension between valuation and investment appraisal approaches. This can lead to different advices being given to lessors by two different departments of the same property consultant – and this is not surprising, because one approach is based on short-term sale price protection while the other is based on long-term cash-flow protection.

Funding

Funding criteria are often critical to the pricing strategies of private investors. Given that the banks place great importance on unexpired lease terms in their risk management procedures, short leases are undesirable from the landlord's perspective.

The observed capitalisation rate damage that can be observed for leases with less than 10 years unexpired – or 15 in some sectors – can be seen as a rational outcome of financing criteria.

Liquidity

One consequence of the valuation process may be that short leases tend to be less liquid. Practitioners commented that it was rare to see a property on the market that had less than 5 years unexpired. Landlords tended to follow one of two strategies. First, they could simply wait until the lease had expired and a new lease negotiated before disposal. Alternatively, they could restructure the lease.

Few landlords appear to be prepared to take on what would be a normal challenge in many other markets, namely, to provide a level of customer service and the resulting continuation of a customer relationship. This may be the result of the market's excessive reliance on the valuation process accompanied by a lack of faith in its use where there is abnormality and little or no comparable evidence.

The portfolio effect

Landlords will be more flexible on multi-let schemes than on stand-alone leases, partly because of the influence of valuers who will penalise the capitalisation rate for a short lease on a single investment but take the 'tone' of lease lengths for the yield on a multi-let estate.

In addition, lenders may be more relaxed about lending against properties let on short lease terms where the property is multi-let, and on schemes including several assets let on flexible lease terms, because of the portfolio effect. However, this is not easily modelled in a lease-pricing system. It therefore represents an advantage for larger owners able to exploit the risk reduction explained by standard portfolio theory.

The price impact of flexible leases will also be affected by the portfolio effect: a department store or anchor store has much greater impact on a shopping centre than other tenants, so the rent impact of a break is much bigger.

Lessor options

Flexible lease pricing provides the parties with more options both in the standard sense and in the financial sense. Lessee options are most obviously introduced by tenants' break clauses. They have a value to the tenant based on the occupation alternatives they provide: remain, move or close down. They have a cost to the lessor based on the potential interruption to cash flow and the associated cost of running and re-letting an empty property. While it is difficult to estimate their value to a tenant using pure financial variables, they can be valued by reference to the landlord's costs.

Interviewees found it relatively easy to find examples of break clauses and to comment on the likely rent impact. Typical were expectations such as a 15% premium for a 5 year break; a 7.5% premium for 10 year break; and 15% plus for both.

Tenants' break options may be countered by lessor options to break, which may cancel any price impacts. Less obviously, the grant of a lease outside the Landlord and Tenant Act 1954 removes a tenant option to stay and grants a lessor option to remove the tenant.

The value of these lessor options is less easy to model than the lessees'. The financial cost of exercising a lessor break can be modelled using financial variables – namely the cost of running and re-letting an empty property – while the benefits of the option (which may include redevelopment options, or the opportunity to relocate other tenants to free up space that could be re-let at a higher rent and many others) are less easily priced.

Part Three

Volatility

Rental growth volatility was not mentioned as an input variable by a single valuer or market participant interviewed. It is clear that this variable is not used explicitly in market pricing. Yet, in theory, it is of significant impact.

8.5.3   *Developing a model for pricing cash flows*

8.5.3.1   *Introduction*

It is apparent that there is a wide variety of factors affecting the financial implications of short leases and break clauses. Valuers are faced with the task of reflecting the rental and capital value implications of this diversity within their appraisals. It is well documented that when facing with relatively novel lease structures, valuers tend to adopt conservative practices. Indeed there are rational grounds for such an approach. Consistent with other appraisal approaches to 'anomalies', the initial research on this topic found that valuers tend to use rather *ad hoc* adjustments to reflect the effects of break clauses (Lizieri and Herd, 1994).

Although it may be argued that any application of generalised risk adjustments by market participants to account for break options should also be used by valuers in assessing market values, previous research has shown that established rules of thumb in valuation practice are often at odds with activities in the market or that there is diversity of application within the market (O'Roarty *et al.*, 1997). Further, given the combination of asset heterogeneity, confidentiality and 'thin' trading, the usefulness of direct comparison methods of valuation will be limited. For break clauses, this drawback will be further exacerbated by the diversity of break clauses.

8.5.3.2   *Simulation approaches*

In this method of analysis, the distribution of possible outcomes is generated by a computer using randomisation based on specified probability distributions. Lizieri and Herd (1994) used simulation as a method of pricing break clauses. They examined approaches to the problem by practitioners and found a notable lack of consistency between valuers and in the internal logic of their assumptions.

They developed a simulation approach to formally account for the probability that tenants may exercise the right to prematurely determine the lease and found evidence of inconsistency in the application of yield adjustments as a remedy for the impact on value of break options. Indeed, they concluded that in general valuers tended to adopt a conservative approach (presenting an opportunity for arbitrage trading). Their model derived the probability of tenant vacation from evidence about an 'average' rate of non-renewal by tenants.

However, given the diversity in the structure of break clauses and the heterogeneity of tenant circumstances, applying 'average' probabilities is just as likely to fail to account accurately for the implications of break clauses. There is information available that can enable an estimation of the probability of tenant vacation to be made.

8.5.3.3   Analytical approaches – using option pricing theory

Although simulation can be used to price financial options, specific mathematical equations have been proposed which generate similar outputs. There has been considerable interest in the potential application of option pricing techniques to property investment and development decisions (Grenadier, 1995; Patel and Sing, 1998; Ward *et al.*, 1998; Rowland, 1999). If the option to vacate is viewed from a typical option perspective, the limitations of such methodologies can be seen.

In a typical option product the investor acquires the right to buy (call option) or sell (put option) an underlying asset before or at a pre-agreed date. In this case, as the problem is concerned with options to vacate, the similarity is with a European put option where the tenant has the right to vacate (sell) at a pre-agreed date. The value of the option is a function of movement in the price of the underlying asset. Logically, the price volatility of the underlying asset is a key determinant of the value of the option with increasing volatility producing higher option values. Although mathematically complex in derivation, the operation of option pricing models is relatively simple. The key variable – volatility – is either estimated from analysis of historic price data or is obtained by analysing implied volatility in transactions.

It can be recognised how the volatility of property rental and yield series can impact on the financial implications of an option to vacate. Where the rental value at the point of potential letting termination is lower than the rent passing, the right to vacate may act as a downward rent review. This point is further analysed in the following. However, reliable application of these pricing models is, therefore, predicated on reliable historic time series and/or adequate transaction data. There are well-documented problems with both these requirements in the commercial property market. Moreover, even in markets which are relatively deep, mis-estimation of volatility is a problem in valuing options (Hodges, 1990).

A good example of the limitations of the application of option pricing models to break clauses is illustrated by Ward (1997). He presents an approach derived from the binomial option pricing model. Ward identifies volatility in rents as the primary factor affecting value-making assumptions about the circumstances in which the tenant will vacate. Pricing outcomes are presented on the basis of a range of assumptions about rental volatility. Moreover, the focus on future rental levels (and associated volatility) ignores

Part Three

the role of other issues such as tenant circumstances and break clause structure. The emphasis on volatility as the primary determinant of option value will be more appropriate where there is uniformity in the structure of the option but may be problematic where there is heterogeneity in the probability of exercise. In a typical European option, the rational investor will always exercise the option when they are 'in the money'. However, in the property market we have seen that each break option is unique in terms of structure of the option and the tenant attitude to exercise.

It is illuminating to contrast this study with the case of pricing upward/downward rent reviews (Ward and French, 1997). In this case, the rationale for the application of option pricing models seems more appropriate. Where the open market rental value is below the rent passing, the rent will always fall in the case of a non-upwards only rent review: the option will be exercised since it is 'in the money'. Ward's break option pricing model assumes that this rule also hold for break clauses. In reality, tenants may choose to exercise the break whether rents have fallen or not and in some cases may be unwilling to use the 'threat' of break to lower the rent. Moreover, in the case of downward rent reviews also, the pricing implications are dependent upon the volatility assumption, and Ward and French (1997) demonstrate the relatively wide range of possible volatility-dependent pricing outcomes.

It is clear that both option pricing and simulation approaches can provide similar solutions to lease pricing issues. However, simulation seems more suitable in this context for a number of reasons.

- It can be carried out using spreadsheet-compatible analytical systems such as Crystal Ball or @RISK.
- The outputs can be integrated into conventional spreadsheet models.
- It is flexible enough to cope with non-standard or unusual situations/assumptions.
- It is relatively transparent and permits the analyst to identify the key determinants of the outputs.

8.5.3.4   OPRent: the system

OPRent is a simulation-based system that is now being adopted in the UK property market. It uses the aforementioned research and theory to change the way in which property owners think about income streams, moving from a deterministic approach to a probabilistic approach. OPRent works by a statistical evaluation of risk through the modelling of the cash flows associated with a range of different elements of flexibility that could be incorporated into a lease. OPRent compares the likely cash flow from a standard lease with that expected from a non-standard lease.

Two illustrative examples of OPRent outputs are used here.

Simulation 1: Moving from a 15-year lease with 5-yearly upward-only rent reviews to a 10-year lease with a 5-year break

Assumptions
Rental value on a standard lease: £100,000 with 1 year rent-free
Lease renewal probability: 20%
Lease break probability: 25%
Expected void: 3 quarters
Void volatility: 3 quarters
Empty property costs: £10,000 a year
Re-letting costs: £25,000
Expected rental growth: 1%
Rental growth volatility: 4%
Target return: 9%

Result
The required year 1 rent increases by 36% (Table 8.A1).

Table 8.A1   Simulation 1 outputs (shorter lease with break).

Year	Cash flow: standard (£)	Cash flow: flexible (£)
1	0	0
2	100,000	135,900
3	100,000	135,900
4	100,000	135,900
5	100,000	135,900
6	108,100	82,492
7	108,100	87,969
8	108,100	104,576
9	108,100	107,424
10	108,100	107,484
11	115,908	25,200
12	115,908	53,931
13	115,908	104,907
14	115,908	113,256
15	115,908	113,256

Explanation. The higher initial cash flow for the flexible lease acts as compensation for the owner, but can be lost at the first review where a break operates. At this point there is a 25% chance of a break being exercised, and the system assumes a 100% chance of any tenant using the break to bring the rent back down to the market level.

After the break, there is a chance of a void and associated costs. The probability of a void falls over time as the property is marketed, and the cash flow improves with every passing quarter. At the lease end in year 10, the chance of a lease renewal is very small and the cash flow recovers only as the probability of a re-letting after an expected void period rises with passing time.

Simulation 2: Moving from a 15-year lease with 5-yearly upward-only rent reviews to a 15-year lease with rent reviews that operate in either direction

Assumptions
Rental value on a standard lease: £100,000 with 1 year rent-free
Lease renewal probability: 20%
Lease break probability: 25%
Expected void: 3 quarters
Void volatility: 3 quarters
Empty property costs: £10,000 a year
Re-letting costs: £25,000
Expected rental growth: 1%
Rental growth volatility: 8%
Target return: 9%

Result
The required year 1 rent increases by 6% (Table 8.A2).

Table 8.A2 Simulation 2 outputs (moving from upward-only reviews).

Year	Cash flow: standard (£)	Cash flow: flexible (£)
1	0	0
2	100,000	105,712
3	100,000	105,712
4	100,000	105,712
5	100,000	105,712
6	114,288	112,322
7	114,288	112,322
8	114,288	112,322
9	114,288	112,322
10	114,288	112,322
11	126,996	119,580
12	126,996	119,580
13	126,996	119,580
14	126,996	119,580
15	126,996	119,580

Explanation. The key here is to compare the expected rental value using 1% rental growth (£112,322 at year 6 and £119,580 at year 11) with the expected cash flows under these two leasing options. The two-way rent review picks up exactly these values, which represent the mean cash flow where rental growth can be higher or lower than expected. The upward-only rent review picks up a higher value, which is defined as the mean cash flow where rental value growth has an expected value and a positively skewed distribution, with zero being the lowest possible value.

In many ways, the more interesting questions raised by this research are to do with the possibility that the result of this technology will be accepted by market participants with a traditional view of property income. This impacts on lease pricing but also has implication for capital values and valuation/pricing/appraisal.

8.5.3.5   Valuation

The implications for pricing are best illustrated by using an example.

Assume the rental value of a property let on a standard lease is £100,000. The market capitalisation rate that would be applied is 7%, and a valuation of £1,428,000 would result.

In DCF terms, a required return or target IRR of 9% might be decided as appropriate. If the price of £1,428,000 is 'correct' the implied perpetuity rental growth rate required to deliver the return is 2.29%. A DCF analysis using these inputs would confirm a present value of the expected income stream of £1,428,000.

Now rental growth volatility of 8% is added to the problem. The value of the standard lease is impacted by this variable, as it includes upward-only rent reviews, which creates a prism through which effective cash-flow growth is magnified. The greater the volatility, the greater the value of the lease with the upward-only review. The following question arises: does the market value of £1,428,000 reflect the impact of rental growth volatility? If so, how can that market price be deconstructed and explained?

A required return of 9% and expected market rental growth of 2.29% produces a value of £1,428,000 only if rental growth volatility takes a value of zero. If we accept that the price is the result of efficient market pricing, and that the market understands the impact of rental growth volatility, one of the inputs must change. This has to be either the required IRR, which will be lower in a world which recognises volatility (8%), or alternatively volatility-adjusted rental growth must be lower (1.1%).

If we do not accept that price is the result of efficient market pricing, and that the market may not understand the impact of rental growth volatility, then we may assume that the 9% IRR and the implied rental growth values are fixed. The valuation then rises to £1,575,000 to take account of volatility. This is a matter for further exploration.

Part Three

8.5.4   The impact of rental growth volatility on pricing and returns

In the following section, we report the results of a set of 720 OPRent simulations and the making explicit of the implicit relationships between these key variables: rental growth, capitalisation rate, IRR and rental growth volatility. What impact do changes in rental growth volatility have on the delivered IRR? What impact do changes in rental growth volatility have on the rate of rental growth required to deliver a required return or IRR? What impact do changes in rental growth volatility have on the appropriate capitalisation rate for pricing a property cash flow to deliver a required IRR?

Results are shown in Figures 8.A1, 8.A2 and 8.A3. A standard 15-year lease with upward-only rent reviews is used in all 720 simulations.

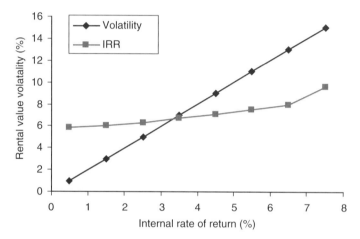

Figure 8.A1   Rental growth volatility and IRR.

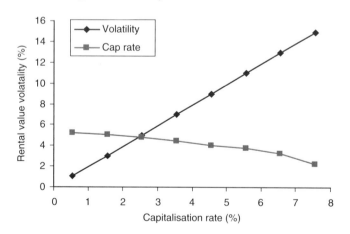

Figure 8.A2   Rental growth volatility and capitalisation rates (%).

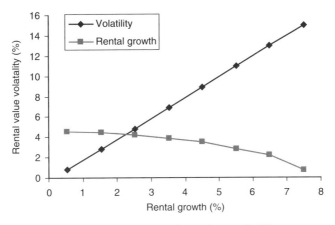

Figure 8.A3   Rental growth volatility and rental growth (%).

Table 8.A3   Rental growth volatility.

High street shops	4.7
Shopping centres	3.7
Retail warehouses	6.4
Business parks	3.3
City and mid-town offices	6.9
West End offices	8.1
Rest of London and provincial offices	4.7
Industrial	3.1
All property	4.8

Source: Investment Property Databank.

Figure 8.A1 shows that IRR increases exponentially with rental growth volatility. If market pricing models ignore volatility, as our research has established, then delivered IRRs are likely to be higher than those modelled by the market. Given a market average of close to 5% (Table 8.A3) the delivered IRR could be underestimated by more than 1%.

Figure 8.A2 shows how capitalisation rates to deliver the required return fall at an increasing rate as rental growth volatility increases. Again, capitalisation rates that are used to value upward-only rent reviews in models which ignore rental value volatility can undervalue by using capitalisation rates that are as much as 1.5% too low at 5% market average rates of volatility.

These findings have significant implications for the pricing of UK property investment, especially those subject to upward-only rent reviews. We suggest that:

- Delivered returns will, all things being equal, exceed the returns modelled in conventional DCF appraisals.

Part Three

- Capitalisation rates should be lower than those used in the market, and both traditional and DCF valuations fail to price the options inherent in the upward-only rent review.
- The rental growth rates required to deliver required returns are lower than market participants believe to be the case.

For a given set of inputs regarding the required IRR, expected rental growth rates and an upward-only rent review pattern, as long as rental growth volatility is expected to exceed zero, simulations approaches are now essential additions to the professional property analyst's (valuer's?) toolkit. These buyers can pay more than they think they can afford for property investments.

Chapter 9
Value and Price: a Case Study

9.1 Introduction

This chapter describes an analysis of the value or worth of an 'over-rented' City of London office building that was sold in 1993 and again in 2006. It illustrates the tension between true 'value' and an appraiser's valuation produced by conventional income valuation techniques. It demonstrates the key importance of international investors and capital markets, and the significance of unusual or alien lease structures.

The case shows how the pricing process should be affected by a greater understanding of the purchaser's view, and how changes in economic fundamentals will create changes in worth before market pricing techniques can adapt to new comparable evidence. In other words, there is a short-term deficiency in all pricing techniques that are based on comparable evidence in a changing market, quite apart from the irrationalities and mathematical inadequacies in conventional models that we hope to have demonstrated.

9.2 The investment

9.2.1 The property

Constructed in 1990, the subject property is an office building of around 15,000 ft^2 constructed on the edge of the central area of the City of London. It was let to a leading firm of lawyers, a private partnership, on a 25-year lease from May 1991 at a rent of £760,000. In early 1993 the estimated rental value (ERV) was around £20–25p.s.f. (in the range of £296,000–370,000). It was owned by an insurance company, which due to poor solvency and an overweight position in property and City offices in particular was very keen to sell. The original valuation date was March 1993.

9.2.2   The economic background

In 1990, on 5 October, Britain joined the Exchange Rate Mechanisum (ERM) at a Deutsche Mark (DM) 2.95 central rate, with 6% margins. The UK economy was suffering: unemployment was rising, interest rates were high, inflation was significant and the first Gulf War was brewing up. All asset markets were performing poorly.

On 20 November, Margaret Thatcher resigned and Norman Lamont was later made chancellor by new Prime Minister John Major. In May 1991, Lamont said recession is 'a price worth paying' (for the high invest rate necessitated by ERM membership). 'The green shoots of economic spring are appearing...'. On 10 July 1992, with base rates at 10%, Lamont was quoted as saying the ERM 'is not an optional extra, an add-on to be jettisoned at the first hint of trouble'. On 16 July, Sterling fell to DM 2.85. Germany raised the discount rate from 8% to 8.75%, further damaging Sterling's entire strength. At the end of July many insurance companies were beginning to suffer potential insolvency. The pound was close to its theoretical lowest point in the ERM, at DM 2.7780. Speculators, including George Soros, were selling sterling short.

On 26 August, Lamont tried to remove any 'scintilla of doubt'. 'We are going to maintain Sterling's parity and we will do whatever is necessary.' The Bank of England spent $1 billion buying pounds. On 28 August, the lira, pound and French franc were hit by wave of Soros-inspired selling. Lamont, as chairman of the finance ministers' council, said: 'A change in the present structure of interest rates would not be an appropriate response to the current tensions.' On 29 August, at the Bath meeting, Lamont tried four times to pressurise Helmut Schlesinger, president of the Bundesbank, into agreeing to cut German rates (but Schlesinger had no authority to do so without his colleagues). On 29 August a compromise statement concluded: 'The Bundesbank in the present circumstances has no intention to increase rates.' This sent the market in the opposite direction to the one Lamont desired. On 8 September, Major said: 'The soft option, the devaluers' option, the inflationary option, would be a betrayal of our future.' On 12 September the lira was devalued by 7%. On 15 September Sterling fell below its floor.

On 'Black Wednesday', 16 September 1992, at 9 a.m., Lamont told Major that interest rates might have to rise. Rates were raised from 10% to 12% at 11 a.m. There was no resulting rise in Sterling, despite massive intervention. The Bank of England was the only buyer at DM 2.7780. It was announced that interest rates would rise to 15% the next morning, but on that evening Lamont accepted that the government would immediately give up its attempt to keep the sterling in the ERM. The pound was then devalued and interest rates began a downward drift.

9.2.3   The property market background

In late 1992, the UK had been in recession for 18 months, and the over-supply of London offices created through the boom of the mid-to late 1980s, coupled with a very weak demand side and rents, which had reached a peak in real terms by 1989, created a potent mixture. Property companies had been squeezed by interest rate rises in the late 1980s, by a scarcity of debt following the record indebtedness of banks and by a fall in investor demand for property. When rents started to tumble in 1991 the final piece in the jig-saw was in place, and the UK saw property company failures, non-performing bank loans and a loss of investor confidence.

In one weekend in October 1992, Canary Wharf announced its insolvency, falls in house prices became the favourite topic in the Sunday supplements, and commercial property markets were badly infected by a widespread malaise.

When, in late 1992, the UK withdrew from the European Exchange Rate Mechanism, interest rates fell, gilt yields fell and Sterling was effectively devalued against the German mark. This marked a turn in investor sentiment. By this time, and after only 2 years, a London office building might have been worth only 50% of its 1990 peak. Rents appeared to be approaching a floor. Yields (capitalisation rates) were at an all-time high in absolute terms and relative to gilts (treasuries) and equities.

Because rents had fallen so much, and following the building boom of 1986–1990, there were many office properties in central London that had been let on new leases at high rents of up to £65p.s.f. and which were now worth only a small proportion of this amount. These were now 'over-rented' buildings, for which (as a result of upward-only rent reviews) the rent passing was likely to continue for a very long time, until a rent review would operate to apply a market rent of more than the original passing rent. In some cases this was not expected to happen before the end of the lease, as inflation and real growth forecasts were both very bearish at the time.

The leasing position in 1992 based on IPD data was set out in Chapter 4. By value 60% of the IPD was let on leases with over 15 years unexpired and virtually all of the let office property in the City of London was over-rented. Rental growth in the City of London office market was measured as negative at −6% in 1990, −24% in 1991 and −29% in 1992, a total fall of 60%. Vacancy rates were between 10% and 20% in the period.

9.2.4   The investment: equity or bond?

Investors were now able to buy a fixed income secured on property with the prospect of an equity conversion at some time in the future. Continental

European purchasers were able to purchase investments that appeared very similar to fixed-interest low-risk bonds, which constituted their natural habitat, at very attractive yields relative both to their domestic bonds (selling at around 6%) and to UK gilts. Not only that, but the currency devaluation meant that a larger building could now be purchased for the same outlay in domestic currency terms, providing a cheap building with the prospect of currency appreciation.

This led to a radical change in the property investment market. Valuers and investors were locked into thought processes and valuation methods based on the concept of property as an equity investment, one which is expected to benefit from income growth and capital appreciation, from both inflation and from real economy growth. Instead, property had become a convertible bond.

The distinction between a bond investment and an equity investment is reflected in the two component parts of a valuation. These are the cash-flow forecast and the discount rate.

9.2.5   The cash flow

The cash flow from a simple bond is fixed in nominal terms for the life of the investment. The cash flow from an equity rises and falls in response to inflation and to growth and decline in the real economy. Hence, forecasts of the cash flow for a bond do not require a view of the future for the economy or of inflation. Forecasts of the cash flow for an equity require both.

UK property in 1993 might fall into the bond category or the equity category. City offices let on upward-only rent reviews, subject to both long leases and over-renting, produce what is effectively a bond that will convert to an equity at the lease end and possibly (if there is a rental boom) before. Forecasts of rental growth for offices are not very important in predicting this cash flow, because the majority of the value lies in the currently contracted rent.

On the other hand, retail warehouses were, in 1993, straightforward property equities. There had been no rent decline of the scale that affected offices; rents continued to rise through 1993; and the cash-flow expectation would have been one of rents rising at each review. The expected cash flow would have been driven by expected inflation and expectations of the real economy, especially consumer expenditure growth in those sectors that constitute the retail warehouse occupier market.

In addition to the bond and equity comparison, the expected cash flow from a property investment is also subject to several unique factors. One is the lease term; another is the fact that property, unlike any other mainstream investment, is a tangible asset which depreciates through physical deterioration and obsolescence; the third is illiquidity. These factors combine to create investments that have very different risk characteristics, which in turn leads to different discount rates.

9.2.6   The discount rate

The discount rate applied to the cash flow from an investment should be the required return, made up of a risk-free rate and a required risk premium. The required risk premium should be determined by the liquidity of the investment and by the sensitivity of the cash flow to shocks created by inaccurate forecasts.

For an equity, the liquidity premium is unlikely to be high or to vary considerably between quoted stocks. The sensitivity of the cash flow (the stream of dividends) to economic shocks will be very important indeed. Examples include the effect on oil shares of unexpected changes in the oil price, and the effect of a change in the sterling exchange rate on the share price of a company with significant overseas earnings. Default risk is also relevant, an extreme example of the effect of an economic shock on the cash flow. Finally, for those investors interested in the real cash flow, shocks to inflation may be important, although the cash flow is to some extent inflation-proof as a result of a generally strong positive relationship between dividends, profits and inflation.

For a bond, the liquidity premium varies to some extent, but the sensitivity of the cash flow to economic shocks is nil. Default risk, on the other hand, is highly relevant, and will be the most important factor in the risk premium. Shocks to inflation will affect bonds more than equities, because the cash flow is fixed in nominal terms, and therefore has no inflation-proofing quality.

For property, the discount rate will be determined by the extent to which the investment is a bond or an equity. Over-rented offices in central London (bonds) will be sensitive to default risk and inflation. Retail warehouses will be sensitive to default risk, shocks to the real economy and, to a much lesser extent, inflation (bearing in mind the fixed nature of rents between reviews). In addition, all property is subject to two further special risks. The first is the extra illiquidity, which affects all property much more than normal bonds and equities and which will lead to an increase in the risk premium. The second is the lease pattern. Long leases and upward-only rent reviews contribute to a quality of income stream that will reduce the risk premium.

9.2.7   The property: cash flow and discount rate

It is clear that the subject property was in 1993 primarily a bond. Its cash flow would be driven by the lease terms, by inflation expectations, by forecasts of the real economy, and by expected depreciation.

Part Three

These factors will all influence an assessment of the investment value/ worth of this investment. In Section 9.4 a full cash-flow valuation illustrates how these factors may be accounted for. Prior to this, Section 9.3 illustrates an approach to a pricing valuation that attempts to account for the factors listed earlier primarily through the capitalisation rate.

9.3   Market valuation

As in all market valuations, the core data required is the passing rent, the ERV and the capitalisation rate. The latter was estimated to be 7.7%. Using this as the basis for both conventional and contemporary valuations, the results were as follows:

a. Conventional core and top-slice approach

Current rental value	£296,000	
YP perpetuity @ 7.7%	12.9870	
		£3,844,156
Overage	£464,000	
YP 23 years 2 months @ 12.4%	7.5269	
	£3,492,470	
Valuation		£7,336,626
Less costs @ 2.75%		£7,140,269
Valuation: say		£7.15m

Notes

a. The term for which the froth – or overage – was expected is dependent upon the valuer's intuitive view regarding whether the real rental value would overtake the passing rent before the final rent review in the lease. The assumption made was that it would not, and therefore the overage was taken to the end of the lease.

b. The overage yield represented a 4% margin over gilts (8.4%) to take into account the additional tenant default risk on the overage as well as illiquidity and normal tenant default risk on the base income.

b. Contemporary short-cut discounted cash flow

To illustrate the contemporary growth-explicit approach, a short-cut discounted cash-flow (DCF) was also undertaken. The required return needed to be determined for a property let at a rack rent and did not include any additional risk premium for the over-rented nature of the asset. The redemption yield on long-dated gilts at the valuation date was 8.4%. Adopting a 2% risk premium generated a target rate of 10.4%. The valuation was as follows:

Implied rental growth

$$(1+g)^5 = \frac{\text{YP perp. @ 7.7%} - \text{YP 5 years @ 10.4%}}{\text{YP perp. @ 7.7%} \times \text{PV 5 years @ 10.4%}}$$

$$(1+g)^5 = \frac{12.987 - 3.7524}{12.987 \times 0.6098} = \frac{9.2346}{7.9195} = 1.16606$$

$$g = 1.16606^{(1/5)} - 1 = 3.1203\% \text{ p.a.}$$

Would the overage be overtaken by ERV before the final review in the lease in just over 18 years' time? £296,000 × 1.031203$^{18.1667}$ = £517,267: the passing rent was expected to remain static until the end of the lease.

Valuation

Rent passing	£760,000	
YP 23 years 2 months @ 11.4%	8.0526	
		£6,119,984
Reversion to ERV	£296,000	
A £1 23 years 2 months @ 3.1203% p.a.	2.0377	
	£603,159	
YP perp. @ 7.7%	12.9870	
PV 23 years 2 months @ 10.4%	0.10105	
	£791,573	
Valuation		£6,911,557
Less costs @ 2.75%		£6,726,576
Valuation: say		£6.75 m

Note: The discount rate used for the term reflected the fact that some of the passing rent was overage, and was therefore a composite yield between the 10.4% applied to the rack rent and the 12.4% applied to the overage.

A market valuation of somewhere between £6.7m and £7.1m was arrived at by a conventional valuation approach. A similar result would have been produced by applying a capitalisation rate of 10% to the rent passing and a small discount to reflect the over-rented nature of the asset.

9.4 Investment appraisal

9.4.1 Cash flow

The cash flow from the property is determined mainly by the lease terms, which created a very over-rented bond-type investment. With over 23 years of the lease remaining, inflation expectations, real rent forecasts and expected depreciation would together determine the pattern of the future ERV and its relationship with the current contracted rent.

Forecasts of inflation at 4% per annum, rental depreciation at 0.75% per annum and nominal rental growth forecasts of –10%, 0%, 0%, 22% and 5%, respectively, in years 1, 2, 3, 4 and 5, with long-term real growth of 1% per annum after year 5, produced an ERV of around £600,000 by the lease end, still less than the contracted rent.

The property was therefore expected to produce a bond-type cash flow until the lease end. After this, it would revert to an equity-type property, which could be valued at that point on the basis of the expected rental value and a forecast yield of 7.7% (the current capitalisation rate used in the market valuation, reflecting a market that has recovered but a building that would then be 25 years old).

Complicating matters somewhat was the fact that the base rent – that component of the cash flow secured by ERV – would change quarter by quarter, as would the overage or froth, as rental values fell or rose.

9.4.2   Discount rate

For a bond-type investment the default risk predominated in the estimation of the risk premium. Over-rented properties are relatively complex in terms of default risk. The base income is defined as that part of the passing rent which is secured both by the covenant, that is, the contractual lease which binds the tenant to pay the rent agreed upon, and by the rental value of the property. The froth or over-rented element is defined as that part of the passing rent which is secured only against the covenant. The base income is doubly secured; the froth income is more exposed to potential default. The risk premium on each element should therefore be different for any tenant other than the most low-risk covenant.   A consulting firm appointed by the insurance company analysed this valuation in the following way. Taking the expected redemption yield on a long gilt (8.4%) as the risk-free rate proxy and a risk premium for the base income of 1.5% to reflect default risk, this produced a required return of 9.9% on the base income. A further 1.5% premium on the over-rented element produced a discount rate of 11.4% for that 'froth'. But even the froth had low default risk. The partnership of lawyers had a joint and several liabilities, had provided personal guarantees against the debts of the partnership, were likely to have substantial personal assets and would be motivated to protect the trading brand of the partnership.

The estimated resale price was discounted at an equity-determined required return, within which the risk premium was set primarily to reflect the real economy risks of predicting the rental value and yield at sale. A premium of 3.25% was chosen, being higher than the base income discount rate, reflecting the expected difference between a standard equity and a low-risk bond. Assuming the froth disappeared at the third review in 15 years' time, these inputs produced an appraised value of £7.6m. This made the conventional valuation look low.

Appraisal 1 shows the appraisal approach used by the consulting firm. The driver is the UK gilt rate, which limits a bid to around £7.6m, above the valuation, but not, as it turned out, competitive.

Appraisal 1: The UK perspective

Annual rent		760,000	Long gilt		8.40%
Annual ERV p.s.f.		20.00			
Total ERV		296,100	Base premium		1.50%
			Froth premium		3.00%
Growth	**Real**	**Nominal**	Property premium		3.00%
Growth 1	−13.46%	−10.00%			
Growth 2	−3.85%	0.00%	**Required return**	**Quarterly**	**Annual**
Growth 3	−3.85%	0.00%	Base	2.39%	9.90%
Growth 4	17.50%	22.20%	Froth	2.74%	11.40%
Growth 5	4.90%	9.10%	Property	2.74%	11.40%
Growth l.g.	1.00%	5.04%			
			Net exit value		659,236
Depreciation p.a.		1.50%	Base value		3,406,636
Depreciation p.q.		0.37%	Froth value		3,522,446
Exit yield		7.70%			
Review costs		2.50%	Total value		7,588,319

ERV = estimated rental values; p.s.f. = per square foot; p.a. = per annum; p.q. = per quarter; l.g. = long term.
Real Estate Strategy
March 1993.

Quarterly cash flow

Review	Quarter	Rent	ERV	Base rent	Froth	Cap/costs
0	1993.50	190,000.00	74,025.00	74,025.00	115,975.00	0.00
0	1993.75	190,000.00	71,833.08	71,833.08	118,166.92	0.00
0	1994.00	190,000.00	69,706.06	69,706.06	120,293.94	0.00
0	1994.25	190,000.00	67,642.02	67,642.02	122,357.98	0.00
0	1994.50	190,000.00	65,639.10	65,639.10	124,360.90	0.00
0	1994.75	190,000.00	65,394.58	65,394.58	124,605.42	0.00
0	1995.00	190,000.00	65,150.97	65,150.97	124,849.03	0.00
0	1995.25	190,000.00	64,908.27	64,908.27	125,091.73	0.00
0	1995.50	190,000.00	64,666.48	64,666.48	125,333.52	0.00
0	1995.75	190,000.00	64,425.58	64,425.58	125,574.42	0.00

Continued

Quarterly cash flow   (Continued)

Review	Quarter	Rent	ERV	Base rent	Froth	Cap/costs
0	1996.00	190,000.00	64,185.58	64,185.58	125,814.42	0.00
0	1996.25	190,000.00	63,946.48	63,946.48	126,053.52	0.00
1	1996.50	190,000.00	63,708.26	63,708.26	126,291.74	0.00
0	1996.75	190,000.00	66,733.99	66,733.99	123,266.01	0.00
0	1997.00	190,000.00	69,903.41	69,903.41	120,096.59	0.00
0	1997.25	190,000.00	73,223.36	73,223.36	116,776.64	0.00
0	1997.50	190,000.00	76,700.98	76,700.98	113,299.02	0.00
0	1997.75	190,000.00	78,097.41	78,097.41	111,902.59	0.00
0	1998.00	190,000.00	79,519.26	79,519.26	110,480.74	0.00
0	1998.25	190,000.00	80,967.00	80,967.00	109,033.00	0.00
0	1998.50	190,000.00	82,441.09	82,441.09	107,558.91	0.00
0	1998.75	190,000.00	83,150.70	83,150.70	106,849.30	0.00
0	1999.00	190,000.00	83,866.41	83,866.41	106,133.59	0.00
0	1999.25	190,000.00	84,588.29	84,588.29	105,411.71	0.00
0	1999.50	190,000.00	85,316.38	85,316.38	104,683.62	0.00
0	1999.75	190,000.00	86,050.73	86,050.73	103,949.27	0.00
0	2000.00	190,000.00	86,791.41	86,791.41	103,208.59	0.00
0	2000.25	190,000.00	87,538.46	87,538.46	102,461.54	0.00
0	2000.50	190,000.00	88,291.94	88,291.94	101,708.06	0.00
0	2000.75	190,000.00	89,051.91	89,051.91	100,948.09	0.00
0	2001.00	190,000.00	89,818.42	89,818.42	100,181.58	0.00
0	2001.25	190,000.00	90,591.52	90,591.52	99,408.48	0.00
1	2001.50	190,000.00	91,371.29	91,371.29	98,628.71	0.00
0	2001.75	190,000.00	92,157.76	92,157.76	97,842.24	0.00
0	2002.00	190,000.00	92,951.00	92,951.00	97,049.00	0.00
0	2002.25	190,000.00	93,751.07	93,751.07	96,248.93	0.00
0	2002.50	190,000.00	94,558.03	94,558.03	95,441.97	0.00
0	2002.75	190,000.00	95,371.93	95,371.93	94,628.07	0.00
0	2003.00	190,000.00	96,192.84	96,192.84	93,807.16	0.00
0	2003.25	190,000.00	97,020.81	97,020.81	92,979.19	0.00
0	2003.50	190,000.00	97,855.91	97,855.91	92,144.09	0.00
0	2003.75	190,000.00	98,698.20	98,698.20	91,301.80	0.00
0	2004.00	190,000.00	99,547.74	99,547.74	90,452.26	0.00
0	2004.25	190,000.00	100,404.59	100,404.59	89,595.41	0.00
0	2004.50	190,000.00	101,268.82	101,268.82	88,731.18	0.00
0	2004.75	190,000.00	102,140.49	102,140.49	87,859.51	0.00
0	2005.00	190,000.00	103,019.65	103,019.65	86,980.35	0.00
0	2005.25	190,000.00	103,906.39	103,906.39	86,093.61	0.00
0	2005.50	190,000.00	104,800.76	104,800.76	85,199.24	0.00
0	2005.75	190,000.00	105,702.82	105,702.82	84,297.18	0.00
0	2006.00	190,000.00	106,612.65	106,612.65	83,387.35	0.00

Continued

Quarterly cash flow   (Continued)

Review	Quarter	Rent	ERV	Base rent	Froth	Cap/costs
0	2006.25	190,000.00	107,530.32	107,530.32	82,469.68	0.00
1	2006.50	190,000.00	108,455.88	108,455.88	81,544.12	0.00
0	2006.75	190,000.00	109,389.40	109,389.40	80,610.60	0.00
0	2007.00	190,000.00	110,330.97	110,330.97	79,669.03	0.00
0	2007.25	190,000.00	111,280.63	111,280.63	78,719.37	0.00
0	2007.50	190,000.00	112,238.48	112,238.48	77,761.52	0.00
0	2007.75	190,000.00	113,204.56	113,204.56	76,795.44	0.00
0	2008.00	190,000.00	114,178.96	114,178.96	75,821.04	0.00
0	2008.25	190,000.00	115,161.75	115,161.75	74,838.25	0.00
0	2008.50	190,000.00	116,153.00	116,153.00	73,847.00	0.00
0	2008.75	190,000.00	117,152.78	117,152.78	72,847.22	0.00
0	2009.00	190,000.00	118,161.17	118,161.17	71,838.83	0.00
0	2009.25	190,000.00	119,178.23	119,178.23	70,821.77	0.00
0	2009.50	190,000.00	120,204.05	120,204.05	69,795.95	0.00
0	2009.75	190,000.00	121,238.70	121,238.70	68,761.30	0.00
0	2010.00	190,000.00	122,282.25	122,282.25	67,717.75	0.00
0	2010.25	190,000.00	123,334.79	123,334.79	66,665.21	0.00
0	2010.50	190,000.00	124,396.39	124,396.39	65,603.61	0.00
0	2010.75	190,000.00	125,467.12	125,467.12	64,532.88	0.00
0	2011.00	190,000.00	126,547.07	126,547.07	63,452.93	0.00
0	2011.25	190,000.00	127,636.32	127,636.32	62,363.68	0.00
1	2011.50	190,000.00	128,734.94	128,734.94	61,265.06	0.00
0	2011.75	190,000.00	129,843.02	129,843.02	60,156.98	0.00
0	2012.00	190,000.00	130,960.64	130,960.64	59,039.36	0.00
0	2012.25	190,000.00	132,087.87	132,087.87	57,912.13	0.00
0	2012.50	190,000.00	133,224.81	133,224.81	56,775.19	0.00
0	2012.75	190,000.00	134,371.54	134,371.54	55,628.46	0.00
0	2013.00	190,000.00	135,528.13	135,528.13	54,471.87	0.00
0	2013.25	190,000.00	136,694.68	136,694.68	53,305.32	0.00
1	2013.50	190,000.00	137,871.27	137,871.27	52,128.73	0.00
0	2013.75	190,000.00	139,057.99	139,057.99	50,942.01	0.00
0	2014.00	190,000.00	140,254.93	140,254.93	49,745.07	0.00
0	2014.25	190,000.00	141,462.16	141,462.16	48,537.84	0.00
0	2014.50	190,000.00	142,679.79	142,679.79	47,320.21	0.00
0	2014.75	190,000.00	143,907.90	143,907.90	46,092.10	0.00
0	2015.00	190,000.00	145,146.58	145,146.58	44,853.42	0.00
0	2015.25	190,000.00	146,395.92	146,395.92	43,604.08	0.00
0	2015.50	190,000.00	147,656.01	147,656.01	42,343.99	0.00
0	2015.75	190,000.00	148,926.95	148,926.95	41,073.05	0.00
0	2016.00	190,000.00	150,208.83	150,208.83	39,791.17	0.00
0	2016.25	190,000.00	151,501.74	151,501.74	38,498.26	0.00
1	2016.50		152,805.79			7,922,682
		Present values		3,406,636	3,522,446	659,236

Part Three

9.5   The international perspective

The eventual German buyer had a subtly different perspective.

Germany has been a low-return property market. The pound had just col-lapsed against the Deutsche mark. The local bond rate was just under 6.9% (while the UK gilt yield was 8.4%). The open-ended funds have a very long-term perspective, and had just been permitted to invest outside Germany. There was no Euro yet, and so the UK was not at the disadvantage it now suffers relative to other Eurobloc markets. In addition, the buyers were driven by the following considerations:

- The cash flow was effectively fixed for 23 years – there was no upside but also no risk.
- The local risk-free rate was lower, and so the discount rate, all things being equal, could be lower than a UK buyer's.
- The risk premium depended on the default risk, the currency risk and the illiquidity: but the default risk was tiny, the currency looked as if it had fallen a long way already and the buyer had a long-term perspective – so the risk could be seen to be low.
- Germany was a low-return market, so this asset would add a lot to the fund's returns.
- UK property – and this was a new building in the City – looked very, very cheap compared with recent prices, especially after the collapse of the pound.

The buyer had a long expected holding period and focused on the eventual exit price on the basis of a 10-year holding period. The holding-period cash flow and the lower required return were the key variables.

On a more visceral level, this appeared to be a lot of building for a low price. German office yields were considerably lower than UK yields – by 200 basis points. The buyer also regarded the income stream as highly secure, protected as it was by both the lease and by the personal liability offered by the partners of the occupying law firm.

In addition, the UK currency stood at a low point against the DM, and yet the domestic risk-free rate was lower than UK gilt. This ran counter to economic logic and appeared to offer an arbitrage opportunity.

Driven by a lower local bond yield, Appraisal 2 shows how the German buyer could have bid up to £1m more, and it is no surprise that this deter-mined the domicile of the eventual buyer.

Appraisal 2:   The international perspective

Annual rent		760,000	Long gilt		6.90%
Annual ERV p.s.f.		20.00			
Total ERV		296,100	Base premium		1.50%
			Froth premium		3.00%
Growth	**Real**	**Nominal**	Prop premium		3.00%
Growth 1	−13.46%	−10.00%			
Growth 2	−3.85%	0.00%	**Required rent**	**Quarterly**	**Annual**
Growth 3	−3.85%	0.00%	Base	2.04%	8.40%
Growth 4	17.50%	22.20%	Froth	2.39%	9.90%
Growth 5	4.90%	9.10%	Property	2.39%	9.90%
Growth l.g.	1.00%	5.04%			
			Net exit value		900,395
Depreciation p.a.		1.50%	Base value		3,868,898
Depreciation p.q.		0.37%	Froth value		3,822,074
Exit yield		7.70%			
Review costs		2.50%	Total value		8,591,367

ERV = estimated rental values; p.s.f. = per square foot; p.a. = per annum; p.q. = per quarter; l.g. = long term.
Real Estate Strategy
March 1993.

Quarterly cash flow

Review	Quarter	Rent	ERV	Base rent	Froth	Cap/costs
0	1993.50	190,000.00	74,025.00	74,025.00	115,975.00	0.00
0	1993.75	190,000.00	71,833.08	71,833.08	118,166.92	0.00
0	1994.00	190,000.00	69,706.06	69,706.06	120,293.94	0.00
0	1994.25	190,000.00	67,642.02	67,642.02	122,357.98	0.00
0	1994.50	190,000.00	65,639.10	65,639.10	124,360.90	0.00
0	1994.75	190,000.00	65,394.58	65,394.58	124,605.42	0.00
0	1995.00	190,000.00	65,150.97	65,150.97	124,849.03	0.00
0	1995.25	190,000.00	64,908.27	64,908.27	125,091.73	0.00
0	1995.50	190,000.00	64,666.48	64,666.48	125,333.52	0.00
0	1995.75	190,000.00	64,425.58	64,425.58	125,574.42	0.00
0	1996.00	190,000.00	64,185.58	64,185.58	125,814.42	0.00
0	1996.25	190,000.00	63,946.48	63,946.48	126,053.52	0.00
1	1996.50	190,000.00	63,708.26	63,708.26	126,291.74	0.00
0	1996.75	190,000.00	66,733.99	66,733.99	123,266.01	0.00
0	1997.00	190,000.00	69,903.41	69,903.41	120,096.59	0.00
0	1997.25	190,000.00	73,223.36	73,223.36	116,776.64	0.00
0	1997.50	190,000.00	76,700.98	76,700.98	113,299.02	0.00
0	1997.75	190,000.00	78,097.41	78,097.41	111,902.59	0.00

Continued

Part Three

Quarterly cash flow   (Continued)

Review	Quarter	Rent	ERV	Base rent	Froth	Cap/costs
0	1998.00	190,000.00	79,519.26	79,519.26	110,480.74	0.00
0	1998.25	190,000.00	80,967.00	80,967.00	109,033.00	0.00
0	1998.50	190,000.00	82,441.09	82,441.09	107,558.91	0.00
0	1998.75	190,000.00	83,150.70	83,150.70	106,849.30	0.00
0	1999.00	190,000.00	83,866.41	83,866.41	106,133.59	0.00
0	1999.25	190,000.00	84,588.29	84,588.29	105,411.71	0.00
0	1999.50	190,000.00	85,316.38	85,316.38	104,683.62	0.00
0	1999.75	190,000.00	86,050.73	86,050.73	103,949.27	0.00
1	2000.00	190,000.00	86,791.41	86,791.41	103,208.59	0.00
0	2000.25	190,000.00	87,538.46	87,538.46	102,461.54	0.00
0	2000.50	190,000.00	88,291.94	88,291.94	101,708.06	0.00
0	2000.75	190,000.00	89,051.91	89,051.91	100,948.09	0.00
0	2001.00	190,000.00	89,818.42	89,818.42	100,181.58	0.00
0	2001.25	190,000.00	90,591.52	90,591.52	99,408.48	0.00
1	2001.50	190,000.00	91,371.29	91,371.29	98,628.71	0.00
0	2001.75	190,000.00	92,157.76	92,157.76	97,842.24	0.00
0	2002.00	190,000.00	92,951.00	92,951.00	97,049.00	0.00
0	2002.25	190,000.00	93,751.07	93,751.07	96,248.93	0.00
0	2002.50	190,000.00	94,558.03	94,558.03	95,441.97	0.00
0	2002.75	190,000.00	95,371.93	95,371.93	94,628.07	0.00
0	2003.00	190,000.00	96,192.84	96,192.84	93,807.16	0.00
0	2003.25	190,000.00	97,020.81	97,020.81	92,979.19	0.00
0	2003.50	190,000.00	97,855.91	97,855.91	92,144.09	0.00
0	2003.75	190,000.00	98,698.20	98,698.20	91,301.80	0.00
0	2004.00	190,000.00	99,547.74	99,547.74	90,452.26	0.00
0	2004.25	190,000.00	100,404.59	100,404.59	89,595.41	0.00
0	2004.50	190,000.00	101,268.82	101,268.82	88,731.18	0.00
0	2004.75	190,000.00	102,140.49	102,140.49	87,859.51	0.00
0	2005.00	190,000.00	103,019.65	103,019.65	86,980.35	0.00
0	2005.25	190,000.00	103,906.39	103,906.39	86,093.61	0.00
0	2005.50	190,000.00	104,800.76	104,800.76	85,199.24	0.00
0	2005.75	190,000.00	105,702.82	105,702.82	84,297.18	0.00
0	2006.00	190,000.00	106,612.65	106,612.65	83,387.35	0.00
0	2006.25	190,000.00	107,530.32	107,530.32	82,469.68	0.00
1	2006.50	190,000.00	108,455.88	108,455.88	81,544.12	0.00
0	2006.75	190,000.00	109,389.40	109,389.40	80,610.60	0.00
0	2007.00	190,000.00	110,330.97	110,330.97	79,669.03	0.00
0	2007.25	190,000.00	111,280.63	111,280.63	78,719.37	0.00
0	2007.50	190,000.00	112,238.48	112,238.48	77,761.52	0.00
0	2007.75	190,000.00	113,204.56	113,204.56	76,795.44	0.00
0	2008.00	190,000.00	114,178.96	114,178.96	75,821.04	0.00

Continued

Quarterly cash flow   (Continued)

Review	Quarter	Rent	ERV	Base rent	Froth	Cap/costs
0	2008.25	190,000.00	115,161.75	115,161.75	74,838.25	0.00
0	2008.50	190,000.00	116,153.00	116,153.00	73,847.00	0.00
0	2008.75	190,000.00	117,152.78	117,152.78	72,847.22	0.00
0	2009.00	190,000.00	118,161.17	118,161.17	71,838.83	0.00
0	2009.25	190,000.00	119,178.23	119,178.23	70,821.77	0.00
0	2009.50	190,000.00	120,204.05	120,204.05	69,795.95	0.00
0	2009.75	190,000.00	121,238.70	121,238.70	68,761.30	0.00
0	2010.00	190,000.00	122,282.25	122,282.25	67,717.75	0.00
0	2010.25	190,000.00	123,334.79	123,334.79	66,665.21	0.00
0	2010.50	190,000.00	124,396.39	124,396.39	65,603.61	0.00
0	2010.75	190,000.00	125,467.12	125,467.12	64,532.88	0.00
0	2011.00	190,000.00	126,547.07	126,547.07	63,452.93	0.00
0	2011.25	190,000.00	127,636.32	127,636.32	62,363.68	0.00
1	2011.50	190,000.00	128,734.94	128,734.94	61,265.06	0.00
0	2011.75	190,000.00	129,843.02	129,843.02	60,156.98	0.00
0	2012.00	190,000.00	130,960.64	130,960.64	59,039.36	0.00
0	2012.25	190,000.00	132,087.87	132,087.87	57,912.13	0.00
0	2012.50	190,000.00	133,224.81	133,224.81	56,775.19	0.00
0	2012.75	190,000.00	134,371.54	134,371.54	55,628.46	0.00
0	2013.00	190,000.00	135,528.13	135,528.13	54,471.87	0.00
0	2013.25	190,000.00	136,694.68	136,694.68	53,305.32	0.00
1	2013.50	190,000.00	137,871.27	137,871.27	52,128.73	0.00
0	2013.75	190,000.00	139,057.99	139,057.99	50,942.01	0.00
0	2014.00	190,000.00	140,254.93	140,254.93	49,745.07	0.00
0	2014.25	190,000.00	141,462.16	141,462.16	48,537.84	0.00
0	2014.50	190,000.00	142,679.79	142,679.79	47,320.21	0.00
0	2014.75	190,000.00	143,907.90	143,907.90	46,092.10	0.00
0	2015.00	190,000.00	145,146.58	145,146.58	44,853.42	0.00
0	2015.25	190,000.00	146,395.92	146,395.92	43,604.08	0.00
0	2015.50	190,000.00	147,656.01	147,656.01	42,343.99	0.00
0	2015.75	190,000.00	148,926.95	148,926.95	41,073.05	0.00
0	2016.00	190,000.00	150,208.83	150,208.83	39,791.17	0.00
0	2016.25	190,000.00	151,501.74	151,501.74	38,498.26	0.00
1	2016.50		152,805.79			7,922,682
		Present values		3,868,898	3,822,074	900,395

9.6   Investment performance

The property was bought for £8 million, and sold in 2001 for £12.5 million. At this point 15 years were still remaining on the lease. The rental value had risen to £40 p.s.f., or £600,000, so the property remained over-rented. The law firm remained in occupation.

The running yield enjoyed by the buyer over the holding period was 9.25%, which compares with a likely 5–6% on a domestic office building of similar quality. The achieved internal rate of return (IRR) was 13.1% in sterling and 17.5% in DM. By 2003, the rental value had collapsed again to £25p.s.f., or £375,000.

9.7   2006: on the market again

The same property was on the market again in 2006. The 2001 buyer was making the most of perceived recent price rises and cashing in. Rental values had recovered in the City to around £37.50p.s.f., but the property was now 15 years old with exactly 10 years to run on its lease. The law firm – which was now less highly regarded – had assigned the lease but remained liable for paying the rent in the event of tenant default. What was it worth in 2006? Who would be the most likely buyer and what would they bid?

Appraisal 3 shows how a value of just over £12m is justified – somewhat disappointing the 2001 buyer. Who buys? A German open-ended fund? Now they have less capital to spend, there is no obvious currency gain to be made because the pound is not at an all-time low, there is less yield advantage because yields are not much higher in London than in Frankfurt, and

Appraisal 3:   The 2006 sale

	Real	Nominal			
Annual rent		760,000	Long gilt		4.50%
Annual ERV p.s.f.		37.50			
Total ERV		555,188	Base premium		1.50%
Inflation		0.025	Froth premium		2.50%
			Property premium		2.50%
Growth	**Real**	**Nominal**			
Growth 1	10.00%	12.75%	**Required rent**	**Quarterly**	**Annual**
Growth 2	5.00%	7.62%	Base	1.47%	6.00%
Growth 3	0.00%	2.50%	Froth	1.71%	7.00%
Growth 4	0.00%	2.50%	Property	1.71%	7.00%
Growth 5	0.00%	2.50%			
Growth l.g.	1.00%	3.53%	Net exit value		5,980,559
			Base value		5,503,736
Depreciation p.a.		1.50%	Froth value		705,291
Depreciation p.q.		0.37%			
Exit yield		6.00%			
Review costs		2.50%	Total value		12,189,585

ERV = estimated rental values; p.s.f. = per square foot; p.a. = per annum; p.q. = per quarter; l.g. = long term.
Baum, Crosby and Co.
October 2006.

Quarterly cash flow

Review	Quarter	Rent	ERV	Base rent	Froth	Cap/costs
0	2005.50	190,000.00	138,796.88	138,796.88	51,203.13	0.00
0	2005.75	190,000.00	142,492.60	142,492.60	47,507.40	0.00
0	2006.00	190,000.00	146,286.73	146,286.73	43,713.27	0.00
0	2006.25	190,000.00	150,181.89	150,181.89	39,818.11	0.00
1	2006.50	190,000.00	154,180.77	154,180.77	35,819.23	0.00
0	2006.75	190,000.00	156,455.91	156,455.91	33,544.09	0.00
0	2007.00	190,000.00	158,764.63	158,764.63	31,235.37	0.00
0	2007.25	190,000.00	161,107.42	161,107.42	28,892.58	0.00
0	2007.50	190,000.00	163,484.78	163,484.78	26,515.22	0.00
0	2007.75	190,000.00	163,885.97	163,885.97	26,114.03	0.00
0	2008.00	190,000.00	164,288.15	164,288.15	25,711.85	0.00
0	2008.25	190,000.00	164,691.31	164,691.31	25,308.69	0.00
0	2008.50	190,000.00	165,095.46	165,095.46	24,904.54	0.00
0	2008.75	190,000.00	165,500.61	165,500.61	24,499.39	0.00
0	2009.00	190,000.00	165,906.75	165,906.75	24,093.25	0.00
0	2009.25	190,000.00	166,313.89	166,313.89	23,686.11	0.00
0	2009.50	190,000.00	166,722.02	166,722.02	23,277.98	0.00
0	2009.75	190,000.00	167,131.16	167,131.16	22,868.84	0.00
0	2010.00	190,000.00	167,541.30	167,541.30	22,458.70	0.00
0	2010.25	190,000.00	167,952.45	167,952.45	22,047.55	0.00
0	2010.50	190,000.00	168,364.60	168,364.60	21,635.40	0.00
0	2010.75	190,000.00	169,198.14	169,198.14	20,801.86	0.00
0	2011.00	190,000.00	170,035.81	170,035.81	19,964.19	0.00
0	2011.25	190,000.00	170,877.62	170,877.62	19,122.38	0.00
1	2011.50	190,000.00	171,723.60	171,723.60	18,276.40	0.00
0	2011.75	190,000.00	172,573.77	172,573.77	17,426.23	0.00
0	2012.00	190,000.00	173,428.15	173,428.15	16,571.85	0.00
0	2012.25	190,000.00	174,286.75	174,286.75	15,713.25	0.00
0	2012.50	190,000.00	175,149.61	175,149.61	14,850.39	0.00
0	2012.75	190,000.00	176,016.74	176,016.74	13,983.26	0.00
0	2013.00	190,000.00	176,888.17	176,888.17	13,111.83	0.00
0	2013.25	190,000.00	177,763.90	177,763.90	12,236.10	0.00
1	2013.50	190,000.00	178,643.98	178,643.98	11,356.02	0.00
0	2013.75	190,000.00	179,528.41	179,528.41	10,471.59	0.00
0	2014.00	190,000.00	180,417.22	180,417.22	9,582.78	0.00
0	2014.25	190,000.00	181,310.43	181,310.43	8,689.57	0.00
0	2014.50	190,000.00	182,208.06	182,208.06	7,791.94	0.00
0	2014.75	190,000.00	183,110.13	183,110.13	6,889.87	0.00
0	2015.00	190,000.00	184,016.67	184,016.67	5,983.33	0.00
0	2015.25	190,000.00	184,927.70	184,927.70	5,072.30	0.00
0	2015.50	190,000.00	185,843.24	185,843.24	4,156.76	0.00

Continued

Part Three

Quarterly cash flow (Continued)

Review	Quarter	Rent	ERV	Base rent	Froth	Cap/costs
0	2015.75	190,000.00	186,763.31	186,763.31	3,236.69	0.00
0	2016.00	190,000.00	187,687.94	187,687.94	2,312.06	0.00
0	2016.25	190,000.00	188,617.15	188,617.15	1,382.85	0.00
1	2016.50		189,550.95			12,617,775
		Present values		5,503,736	705,291	5,980,559

the small differential in local bond yields is now reflected in the currency markets – no arbitrage is available. But, for a UK pension fund, this could be just right. The City office market is expected to perform well and 10 years remaining on a lease to a law firm is low risk. Property is now much more attractive as an asset class, and the risks perceived by the market participants in 1993 are no longer being priced.

9.8   Summary

In 1993, the market valuation exercise produced a valuation of around £7m. A DCF investment appraisal, using reasonably compatible inputs, produced an estimate of £7.6m. Yet, the building was soon the subject of a bid from an overseas purchaser at a figure of £8m, and it became clear that more could have been paid.

The pricing valuations were based on evidence derived from the market. However, this evidence may have been based on historic transactions or, more likely, on valuers' estimates of what the yields and rents would be if evidence existed. In late 1992/early 1993, in a changing market, historic transactions would not reflect the ERM exit, lower gilt yields and the new interest of overseas buyers. Changes in such economic fundamentals can only be reflected in traditional pricing techniques intuitively.

In hindsight, there are two reasons for the underestimate from a UK perspective. First, the value of this property was dominated by the fixed-cash-flow element underpinned by the upward-only rent review and the ability of the tenant to continue to pay the rent. Once it has been decided that the tenant is not likely to default, the bond investor can virtually forget the property risks and concentrate on interest rate risk. This would reduce the discount rate and increase the value. Second, in 1993, the prospects of falling interest rates would create possibilities of capital value growth, which could be realised when interest rates were forecast to be at their lowest level. A shorter holding period would have thrown up a higher exit value and (probably) a higher present value.

From an international perspective, specifically in this case, German, other issues come into play. The cash flow was different and the discount rate was different. The cash flow would be converted back into DM and then Euros, and so the prospect of currency appreciation became an issue and the cash flow looked more attractive. The local risk-free rate was lower; so the discount rate was lower.

By 2001 and 2006, the experience of both local and international investors with fixed, bond-type cash flows was greater and the use of cash flows analysis to advise purchasers and sellers had become standard practice in the UK (Baum *et al.*, 2000). Unlike in 1993, when valuations were obviously wrong because of a combination of valuers not recognising market change and using inappropriate techniques, in 2001 and 2006 more rational valuations can be produced because of a better understanding of investment value and the use of DCF to appraise sales and purchases. It also shows that valuation using conventional techniques based on comparison can be divorced from the capital markets. In addition, individual purchasers, or groups of purchasers, may be the marginal buyers at any time. Hence, investment appraisal will always drive market value, and valuers who ignore this rule will not be able to recognise inappropriate valuations and will fail to serve their clients.

Chapter 10
Conclusions

We began this book by distinguishing between market valuation and investment appraisal. This distinction continued throughout the text and culminated in the separate treatment of property investment valuation in Part Two and property investment appraisal methods in Part Three. In attacking the subject in this way, we reflect the view held by many practising valuers that these are fundamentally different functions and that, as a consequence, different models might be appropriate for each.

However, the reader will have noted that there is little variation in the basic models we demonstrate for both valuation and appraisal. We propose an explicit-cash-flow model for appraisal; and, while we have been careful to make some effort towards an impartial presentation, we have to conclude by proposing (simplified) explicit-cash-flow models for general use in market valuations. The major technical difference between a market valuation and an appraisal of worth is the increase in the number of inputs included in an investment appraisal involving the use of forecasts rather than a market analysis (to identify implied growth). These are different functions; yet the approaches to them are complementary.

Widespread adoption of our recommendations for market valuations would be seen as radical in the UK, but this would not be the case in several other markets. The models we favour appear to replace a tried-and-tested conventional implicit-yield model with a dangerously subjective contemporary explicit cash-flow model, forcing the valuer into the hazardous science of forecasting.

We hope we have demonstrated that this is not so. While our examination of market valuation models prior to the appearance of the reverse yield gap (Chapter 4) shows that conventional techniques had a logical basis, they were at that time explicit-cash-flow projections, and they were based on the concept of risk-adjusted, opportunity-cost target rates, thereby enabling an investment decision relating property to the alternatives to be made. Our recommendation is not, therefore, radical; it is a return to pre-reverse yield gap logic. The revolution that radically altered the logical base of conventional valuation techniques was the creeping and gradual effect of inflation, which replaced the explicit-cash-flow model by a new, growth-implicit, all-risks yield technique, riddled (as we show in Chapter 4) with unforeseen errors, irrationalities and difficulties, but made seemingly innocuous by its familiar appearance.

In addition, we reject the aforementioned charge that explicit-cash-flow market valuation models are dangerously subjective and necessitate the use of forecasts. The latter problem is avoided by the analysis of market-growth expectations, which we demonstrated in detail in Chapter 5. This does nonetheless leave us with the problem that the target rate or required return remains a subjective choice, and the adoption of growth-explicit contemporary models will create a period of temporary uncertainty while valuers are unused to choosing the appropriate risk premium and discount rate. But this is done elsewhere – Sweden is an example – and a number of *ad hoc* surveys also exist in the UK (DTZ, 1999, 2004), and these will facilitate the choice of risk premium and discount rate. We have shown in Chapter 6 that, within reasonable boundaries, errors in the choice of required return in the appraisal/valuation process for freeholds will be cancelled out by the impact on implied rental growth. In any case, where (as is typical) the perfect comparable does not exist, the conventional model necessitates subjective adjustment. And, as we showed in Chapter 6, changing the required return in contemporary freehold valuations has much less effect upon the result than changing the capitalisation rate in a conventional valuation, which lacks the inbuilt safety net of the discounted-cash-flow (DCF) method.

We do not make a case for the adoption of any particular presentation of the contemporary market valuation model. We suggest three alternatives: an explicit-cash-flow projection with (for freeholds) a cutoff point to simulate re-sale short-cut DCF model, and a real value/arbitrage model.

The former is popular in the US, is capable of producing a rational solution and also has the advantage of sharing a common basis with our model for property investment appraisal, which is not, as far as we can judge, controversial.

The other two have the advantage that they are presented in an almost identical format to the conventional model, highlighting the real difference between conventional and contemporary market valuation techniques (the yield differences within the individual parts of the valuation). Adjusted slightly (to Wood's design), they present a basis for real return analysis, likely to be of increasing value. It seems to us that a comparison and reconciliation of the explicit and short cut DCF, arbitrage and real value models we presented in Chapters 5, 6 and 7 is the source of a thorough understanding of a framework for property investment appraisal, and we must leave it to the reader to choose his or her own means of presentation based upon what we would hope to be an enhanced perception of underlying theory.

The first and third editions of this book were written during booming property investment markets in the UK. The second edition of this text was written against the backdrop of a recession leading to substantial falls in some property values. It may have been thought that methods developed to deal with rising markets would not work in the context of a falling or collapsed market. This has proved to be spectacularly incorrect, and the early-1990s' recession provided the advocates of contemporary approaches with enormous justification. Some of the conventional applications to over-rented property valuations were seen to be technically inept, and attempts to adjust them to meet the new circumstances proved woefully inadequate. Those inadequacies were accepted by a large number of practitioners. Having re-appraised their techniques, those practitioners perceived the advantages of the growth-explicit alternatives that, having a rational foundation, adjusted naturally and painlessly to other situations. Contemporary techniques are now being taken far more seriously than they were before 1990. Nonetheless, the booming market of the early years of the new millennium has taken the pressure off – but for how long?

The tests of a valuation model are, we suggested in Chapter 1, accuracy and rationality. Accuracy has proved difficult to test; the potential for inaccuracy is therefore perhaps a preferable yardstick. Inaccuracy is best avoided by the application of a rational methodology. Conventional valuations are not rational. It is not rational to value a fixed income at a growth-implicit yield; it is not rational to value a leasehold profit rent at a rate of return based on freehold yields.

Whether it is rational that investment worth, especially to a group of purchasers, should be distinguishable from market value is a more open question. Speculators can influence short-term movements in market prices, which are not always heavily influenced by the longer-term investment value modelled by cash-flow techniques. However, this is not an excuse for adopting irrational models. Short-term speculation can never be explained by a valuation model of the type presented in this book.

The role of the valuer/appraiser is founded upon the two functions of investment appraisal and market valuation. One follows the other. As more and more property investment analysis is performed explicitly, the stronger will the motivation become for valuations to be carried out on the same basis. This process has begun, but the pace of change needs to accelerate. When property investment appraisal becomes rational, we will not only see an improvement in the quality of valuations but we will, at the same time, witness a valuation profession capable of performing comparative investment appraisals, influencing investment decisions and attaining a respected advisory role. We may even see an improvement in the efficiency of the property investment market.

Meanwhile, the adoption of explicit appraisal models by increasingly sophisticated investors has stimulated a drive for improved information in the property investment markets. Empirical research in these markets has begun to command a premium. We now know more about investors' criteria for their required return, their attitude to risk, the impact of depreciation upon return and its relationship to rental growth implications, and ways to forecast property investment performance. While much work still remains to be done, research into all of these areas continues.

But good information applied within a faulty model is worthless. Only by the adoption of rational appraisal models will property professionals be able to utilise the increasing volume of property market intelligence, which is now available, and to command a position of respect within the wider investment community.

Part Three

Bibliography

Adair, A. and N. Hutchison (2005) The reporting of risk in real estate appraisal property risk scoring. *Journal of Property Investment and Finance*, 23(3): 254–68.

Adair, A., M.L. Downie, S. McGreal and G. Vos (eds) (1996a) *European Valuation Practice: Theory and Techniques*. London: E & FN Spon.

Adair, A., N. Hutchison, B. MacGregor, S. McGreal and N. Nanthakumaran (1996b) An analysis of valuation variation in the UK commercial property market: Hager and Lord revisited. *Journal of Property Valuation and Investment*, 14(5): 34–47.

Bailey, C., C. White and R. Pain (1999) Evaluating qualitative research: Dealing with the tension between 'science' and 'creativity'. *AREA*, 31(2): 169–83.

Ball, M. Lizieri, C. and MacGregor B. (1998). *The Economics of Commercial Property Markets*. London: Routledge.

Ball, M., Lizieri and B. MacGregor (2000) *The Economics of Commercial Property Markets*. London: Routledge.

Bannier, C., F. Fecht and M. Tyrell (2006) *Open-End Real Estate Funds in Germany – Genesis and Crisis*. Working Paper No 165, Finance and Accounting. Johann Wolfgang Goethe-Universitat, Frankfurt-am-Main. www.finance.uni-frankfurt. de/wp/1248.pdf.

Barkham, R. and D. Geltner (1994) Unsmoothing British valuation-based returns without assuming an efficient market. *Journal of Property Research*, 11: 81–95.

Baum, A. (1982) The enigma of the short leasehold. *Journal of Valuation*, 1: 5–9.

Baum, A. (1984a) The all risks yield: Exposing the implicit. *Journal of Valuation*, 2: 229–37.

Baum, A. (1984b) The valuation of reversionary freeholds: A review. *Journal of Valuation*, 3: 53–73.

Baum, A. (1985) Premiums on acquiring leases. *Rent Review and Lease Renewal*, 5: 212–22.

Baum, A. (1988a) Depreciation and property investment appraisal. In A. MacLeary and N. Nanthakumaran (eds) *Property Investment Theory*. London: Spon.

Baum, A. (1988b) *A Critical Examination of the Measurement of Property Investment Risk*. Working Paper No 22, Department of Land Economy, University of Cambridge.

Baum, A. (1991) *Property Investment Depreciation and Obsolescence*. London: Routledge.

Baum, A. (2003a) Pricing the options inherent in leased commercial property: A UK case study. Paper delivered at the European Real Estate Society Conference, June.

Baum, A. (2003b) *OPRent Research Report 2003*. Reading, MA: OPS.

Baum, A. and D. Butler (1986) The valuation of short leasehold investments. *Journal of Valuation*, 4: 342–53.

Baum, A. and N. Crosby (1995) Over-rented properties: Bond or equity? A case study of market value, investment worth and actual price. *Journal of Property Valuation and Investment*, 13(2): 31–40.

Baum, A. and G. Sams (2007) *Statutory Valuations* (3e). London: Estates Gazette.

Baum, A. and J.A. Schofield (1991) *Property as a Global Asset*. Reading, MA: Centre for European Property Research, University of Reading.

Baum, A. and P. Struempell (2005) Managing specific risk in property portfolios. Paper delivered at the International Real Estate Research Symposium, Kuala Lumpur, April.

Baum, A. and S.M. Yu (1984) The valuation of leaseholds: A review. *Journal of Valuation*, 3: 157–67 and 229–42.

Baum, A. and S.M. Yu (1985) The valuation of leaseholds: A review. *Journal of Valuation*, 3: 157–67 and 230–47.

Baum, A., N. Crosby and B. MacGregor (1996) Price formation, mispricing and investment analysis in the property market. *Journal of Property Research*, 13(1): 36–49.

Baum, A., N. Crosby P and P. McAllister (2001) *Pricing Lease Terms in the Retail Sector, University of Reading*. Working Paper, Department of Land Management, University of Reading.

Baum, A., D. Mackmin and N. Nunnington (2006) *The Income Approach to Property Valuation* (4e). London: Estates Gazette.

Baum A., N. Crosby P. Gallimore, A. Gray and P. McAllister (2000a) *The Influence of Valuers and Valuations on the Workings of the Commercial Property Investment Market*. London: Royal Institution of Chartered Surveyors/Investment Property Forum/Jones Lang LaSalle Education Trusts.

Baum, A., N. Crosby P. Gallimore, P. McAllister and A. Gray (2000b) *The Influence of Valuers and Valuations on the Workings of the Commercial Property Investment Market*. London: IPF/JLL/RICS.

Baum, A., M. Callender, N. Crosby, S. Devaney, V. Law and C. Westlake. (2005) *Depreciation in Commercial Property Markets*. London: Investment Property Forum.

Beattie, V., R. Brandt and S. Fearnley (1999) Perceptions of auditor independence: UK evidence – a pedagogical note. *Journal of International Accounting, Auditing and Taxation*, 8(1): 67–104.

Blundell, G. and C. Ward (1999) *The Accuracy of Valuations – Expectations and Reality*. Working Paper, Department of Land Management, University of Reading.

Bibliography

Bornand, D. (1985) Conveyancing of commercial property investments. *Solicitors Journal*, August 9 and 16.

Bowcock, P. (1983) The valuation of varying incomes. *Journal of Valuation*, 1: 366–76.

Branch, B. (1985) *Investments: A Practical Approach*. Chicago, IL: Longman.

Brealey, R., S. Myers and F. Allen (2005) *Corporate Finance*, New York: McGraw Hill/Irwin. Previously titled *Principles of Corporate Finance*. First edition: 1984, Sixth edition: 2000, Seventh edition: 2003. Brealey and Myers.

Brigham, E. and M. Ehrhardt (2005) *Financial Management: Theory and Practice*, Orlando: Harcourt College Publishers, Thomson South Western.

Brown, G. (1985) An Empirical Analysis of Risk and Return in the U.K. Commercial Property Market. Unpublished Ph.D. thesis, University of Reading.

Brown, G. and G. Matysiak (2000a) Sticky valuations, aggregation effects and property indices. *Journal of Real Estate Finance and Economics*, 20(1): 49–66.

Brown, G. and G. Matysiak (2000b) *Real Estate Investment: A Capital Market Approach*. Harlow: Financial Times/Prentice Hall.

Brown, G., G. Matysiak and M. Shepherd (1998) Valuation uncertainty and the Mallinson Report. *Journal of Property Research*, 15: 1–13.

Bruhl M. (2001) *Real Estate Valuations: Standards and Models of Professional Organisation*. Conference paper to RICS Europe, Brussels, September.-BVI (2006). *BVI Press Release January 24th*. Frankfurt am Main. Bundersverband Investment und Asset Management e. V.

BVI (undated) *Open Ended Real Estate Investment Funds – an Investment in Solid Value*. Frankfurt am main: Bundersverband Investment und Asset Management .

Byrne, P. (1996) Risk, Uncertainty and Decision-Making in Property Development. London: Spon.

Carsberg, B. (2002) *Property Valuation – The Carsberg Report*. London: Royal Institution of Chartered Surveyors.

Clayton, J., D. Geltner and S. Hamilton (2001) Smoothing in commercial property valuations: Evidence from individual appraisals, *Real Estate Economics*, 29: 337–60.

Colam, M. (1983) The single rate valuation of leaseholds. *Journal of Valuation*, 2: 14–18.

Cole, R., D. Guilkey and M. Miles (1986) Towards an assessment of the reliability of commercial appraisals. *The Appraisal Journal*, 54(3): 422–32.

Corporate Intelligence Group (1993) Market Research Survey. Reported in *DoE Consultation Paper on Commercial Property Leases: Response by the Investment Property Forum*. London: Investment Property Forum.

Crosby, N. (1983) The investment method of valuation: A real value approach. *Journal of Valuation*, 1: 341–50 and 2: 48–59.

Crosby, N. (1985) *The Application of Equated Yield and Real Value Approaches to the Market Valuation of Commercial Property Investments*. Unpublished Ph.D thesis, University of Reading.

Crosby, N. (1986) The application of equated yield and real value approaches to market valuation: Equivalent yield or equated yield approaches. *Journal of Valuation*, 4: 261–74.

Crosby, N. (1987) A Critical Examination of the Rational Model. *Research Papers in Land Management and Development*, Appraisal: No 1, Department of Land Management and Development, University of Reading.

Crosby, N. (1991) The practice of property investment appraisal: Reversionary freeholds in the U.K. *Journal of Property Investment and Valuation*, 9: 109–22.

Crosby, N. (1996a) United Kingdom. In Adair, A., M.L. Downie, S. McGreal and G. Vos (eds) *European Valuation Practice: Theory and Techniques*. London: E & FN Spon.

Crosby, N. (1996b) Valuation and arbitrage: A comment. *Journal of Property Research*, 13: 211–20

Crosby, N. (2000) Valuation accuracy, variation and bias in the context of standards and expectations, *Journal of Property Investment and Finance*, 18(2): 130–61.

Crosby, N. (2006a) Bank lending valuations of commercial property: Learning from mistakes? Keynote address to the International Valuation Conference of the Australian Property Institute and the Property Institute of New Zealand, Cairns, May.

Crosby, N. (2006b) Evaluating the valuers. *IPE Real Estate*, July/August: 2–3.

Crosby, N. (2006c) An evaluation of the policy implications for the UK of the approach to small business tenant legislation in Australia. University of Reading Research Report. www.rdg.ac.uk/rep/ausleaserpt.pdf and www.rdg.ac.uk/rep/ausleaseapp.pdf.

Crosby, N. and S. Murdoch (2000) The influence of procedures on rent determination in the commercial property market of England and Wales. *Journal of Property Investment and Finance*, 18(4): 420–44.

Crosby, N., N. French and C. Ward (1993) Valuation accuracy: A self-fulfilling prophecy? RICS Cutting Edge Research Conference, London, September.

Crosby, N., N. French and C.W.R. Ward (1997a) Contemporary UK market valuation methods for over-rented properties: A framework for risk adjustment. *Journal of Property Research*, 14: 99–115.

Crosby, N., G. Newell, G. Matysiak, N. French and W. Rodney (1997b) Client perception of property investment valuation reports in the UK. *Journal of Property Research*, 14(1): 27–47.

Crosby, N., A. Baum and S. Murdoch (1998a) The contribution of upward-only rent reviews to the capital value of UK property. *Journal of Property Research*, 15: 105–20.

Crosby, N. A. Lavers and H. Foster (1998b) Commercial property loan valuations in the UK: Implications of current trends in valuation practice and legal liability. *Journal of Property Research*, 15(3): 183–209.

Crosby, N., A. Lavers, and S. Murdoch (1998c) Property valuation variation and the margin of error in the UK. *Journal of Property Research*, 15(4): 305–30.

Crosby, N., C. Lizieri and S. Murdoch (1998d) Changing lease structures in real estate office markets. Paper delivered at ERES/AREUEA Conference, Maastricht.

Crosby, N., N. Lizieri and S. Murdoch (1998e) Bank lending valuations on commercial property: Does the European mortgage lending value add anything to the process? *Journal of Property Investment and Finance*, June 18(1): 66–83.

Crosby, N., C. Hughes and S. Murdoch (2005) *Monitoring the 2002 Code of Practice for Commercial Leases*. London: Office of the Deputy Prime Minister.

Cypher, M. and A. Hansz (2003) Does assessed value influence market value judgments? *Journal of Property Research*, 20(4): 305–18.

Damodaran, A. (2001) *The Dark Side of Valuation*. New Jersey: Prentice Hall.

Denzin, N. and Y. Lincoln (1997) *The Handbook of Qualitative Research*. London: Sage.

DETR (2000) *Monitoring the Code of Practice for Commercial Leases*. London: Department of the Environment, Transport and the Regions.

Diaz III, J. (1990a) How appraisers do their work: A test of the appraisal process and the development of a descriptive model. *Journal of Real Estate Research*, 5(1): 1–15.

Diaz III, J. (1990b) The process of selecting comparable sales. *The Appraisal Journal*, 58(4): 533–40.

Diaz III, J. (1997) An investigation into the impact of previous expert value estimates on appraisal judgment. *Journal of Real Estate Research*, 13(1): 57–66.

Diaz III, J. (1999) The first decade of behavioral research in the discipline of property. *Journal of Property Investment and Finance*, 17(4): 326–32.

Diaz III, J. and A. Hansz (1997) How valuers use the value opinion of others. *Journal of Property Valuation and Investment*, 15(3): 256–60.

Diaz III, J. and A. Hansz (2001) The use of reference points in valuation judgment. *Journal of Property Research*, 18(2): 141–8.

Diaz III, J. and M. Wolverton (1998a) A longitudinal examination of the appraisal smoothing process. *Real Estate Economics*, 26(2): 349–56.

Diaz III, J. and M. Wolverton (1998b). A longitudinal examination of the appraisal smoothing hypothesis. *Real Estate Economics*, 26(2): 349–58.

Diaz III, J., P. Gallimore and D. Levy (2004) Multicultural examination of valuation behaviour. *Journal of Property Investment and Finance*, 22(4): 339–46.

Downie, S. McGreal and G. Vos (eds) *European Valuation Practice: Theory and Techniques*, London: E & FN Spon.

Downie, M.L., K.W. Schulte and M. Thomas (1996) Germany. In A. Adair, M.L. Drivers, J. (1997) *Commercial Leases – A Permanent Revolution*. Drivers Jonas Research, London.

DTZ (1999) *Money into Property*. London: DTZ Debenham Tie Leung.

DTZ (2004). *Money into Property*. London: DTZ Debenham Tie Leung.

Edelstein, R.H. and D.C. Quan (2006) How does appraisal smoothing bias real estate returns measurement? *Journal of Real Estate Finance and Economics*, 32(1): 41–60.

EMF (1999) *The Valuation of Property for Lending Purposes in the EU*. Brussels: European Mortgage Federation.

Enever, N. (1981) *The Valuation of Property Investments* (2e). London: Estates Gazette.

Fisher, I. (1930) *The Theory of Interest*. Philadelphia, PA: Porcupine Press.

Fisher, J., M. Miles and B. Webb (1999) How reliable are commercial appraisals? Another look. *Real Estate Finance*, 16(3): 16–26.

Fisher, J.D. and G.H. Lentz (1990) Business enterprise value in shopping malls : An empirical test. *Journal of Real Estate Research*, 5(1): 167–75.

Fisher, J.D., D. Gatzlaff, D. Geltner and D. Haurin (2003) Controlling the impact of variable liquidity in commercial real estate indices. *Real Estate Economics*, 31(2): 269–303.

Fraser, W.D. (1977) The valuation and analysis of leasehold investments in time

Fraser, W.D. (1984) *Principles of Property Investment and Pricing*. London: Macmillan.

Fraser, W.D. (1985a) Rational models or practical methods. *Journal of Valuation,* 3: 253–8.

Fraser, W.D. (1985b) Gilt yields and property's target return. *Estates Gazette,* 273: 1291–4.

Fraser, W.D. (1993) *Principles of Property Investment and Pricin* (2e). London: Macmillan.

French, N. and L. Gabrielli (2004) The uncertainty of valuation. *Journal of Property Investment and Finance,* 22(6): 484–500.

French, N. and C.W.R. Ward (1995) Valuation and arbitrage. *Journal of Property Research,* 12(1): 1–11.

French, N. and C.W.R. Ward (1996) Applications of the arbitrage method of valuation. *Journal of Property Research,* 13(1): 47–56.

Gallimore, P. (1994) Aspects of information processing in valuation judgement and choice. *Journal of Property Research,* 11(2): 97–110.

Gallimore, P. (1996) Confirmation bias in the valuation process: A test for corroborating evidence. *Journal of Property Research,* 13(4): 261–73.

Gallimore, P. and M. Wolverton (1997) Price knowledge induced bias: A cross-cultural comparison. *Journal of Property Valuation and Investment,* 15(3): 261–73.

Gallimore, P. and M. Wolverton (2000) The objective in valuation: A study of the influence of client feedback. *Journal of Property Research,* 17(1): 47–58.

Geltner, D. (1993) Estimating market values from appraised values without assuming an efficient market. *Journal of Real Estate Research,* 8(3): 325–45.

Geltner, D., R. Graff and M. Young (1994) Random disaggregate appraisal error in commercial property evidence from the Russell-NCREIF Database. *Journal of Real Estate Research,* 9(4): 403–19.

Geltner, D., B.D. MacGregor and G. Schwann (2003) Appraisal smoothing and price discovery in real estate markets. *Urban Studies,* 40(5/6): 1047–64.

Geltner, D., N.G. Miller, J. Clayton and P. Eichholtz (2007) *Commercial Real Estate: Analysis and Investments,* Thomson South Western.

Gitman, L. (2006) *Fundamentals of Investing* (9e). Boston, MA: Addison Wesley.

Gordon (1958) Reported in Brigham, E. (1982) *Financial Management: Theory and Practice* (4e). Chicago, IL: Dryden Press.

Graff, R. and J. Webb (1997) Agency costs and inefficiency in commercial real estate. *Journal of Real Estate Portfolio Management,* 3(1): 19–37.

Gray, K.J. and P.D. Symes (1981) *Real Property and Real People.* London: Butterworth.

Greaves, M.J. (1972a) Discounted cash flow techniques and current methods of income valuation. *Estates Gazette,* 223: 2147–55 and 2339–45.

Greaves, M.J. (1972b) *The Investment Method of Property Valuation and Analysis: An Examination of Some of its Problems.* Unpublished Ph.D. thesis, University of Reading.

Greaves, M.J. (1985) The valuation of reversionary freeholds: A reply. *Journal of Valuation,* 3: 248–52.

Greer, G.E., M.D. Farrell and P.T. Kolbe (1996) *Investment Analysis for Real Estate Decisions* (5e). Chicago, IL: Dearborn Financial Publishing.

Grenadier, S. (1995) Valuing lease contracts: A real-options approach. *Journal of Financial Economics,* 38: 297–331.

Grenadier, S. (2003) *An Equilibrium Analysis of Real Estate Leases*. National Bureau of Economic Research Working Paper 9475, Cambridge, Massachusetts.

Gwin, C. R. and C. L. Maxam (2002) Why do real estate appraisals nearly always equal offer price? *Journal of Property Investment and Finance*, 20(3): 242–53.

Hackenbrack, K. and M. Nelson (1996) Auditors' incentives and their application of financial accounting standard. *The Accounting Review*, 14(1): 43–59.

Hamill, J. (1993) Incentive problems and general partner compensation in limited real estate investments. *Journal of American Real Estate and Urban Economics Association*, 21(2): 131–40.

Hansz, J.A. and J. Diaz (2001) Valuation bias in commercial appraisal: A transaction price feedback experiment. *Real Estate Economics*, 29(4): 553–65.

Hansz, J.A. (2004) The use of a pending mortgage reference point in valuation judgment. *Journal of Property Investment and Finance*, 22(3): 259–68.

Hargitay, S. and S.M. Yu (1992) *Property Investment Decisions: A Quantitative Approach*. London: Spon.

Herring, R. and S. Wachter (1999) *Real Estate Booms and Banking Busts: An International Perspective*. Wharton Financial Institutions Center Working Paper No 99-27, The Wharton School, University of Pennsylvania.

Hillier, F.S. (1963) The derivation of probabilistic information for the evaluation of risky investments. *Management Science*, 9: 443–57.

Hoesli, M. and B. MacGregor (2000) *Property Investment*. London: Longman.

Huberman, A. and M. Miles (1997) Data management and analysis methods. In N. Denzin and Y. Lincoln (eds) *The Handbook of Qualitative Research*, London: Sage.

IPD (1991) *Property Investors Digest*. London: Investment Property Databank.

IPD (2004) *Property Investors Digest*. London: Investment Property Databank.

IPD/DJ (2003) *Variance in Valuations* (7e). London: Drivers Jonas/Investment Property Databank.

IVSC (2005) *International Valuation Standards 2003* (7e). London: International Valuation Standards Committee.

Jacob, N. and B. Pettit (1984) *Investments*. Irwin: Homewood.

Jaffe, A (1977) Is there a new internal rate of return literature? *AREUEA* 4: 483.

Jenkins, J. and J. Lowe (1999) Auditors as advocates for their clients: Perceptions of the auditor–client relationship. *Journal of Applied Business Research*, 15(2): 73–81.

Jensen, M. (1994) Self-interest, altruism, incentives and agency theory. *Journal of Applied Corporate Finance*, Summer, 7(2): 40–5.

JLL (2006) *Real Estate Transparency Index*. Chicago, IL: Jones Lang LaSalle.

Key, T. (2004) Transactions activity: Empirical evidence. In C. Lizieri, S. Bond, N. Crosby, M. Callender, S. Hwang, T. Key, G. Matysiak, P. McAllister and C. Ward (eds) *Liquidity in Commercial Property Markets*. Research Report. London: Investment Property Forum.

Kilbinger, S.S. (2006) Run on German real estate funds exposes flaws in regulation. *Wall Street Journal Online*, www.realestatejournal.com/reits/20060131-kilbinger.html.

Kincaid, D. and J. Murdoch (2003) Negligent valuations: Passing the buck. *Australian Property Journal*, February: 323–8.

Kinnard, W., M. Lenk and E. Worzala (1997) Client pressure in the commercial appraisal industry: How prevalent is it? *Journal of Property Valuation and Investment*, 15(3): 233–44.

Kurzrock, B.M. (2006) Extending the index time series: The performance of the German property market from 1989 to 2005. Paper to the European Real Estate Society Conference, Weimar, June.

Lai, T. and K. Wang (1998) Appraisal smoothing: The other side of the story. *Real Estate Economics*, 26: 511–35.

Lee, J. and G. Zhaoyang (1998) Low balling, legal liability and auditor independence. *Accounting Review*, 73(4): 533–56.

Levy, D. (2006) *Conceptualizing the Influence of Clients on Valuations*. Unpublished Ph.D. thesis, The University of Auckland.

Levy, D. and E. Schuck (1999) The influence of clients on valuations. *Journal of Property Investment and Finance*, 17(4): 380–400.

Levy, D. and E. Schuck (2005) The influence of clients on valuations: The clients' perspective. *Journal of Property Investment and Finance*, 23(2): 182–201.

Lizieri, C. (1997) The changing market for business space: Occupier requirements, market response and valuation impacts. Paper delivered at RICS The Cutting Edge Research Conference, Dublin.

Lizieri, C. and G. Herd (1994) Valuing and appraising new lease forms: The case of break clauses in office markets. Proceedings of RICS The Cutting Edge Property Research Conference, London, September.

Lizieri, C. S. Bond, N. Crosby, M. Callender, S. Hwang, T. Key, G. Matysiak, P. McAllister and C. Ward (2004) *Liquidity in Commercial Property Markets*. Research Report. London: Investment Property Forum.

MacGregor, B.D., *et al.* (1985) *Land Availability for Inner City Development*. Reading, MA: Department of Land Management, University of Reading.

Mallinson, M. (1994) *Commercial Property Valuations*. Report of the RICS Committee. London: RICS.

Markowitz, H. (1959) *Portfolio Selection – Efficient Diversification of Investments. New Haven*, CT: Yale University Press.

Marriott, O. (1967) *The Property Boom*. London: Pan.

Marshall, P. (1976) Equated yield analysis. *Estates Gazette*, 239: 493–7.

Marshall, P. (1979) *Donaldsons Investment Tables*. London: Donaldsons.

Mason, R. (1978) Versatility in existing method. Presented at Investment and Management Surveyors Conference, Nottingham, June.

Matysiak, G. and P. Wang (1995) Commercial property prices and valuations: Analysing the correspondence. *Journal of Property Research*, 12: 181–202.

Maurer, R., F. Reiner and R. Rogalla (2004) Return and risk of German open-ended funds. *Journal of Property Research*, 21(3): 209–33.

McAllister, P. (2000) *Pricing Short Leases and Break Clauses Using Simulation Methodology*. Department of Land Management Working Paper. University of Reading.

McAllister, P. and B. O'Roarty (1998) The legal and valuation implications of break clauses: A behavioural perspective. Paper delivered at RICS Cutting Edge conference, de Montfort University.

McAllister, P. and B. O'Roarty (1999) Pricing break clauses: A fundamental approach. Paper delivered at the RICS Cutting Edge Conference, Cambridge.

McAllister, P., A. Baum, P. Gallimore and A. Gray (2003) Appraiser behaviour and appraisal smoothing: Some qualitative and quantitative evidence. *Journal of Property Research*, 20(3): 262–80.

McIntosh, A.P.J. (1983) The rational approach to reversionary leasehold property investment valuations. In D. Chiddick and A. Millington (eds) *Land Management; New Directions*. London: Spon.

Mehdi, N. (2003) *The Capitalisation of Business Rates: An Empirical Study of Tax Incidence in Six London Boroughs*. Ph.D. Dissertation, London School of Economics.

Miller, G. and R. Dingwall (1997) *Context and Method in Qualitative Research*. London: Sage.

Molho, I. (1997) *The Economics of Information: Lying and Cheating in Markets and Organisations*. Oxford: Blackwell.

Montier, J. (2002) *Behavioural Finance: Insights into Irrational Minds and Markets*. Chichester: John Wiley & Sons.

Neuman, W. (1997) *Social Research Methods*. London: Allyn and Bacon.

Newell, G. (1999) The quality of valuation reports in Australia. *Australian Property Journal*, 35(7): 605–8.

Newell, G. and R. Kishore (1998a) The accuracy of commercial property valuations. Paper presented at the 4th Pacific Rim Real Estate Society Conference, Perth, January.

Newell, G. and R. Kishore (1998b) Are valuations an effective proxy for property sales? *The Valuer and Land Economist*, 35(2): 150–3.

Newell, M. (1986) The rate of return as a measure of performance. *Journal of Valuation*, 4: 130–42.

Norris, C. (1884) *The Appraiser, Auctioneer, Broker, House and Estate Agent, and Valuer's Pocket Assistant*. London: Crosby Lockwood.

O'Roarty, B., S. McGreal and A. Adair (1997) The impact of retailers' store selection criteria on the estimation of retail rents. *Journal of Property Valuation and Investment*, 15(2): 119–30.

Parker, D. (1998) Valuation accuracy – an Australian perspective. Paper presented at the 4th Pacific Rim Real Estate Society Conference, Perth, January.

Patel, K. and T.F. Sing (1998) Application of contingent claim valuation (real option) model for property investment analysis. Paper delivered at RICS 'Cutting Edge' Conference, de Montfort University.

Quan D.C. and J.M. Quigley (1991) Price formation and the appraisal function in real estate markets. *Journal of Real Estate Finance and Economics*, 4: 127–46.

Reilly, F. and K. Brown (2002) *Investment Analysis and Portfolio Management* (7e). South Western.

Reynolds, K. (1997) Can tenants use break clauses to re-negotiate rents downwards? In *Proceedings of Henry Stewart Conference Studies*, Break Clauses, London.

RICS (1992) *Valuation Guidance Manual (The White Book)*. London: RICS.

RICS (1997) *Commercial Property Valuation: An Information Paper*. London: RICS.

RICS (2002) *Property Valuation (Carsberg Report)*. London: RICS.

RICS (2003) *RICS Appraisal and Valuation Standards* (5e). London: RICS.

RICS/IPD (2005) *Valuation Accuracy Report*. London: RICS.

Robinson, J. (1986) Dual rate DCF analysis. *Journal of Valuation*, 4: 143–57.

Robinson, J. (1987) Cash flows and risk analysis. *Journal of Valuation*, 5: 268–89.

Rose, J. (1985) *The Dynamics of Urban Property Development*. London: Spon.

Rowland, P. (1999) Pricing lease covenants: Turning theory into practice. Paper delivered at PRRES Conference, Kuala Lumpur.

Ruchardt, K. (2003) *Mortgage Lending Value*. Frankfurt-am-Main: Fritz Knapp Verlag.

Rutterford, J. and M. Davison (2007) *Introduction to Stock Exchange Investment* (4e). Basingstoke: Palgrave MacMillan.

Sharpe, W. F. and G. Alexander (1990) *Investments* (4e). New Jersey: Prentice Hall.

Slessenger, E. and R. Ballaster (1994) Tenants' break clauses. *Estates Gazette*, Issue 9446: 196–7.

Smolen, G. and D. Hambleton (1997) Is the real estate appraiser's role too much to expect? *The Appraisal Journal*, 65(1): 9–17.

Solt, M. and N. Miller (1985) Managerial incentives: Implications for the financial performance of real estate assets. *Journal of American Real Estate and Urban Economics Association*, 13(4): 404–23.

Stork, H.U. and C. Humphreys (1996) Valuation for loan security. In A. Adair, M.L. Downie, S. McGreal and G. Vos (eds) *European Valuation Practice: Theory and Techniques*. London: E & FN Spon.

Strutt and Parker/IPD (2006) *Annual Lease Events Review*. London: Strutt and Parker/Investment Property Databank.

Sykes, S.G. (1981) Property valuation: A rational model. *The Investment Analyst*, 61: 20–6.

Sykes, S.G. (1983a) Valuation models: action or reaction. *Estates Gazette*, 267: 1108.

Sykes, S.G. (1983b) The assessment of property risk. *Journal of Valuation*, 1: 253–67.

Sykes, S.G. and A. Mcintosh (1982) Towards a standard property income valuation model: Rationalisation or stagnation. *Journal of Valuation* 1: 117–35.

Trott, A. (1980) *Property Valuation Methods: Interim Report*. London: Polytechnic of the South Bank, RICS.

Ward, C. (1997) Risk neutrality and the pricing of specific financial aspects of UK leases. Paper delivered at RICS 'Cutting Edge' Research Conferences, Dublin.

Ward, C. and N. French (1997) The valuation of upwards only rent reviews: An option pricing model. *Journal of Property Valuation and Investment*, 15(2): 171–82.

Ward, C., P. Hendershott and N. French (1998) Pricing upwards only rent review clauses: An international perspective. *Journal of Property Valuation and Investment*, 16(5): 447–54.

Waters, J. (2000) *Valuers' Compliance with the Reporting Standards of the RICS 'Red Book'*. London: Royal Institution of Chartered Surveyors.

Webb, B. (1994) On the reliability of commercial appraisals: An analysis of properties sold from the Russell-NCREIF Index. *Real Estate Finance*, 11(1): 62–5.

Windsor, C. and N. Ashkansay (1995) The effect of client management bargaining power, moral reasoning development and belief in audit. *Accounting, Organizations and Society*, 20: 7–8 and 701–21.

Wolverton, M.L. and P. Gallimore (1999) Client feedback and the role of the appraiser. *Journal of Real Estate Research*, 18(3): 415–32.

Wood, E. (1972) *Property Investment – A Real Value Approach*. Unpublished Ph.D. thesis, University of Reading.

Bibliography

Wood, E. (1973) Positive valuations: A real value approach to property investment. *Estates Gazette*, 226: 923–5, 115–17 and 1311–13.

Worzala, E., M. Lenk and W. Kinnard Jr (1998) How client pressure affects the appraisal of residential property. *Appraisal Journal*, 66(4): 416–28.

Wurtzebach, C. and A. Baum (1993) International property investment. In S. Hudson-Wilson and C. Wurtzebach (eds) *Managing Real Estate Portfolios*. Boston: Wiley.

Yavas, A. and P. Colwell (1999) Buyer brokerage: Incentive and efficiency implications. *Journal of Real Finance and Economics*, 18(3): 257–77.

Zhang, P. (1999) A bargaining model of auditor reporting. *Contemporary Accounting Research*, 16(1): 167–85.

Zimbelman, M. and W. Waller (1999) An experimental investigation of auditor–auditee interaction under ambiguity. *Journal of Accounting Research*, 37: 135–56.

Zorn, T. and J. Larsen (1986) The incentive effects of flat-fee and percentage commissions for real estate brokers. *Journal of American Real Estate and Urban Economics Association*, 14(1): 46–57.

Index

Numbers in **bold** indicate pages containing charts/diagrams/examples in boxes/graphs/illustrations/tables

Index